THE COVENANT
OF THE TORCH

"Remember the days of old,
Consider the years of all generations.
Ask your father, and he will inform you,
Your elders, and they will tell you."

—Deuteronomy 32:7

THE COVENANT
OF THE TORCH

A Forgotten Encounter in the History of
the Exodus and Wilderness Journey

Rev. Abraham Park, D.Min., D.D.

PERIPLUS EDITIONS
Singapore • Hong Kong • Indonesia

Published by Periplus Editions (HK) Ltd., with editorial offices at 61 Tai Seng Avenue, #02–12, Singapore 534167.

Copyright © 2010 Periplus Editions (HK) Ltd.
First Korean edition published by Huisun in 2007. www.pyungkang.com

Photographs © 2010 Hanan Isachar /www.isachar-photography.com

Scripture quotations taken from the New American Standard Bible®, Copyright © 1960, 1962, 1963, 1968, 1971, 1972, 1973, 1975, 1977, 1995 by The Lockman Foundation.

Library of Congress Cataloging-in-Publication Data
Park, Abraham.
 The covenant of the torch : a forgotten encounter in the history of the exodus and wilderness journey / by Abraham Park.
    p. cm.
Includes bibliographical references and index.
ISBN 978-0-7946-0631-2 (hardcover)
1. Exodus, The. I. Title.
BS1199.E93P37 2010
231.7'6--dc22
                              2009041914

Distributed by:

North America, Latin America & Europe
Tuttle Publishing
364 Innovation Drive North Clarendon,
VT 05759-9436 U.S.A.
Tel: 1 (802) 773-8930
Fax: 1 (802) 773-6993
info@tuttlepublishing.com
www.tuttlepublishing.com

Asia Pacific
Berkeley Books Pte. Ltd.
61 Tai Seng Avenue #02-12
Singapore 534167
Tel: (65) 6280-1330
Fax: (65) 6280-6290
inquiries@periplus.com.sg
www.periplus.com

Japan
Tuttle Publishing
Yaekari Building, 3rd Floor,
5-4-12 Osaki, Shinagawa-ku,
Tokyo 141-0032
Tel: 81 (03) 5437 0171
Fax: 81 (03) 5437 0755
tuttle-sales@gol.com

Indonesia
PT Java Books Indonesia
Jl. Rawa Gelam IV No. 9
Kawasan Industri Pulogadung
Jakarta 13930
Tel: (62) 21 4682-1088
Fax: (62) 21 461-0206
cs@javabooks.co.id

Printed in Singapore

13 12 11 10   10 9 8 7 6 5 4 3 2 1

Contents

Introduction

A Forgotten Encounter

Man was originally created in the image of God (Gen 1:26; 2:7; 5:1; 9:6; Col 3:9–10), but fell because of sin, becoming totally incapable, corrupt, and without the ability to do good or save himself (Job 15:16; Ps 14:1–3; 51:5; 53:1; Isa 44:20; Jer 17:9). God, however, gave the greatest gift–the Bible (special revelation)–to mankind through His abounding grace, mercy, and endless compassion. The 66 books of the Bible are inspired by the Holy Spirit. Hence, the Bible is completely the inerrant Word of God, which contains His wondrous and immeasurable plan for the redemption of fallen man that was predestined before time. God manifested His divine administration of redemption through the "covenant," establishing a new covenant of grace with His people in each era. Among God's various covenants, the "covenant of the torch" made with Abraham is the most significant because it is the condensed summary of God's administration in the history of redemption. The elements of God's kingdom, which are "descendants" and "land," are clearly addressed in the covenant of the torch.

For the past few decades I have knelt in prayer and struggled over the covenant of the torch, researching its chronology and studying in depth the vast process of its fulfillment. I believe that the most fundamental and important aspects of God's administration in the history of redemption are made clearer to us through an understanding of its chronology. A clear understanding of the chronological flow of biblical events authenticates, in our rational minds, their historicity. Moreover, it reveals the culture of the times and helps create links with the preceding and succeeding historical events. Furthermore, threading the chronologies together under the theme of "God's administration in the history of redemption" brings the recorded biblical events to life so that they pulsate in our hearts today and turn into a history full of the power of life.

As I delved deeper into the study of the covenant of the torch, I was able to confirm the underlying truth that God most definitely fulfills the Word He has spoken (Matt 5:18; 24:34-35). For Christians on their journey of faith in the spiritual wilderness (i.e., church; Acts 7:38 KJV), God's faithfulness with regard to His covenants is the assurance of salvation, foundation of eternal hope and confirmation of faith.

The Genesis Genealogies: God's Administration in the History of Redemption dealt with the history of redemption from the first man, Adam, to the father of faith, Abraham, with a focus on the genealogies of the godly descendants. In this book, *The Covenant of the Torch: A Forgotten Encounter in the HIstory of the Exodus and Wilderness Journey*, I tried to organize the process of fulfilling the covenant of the torch chronologically from Abraham until Israelites' settlement in the land of Canaan.

Mankind has forgotten many things since the fall of Adam. We have forgotten the Word of God, all the blessings and abounding *agape* love in God's covenant, and the precious memories of grace from the times we spent with God. The root of this problem is their forgotten encounter with God. The encounter with God is the most important starting point of our lives. It is the driving force behind life and the confirmation of eternal life. I earnestly hope that we may recover our forgotten encounter with God through the covenant of the torch and the process of its fulfillment. This encounter will last for all eternity.

✳ ✳ ✳ ✳ ✳

As I look back to the days which have lived, I confess that it is completely by the grace of our living God that this old servant is still alive today to share the gospel of the cross and the blood of our Lord—the gospel of glory. It is the power of Christ's precious blood shed on the cross that forgave all my sins and saved me though I was the foremost of all sinners. Truly, the cross of Jesus Christ is eternal; it is a complete victory and the only hope for all mankind. I am a only a sinner greatly indebted to our Lord's great love and the gospel of the cross (Rom 1:14). For this reason, I prayed and vowed in my heart 47 years ago to pray for at least two hours and read the Bible at least three hours each day. By God's sovereign grace, I have prayed and read the Bible to this day, without missing a single day. My focus has not strayed from walking the solitary path centered on only the Bible. Until the day of my last breath in this life that God has granted me, I will push forward with prayer and the Word, and boast only of the cross (1 Cor 2:2; Gal 6:14).

This year marks the fifty-first year since this inadequate servant has served this church, the body of our Lord. I have exerted all my efforts in maintaining the orthodox faith by continuously studying Calvinism and the reformed orthodox theology taught by my predecessor of faith, Dr. Hyung Yong Park. Although there were times of struggle when I faced great obstacles because of authorities who had misunderstood my faith and attempted to destroy it, they were actually struggles against the darkness within me. The Word of God was my only consolation and hope during those times.

I started preaching what I wrote in this book in 1968. Recently, I revised and supplemented the content and shared it both in and out of the country through messages entitled "The Faithful God Who Remembers and Fulfills His Covenant" (Josh 21:45; 23:14). This book is a summary of the grace shared through those sermons. By the help of God's good hands, I began writing this book in December of 2007 and finished in May of 2008. This book is far from being perfect and may contain parts that are unsatisfactory to some readers. Nevertheless, I release my humble work into this world with a sincere hope that the God, who delivered His message through the mouth of a donkey, would also speak through this inadequate servant (Num 22:28).

History is flowing full force toward the completion of redemption which God has predestined. It is appointed for men to die once, and after this comes judgment (Heb 9:27). Eighty years have passed already in my life and there is nothing else left for me except to enter the kingdom of God.

Jesus said in Matthew 12:36–37, "And I say to you, that every careless word that men shall speak, they shall render account for it in the day of judgment; for by your words you shall be justified, and by your words you shall be condemned." I find serenity with a reverent heart before God, as I am reminded of the short time that remains in my sojourn. The tongue of man is a restless evil that no one can tame and full of deadly poison (Jas 3:8). If we mean to love life and see good days, we must refrain our tongues from uttering evil and our lips from speaking guile (1 Pet 3:10; Rev 21:8; 22:15). At the end of life which is as short as a watch in the night, I am stricken anew with the realization that we need to sincerely serve God with a good conscience (Acts 23:1).

The darkness of the spiritual realm that covers the entire world seems to be a sign that we are at the dawn of a new work. God said, "Pursue peace with all men, and the sanctification without which no one will see the Lord" (Heb 12:14). Christians who yearn for the Second Coming of Jesus Christ need to forgive each other generously with Christ's fervent love (Matt 18:21–22) and live in peace with one another through deep understanding (1 Thess 5:13).

I sincerely hope that God's churches may overcome this world (1 John 5:4) and become His own people who are zealous for His good deeds (Eph 2:10; Titus 2:14), so that we may become spotless and blameless in peace until the coming of our Lord Jesus Christ (1 Thess 5:23; 2 Pet 3:14). I pray that the river of the Lord's delight may overflow in the lives of all who read this book (Ps 36:8). Hallelujah!

Finally, I would like to express my heart of thanksgiving to my fellow ministers, elders, leaders, the beloved congregation of Pyung Kang Che-il Church, and my wife and children for always praying for this servant. I also offer my heartfelt thanks to the people who have helped arrange the drafts of this book until its completion.

May 17, 2008
Servant of Jesus Christ,
On the sojourner's journey to heaven,
Rev. Yoon-Sik Park

List of Abbreviations

Bible Versions

KJV   King James Version
NASB   New American Standard Bible*
NIV   New International Version
NKJV   New King James Version
NLT   New Living Translation
NRSV   New Revised Standard Version

Reference Works

BDAG   Bauer, Walter. *A Greek-English Lexicon of the New Testament and Other Early Chrisitan Literature*. Revised and augmented by F. Wilbur Gingrich and Frederick W. Danker. Chicago, 1979

BDB   Brown, F., S. R. Driver, and C. A. Briggs. *A Hebrew and English Lexicon of the Old Testament: With an Appendix Containing the Biblical Aramaic*. Oxford, 1952

HALOT   Koehler, L., W. Baumgartner, and J. J. Stamm. *The Hebrew and Aramaic Lexicon of the Old Testament*. Translated and edited under the supervision of M. E. J. Richardson. 4 vols. Leiden: 1994–1999

ISBE   *International Standard Bible Encyclopedia*. Edited by G. W. Bromiley. 4 vols. Grand Rapids, 1979–1988

TDOT   *Theological Dictionary of the Old Testament*. Edited by G. Johannes Botterweck, Helmer Ringgren, and Heinz-Josef Fabry. Translated by Douglas W. Stott. 15 vols. Grand Rapids, 1999

TWOT   *Theological Wordbook of the Old Testament*. Edited by R. L. Harris and G. L. Archer. 2 vols. Chicago, 1980

* Bible verses quotes in this book are from the New American Standard Bible unless indicated otherwise.

PART ONE

The Covenant of the Torch and God's Administration in the History of Redemption

CHAPTER 1

Jesus Christ, the Center of the Divine Administration of Redemption

When God created man, He created him in His own image (Gen 1:26–27) and entrusted to him the ownership and dominion over the entire universe (Gen 1:28). However, Adam and Eve, the ancestors of mankind, were proud, lacked faith, and disobeyed the Word. As a result, they lost the power to subdue and rule over the world. God had commanded Adam, "But from the tree of the knowledge of good and evil you shall not eat, for in the day that you eat from it you shall surely die" (Gen 2:17), but he listened to the words of the serpent through Eve rather than the Word of God. This caused the fall of man and their banishment from the Garden of Eden (Gen 3:24).

Created in God's likeness, man was to commune with Him and live eternally (Prov 3:32; Eccl 3:11); however, as a result of sin, they fell to the status of beings destined to die (Rom 5:12; 6:23; Eph 2:1; Col 2:13; Heb 9:27). Mankind became subordinate to the devil who holds the power of the air and is the object of God's fearful wrath (Eph 2:2–3).

Redemption achieved through Jesus Christ was the only means to save fallen sinners. The word redemption refers to a person acting to save another person from severe distress, illness, or great danger. It can also refer to the act of saving someone by giving a ransom payment. In other words, it is the recovery of ownership or a freedom from oppression after making proper payment, and the freedom to move from a confined space into a spacious one.

1. Jesus Christ, the Center of the History of Redemption

The word *redemption* in the original language is written in different forms of Greek: λυτρόω (*lytroō*, "to redeem" [Luke 24:21; Titus 2:14; 1 Pet 1:18–19]), λύτρον (*lytron*, "ransom" [Matt 20:28; Mark 10:45]), and λύτρωσις (*lytrōsis*, "redemption, atonement" [Luke 1:68; 2:38; Heb 9:12]). The underlying meaning of these words concerns the act of making the proper payment to obtain ownership. But these words take on a profound meaning when they are used in connection with Jesus Christ.

First, Jesus Christ paid the ransom for all sinners whom God had predestined, according to His plan for redemption, so that they may be saved and become His children in Christ (Matt 22:14; Rom 8:29–30; 11:5; Eph 1:4–5, 11; 1 Pet 1:2). This is the absolute predestination determined before creation (Eph 1:4–5; 3:11; 2 Tim 1:9). Absolute predestination is not based on a person's good works, meritorious deeds, or effort. It is determined only by God's sovereign will. Jesus Christ paid the price on the cross and redeemed the people predestined for salvation.

Second, Jesus Christ paid the price with His blood. The price that Jesus Christ paid to redeem us from sin and death was His own precious blood. We were not saved by perishable things like precious gold or silver, but by the precious blood of Jesus Christ, unblemished and spotless as that of a lamb (1 Pet 1:18–19).

Third, those who are redeemed are Jesus Christ's own possession, they are bought with the cost of His precious blood (1 Cor 6:19–20; 7:22–23). History did not flow aimlessly after the fall of mankind, but worked for the purpose of redeeming the saints chosen in Jesus Christ before the foundation of the world (Eph 1:4). Thus, the focus of the administration in the history of redemption is the salvation of fallen mankind, with Jesus Christ standing at the center of that work. Jesus Christ is the only true Savior who can save His chosen people (Matt 1:21; Luke 2:11; John 4:42; Acts 4:12; 5:31; 1 John 4:14).

When Jesus Christ came to this earth through the virgin Mary (Isa 7:14; Matt 1:18–21), He possessed both perfect divinity and perfect humanity (John 1:14; Phil 2:6–8). Jesus the incarnate God—the Word which became flesh—is both perfectly God and perfectly man (John 1:1, 14, 18). Jesus Christ is the atoning sacrifice (Rom 3:25; 1 John 2:2) and the Lamb who takes away the sins of His chosen people (John 1:29).

The history of this earth is centered on Jesus Christ, fulfilled through Him, and will be completed through His Second Coming. The Bible refers to Jesus, who stands at the center of God's history of redemption, as God's mystery (Col 2:2). Colossians 1:26–27 reveals four things about this mystery.

Colossians 1:26–27 … that is, the mystery which has been hidden from the past ages and generations, but has now been manifested to His saints, [27]to whom God willed to make known what is the riches of the glory of this mystery among the Gentiles, which is Christ in you, the hope of glory.

First, this mystery has been hidden (Col 1:26). The word *mystery* is μυστήριον (*mysterion*) in Greek, signifying an unrevealed truth or a truth hidden to the outside world. The word *hidden* is ἀποκεκρυμμένον (*apokekrymmenon*) in Greek, a perfect passive participle form of ἀποκρύπτω (*apokryptō*). It reveals the truth that God is the one who has hidden the mystery. Thus, it cannot be understood by human wisdom or ability; it can be understood only when God reveals it. This mystery is the profound mystery of God's redemptive work made known to His people through revelations. It is the will of God (1 Cor 2:7; 4:1; Eph 3:3). In the Bible, God's holy work of salvation, the Second Coming of Jesus Christ, the kingdom of God, the gospel, and so forth are part of the mystery (Matt 13:11; Mark 4:11; Eph 6:19; Rev 10:7; cf. Amos 3:7).

Second, this mystery has been hidden from past ages and generations (Col 1:26). Here, the word *ages* is the plural form of the Greek word αἰών (*aiōn*), meaning "eternal," and the word "generations" is the plural form of the Greek word γενεά (*genea*), meaning "generation." Thus, the phrase "past ages and generations" means "from eternity and each continuing generation" and can be used interchangeably. Ephesians 3:9 uses the phrase "from the beginning of the world" (KJV), while 1 Corinthians 2:7 uses "before the ages" (NASB).

Third, this mystery has now been manifested to His believers (Col 1:26). Here, the Greek expression is νῦν δέ (*nyn de*), meaning "but now." This means that the mystery of God, which has been hidden until now, has been manifested (Rom 16:25–26). On the other hand, the word "manifested" in Greek is ἐφανερώθη (*ephanerōthē*), a passive form of the verb φανερόω (*phaneroō*). The mystery of the work of salvation through Jesus Christ can be understood only when God reveals it to His believers.

Fourth, this mystery has to be richly manifested, even among the Gentiles. Colossians 1:27 states, "To whom God willed to make known what is the riches of the glory of this mystery among the Gentiles, which is Christ in you, the hope of glory." "Gentiles" refers to all people not of Jewish descent, including those who serve other gods (Rom 11:11; 15:9; Gal 2:8). The Gentiles were originally excluded from the covenant of God, but God gave them the precious gift of salvation through the redemptive work of Jesus Christ (Acts 26:17–18; Rom 11:11, 25; Gal 1:16; 3:8, 14; Eph 2:11–14; 3:6). There are numerous prophesies in the Old Testament regarding the glorious salvation of the Gentiles (Gen 22:18; 28:14; Isa 54:2–3; Mal 1:11).

God's work was centered on the Jews until the coming of Jesus Christ. However, God's work expanded to include the Gentiles after Jesus' atoning work on the cross. Romans 2:28–29 states that an outward Jew is a Jew by lineage, but an inward Jew transcends the boundaries of lineage and is one who confesses faith in Jesus Christ (Gal 3:7–9, 26–29). Now, Jew or Greek, slave or free, man or woman, all people are one in Jesus Christ (Gal 3:28). The gospel of the cross became the power of God that gives salvation to all believers—both Jews and Gentiles (Rom 1:16).

The riches of the glory that the Gentiles receive through salvation is known as the "glory of the mystery" (Col 1:27). This is why the apostle Paul confessed that he is honored to be called the servant of Christ for the Gentiles (Rom 11:13). We must also preach this mystery of the gospel to all the people so that the glory of the mystery may be richly manifested on the earth.

2. Jesus Christ's Work of Atonement

The work of atonement refers to the specific work of Jesus Christ for the forgiveness of our sins. It is the work of paying the price of our sins according to God's plan and providence for the salvation of mankind. This work of atonement is the height of God's work of salvation and the essence of the Christian gospel.

(1) The redemptive work of the cross and God's will

Sinners must receive the forgiveness of their sins in order to be saved (Eph 1:7; Col 1:14). Jesus Christ came to this earth for the complete redemption of the chosen people (John 1:29; Heb 9:26; 1 John 3:5). This redemption was achieved when Jesus Christ came to this earth, shed His blood and died on the cross (1 Pet 1:18-19). He spoke publicly to His disciples about how His suffering on the cross and His death were predestined as part of God's plan of salvation.

> **Matthew 26:24** The Son of Man is to go, just as it is written of Him; but woe to that man by whom the Son of Man is betrayed! It would have been good for that man if he had not been born.

Luke 22:22 For indeed, the Son of Man is going as it has been determined; but woe to that man by whom He is betrayed!

During His public life, Jesus spoke four times regarding the redemptive work to be done on the cross through His death (Matt 16:21–28; 17:22–23; 20:17–19; 26:1–2). Every time He warned about His death on the cross, He used the Greek word δεῖ (*dei*), meaning "for certain," "it is necessary," "must," and "ought to" in order to emphasize its inevitability (Matt 16:21; Mark 8:31; Luke 9:22; 24:7).

Not grasping the importance of the work of redemption, Peter said, "God forbid it, Lord! This shall never happen to You." In response, Jesus rebuked him, "Get behind Me, Satan! You are a stumbling block to Me; for you are not setting your mind on God's interests, but man's." (Matt 16:23; Mark 8:33).

Jesus Christ willingly obeyed God's eternal plan and providence by dying on the cross. He stood ahead of His disciples and went up to Jerusalem on the last day of His public life (Mark 10:32; Luke 19:28) and said, "Behold, we are going up to Jerusalem, and all things which are written through the prophets about the Son of Man will be accomplished" (Luke 18:31). On the night He was captured, He sang hymns with His disciples as He crossed the Kidron Valley and went to the Mount of Olives (Matt 26:30; Mark 14:26; John 18:1).

On the Mount of Olives, Jesus prayed until beads of sweat turned into great drops of blood. Then a multitude carrying swords and clubs came looking for Him. "Knowing all the things that were coming upon Him" (John 18:4), Jesus boldly said to them, "I am He" (John 18:6), and allowed Himself to be taken. As Jesus was about to be captured by the Roman soldiers, Peter struck Malchus, a slave of the high priest, and cut off his ear. At this, Jesus said, "Stop! No more of this!" and touched his ear and healed him (Luke 22:51). Then as Jesus said to Peter, "Or do you think that I cannot appeal to My Father, and He will at once put at My disposal more than twelve legions of angels? How then shall the Scriptures be fulfilled, that it must happen this way?" (Matt 26:53–54), He bore the cross according to the Scriptures.

Jesus Christ, in order to achieve a perfect reconciliation between God and man (Rom 5:10–11; Eph 2:13–18), strove toward the fulfillment of redemption through the cross according to God's predetermined will. At last, He achieved what He so desired through His death on the cross and declared, "It is finished" (John 19:30).

(2) The foreshadowing of the work of redemption

God is holy and righteous and does not tolerate sin. Thus, no one can meet with God if one has sin. In the Old Testament, God made people bring offerings before Him as a foreshadowing of the redemptive work of Jesus Christ. The closest foreshadowing of the redemptive work can be found in the example of the "scapegoat" (*'ăzā'zēl*) found in Leviticus 16:6–10, 20–22, 26. The word עֲזָאזֵל (*'ăzā'zēl*) means "entire removal." Aaron, the high priest, would lay both of his hands on the head of the scapegoat and transfer all the sins and unrighteousness of the Israelites onto the scapegoat and send it away into the wilderness to become food for the fierce predators (Lev 16:21–22). Thus, the scapegoat foreshadows how Jesus, who is without sin, would bear the sins of the chosen people and be thrown outside the city gates to die on the cross (Heb 13:12).

In the Old Testament, the first prerequisite for an offering was that it be without blemish (Exod 12:5; 29:1; Lev 1:3; Num 6:14; 19:2), because it foreshadowed Jesus Christ who was to come. God did not accept offerings that are worthless, abominable, blind, sick, or lame (Isa 1:11–17). He warned that those who make such offerings will be cursed (Mal 1:7–14).

Jesus Christ was an unblemished and spotless lamb. He was a perfect offering, without sin (1 Pet 1:19). Jesus neither sinned (1 Pet 2:22) nor did He know sin (2 Cor 5:21). He was without sin from the beginning (1 John 3:5), and in Him there was no evil (Heb 7:26).

Because Jesus Christ, being without sin, became our sacrifice of redemption, God's righteousness was completely satisfied while demonstrating His *agapē* love to us. Jesus was cursed according to the law on behalf of sinners (Gal 3:13) and bore their sins (1 Pet 2:24; cf. Isa 53:6). As a result, our sins were transferred to Jesus, and His righteousness was given to us as a free gift (Rom 3:22–24; 4:25; 2 Cor 5:21). Finally, true freedom was restored and eternal life was given (Rom 6:23; 8:1–2) to the humanity that was groaning under the weight of sin and death.

(3) The suffering Jesus endured on behalf of sinners

The suffering that Jesus endured was the atonement for the redemption of His chosen people. The entire thirty-three years of Jesus' life, from the very moment He came to this earth in the form of man, was a continuance of the horrendous suffering that He had to bear for all of our sins.

This unspeakable pain was for the fulfillment of His redemptive work.

During the final week of His short life of thirty-three years, all the forces of evil gathered their strength to attack Jesus. He was oppressed and afflicted beyond His strength. On His way to the Garden of Gethsemane, Jesus revealed His distressed heart to three of His disciples (Mark 14:32–34).

> **Matthew 26:37–38** And He took with Him Peter and the two sons of Zebedee, and began to be grieved and distressed. [38]Then He said to them, "My soul is deeply grieved, to the point of death; remain here and keep watch with Me."

Jesus left eight of His disciples at the foot of the mountain and took three disciples to pray with Him (Matt 26:36; Mark 14:32). However, they became exhausted with fatigue and fell asleep, so Jesus was left alone to pray. He fell to the ground (Mark 14:35), knelt down (Luke 22:41), fell on his face (Matt 26:39), and offered up prayers with loud cries and tears that resounded throughout the Garden of Gethsemane (Heb 5:7).

Knowing what was going to happen to Him (Mark 10:32), in His last earnest prayer at Gethsemane, Jesus must have squeezed every drop of oil from His flesh, heart, and soul until He felt like His heart would burst and His intestines would tear. This pain was the beginning of the cross. When Jesus prayed, "Yet not My will, but Thine be done" (Luke 22:42), God could not bear to look upon His suffering and anguish any longer and sent an angel from heaven to strengthen Him (Luke 22:43). In the meantime, Jesus prayed even more earnestly, and His sweat became like drops of blood, falling upon the ground (Luke 22:44).

As soon as Jesus finished praying, more than 200 soldiers came looking for Him (John 18:3).[1] With Judas' kiss, which was a prearranged sign, they seized Jesus as if He were a thief (Matt 26:55), tied Him up with a rope (Mark 14:44), and dragged Him away bound like a beast (John 18:12). Jesus was brought before Annas (John 18:13), Caiaphas (Matt 26:57–68), the council of the Sanhedrin (Luke 22:66), Pilate (Mark 15:1), Herod (Luke 23:7), and Pilate again (Luke 23:11–25), respectively, until finally He was dragged up to Golgotha to be crucified on the cross (Matt 27:31; Mark 15:20; Luke 23:26).

When Jesus was questioned by Annas, one of the officers struck Him (John 18:22). After His death sentence was confirmed in the courtyard of Caiaphas the high priest, the religious leaders spat in Jesus' face. They then covered His face with a cloth, struck Him, and taunted Him by saying, "Prophesy to us, you Christ; who is the one who hit you?" (Matt 26:66–68). The servants followed the others and struck Him with the palms of their hands (Mark 14:64–65).

After being scourged and sentenced to crucifixion by Pilate, Jesus was dragged to the governor's courthouse, the Praetorium, where He was ridiculed and mocked before the entire Roman cohort (Matt 27:26–30; Mark 15:15–20; John 19:1). Thick whips normally were split into three strands at the end, while other whips were split into nine thinner strands with pieces of metal or bone attached at each tip. Each time the whip was lashed, the tips dug in and tore off a piece of flesh. According to the seven great prophecies in Psalm 38, there was not one place on Jesus' flesh that was sound (Ps 38:3). Every lashed area was torn up, and His back looked like a field with furrows plowed.

> **Psalm 129:3** The plowers plowed upon my back; they lengthened their furrows.

It was a cold dawn (John 18:18), and Jesus could hardly hold Himself up after losing so much blood from the ruthless beatings. Just as the author of the book of Psalms prophesied, His bones were wounded, fractured, and out of joint (Ps 22:14). By the time the soldiers propped Him up, His face was unrecognizable. His face was swollen and covered with blood. Indeed, it did not even look human.

> **Psalm 22:6** But I am a worm, and not a man, a reproach of men, and despised by the people.

The prophet Isaiah prophesied 750 years before Jesus' time that all the people would turn their faces away to avoid looking upon Jesus' appalling appearance.

> **Isaiah 53:3** He was despised and forsaken of men, a man of sorrows, and acquainted with grief; and like one from whom men hide their face, He was despised, and we did not esteem Him.

The Roman soldiers cruelly placed a crown of thorns on Jesus' head to mock Him, mercilessly stripped Him, and clothed Him with a scarlet robe to further ridicule Him (Matt 27:28; Mark 15:17; John 19:2). They stomped over His holy body with their dirty feet and treated Him like a worm (Isa 51:23). Furthermore, they spat on Him and beat Him on the head pitilessly with reeds (Mark 15:17–19; John 19:2-3).

> **Matthew 27:29–30** And after weaving a crown of thorns, they put it on His head, and a reed in His right hand; and they kneeled down before Him and mocked Him, saying, "Hail, King of the Jews!" [30]And they spat on Him, and took the reed and began to beat Him on the head.

Here, the word *beat* (ἔτυπτον, *etypton*) refers to the act of striking with the hand, fist, feet, stick, staff, whip, or some other weapon. It is in the iterative imperfect tense of τύπτω (*typto*), referring to a repeated action in the past. This indicates that the Roman soldiers took turns striking Jesus over and over until their malicious desires were satiated. Meanwhile, Jesus bled heavily from His head where the crown of thorns had pierced deeply into the skull. The excruciating pain only grew more and more intense. All the indescribable afflictions that our Lord had to endure were because of our sins and transgressions (Isa 53:5, 8). Knowing all of this, do we not still turn away from the cross, reject it, and look upon it with contempt while claiming that we believe in Jesus? The prophet Isaiah's heartwrenching lament, "And we did not esteem Him," is truly the message that each of us must inscribe in the depth of our hearts (Isa 53:3).

(4) The work of redemption fulfilled on the cross

After the agonizing climb up the hill of Golgotha, Jesus was treated like a wicked criminal when he was crucified alongside the two actual criminals. He was subjected to the unspeakable shame of being crucified completely naked in broad daylight before a mob of people (Matt 27:38; Mark 15:27; Luke 23:33; John 19:18).

Jesus spoke seven times during the six hours on the cross. He spoke three times between the third (9 a.m. [Mark 15:25]) and the sixth hour (noon [Luke 23:34, 43; John 19:26]). Between the sixth and the ninth hour (3 p.m.), darkness fell over the whole land (Matt 27:45; Mark 15:33; Luke 23:44). Just before He died, around the ninth hour, He spoke four more times (Matt 27:45–46; John 19:28, 30; Luke 23:46).

The six hours on the cross were a compression of Jesus' life and the culmination of the history of redemption. It is not an overstatement to say that Jesus lived thirty-three years of His life for those six hours on the cross. They contain the completion of God's work of redemption, His judgment upon Satan, and the ultimate triumph of the saints (Col 2:13–15).

Jesus delivered seven immortal messages during the six hours on the cross. The first of the messages was the proclamation of atonement.

> **Luke 23:34** But Jesus was saying, "Father, forgive them; for they do not know what they are doing." And they cast lots, dividing up His garments among themselves.

In this verse, the word *but* is δὲ (*de*) in Greek, meaning "however" or "but." It expresses the boundless *agapē* love of God through which He pronounced atonement without cause. Even as Jesus was on the wretched cross at Golgotha, He prayed for the forgiveness of those who drove nails through Him and hurled abuses at Him. During His ministry, Jesus taught His disciples to forgive their brothers, saying, "I do not say to you, up to seven times, but up to seventy times seven" (Matt 18:22). Here, on the cross, was an amazing demonstration of His teaching.

> **Matthew 5:44** But I say to you, love your enemies, and pray for those who persecute you.
> **Matthew 5:46** For if you love those who love you, what reward have you? Do not even the tax collectors do the same?

Jesus' sixth message on the cross, recorded in John 19:30 was, "It is finished" (τετέλεσται, *tetelestai*), in the perfect tense of τελέω (*teleō*). This end is not an incomplete end, but a total completion of the originally intended plan. Thus, Jesus' work of redemption was already completed on the cross, and emphasis is placed on the eternal efficacy of that work.

At last, Jesus cried out with a loud voice, "Father, into Thy hands I commit My spirit" (Luke 23:46), and breathed His last. To confirm Jesus' death, the Roman soldiers pierced His side with a spear, and immediately blood and water came out (John 19:34). Jesus shed blood and water on the cross for all sinners and died, completing His work of salvation.

(5) The reconciliation and the attitude of the saints concerning Jesus' work of atonement

(i) Reconciliation, the result of Jesus' atoning work

The word *reconciliation* signifies the recovered state of harmony between God and man after sin had created a hostile relationship. Before Adam and Eve sinned, there was a close fellowship between God and man. Man communed with God and worshiped only Him. Furthermore, man ruled over all the creatures on the earth (Gen 1:26, 28; 2:15).

After sin entered, however, not only was that close relationship cut off and ruined, but also it became hostile. Consequently, mankind became enemies with God (Rom 5:10). As a result of sin, mankind became totally fallen and corrupt, and experienced a total depravity (Job 15:16; Ps 14:1–3; 51:5; 53:1; Isa 44:20; Jer 17:9). This is what John Calvin argues is the state of mankind after the fall. Consequently, the corruption of the flesh, the nature of sin, and the presence of the old self utterly deprived mankind of the ability to consider changing the hostile relationship to an amicable one.

For fallen mankind, Jesus Christ is truly the only way of restoring the relationship with God (John 14:6). God the Father, in His mercy, compassion, and *agapē* love, sent His only begotten Son into this world (John 3:16) so that He may become an atoning sacrifice (Rom 3:25). 2 Corinthians 5:18 states, "Now all these things are from God, who reconciled us to Himself through Christ, and gave us the ministry of reconciliation."

The Hebrew word for *reconciliation* in the Old Testament is כָּפַר (*kāpar*), and the Greek word used in the New Testament is καταλλαγή (*katallagē*). Both signify the act of reconciliation (Rom 5:11; 11:15; 2 Cor 5:18–19). Sin separated mankind far apart from God, but the cross allowed them back to the bosom of God, reconciling God and mankind (2 Cor 5:18; Col 1:20–22).

> **Romans 5:11** And not only this, but we also exult in God through our Lord Jesus Christ, through whom we have now received the reconciliation.
>
> **Colossians 1:20** ... and through Him to reconcile all things to Himself, having made peace through the blood of His cross; through Him, I say, whether things on earth or things in heaven.
>
> **Ephesians 2:13** But now in Christ Jesus you who formerly were far off have been brought near by the blood of Christ.

Although mankind had fallen far away from God, the blood of Jesus Christ brought them back to Him. Mankind had become the slave of death, but by the grace of atonement they were given eternal life (John 3:16; 1 John 2:25).

Jesus completed the work of atonement once and for all on the cross (Rom 6:10; Heb 7:27; 9:12, 26; 10:2, 10; 1 Pet 3:18). Mankind was cleansed for eternity by a single offering (Heb 10:14). There is no need for another offering for sin (Heb 10:18). Anyone who draws near to God through Christ will be saved (Heb 7:25). Besides the blood that Christ shed on the cross, there is no other method of atonement, and there is no other name other than Jesus Christ that brings salvation (Acts 4:12).

Historically speaking, Jesus Christ's sacrifice is the most noble and valuable among all others. No price can be given for the *agapē* love of God that seeks to save all the chosen in Christ (Eph 1:4). Psalm 49:8 states, "For the redemption of his soul is costly, and he should cease trying forever." Redemption of life cannot be achieved even with all the wealth in the world, but God achieved it through Jesus Christ.

(ii) The attitude of the redeemed saints

We are all eternally indebted to Jesus' redemptive love (Rom 1:14), for we are unable to repay Him in all our lifetime. What ingratitude if we forget His grace in our lives! How could we forget the cross of Jesus Christ when He was whipped and beaten for our sins (1 Cor 2:2)? The redemption we received through the cross is not a disposable doctrine that we use once and throw away. The cross must not become an accessory item that we wear on our necks without much thought or emotion. The cross holds the unique power to save. It is the source of God's wisdom. It lies at the center of the Christian gospel; without the cross, there would be no Christianity.

As long as we are on this earth, we must love God with all our lives and boast only of the cross. Galatians 6:14 states, "But may it never be that I should boast, except in the cross of our Lord Jesus Christ, through which the world has been crucified to me, and I to the world."

Anyone who boasts only of the cross has been also crucified on the cross (Gal 2:20). Furthermore, all such persons have crucified their greed and lusts on the cross (Gal 5:24). Thus, there would be nothing left to boast about but the cross if they have crucified everything on the cross. The person who boasts of the cross despises every deceitful way (Ps 119:104) and strives against sin to the point of bloodshed (Heb 12:4).

The way to boast of the cross is to preach the life given on the cross, the gospel of eternal life to the souls who are groaning under the shadow of death. If we believe in God and love Him, then we must preach the gospel of the cross with all of our strength (Acts 4:20). Woe will befall us if we do not make restitution for the grace of atonement that we have received (1 Cor 9:16). We must become God's own people who strive to preach the gospel of the cross in season and out of season until we enter heaven's gate (2 Tim 4:2; Titus 2:14).

CHAPTER 2

The Divine Administration of Redemption and the Covenant

The Bible contains the infallible blueprint of God's great plan for the salvation of mankind. All of God's numerous works that are accomplished according to His plan are also called His *divine administration*. The force that propels God's administration is His covenant and its fulfillment. In other words, the link that connects God's work of salvation in each era is His covenant (also called agreement or promise) and its fulfillment.

The Bible is divided into two major parts: the Old Testament and the New Testament. The Old Testament is a covenant of the coming of Jesus Christ, while the New Testament is a covenant of Jesus Christ as the essential fulfillment (Luke 24:27, 44) and His Second Coming (Acts 1:11; Rev 1:7).

In Matthew 26:28, Jesus says, "For this is My blood of the covenant, which is poured out for many for forgiveness of sins." The blood that Jesus Christ shed for all mankind is the blood of the covenant (Zech 9:11; Mark 14:24; Heb 9:20; 10:29; 13:20). The shedding of Jesus' precious blood on the cross was not a spontaneous event, but a long-promised event. This is the message conveyed in the phrase, "the blood of the covenant." Jesus came according to the promise of the Old Testament (Gen 3:15; Gal 3:19). He came at the fullness of time (Gal 4:4; Mark 1:15), at the right time (Rom 5:6), and with a view to an administration suitable to the fullness of the times (Eph 1:9–10). He died according to the Scriptures (1 Cor 15:3) and was resurrected according to the Scriptures (1 Cor 15:4). At the proper time, He will surely come again to this earth to fulfill the promise of His Second Coming (1 Tim 6:15).

The covenant and its fulfillment as revealed in the Bible play a vital role in properly understanding God's administration of salvation. Even to this day, the work to fulfill the covenant has progressed according to God's perfect plan. It is continuously being fulfilled today and will continue to be fulfilled in the future according to His administration until it is complete.

1. The Meaning of the Word *Covenant*

(1) Hebrew – בְּרִית (*bĕrît*)

The word *covenant* is בְּרִית (*bĕrît*) in Hebrew and refers to a mutual agreement between two parties. However, the covenant between God and His people is a unilateral agreement, with the emphasis on God's sovereignty in its implementation because God is the Creator and mankind is the creature. By nature, God and human beings cannot be equal. In Genesis 6:18, God says, "But I will establish My covenant with you." God is the One who establishes the covenant, and He is the rightful possessor of that covenant.

The word בְּרִית (*bĕrît*) also means "to break apart." The word originates from an Ancient Near Eastern practice of cutting an offering into two pieces when an important covenant was established (Gen 15:10; Jer 34:18). This act signified that if either of the two parties in the agreement does not keep his part of the agreement, he will also be torn into two pieces like the offering.

(2) Greek – διαθήκη (*diathēkē*)

In the Septuagint, בְּרִית (*bĕrît*) often is translated as διαθήκη (*diathēkē*), which is a combination of the word δια, (*dia*, prefix for "two") and the word τίθημι (*tithēmi*, "to put," "to place," or "to lay"). Thus, the compound word means "to place (or settle) between the two." The covenant is made between two parties: God and His people in the Bible. The word διαθήκη (*diathēkē*) is also used to mean "a will" (Heb 9:16–17). Normally, a covenant is made between two parties, but a will is given unilaterally. Just as a dying person unilaterally leaves behind final words (i.e., will) for the family, so too, is God's covenant made exclusively by His sovereign power.

When considering the root meaning of the word *covenant*, one can see that the ultimate conclusion after entering into a covenant with God is for God and man to become one through a spiritual bond, thus forming a personal relationship. Accordingly, God's use of the covenant as a tool to advance the plan of salvation is a clear display of His love toward mankind and strong will to save them.

2. Characteristics of the Covenant with God

(1) The unilateral and sovereign covenant

Although a covenant is an agreement between God and man, it is always initiated by God. In love, God drew near to fallen mankind to save them (1 John 4:10, 19) because human beings are God's creation but lost the ability to enter into a covenant with God since the fall.

Thus, the covenant with God is unilateral by nature and is the sovereign covenant of His grace. Even when God's people strayed from faithfully adhering to the covenant, He forgave them when they repented (Jer 33:8; 36:3). Furthermore, God Himself restored the covenant (Jer 31:31–34) and renewed it again (Ezek 16:60–63; Rom 11:27).

We have received a new covenant in Christ. As a result, we have an eternal hope that keeps us from wavering no matter how difficult our circumstances may be. This covenant is our greatest comfort and the guarantee of the ultimate victory for those who wait for His Second Coming.

(2) The eternal covenant

The greatest characteristic of the biblical covenant is that once a covenant is made, it is unchanging and faithfully fulfilled. This is why we call it the "eternal covenant" (Gen 17:13, 19; 2 Sam 23:5; 1 Chr 16:17; Ps 105:8; Ezek 16:60; 37:26). The Word of God possesses eternal efficacy. Thus, once it is proclaimed, it is definitely fulfilled (Ps 119:160; Isa 40:8; 55:11).

> **1 Kings 8:56** Blessed be the LORD, who has given rest to His people Israel, according to all that He promised; not one word has failed of all His good promise, which He promised through Moses His servant.

God's covenant is not altered by any human condition or time. It can never be nullified or made void, and it can never be cancelled or terminated. Before this generation passes, all that He has planned will be fulfilled (Matt 24:34). He will fulfill His word with perfection, and He will not delay (Hab 2:3; Heb 10:37; Rev 1:1; 22:6).

Ezekiel 12:28 Therefore say to them, "Thus says the Lord God, 'None of My words will be delayed any longer. Whatever word I speak will be performed,'" declares the Lord God.

The covenant of the torch, which we will address in this book, is an eternal covenant. Psalm 105:8–10 states, "He has remembered His covenant forever, the word which He commanded to a thousand generations, the covenant which He made with Abraham, and His oath to Isaac. Then He confirmed it to Jacob for a statute, to Israel as an everlasting covenant." Once God takes an oath confirming it as a statute, the covenant becomes an eternally unchanging covenant.

3. Types of the Covenant

The Bible is a historical account based on God's covenant. Through the covenant, God promised redemption in Jesus Christ. Thus, the main contents of the covenant are Jesus Christ and the redemption fulfilled through Him, which is eternal life (1 John 2:25). In Titus 1:2, the apostle Paul says that he is writing, "in the hope of eternal life, which God, who cannot lie, promised long ages ago." Thus, this promise of eternal life can be traced all the way back to the eternal world before creation. There are many different types of covenants in the Bible, but the covenants that appear after creation include the covenant of works, the covenant of redemption, and the covenant of grace.

(1) The covenant of works

After God established the Garden of Eden toward the east, He placed Adam there (Gen 2:8). In the garden, God entered into the covenant of works with Adam, who represents all humanity (Hos 6:7). Then God said to him, "But from the tree of the knowledge of good and evil you shall not eat, for in the day that you eat from it you shall surely die" (Gen 2:17). This covenant, which God established with Adam concerning the tree of life and the tree of the knowledge of good and evil, is called the covenant of works because Adam's life depended on his works.

The ultimate promise in this covenant of works is eternal life (1 John 2:25). If Adam and Eve had treasured, cherished, believed, and obeyed this divine Word wholeheartedly with fear, they would have eaten the fruit from the tree of life and lived eternally (Gen 3:22).

However, Eve listened to the words of the serpent, which were in complete opposition to God's covenant. The serpent completely altered God's Word by asserting, "You surely shall not die" by eating the fruit of the tree of the knowledge of good and evil (Gen 3:4). The serpent also tempted her with a lie that they could be like God: "For God knows that in the day you eat from it your eyes will be opened, and you will be like God, knowing good and evil" (Gen 3:5). As Eve's heart became tempted, she began to believe in the serpent's lies. Thus, with a proud desire to become like God, she reached out her hand for the fruit of that tree and ate it (Gen 3:6). Then, she became another tempter and gave the fruit to her husband, Adam. He too, ended up eating that fruit (Gen 3:6). Hence, the first man and woman committed the sin of disbelief, disobedience, and pride.

In this manner, the covenant of works that had been established by the Word of God was breached. The consequent condemnation that was poured upon mankind was enormous. Because of Adam, the ground was cursed to yield thorns and thistles, and in toil Adam was to eat of it all the days of his life (Gen 3:17–19). Adam and Eve were destined to die as a result of their sins (Rom 5:12). They received the sentence, "For you are dust, and to dust you shall return," (Gen 3:19) and were cast out from the beautiful Garden of Eden, an actual, historical entity (Gen 3:24). After expelling Adam and Eve from the garden, God placed cherubim and a flaming sword that turned in every direction to the east of the garden to guard the way to the tree of life (Gen 3:24). God has shown that those who break the covenant simply cannot live forever.

Thus, "sin" caused mankind to fall. This fall caused a total separation from God that resulted in their expulsion from the garden and the stark darkness of despair in their lives (Isa 59:2). As a result of the breached covenant of works, the once noble mankind—originally created to live in eternity with God—fell and became children of wrath and beings under the curse of death who cannot escape judgment (Eph 2:3).

(2) The covenant of redemption

The covenant of redemption is the covenant that God established from before the ages to save fallen mankind. To restore a humanity expelled from Eden because they could not keep the covenant of works, God entered into a covenant with Jesus Christ, the Holy Son, and promised to accomplish the covenant through Him. In other words, the covenant of works, which Adam could not keep, was now enacted through Jesus. To do this, God the Father required two things from Jesus Christ.

First, Jesus must put on the form of humanity by coming as the seed of the woman (Gen 3:15; Gal 4:4–5; Heb 2:11–15). When mankind faced eternal destruction because of their transgression and fall, God did not simply abandon them (Isa 59:16); He made a firm promise to save them through the seed of the woman. The one who came as the seed of the woman at the fullness of time (Gal 4:4)—the only begotten Son who was in the bosom of the Father from before the beginning (John 1:14, 18) and was conceived by the Holy Spirit in the body of the virgin Mary (Matt 1:23; cf. Isa 7:14)—was indeed Jesus Christ.

By taking the form of flesh and blood, Jesus Christ achieved a hypostatic (personal) union of divinity and humanity. While He was on this earth, He was God-Man—the true God and true man.

Second, Jesus was to pay the penalty of sin on the cross, thereby satisfying the righteousness of the law (Gal 3:10–13). By bearing the transgressions of sinners and accepting their penalty on their behalf, Jesus undertook the work of atonement for their transgressions. Because the first Adam could not keep the covenant of works, Jesus Christ had to come and shed His blood on the cross, to fulfill the righteousness of the law and accomplishing the requirements of the covenant without fail (Heb 7:22; 8:6).

With the redeeming covenant that Jesus Christ has fulfilled on the cross, God the Father forgave the sins of the people who belong to Him and bestowed upon them the grace of justification (Rom 3:21–24). Therefore, the covenant of redemption is the lawful foundation for the fulfillment of the covenant of grace.

(3) The covenant of grace

While the covenant of redemption was made between God and Jesus Christ for the purpose of redeeming fallen mankind, the covenant of grace is made between God and fallen mankind. It is based upon the foundation of the covenant of redemption, in which sinners can find salvation and eternal life by believing in Jesus Christ. Considering that even faith in Christ—which is the sole requirement for salvation—is a free gift (i.e., grace) from God (Eph 2:8), we can conclude that the covenant of grace is entirely founded upon His unilateral grace. Neither our faith nor our repentance qualifies as the meritorious requirements for this covenant of grace.

In the covenant of works, men are given the task and obligation to carry out the covenant. However, because the covenant of grace is established in Christ, He is the One who guarantees to carry out the covenant. Humanity is merely a recipient under the covenant of grace through which eternal life is guaranteed through Christ. Thus, unlike the covenant of works, the covenant of grace requires no conditions, for it is laid upon the foundation of His boundless love, a gift freely bestowed through the One willed by God (John 3:15).

Indeed, the covenant of grace is the covenant of God's sovereign love that He bestows upon His people. This covenant of grace emerges in various forms throughout the history of redemption.

4. The Gradual Expansion of Covenantal Revelations

(1) Covenants in the Old Testament

The relationship between God and mankind was severed when Adam, the forefather of humanity, disobeyed the Word of God (Gen 2:17) and ate of the fruit of the tree of the knowledge of good and evil. To restore this broken relationship, God elected Israel as His chosen people and made a covenant with them. Since then, God has been progressing toward the completion of the history of salvation by gradually fulfilling that covenant. Therefore, many covenants that appear in the Old Testament are the gradual expansion of revelations for the salvation of sinful mankind.

The very first revelation regarding the covenant is the "seed of the woman" promised in Genesis 3:15. This was the first covenant that vividly conveyed God's will to save fallen mankind. All covenants, which are to be revealed gradually and vividly as the history of redemption progresses, stem from this covenant. God's covenants were gradually developed into different forms in each time period throughout the history of the Old Testament. Such varying forms include the covenant with Noah (Gen 9), the covenant with Abraham (Gen 15; 17), the covenant with Moses (Exod 19; 24), the covenant with David (2 Sam 7; 1 Kgs 8:25; Ps 132:11), the new covenant through Jeremiah (Jer 31:31–34), and the everlasting covenant with Ezekiel (Ezek 16:60–63).

(2) The covenant with Abraham

God established a covenant with Abraham on seven occasions:

- First, God called Abraham and made His first promise in Genesis 12:1–3.
- Second, in Genesis 12:7, God promised the land of Canaan for the first time.
- Third, in Genesis 13:15–18, God once again gave a promise concerning the land of Canaan and Abraham's descendants.
- Fourth, in Genesis 15, God reconfirmed His promise concerning the land of Canaan and Abraham's descendants through the covenant of the torch.
- Fifth, in Genesis 17:9–14, God established the covenant of circumcision.
- Sixth, in Genesis 18:10, God once again promised the birth of Isaac.
- Seventh, in Genesis 22:15–18, after Abraham offered up Isaac as a sacrifice, God gave His final confirmation of all the covenants He had made with Abraham thus far.

The covenants that God made with Abraham become the focal point of the history of redemption that has progressed since then. Throughout the course of history, when the Israelites were rescued from their bondage in Egypt, when they conquered the land of Canaan, and at the establishment of the powerful dominion of David, they cried out for God's mercy by relying on the "covenant" which God had promised Abraham (Exod 32:13; Deut 9:27; 1 Kgs 18:36; 1 Chr 29:18). In return, God remembered the "covenant" with Abraham and helped them (Exod 2:24; 6:5; Lev 26:42, 45; Deut 9:5; 1 Chr 16:15–18; 2 Kgs 13:23; Luke 1:72–73).

> **Psalm 105:7–10** He is the LORD our God; His judgments are in all the earth. [8]He has remembered His covenant forever, the word which He commanded to a thousand generations, [9]the covenant which He made with Abraham, and His oath to Isaac. [10]Then He confirmed it to Jacob for a statute, to Israel as an everlasting covenant.

(3) The redemptive and historical meaning of the covenant of the torch

Of the numerous covenants in the Old Testament and the seven covenants established with Abraham, the covenant that most explicitly and vividly conveys the intention behind the covenant of grace is the one of the "flaming torch" found in Genesis 15. The divine history of salvation for all humanity becomes clearly outlined in the covenant of the torch which God established with Abraham. The covenant of the torch historically implies the restoration of the nation of Israel, but it ultimately bears the great purpose in redemptive history of restoring fallen mankind's lost "land" and the "people" of that nation. Concerning this, Erich Sauer states, "From the point of view of the history of salvation this is the most significant covenant-making of the Old Testament (Gen. 15:9–18)."[2]

Indeed, the covenant of the torch is the clearest manifestation of the administration of God in the history of redemption, which accomplishes the election of His people, their growth and the formation of their nation, and their possession of their dwelling place, the land of Canaan. There are two major reasons for this.

(i) It is a covenant established with a "torch" that passed between the pieces of the animals that were cut in two.

According to the Ancient Near Eastern customs of establishing a treaty (or covenant) around the fifteenth century BC, when the Pentateuch was recorded, the parties that are establishing the covenant must cut sacrificial animals in two pieces and pass between the pieces in front of many witnesses. This custom was carried out as an act of swearing an oath to keep the covenant, agreeing that whoever fails to keep the covenant will be cut into pieces like the animals (Jer 34:18-21).

A unique phenomenon that happened when God was making the covenant with Abraham is a flaming torch, which passed between the pieces of the animals. Since the torch symbolizes God's presence (Exod 13:21; 19:18; 20:18-20; Deut 4:11-12; 5:23-24; Isa 62:1), the party that passed between the pieces was God. This was an emphatic expression of God's will that He would certainly fulfill this covenant.

(ii) It was a definite promise concerning the establishment of God's kingdom

Of the many covenants in the Old Testament, the covenant that contains the most details concerning the kingdom of God is the "covenant of the torch." Genesis 15:7 states, "And He said to him, 'I am the LORD who brought you out of Ur of the Chaldeans, to give you this land to possess it.'" Through the covenant of the torch, God proclaimed that He would surely give the land of Canaan to Abraham's descendants. Additionally, God promised that they would enter Canaan in the fourth generation from Abraham (Gen 15:16), and God even delineated the boundaries of Canaan (Gen 15:18).

The covenant of the torch is not limited to the fleshly descendants of Abraham. Ultimately, it is the promise given to all the spiritual descendants of Abraham—those who receive salvation through their faith in Jesus Christ (Rom 9:7–8; Gal 3:7, 27–29). If God established an everlasting covenant to give the land of Canaan to Abraham and his descendants (Ps 105:8–11), that covenant is still valid today for the believers who have received the promise of the kingdom of heaven.

Therefore, the covenant of the torch is not merely a covenant from the past. It is a covenant of great importance that will be finally accomplished through the saints who fervently hope for the kingdom of God and believe in Jesus Christ as their Lord and Savior.

PART TWO

The Covenant of the Torch
and the Four Generations

CHAPTER 3

The Content and
Confirmation of the Covenant

1. The Content of the Covenant

God's covenant of the torch established with Abraham in Genesis 15 is a covenant concerning Abraham's "descendants" and the "land of Canaan" where they were to dwell.

(1) The promise concerning the descendants

The covenant of the torch promises the election and prosperity of godly descendants who will accomplish God's administration in the history of redemption. Genesis 15:1–6 deals with the promise concerning the descendants.

> **Genesis 15:4–5** Then behold, the word of the Lord came to him, saying, "This man will not be your heir; but one who shall come forth from your own body, he shall be your heir." ⁵And He took him outside and said, "Now look toward the heavens, and count the stars, if you are able to count them." And He said to him, "So shall your descendants be."

This passage clearly illustrates how God's kingdom will be established through Abraham's descendants. Because Abraham believed in this promise of "descendants," God attributed it to him as righteousness (Gen 15:6).

The history of redemption up until the covenant of the torch was a period of finding one "godly descendant" to establish the kingdom of God in the future. The history of redemption after the covenant of the torch establishes that the godly descendants of that "one man" will build a nation and fill the whole earth so that God's kingdom will be complete (Gen 15:5). Thus, the history of redemption that once worked through one individual and his family became expanded through a nation and out to the entire world; such a turning point was made possible by the covenant of the torch.

(2) The promise concerning the land

The covenant of the torch promises that the land of Canaan will be granted to the godly descendants who will carry out God's plan of redemption (Gen 15:7–21).

> **Genesis 15:7** And He said to him, "I am the LORD who brought you out of Ur of the Chaldeans, to give you this land to possess it."

The message of Genesis 15:13–21 is the promise that the descendants of Abraham would become strangers in a foreign land where they would be oppressed for 400 years, and that they would return to Canaan in the fourth generation.

This is a detailed description of the covenant of the torch:

- First, Abraham's descendants would become strangers in a foreign land where they would be oppressed for 400 years, but they would evenutally come out with great possessions (Gen 15:13–14).
- Second, Abraham would be buried at a good old age and return to his fathers in peace (Gen 15:15).
- Third, the Israelites' return to the land of Canaan would be accomplished in the fourth generation (Gen 15:16).
- Fourth, God outlined the boundaries of the land of Canaan— from the river of Egypt as far as the great river Euphrates—that would be given to the descendants of Abraham (Gen 15:18–21).

2. The Confirmation of the Covenant

After God disclosed the contents of the covenant, He confirmed it with a *smoking oven* and a *flaming torch* (Gen 15:17).

(1) The smoking oven (תַּנּוּר עָשָׁן, *tannûr ʿāšān*)

After having watched for the birds of prey and driven them away when they came down upon the carcasses, Abraham waited tirelessly for the divine presence until the sun went down. At long last, the very first thing that finally appeared over the dedicated sacrifices was a smoking oven (Gen 15:17).

A smoking oven refers to the hot furnace used to melt and refine metal. This foreshadows the severe suffering that the Israelites would face in the future. Gold that passes through a hot furnace comes forth refined as pure gold (Job 23:10). The 400 long and dreary years in Egypt, like being in the "iron furnace of Egypt" (Deut 4:20; 1 Kgs 8:51; Jer 11:4), were the process of purification intended by God to refine the Israelites as pure gold.

It may have seemed torturous and difficult at the time, but herein lies God's administration in the history of redemption: to cause Israel's faith to mature through such trials of affliction (Jas 1:2–4), raise them into a "great nation" that trusts only in God (Gen 46:3), and establish them as the true possessors of the land of Canaan.

(2) The flaming torch (לַפִּיד אֵשׁ, lappîd 'ēš)

After the appearance of the smoking oven, a flaming torch passed between the two pieces of the sacrifice (Gen 15:17). The flaming torch blazing in the darkness that followed the sunset was a clear and undeniable confirmation. Such a vivid image of the brightly illuminating flames of the torch extinguishing the surrounding darkness was a powerful assurance that God certainly would accomplish all that He had promised Abraham.

In the Bible, fire often is used to signify God's glorious presence and His divine manifestation (Isa 10:17; 62:1). The pillar of fire during the wilderness journey was the fire of God's presence in the midst of the Israelites (Exod 13:21). God often descended in fire (Exod 19:18; 20:18) and spoke from the midst of the fire (Deut 4:11–12, 15, 36; 5:23–24). The torch that appears in the covenant given to Abraham clearly represents the presence of God Himself. Hence, the flaming torch passing between the pieces of the sacrifice was none other than God Himself. This signifies that God will assume total responsibility for the covenant.

One important point to be noted here is that the smoking oven has the denotation of continuously smoking (עָשָׁן, 'āšān), and the torch also signifies a continuity (אֵשׁ, 'ēš).

This illustrates the living and active power at work (Heb 4:12), as well as God's zeal that ceaselessly works to fulfill the salvation of His people (2 Kgs 19:31; Isa 9:7; Ezek 39:25; 2 Cor 11:2). In *Webster's Revised Unabridged Dictionary* the word *zeal* is defined as "passionate ardor in the pursuit of anything" and "eagerness in favor of a person or cause."

God has continued the work of salvation through His zeal, which inspired the hearts of numerous men of faith such as Abraham throughout the generations.

The appearance of the smoking oven and the flaming torch provides three important lessons about the salvation of Abraham's descendants who are under the covenant of Christ's blood today.

First, it confirms that we certainly will experience the presence of the living God as long as we cast away our "birds of prey," the forces of darkness, and persevere even though God's answer may seem to be delayed.

Second, it shows that the flaming torch will brighten our dark night even when we undergo severe trials and fiery tests and feel as if we cannot see what is ahead because of the darkness surrounding the smoking furnace. We are guaranteed victory because God is ever-present and participates in our afflictions (Isa 63:9).

Third, the smoking furnace and the flaming torch will always complement each other and work together until the salvation of the saints is complete. Both are products of God's providence founded upon His boundless love. The smoking furnace is a tool that tries us and refines us to perfect our salvation. The flaming torch is a symbol of God's great consolation and His Immanuel love.

3. The Covenant and God's Faithfulness

In our journey toward the fulfillment of the covenant of the torch, we cannot help but confess one thing: God's Word most certainly is fulfilled in history without leaving out a single jot or tittle. The covenant of the torch clearly depicts a blueprint of the grand history of redemption, confirming that this history of redemption, which began with the fall of Adam, will surely see its conclusion at the end of human history.

The words of mankind are deceitful and void because they stem from hearts that are terribly corrupt and deceitful; their words bear no efficacy. Psalm 62:9 states, "Men of low degree are only vanity, and men of rank are a lie; in the balances they go up; they are together lighter than breath." The psalmist, in the midst of severe suffering, confessed, "All men are liars" (Ps 116:11).

The Word of God, however, is the truth that will definitely be kept; it will never end in vain. It certainly will accomplish His pleasing will and return in fruition (Isa 55:11). God does not take back His Words before they are fulfilled (Num 23:19), because He speaks from perfect discernment, complete knowledge, total planning, and eternal providence. Thus, nothing can stand in the way of His Word, for it never withers or fades, but the Word of our God stands forever (Isa 40:8). There is no deceit in the One who speaks (Heb 6:18), and He is always the same forever (Heb 13:8).

Our God is always faithful (Rom 3:3; 1 Cor 1:9; 10:13; 2 Cor 1:18; 2 Thess 3:3; Titus 1:9; 3:8; Heb 11:11; 1 Pet 4:19; 1 John 1:9).

> **1 Thessalonians 5:24** Faithful is He who calls you, and He also will bring it to pass.
>
> **2 Timothy 2:13** If we are faithless, He remains faithful; for He cannot deny Himself.

In *Webster's Revised Unabridged Dictionary* the word *faithful* is defined as "full of faith, or having faith; disposed to believe, especially in the declarations and promises of God." In Greek, the word *faithful* is πιστός (*pistos*), derived from πείθω (*peithō*), meaning "to induce one to believe, to have confidence, and to put trust." Since our "faithful" God establishes and advances forward to fulfill the covenant of the torch, this covenant will carry out His administration in the history of redemption and undoubtedly be fulfilled.

Today, the assurance of salvation and the triumph of believers also remain in the faithfulness of God. Hebrews 6:17 tells us, "In the same way God, desiring even more to show to the heirs of the promise the unchangeableness of His purpose, interposed with an oath." The hope of saints must not falter, but must remain steadfast as long as the promise of God remains as our goal and purpose.

CHAPTER 4

The Time of Ratification

The covenant of the torch (Gen 15) was ratified after Abraham had rescued his nephew Lot in the battle between the kings of northern and southern Canaan and after his encounter with Melchizedek (Gen 14). It was also before Abraham took Sarah's maidservant, Hagar (Gen 16), whom he took after living ten years in Canaan. Therefore, the covenant of the torch was ratified in Abraham's tenth year in Canaan in 2082 BC when he was 84 years of age.

1. The Calculation of the Year of the Exodus

The exodus of the Israelites was the fulfillment of the covenant that God had made with Abraham. Through the covenant of the torch, God promised Abraham that his descendants would become strangers in a foreign land, where they would be enslaved and oppressed for 400 years, and return in the fourth generation (Gen 15:13–16). The question that arises here is, "When did the exodus take place?" To determine the year in which the covenant of the torch was established, we must calculate in reverse, starting from the year of the exodus.

There are two major theological methodologies for determining the year of the exodus. The "early date" theory dates the exodus to the fifteenth century BC, while the "late date" theory dates the exodus to the thirteenth century BC. Many theologians today support the "early date" theory.

The "late date" theory presumes that the exodus occurred during the reign of the Egyptian king Rameses II (1290–1224 BC). It also presumes that the pharaoh who tried to kill Moses (Exod 2:15) was the father of Rameses II, Seti I (1312–1289 BC).

The "early date" theory presumes that the exodus occurred in 1446 BC, during the reign of the Egyptian king Amenhotep II (1450 BC–?). Thus, the pharaoh who tried to kill Moses would have been Thutmose

III (1504 BC–1450 BC) from the 18th Dynasty of Egypt. Many evangelical theologians support this view.

Based on the Bible, the "early date" theory seems more appropriate than the "late date" theory as suggested by the reasons below:

(1) The "early date" agrees with the historical record in 1 Kings 6:1

1 Kings 6:1 states, "Now it came about in the four hundred and eightieth year after the sons of Israel came out of the land of Egypt, in the fourth year of Solomon's reign over Israel, in the month of Ziv which is the second month, that he began to build the house of the LORD." 2 Chronicles 3:2 cites the exact year, month, and date: "And he began to build on the second day in the second month of the fourth year of his reign."

According to history, Solomon was enthroned as the king of Israel in 970 BC; thus, the fourth year of his reign was 966 BC. Adding 480 years in accordance with the record in 1 Kings 6:1 puts the exodus at exactly 1446 BC.

The "late date" theory perceives the 480 years as a symbolic number that represents the 12 generations (i.e., 12 x 40 years). However, the advocates of the "late date" theory assert that one generation is actually only about 25 to 30 years, Accordingly, 12 generations would not amount to 480 years. The original Hebrew text of 1 Kings 6:1 makes no mention of 12 generations. Therefore, the "late date" theory holds little credibility.

(2) The "early date" theory agrees with Judges 11:26

Judges 11:26 states, "While Israel lived in Heshbon and its villages, and in Aroer and its villages, and in all the cities that are on the banks of the Arnon, three hundred years, why did you not recover them within that time?"

Thus, 300 years passed from the beginning of the Canaan conquest until the time of Jephthah's reign. The period of the judges, which came after the conquest of Canaan, can be considered 340 years because the time from the end of Jephthah's rule and the beginning of King Saul's reign, which includes the prophet Samuel's ministry, is considered to be 56 years.[3] Then, adding to this 84 years and 6 months (the sum of 40 years of King Saul's reign [Acts 13:21], 40 years and 6 months of

King David's reign [2 Sam 5:4–5], and four years of Solomon's reign [1 Kgs 6:1]) would make the time between the conquest of Canaan and the construction of the temple of Solomon at least 424 years and 6 months.

The wilderness journey (Num 14:33–34) and the period of the Canaan conquest generally are viewed as 40 years and 16 years respectively (refer to p. 236–37. The Duration of the Conquest of Canaan, in Chapter 14, The Conquest of Canaan). Thus, adding 40 years and 16 years to 424 years and 6 months yields approximately 480 years.

According to this calculation, therefore, it took 480 years from the time of the exodus until the construction of the temple of Solomon; hence, the year of the exodus becomes 1446 BC (480 years + 966 BC, the fourth year of Solomon's reign) and demonstrates that the "early date" theory is in agreement with the overall biblical standpoint.

40 years in the wilderness	300 years / 16 years of Canaan conquest	from the entry into Canaan to dwelling in Canaan until Jephthah (Judg 11:26)	Approx. 56 years after Jephthah, including Samuel's reign	40 years of Saul's reign	Approx. 40 years of David's reign	4 years of Solomon's reign
		Approx. 340 years of the period of the judges		Approx. 84 years		

40 years + 16 years + approx. 340 years (time of the judges) + approx. 84 years = 480 years
966 BC + 480 years = 1446 BC (year of the exodus)

2. The Calculation of the Time of Ratification

(1) The Israelites entered Egypt in 1876 BC

Adding 430 years (the duration of the Israelites' dwelling in Egypt [Exod 12:40–41; Gal 3:17]) to the year of the exodus results in 1876 BC as the year the Israelites entered Egypt.

1446 BC (year of the exodus) + 430 years = 1876 BC

(2) Jacob was born in 2006 BC

Jacob was 130 years old when he entered Egypt (Gen 47:9).

1876 BC + 130 years = 2006 BC

(3) Isaac was born in 2066 BC

Isaac was 60 years old when he became the father of Jacob. (Gen 25:26).

2006 BC + 60 years = 2066 BC

Incidentally, at the time of Isaac's birth (2066 BC), Abraham was 100 years old (Gen 21:5).

(4) The covenant of the torch was ratified in 2082 BC

Abraham took Hagar after having dwelled in Canaan for ten years, when he was 85 years old (Gen 12:4; 16:3). Abraham was 86 years old when Ishmael was born to him through Hagar (Gen 16:16). Therefore, the covenant of the torch was ratified when Abraham was 84 years old, before taking Hagar as his wife. This was 16 years before Isaac's birth (100 − 84 = 16). Therefore, it can be deduced that 2082 BC was the year for the ratification of the covenant of the torch.

2066 BC + 16 years = 2082 BC

CHAPTER 5

The Meaning of the Prophecy "In the Fourth Generation They Will Return"

Genesis 15:13–16 And God said to Abram, "Know for certain that your descendants will be strangers in a land that is not theirs, where they will be enslaved and oppressed 400 years. ¹⁴But I will also judge the nation whom they will serve; and afterward they will come out with many possessions. ¹⁵And as for you, you shall go to your fathers in peace; you shall be buried at a good old age. ¹⁶Then in the fourth generation they shall return here, for the iniquity of the Amorites is not yet complete."

God said that the period of the Israelites' enslavement in a foreign land would be 400 years (Gen 15:13). Afterwards, in Genesis 15:16, He said that Abraham's descendants would return to the land of Canaan in the fourth generation.

There are a few different theological perspectives on this matter. The majority of theologians, commentators, and pastors wrongly interpret the 400 years in Genesis 15:13 as being the same as the four generations in Genesis 15:16. In this view, one generation is equivalent to 100 years, which means 400 years would be four generations. They assert that although the 400 years and the four generations refer to the same amount of time, it was expressed differently for emphasis. This argument construes one generation as "the entire lifespan of a person," approximating that the average lifespan is about 100 years. In this way, the 400 years and four generations are in agreement, and there would be no need to give further consideration about the time of its fulfillment.

1. Calculating One Generation as One Hundred Years: The View that 400 Years (Gen 15:13) Are Equivalent to Four Generations (Gen 15:16)

The following are views that the "400 years" and the "four generations" are the same time for the fulfillment of the covenant of the torch.

(1) "Apparently the two periods are equated, so one generation equals 100 years."

(Gordon J. Wenham, *Genesis 1–15*, Word Biblical Commentary 1 [Waco, TX: Word, 1987], 332).

(2) "[400] is an employment of a round number, something not uncommon in Scripture. The mention in Genesis 15:16 that the return would be 'in the fourth generation' may be explained in terms of the length of a generation in Abraham's experience. God knew that Abraham would be one hundred at Isaac's birth."

(Leon J. Wood, *A Survey of Israel's History*, Rev. David O'Brien [Grand Rapids: Zondervan, 1986], 66).

(3) "Since Abram had his first child at 100 years of age, a generation here is 100 years (Gen 21:5). Thus after the 400 years Abram's descendants would come back into the Promised Land."

(Sun Lin Theological Research Institute, *The Complete Biblical Library: The Old Testament Study Bible*, vol. 1, *Genesis* [Springfield, MO: World Library Press, 1994], 127).

(4) "God said they would be in an alien land 400 years.... This was indicated to be equivalent to 'four generations,' perhaps since men were still living to be one hundred years of age."

(Henry M. Morris, *The Genesis Record: A Scientific and Devotional Commentary on the Book of Beginnings* [Grand Rapids: Baker, 1976], 327).

(5) "'In the fourth generation' means about 400 years, calculating each generation to 100 years."

(Paul Yonggi Cho, *Genesis Exegesis*, vol. 1 [Seoul: Seoul Word Press, 1998], 246).

(6) "... also refers 400 years to 4 generations by considering 100 years to 1 generation. There is no need for much attention in trying to figure out these years."

(Ji Il Pang, *The Exegesis of Genesis* [Seoul: Dong Jin Culture, 1989], 145).

(7) "God prophesied that the Israelites would remain in Egypt for 400 years and the exact years were 430 years (Exod 12:40). The 'four generations' can be figured by estimating the average lifespan during that time as 100. This was a period from the time the 70 of Israel's family went into the land of Egypt until they cleared out from the life of afflictions in Egypt."

(Yong-Kuk Wone, *A Commentary on Genesis* [Seoul: Se Shin Culture, 1990], 295).

(8) "It seems that the 400 years are expressed as four generations, considering 100 years as one generation based on Abram's age when he begot his son."

(Won-Tae Suk, *A Commentary on Genesis* [Seoul: Gyung Hyang, 2002], 191).

(9) "Here, the 'fourth generation' is another expression that refers to 400 years on the basis of Abraham's age (100) when he had his son."

(Won-Tae Suk, *A Commentary on Hebrews* [Seoul: Gyung Hyang, 2005], 227).

(10) "The word 'generation' in verse 16 is *dor* in Hebrew and refers to time, generation, or dwelling. Thus, this word does not contradict the expression 'in fourth generation' in verse 13."

(Il-Oh Chung, *Interpretation of Genesis* [Seoul: Solomon, 2004], 202).

(11) "This part symbolically expresses the 100 years as one generation and thus equates the 400 years to four generations."

(Sang Ho Lee, *Hebrew Morphology and Exegesis Bible Series: Genesis* [Seoul: Sung Kwang Culture, 1996], 227).

(12) "400 years is an absolute number and the 'four generations' is used similar to 'four centuries.'"

(The New Thompson Thompson Reference Commentary Bible Editing Committee, ed., *The Thompson Reference Commentary Bible* [Seoul: Bible Material Publisher, 1989], 18).

(13) "In comparison to the 400 years in v. 13, it seems that one generation was considered 100 years, time from birth to death of a man (Keil). This is sufficiently possible considering the average lifespan of the time was at least 100–120 (Murphy)."

(Disciples Publishing House, *The Grand Bible Commentary: With Comprehensive and Synthetic Exegetical Study Methods* [Seoul: Bible Study Material Publisher, 1991–1993], 1:498).

(14) "One hundred years are considered one period and thus 'in fourth generation' signifies 'in 400 years.'"

(Disciples Publishing House, *The Oxford Bible Interpreter* [Seoul: Bible Study Material Publisher, 2002], 1:171).

(15) "The 'fourth' in the phrase, 'fourth generation' is an approximate number, not a definite one. In comparison to the '400 years' in verse 13, it can be construed that one generation is considered 100 years and that the numbers used here are approximate."

(Samuel Chun, *The Christian Literature Society of Korea 100th Year Anniversary Bible Commentary Series*, vol. 1 [Seoul: Christian Literature Society of Korea, 2001], 231).

(16) "Since four generations cover more than 400 years, we see that the word reckons a hundred years to a generation, according to the computation prevalent at the time of speaking."

(H. C. Leupold, *Exposition of Genesis* [Grand Rapids: Baker, 1942], 1:486).

(17) "Thus the sojourn in Egypt is to last 400 years, so that דור (as in Nestor, γενεα, ii. 1. 250) is a seculum of 100 years—a round number."

(Franz Delitzsch, *New Commentary on Genesis*, vol. 2 [Minneapolis: Klock & Klock Christian Publishers, 1978], 10).

(18) "But, more correctly, the fourth generation, calculating 100 years to a generation. 'Caleb was the fourth from Judah, and Moses from Levi, and so doubtless many others.'"

(H. D. M. Spence and Joseph S. Exell, eds., *The Pulpit Commentary*, vol. 1, *Genesis* [Peabody, MA: Hendrickson, 1950], 221).

(19) "*In the fourth generation*. This statement agrees with the passages which assign only four generations from Joseph to Moses (Ex. vi. 16–20, Nu. xxvi. 5–9), or five to Joshua (Jos. vii. 1). If the v. is by the same writer as v. 13, he must, in accordance with traditional ages of the patriarchs, have reckoned a 'generation' at 100 years."

(S. R. Driver, *The Book of Genesis* [London: Methuen, 1904], 177).

2. Are 400 Years Equivalent to Four Generations?

As is evident from the previous excerpts, many theologians and pastors view the 400 years and the four generations as interchangeable time periods expressed differently. However, there are problems that arise from this interpretation.

First, the average lifespan of the patriarchs who lived in the ten generations prior to Abraham far exceeded 100 years. The lifespan of the patriarchs during that time were as follows: Noah lived 950 years (Gen 9:29); Shem, 600 years; Arpachshad, 438 years; Shelah, 433 years; and Eber, 464 years (Gen 11:10–17). Without question, the general lifespan was drastically shortened after the Tower of Babel; however, Peleg still lived 239 years; Reu, 239 years; Serug, 230 years; Nahor, 148 years; and Terah, 205 years (Gen 11:18–25, 32).

If God had equated 100 years to one generation and accordingly, 400 years to four generations, then the average lifespan of the patriarchs contemporaneous to Abraham would have been about 100 years. However, the average lifespan at that time far exceeded 100 years.

This argument is also valid for the generations that came after Abraham. The average lifespan exceeded 140 years even for some of the main figures in the Bible, such as Abraham, who lived to the age of 175 (Gen 25:7); Isaac, 180 (Gen 35:28–29); Jacob, 147 (Gen 47:28); Joseph, 110 (Gen 50:22); and Moses, 120 (Deut 34:7).

Even among the 20 immediate descendants of Adam down to Abraham, there was not one person who died around the age of 100. Thus, calculating 100 years as one generation and interpreting 400 years of slavery as four generations is unpersuasive.

Second, the 400 years and four generations are measured differently altogether. We must ponder deeply as to why God has distinctively described the time of the fulfillment of the covenant of the torch as "400 years" in Genesis 15:13 and the "fourth generation" in Genesis 15:16. The "400 years" refer to the length of time that it would take for the fulfillment of the covenant, while the "fourth generation" refers to the number of generations or number of people. Thus, different units are used in calculating the 400 years and the four generations.

In particular, the word *generation* in the phrase "in the fourth generation" is דּוֹר (*dôr*) in Hebrew, meaning "period," "generation," or "dwelling." Unlike the assertions of the commentators noted above, this word refers not to an individual's entire lifetime, but to the time period from the birth of an individual until he grows up and fathers the next generation. In other words, it refers to the time it takes for a child to grow to adulthood and give birth to another child. Hence, one generation is generally estimated to be about 30 years.

An examination of the generations starting from Noah's first son, Shem (eleventh generation), to Abraham (twentieth generation) suggests that the birth of the first sons generally began the next generation when their fathers were around 30 years old. This pattern emerged after the birth of Arpachshad, who was born when his father, Shem, was 100 years old because of the special circumstances surrounding the flood.

Genesis 11:12 And Arpachshad lived thirty-five years, and became the father of Shelah.

Genesis 11:14 And Shelah lived thirty years, and became the father of Eber.

Genesis 11:16 And Eber lived thirty-four years, and became the father of Peleg.

Genesis 11:18 And Peleg lived thirty years, and became the father of Reu.

Genesis 11:20 And Reu lived thirty-two years, and became the father of Serug.

Genesis 11:22 And Serug lived thirty years, and became the father of Nahor.

Genesis 11:24 And Nahor lived twenty-nine years, and became the father of Terah.

Thus, based on the verses above, equating approximately 30 years to one generation is a more accurate assessment. Furthermore, nowhere else in the Bible is the word דוֹר (*dôr*) used to refer to the time span of one hundred years.[4]

There were ten generations, which totaled 490 years, from the time when Noah had his firstborn Shem at the age of 502 (Gen 5:32; 11:10) until Abraham had Isaac.

Furthermore, it is said that Job, who presumably lived during the patriarchal age, lived an additional 140 years after his tribulation and lived to see four generations of his descendants.

> **Job 42:16** And after this Job lived 140 years, and saw his sons, and his grandsons, four generations.

In this case, one generation is calculated much shorter than 100 years. Thus, the argument that 400 years equates to four generations seems unpersuasive.

Therefore, 400 years and four generations cannot be referring to the same period of time. They are two different prophecies that say two different things in the covenant of the torch. The prophecy about 400 years (Gen 15:13) is in reference to the number of years that the Israelites would be in slavery under the Egyptians, whereas the prophecy of the fourth generation (Gen 15:16) refers to the generation (דוֹר, *dôr*) in Abraham's line which would "return" to the land of Canaan.

✳ Here, the relationship between the 400 years and the four generations is exposited for the first time in history.

CHAPTER 6

The Starting Point of the Four Generations

Another important issue in the study of the fulfillment of the proph-ecy in Genesis 15:16 is the question about when the four generations begin. There are two major approaches among the scholars. The most prominent is the viewpoint that the four generations begin from the time when Abraham's descendants (the sons of Jacob) entered Egypt. The other viewpoint is that the generations begin from Abraham.

1. The Viewpoint that Four Generations Are Counted from the Time When Abraham's Descendants Settled in Egypt

Genesis 15:16 states, "Then in the fourth generation they shall return here, for the iniquity of the Amorites is not yet complete." Some theolo-gians, such as James Montgomery Boice, assert that the pronoun "they" in Genesis 15:16 refers only to Abraham's "descendants who entered Egypt."[5] They hold that Jacob's son who moved to Egypt was the first generation, and Moses was the fourth generation (Exod 6:16–20; 1 Chr 6:1–3). They construct the four generations as Levi, Kohath, Amram, and Moses. Other theologians, such as Peter S. Ruckman[6] and H. L. Willmington,[7] also support this view that the four generations are those from the time of Levi to Moses. Somewhat similarly, S. R. Driver inter-prets that the four generations begin with Joseph (not Levi, his brother) and continues to Moses.[8]

However, the number of generations between Levi and Moses is ac-tually more than four, and thus the view that the four generations begin with Levi is inaccurate. Many generations were omitted in the genera-tions from Levi to Moses.[9] According to the interpretation of Numbers 1 in *The Grand Bible Commentary*, we can deduce that there were six to seven generations between Moses' father Amram and Kohath, who ap-pear in Exodus 6:16–20 and 1 Chronicles 6:1–3.[10]

Calculation of the Omitted Generations from Kohath to Amram and Moses		
Kohath's longevity: 133 years (Exod 6:18) (assuming that he was 1 year old when entering Egypt)	430 years – 133 years – 80 years = 217 years (gap)	Moses' age at the exodus: 80 years (Exod 7:7)
	Amram's longevity: 137 years (Exod 6:20)	
Total stay in Egypt: 430 years (Exod 12:40–41)		

The Bible shows that Levi had already fathered Kohath when he arrived in the land of Egypt with his father, Jacob (Gen 46:8, 11). Kohath died in Egypt at the age of 133 (Exod 6:18). Moses was born 80 years prior to the exodus (Exod 7:7), and the amount of time that the Israelites dwelled in Egypt was 430 years (Exod 12:40–41). Subtracting Kohath's longevity of 133 years and Moses' age of 80 years at the time of exodus from the Israelites' 430 years of dwelling in Egypt leaves a gap of 217 years, even if we assume that Kohath was at least one year old when he entered Egypt (430 – 133 – 80 = 217). Since Kohath's son Amram lived 137 years (Exod 6:20), it is impossible for Amram to have been the only generation that lived during the 217 years. Consequently, there must have been many more generations that lived between Kohath and Moses (besides Amram), but they have been omitted.

In contrast, all of the generations in the genealogy of Joshua were recorded without omission. This genealogy records 12 generations between Jacob and Joshua (cf. "Abraham's Genealogy", see pg. 313).

Jacob[1] – Joseph[2] – Ephraim[3] – Beriah[4] – Resheph[5] – Telah[6] – Tahan[7] – Ladan[8] – Ammihud[9] – Elishama[10] – Non (Nun)[11] – Joshua[12]

(1 Chr 7:23–27)

In light of the facts above, it becomes evident that calculating the "four generations" from the time when Abraham's descendants entered Egypt is simply not in accordance with the Bible.

2. The Viewpoint that Four Generations Are Counted from Abraham

In order to solve this problem, we need to examine closely the actual scene of Genesis 15. Through the text in which God spoke to Abraham, we can clearly understand how He revealed the details of the covenant of the torch and with whom the four generations begin.

According to Genesis 15:12–16, God spoke of four things when the sun was going down and a deep sleep had fallen upon Abraham.

- First, Abraham's descendants would become strangers in a land that is not theirs and would be enslaved and oppressed for 400 years (v. 13).
- Second, God would judge the nation whom they were to serve, and they would come out with many possessions (v. 14).
- Third, Abraham would live to a good old age and return to his fathers in peace (v. 15).
- Fourth, Abraham's descendants would return to the land in the fourth generation (v. 16).

After God had told Abraham that his descendants would become strangers in a foreign land where they were to be enslaved and oppressed for 400 years (Gen 15:13), God went on to say that He would judge that land, and Abraham's descendants would come out with many possessions after 400 years (Gen 15:14).

15:13 וַיֹּאמֶר לְאַבְרָם יָדֹעַ תֵּדַע כִּי־גֵר יִהְיֶה זַרְעֲךָ בְּאֶרֶץ לֹא

wayyōʾmer lěʾabrām yādōaʿ tēdaʿ kigēr yiyeh zarʿăkā běʾereṣ lōʾ

(15:13) לָהֶם וַעֲבָדוּם וְעִנּוּ אֹתָם אַרְבַּע מֵאוֹת שָׁנָה

lāhem waʿăbādūm wěʿinnû ʾōtām ʾarbaʿ mēʾōt šānâ

15:14 וְגַם אֶת־הַגּוֹי אֲשֶׁר יַעֲבֹדוּ דָן אָנֹכִי וְאַחֲרֵי־כֵן

wěgam ʾethaggôy ʾăšer yaʿăbōdû dān ʾānōkî wěʾaḥărêkēn

(15:14) יֵצְאוּ בִּרְכֻשׁ גָּדוֹל

yēṣʾû birkūš gādôl

God spoke of all that would happen from the time when Abraham's descendants first moved to Egypt until the time of their exodus; He spoke of each stage: from the beginning of their lives under slavery, during slavery until their departure from Egypt. Then, God changed the focus back to Abraham who was receiving the revelation at the time. After speaking of the dismal future of Abraham's descendants, God returned His focus directly to Abraham and blessed him with longevity saying, "And as for you, you shall go to your fathers in peace; you shall be buried at a good old age" (Gen 15:15).

וְאַתָּה תָּבוֹא אֶל־אֲבֹתֶיךָ בְּשָׁלוֹם תִּקָּבֵר בְּשֵׂיבָה טוֹבָה

ṭôbâ   bĕśêbâ   tiqqābēr   bĕšālôm   ʾel ʾăbōtêkā   tābôʾ   wĕʾattâ ⁽¹⁵:¹⁵⁾

Immediately following this, God said, "Then in the fourth generation they shall return here" (Gen 15:16). The pronoun "they" in this verse refers to the descendants of Abraham, the receiver of the revelation. Thus, according to the context of this passage, it is correct to consider Abraham as the starting point of the four generations.

The association between the first part of Genesis 15:16, "Then in the fourth generation they shall return here..." and the latter part of the same verse, "...for the iniquity of the Amorites is not yet complete," further confirms this interpretation.

וְדוֹר רְבִיעִי יָשׁוּבוּ הֵנָּה כִּי לֹא־שָׁלֵם עֲוֹן

ʿāwōn   lōʾšālēm   kî   hēnnâ   yāšûbû   rĕbîʿî   wĕdôr ¹⁵:¹⁶

הָאֱמֹרִי עַד־הֵנָּה

ʿadhēnnâ   hā ʾĕmōrî ⁽¹⁵:¹⁶⁾

In Hebrew, the word *yet* in the latter part of Genesis 15:16 is עַד־הֵנָּה (ʿadhēnnâ). הֵנָּה (hēnnâ) means "here" and "now," and עַד (ʿad) means "as far as" or "even to." The Amorites were in sin even until the time when Abraham was receiving this revelation, but the state of their iniquity was not yet complete. In the future, when the iniquity of the Amorites becomes complete, the descendants of Abraham will possess the land of Canaan. This would happen in the "fourth generation," which begins with Abraham since he is the one who received the promise at the time.

The conjunction *for*, which connects the first and second clauses of Genesis 15:16, is also a clue that the four generations begin with Abraham. In Hebrew, the word *for* is כִּי (kî), a conjunction that leads to the explanation of the cause, indicating the closeness of the two clauses it is connecting. If the judgment that the iniquity of the Amorites is not yet complete is referenced to Abraham, who is presently speaking with God, then it is correct for God's statement "in the fourth generation they will return" to be calculated in reference to Abraham's time.

Accordingly, the most accurate view that fully coincides with the original biblical text is that the four generations begin with Abraham, who received the revelation, and not from the time the Israelites entered Egypt. The covenant of the torch that God gave to Abraham and his descendants must be fulfilled because it is the Word of God (Isa 55:10–11; Matt 5:18; Luke 21:33). If the beginning of the four generations is Abraham, then it is also important to find out who are properly considered the second, third, and fourth generations. In His search for a king, God recognized David, the youngest son of Jesse. Yet, David was not even considered good enough to be king by his own father. People look at the outward appearance, but God searches the heart (1 Sam 16:7).

God sees faith in people (Matt 9:2; Mark 2:5; Luke 5:20) and delights in it (Heb 11:6). Thus, all the men related to the four generations—the ones who fulfill the Divine covenant—must have been men of faith after God's own heart (1 Sam 13:14; Acts 13:22). These four generations were to be extraordinary generations that would accomplish God's administration in the history of redemption.

לכל בר דעת דרך המסעות ארבעים שנה במדבר והרוחב והאורך של ארץ הקדושה מנהר ב[...]

עמלק

מדבר צין הוא קדש

ים המלח

עיר כרמל

השור

שבט

באר שבע

שמעון

שבט

ארץ פלשתים

מדבר שור

מדבר פארן

מדבר סיני

לוח המסעות במדבר
אשר על פי ה' יסעו ועל פי ה' יחנו

א' רעמסס	טז' רתמה	לט' הרהגדגד
ב' סכת	יז' רמן פרץ	ל' ימבתה
ג' אתם	יח' לבנה	לא' עברנה
ד' פיהחירת	יח' רסה	לב' עציונגבר
ה' מרה	יט' קהלתה	לג' מדברצין
ו' אילם	ך' הרספר	לד' הרההר
ז' ים סוף	כא' חרדה	לה' צלמנה
ח' מדבר סין	כב' מקהלה	לו' פונן
ט' רפקה	כג' תחת	לז' אבת
יו' אלוש	כד' תרח	לח' דיבנגד
יא' רפידם	כה' מתקה	לט' עלמן ודבל'
יב' מדברסיני	כו' חשמנה	מ' הרי עברים
יג' קברתהתאוה	כז' מסרות	מא' ערבה מואב
יד' חצרות	כח' בני יעקן	

אלכסנדרי

ארץ גשן

פתם

שדה

צען

פיתום

נחלים

PART THREE

The History of the Patriarchs

God's work of salvation advanced through the godly descendants of Seth after Adam and Eve's fall and their banishment from the Garden of Eden. God had commanded Noah, a descendant of Seth, to build an ark, and He judged the world through the flood. However, even after the judgment of the flood, mankind constructed the Tower of Babel in an attempt to challenge God. God chose Abraham, a descendant of Shem, from the midst of the sinful world, called him out of Ur of the Chaldeans, and led him to the land of Canaan.

After God called Abraham to Canaan, He entered into the covenant of the torch with Abraham (Gen 15). Through this covenant, God demonstrated how the Promised Land of Canaan would be given to the godly descendants.

Thus, the lives of these four patriarchs—Abraham, Isaac, Jacob, and Joseph—play vital roles in the fulfillment of the covenant as part of God's plan for salvation. After God first initiated the covenant with Abraham, He also reconfirmed the contents of the covenant with his descendants as He continued to advance its fulfillment. In this chapter, by organizing the lives of these four patriarchs into a chronology, we will closely examine how God fulfilled his covenant through them.

Chart: The Chronology of the Patriarchs: Abraham, Isaac, Jacob, and Joseph

(360 years, from 2166 to 1806 BC)[11]

Year (BC)	Main Event	Content
2166	Birth of Abraham	① Terah begot Abraham in Ur of the Chaldeans at the age of 70 (Gen 11:26). ② At the birth of Abraham, Noah was 892 years old, and Abraham lived contemporaneously with Noah for 58 years. ✳ All ten generations of patriarchs preceding Abraham, from Noah to Terah, were alive at the time of Abraham's birth (Noah, Shem, Arpachshad, Shelah, Eber, Peleg, Reu, Serug, Nahor, Terah [Gen 10:21–25; 11:10–26]). ③ It was about 292 years after the judgment of the flood when idol worship was spreading in Ur of the Chaldeans. Abraham's father, Terah, was also an idol worshiper (Josh 24:2, 14).
2091	Calling of Abraham	① Abraham was 75 years old (Gen 12:4). • First calling: He was called from Ur of the Chaldeans "before he lived in Haran" (Acts 7:2), and he departed with his father, Terah, and arrived at Haran (Gen 11:26–32; 15:7; Neh 9:7; Acts 7:2–4). • Second calling: He received the calling "Go forth from your country, and from your relatives and from your father's house" (Gen 12:1), and he went to Canaan (Gen 12:5).
2082	Ratification of the Covenant of the Torch	① Abraham was approximately 84 years old. ② It was about ten years since his arrival at Canaan (Gen 16:3). ③ God gave Abraham the promise regarding the "descendants" (Gen 15:1–6) and the "land" (Gen 15:7–21).
2080	2ND YEAR OF THE COVENANT Birth of Ishmael	① Abraham was 85 years old when he took Sarai's maidservant, Hagar, and 86 years old when Ishmael was born (Gen 16:3,16). ② Ishmael was born 14 years before Isaac (Gen 16:1–16; 21:5).

Year (BC)	Main Event	Content
2067	**15TH YEAR OF THE COVENANT** Covenant of Circumcision	① Abraham was 99 years old, and Ishmael was 13 years old (Gen 17:1, 24–25). ② After renaming Abraham (Gen 17:5), God established the covenant of circumcision (Gen 17:9–14) and renamed Sarah (Gen 17:15–16). Abraham, Ishmael, and all the males in the household received circumcision (Gen 17:23–27). ③ God gave the name *Isaac* to their future son and told Abraham when he would be born (Gen 17:19; 18:10).
2066	**16TH YEAR OF THE COVENANT** Birth of Isaac	① Abraham was 100 years old (Gen 21:5; Rom 4:19). ✳ The godly ancestors—Shem (age 490), Arpachshad (age 390), Shelah (age 355), and Eber (age 325)—were alive at the time of Isaac's birth. ② "Then the Lord took note of Sarah as He had said ('one who shall come forth from your own body, he shall be your heir' [Gen 15:4]), and the Lord did for Sarah as He had promised"; and Isaac was born "at the appointed time of which God had spoken to him" and was circumcised on the eighth day of birth (Gen 21:1–4).
2063	**19TH YEAR OF THE COVENANT** Hagar and Ishmael driven out	① Hagar and Ishmael were driven out because Ishmael mocked Isaac during the great feast Abraham made on the day that Isaac was weaned (Gen 21:8, 9–21). ② Traditionally, Hebrew children are weaned three years after birth (cf. Moses [Exod 2:9–10]; Samuel [1 Sam 1:22]). Thus, Abraham was 103 years old, Isaac was 3, and Ishmael was 17 (since he is 14 years older than Isaac) when Hagar and Ishmael were driven out.
2041–2030 (estimated)	**41ST–52ND YEAR OF THE COVENANT** Isaac offered as a sacrifice on a mount in Moriah	① Isaac's mother, Sarah, died at the age of 127, which was after Abraham's test to give Isaac as a burnt offering. (Gen 23:1). Thus, Isaac could not have been 37 years old when Abraham was told to sacrifice him (Sarah had Isaac at the age of 90.) Thus, it is estimated that Isaac was approximately 25 to 36 years old, and Abraham was approximately 125 to 136. ② This was God's confirmation of the covenant with Abraham (Gen 22:1–18; Heb 11:17). ③ Abraham experienced the providence of "Jehovah Jireh" and received the promise of blessing that his seed will possess the gate of their enemies and in his seed all the nations of the earth will be blessed (Gen 22:14–18).
2031	**51ST YEAR OF THE COVENANT** Death of Terah, Abraham's father	① Abraham's father, Terah, died in Haran at the age of 205 (Gen 11:32). ② Since Terah fathered Abraham at the age of 70 (Gen 11:26), Abraham was 135 years old and Isaac was 35 at this time.

Year (BC)	Main Event	Content
2029	**53RD YEAR OF THE COVENANT** Death of Sarah, Abraham's wife	① Sarah, "mother of nations" (Gen 17:16), lived 127 years (Gen 23:1). Abraham was 137 years old and Isaac was 37 at this time. ✳ This was before Isaac was married (Gen 25:20). ② Abraham purchased the "cave of Machpelah" the year Sarah died (Gen 23:2–20). ✳ The cave of Machpelah is the first historical place to become fundamental evidence for claiming the possession of the Promised Land.
2026	**56TH YEAR OF THE COVENANT** Marriage of Isaac	① At the age of 40, Isaac married Rebekah, the daughter of Bethuel (Gen 24; 25:20), the son of Nahor and Milcah (Gen 22:20–23). Abraham was 140 years old at this time. ② It is notable that neither Abraham, the father, nor Isaac went to choose a wife for Isaac. Instead, the old servant Eliezer was sent for the task because they had placed complete trust in God's providence.
After 2026	**AFTER THE 56TH YEAR OF THE COVENANT** Abraham takes Keturah as wife	① It was after Abraham was past the old age of 140 that he took a second wife (Gen 25:1–6). ② Abraham had six children through his second wife, Keturah: Zimran, Jokshan, Medan, Midian, Ishbak, and Shuah. This must have been possible because Abraham was blessed with better health after the birth of Isaac.
2006	**76TH YEAR OF THE COVENANT** Birth of Jacob and Esau	① After 20 years of marriage, at the age of 60, Isaac became the father of twins, Esau and Jacob, as a result of his prayers (Gen 25:21–26). ② Abraham was 160 years old at that time. Since Abraham lived until he was 175 years of age, the three generations of the covenant (Abraham, Isaac, and Jacob) dwelt in tents together (Heb 11:9). ✳ The godly ancestors Shem (age 550), Shelah (age 415), and Eber (age 385) were alive at the time of Jacob's birth. ③ Isaac's wife, Rebekah, received a revelation that "the older shall serve the younger" (Gen 25:23).
1991	**91ST YEAR OF THE COVENANT**	① Abraham, "father of many nations" (Gen 17:5), lived 175 years. He died at a ripe old age satisfied with life, and was gathered to his people (Gen 25:7–8). ✳ This is fulfillment of the prophecy in the covenant of the torch "You shall go to your fathers in peace; you shall be buried at a good old age" (Gen 15:15).

Year (BC)	Main Event	Content
	Death of Abraham	② His sons Ishmael and Isaac buried him in the cave of Machpelah (Gen 25:9). Isaac was 75 years old, Ishmael was 89, and Jacob and Esau were 15 at this time. ✽ The godly ancestors Shem (age 565), Shelah (age 430), and Eber (age 400) were alive at the time of Abraham's death. (Shem lived until Isaac was 110 years old and Jacob was 50; Shelah lived until Isaac was 78 years old and Jacob was 18; and Eber lived until Isaac was 139 years old and Jacob was 79.)
1966	116TH YEAR OF THE COVENANT Marriage of Esau	① Esau married at the age of 40, much earlier than his brother (Gen 26:34). His father, Isaac, was 100 years old at that time. ✽ Jacob married at the age of 83 in Paddan-aram (Gen 29:18–30). ② Esau took Gentile daughters of Hittites as wives: Judith, the daughter of Beeri the Hittite, and Basemath, the daughter of Elon the Hittite (Gen 26:34). These marriages brought grief upon Isaac and Rebekah (Gen 26:35; 27:46). ③ After Jacob left Canaan, Esau married for the third time, this time to Mahalath, the daughter of Ishmael and the sister of Nebaioth (Gen 28:6–9). ✽ Genesis 36:2–3 records Esau's three wives as follows: Adah, the daughter of Elon the Hittite; Oholibamah, the daughter of Anah and granddaughter of Zibeon the Hivite; and Basemath, the daughter of Ishmael and sister of Nebaioth.
1943	139TH YEAR OF THE COVENANT Death of Ishmael	① Ishmael, the son of Hagar (Abraham's concubine), died at 137 years of age (Gen 25:17). Isaac was 123 years old and Jacob was 63 at this time. ② Ishmael died 48 years after his father Abraham had died (Gen 25:7).
1930	152ND YEAR OF THE COVENANT Jacob receives the blessing of the firstborn and flees	① It was by God's sovereign providence that Jacob received the blessing of the firstborn (Gen 27:1–40; Rom 9:10–13). ② It is estimated that Jacob was 76 years old at that time, and his father, Isaac, was 136 years old with eyes too dim to see because of old age (Gen 27:1). ③ By the command of his father, Isaac, Jacob fled from his brother, Esau, to his uncle Laban's house in Paddan-aram (Gen 28:1–5).

Year (BC)	Main Event	Content
1923	**159TH YEAR OF THE COVENANT** Marriage of Jacob	① Jacob married at the old age of 83 (Gen 29:18–30). This was after he worked for his uncle Laban for seven years from the time he had first fled to Paddan-aram at the age of 76. ② Jacob labored for Laban seven years in order to have Rachel (Laban's second daughter) as his wife, but Laban deceived him and gave him Leah (his first daughter) instead. Then, Jacob agreed to work seven additional years for Rachel and took her as wife seven days after the agreement. Thus, Jacob labored a total of 14 years for Laban in order to have Rachel (Gen 29:27–28).
1916	**166TH YEAR OF THE COVENANT** Birth of Joseph	① Jacob begot Joseph, the first son through Rachel, at the age of 90 (Gen 30:22–24). ② Joseph was Jacob's eleventh son and was considered special because he was given by God when "God remembered Rachel" (Gen 30:22). ③ Joseph reunited with his father, Jacob, after seven years of plenty and two years of famine, in the tenth year (Gen 45:6, 11). Joseph was 40 years old because it was the tenth year after he became the second-in-command under Pharaoh in Egypt (Gen 41:46). Jacob was 130 years old (Gen 47:9) according to his confession during his meeting with the pharaoh. Therefore, Jacob was 90 years old when Joseph was born.
1900 (estimated)	**182ND YEAR OF THE COVENANT** Birth of Benjamin and Death of Rachel	① Over a period of seven years, after Jacob had married his two wives, he had 11 sons and one daughter, excluding Benjamin. ② When Rachel gave birth to Benjamin, Jacob was at an old age of approximately 106 and Isaac, approximately 166. Rachel's first son, Joseph, was approximately 16 years old (Gen 35:16–18). ③ Benjamin was "a little child of [Jacob's] old age" born through Rachel and was a son whom Jacob especially loved (Gen 44:20).
1899	**183RD YEAR OF THE COVENANT** Joseph sold to Egypt	① Joseph was 17 years old when he was sold to Egypt (Gen 37:2, 12–36). Isaac was 167 years old and Jacob was 107 at the time. Since Isaac was still alive at the time, he shared Jacob's grief over losing Joseph. ② Joseph was approximately 16 years old (Gen 35:27) when Jacob returned to Isaac in Hebron. It is estimated that Joseph stayed with his grandfather Isaac for about one year before he was sold into Egypt. Although short, it was a precious time in which to inherit the covenantal faith. ③ The 13 years of affliction before Joseph became second-in-command in Egypt at the age of 30 was God's special providence (Gen 45:5–8; 50:20; Ps 105:16–23).

Year (BC)	Main Event	Content
1886	**196TH YEAR OF THE COVENANT** Death of Isaac	① Isaac lived 180 years (Gen 35:28–29). Jacob was 120 years old and Joseph was 30 years old at this time. Joseph could not witness Isaac's death because he was in Egypt. ② Isaac died in the fifty-seventh year after his brother Ishmael died. Ishmael was 14 years older than Isaac (Gen 16:16; 25:17). Thus, Isaac enjoyed the greatest longevity among the four patriarchs of the covenant.
1886	**196TH YEAR OF THE COVENANT** Ascension of Joseph to second-in-command	① Joseph was 30 years old when he became second-in-command and Jacob was 120 (Gen 41:46). ② Isaac died probably in the year that his grandson Joseph became second-in-command. ③ Joseph was in charge of Potiphar's house from the time he was 17 years old (Gen 39:7–23). He was jailed for two years after ten years of service (Gen 41:1). Through God's providence, Joseph interpreted the dreams of two fellow prisoners (Gen 40). He later interpreted Pharaoh's dreams, which gave him the opportunity to become second-in-command of Egypt (Gen 41).
1885–1879	**197TH–203RD YEAR OF THE COVENANT** Seven years of plenty	① Two sons, Manasseh and Ephraim, were born to Joseph through Asenath, the daughter of the priest Potiphera (Gen 41:47-53), "before the year of famine came," which was during the seven years of plenty (Gen 41:50). ② *Manasseh* means "to forget," and *Ephraim* means "fruitful" (Gen 41:51–52). These names embody God's great love and providence toward Joseph.
1878–1872	**204TH–210TH YEAR OF THE COVENANT** Seven years of famine	① There was famine in all the lands, but there was bread in all the land of Egypt, where Joseph was (Gen 41:54-57). ② Joseph reunited with his father and brothers after the seven years of plenty and two years of famine, in the third year of the famine (Gen 45:6, 11; 46:28–30). ③ Joseph's brothers bowed down to him in fulfillment of his dream (Gen 42:6; 43:26, 28; 44:14).
1876	**206TH YEAR OF THE COVENANT** Migration of the 70 members of Jacob's family to Egypt	① Jacob was 130 years old and Joseph was 40 years old (Gen 47:9) when Jacob's family moved to Egypt (Gen 46). ② The migration occurred in Joseph's tenth year as second-in-command, after the seven years of plenty, during the third year of the famine (Gen 45:6, 11). ③ The number of people who came to Egypt, excluding the wives of Jacob's sons, was 66 (Gen 46:26). Including Jacob, Joseph, and his two children (Manasseh and Ephraim), Jacob's family numbered 70 in all (Gen 46:27).

Year (BC)	Main Event	Content
		④ The place where they settled in Egypt was in the land of Goshen, a border area good for raising livestock (Gen 46:28–34; 47:1–12). Their settlement in Goshen was God's special providence; it was according to His amazing plan for salvation—protecting the purity of Israel's faith and allowing them to grow to become a great nation—so that He might lead them back to Canaan.
1859	223RD YEAR OF THE COVENANT Death of Jacob and his funeral	① Jacob had lived in the land of Egypt for 17 years before he was "gathered to his people" at the age of 147 (Gen 47:28; 49:29–33). ② Since Joseph was 57 years old and still in power, Pharaoh extended his great favor so that there was a grand funeral procession (Gen 50:1–14). ③ Earlier, Jacob called his son Joseph and made Joseph place his hand under Jacob's thigh and swear to bury him in Canaan (Gen 47:28–31). ④ At his death, Jacob drew his feet into the bed (straight together without scattering) and was peacefully gathered to his people (Gen 49:33).
1806	276TH YEAR OF THE COVENANT Death of Joseph	① Joseph spent most of his life in Egypt from the time he was 17 years old until his death at age 110. Although he had held a high position in Egypt, he was merely embalmed and did not have an elaborate funeral (Gen 50:22–26). ② Before his death, Joseph, looking forward to returning to the land of Canaan, told his people that God would take care of them, and he made them swear to take his bones up from Egypt (Gen 50:24–25; Heb 11:22). ✴ Joseph was buried at Shechem in the land of Canaan (Josh 24:32). ③ Joseph lived for another 53 years after the death of his father, Jacob, allowing Jacob's family to live under his care during that time (Gen 50:22–23).

CHAPTER 7

The History of Abraham

1. The Birth of Abraham (Gen 11:26), 2166 BC

Noah's age, 892; Shem's age, 390; Terah's age, 70.
Abraham and Noah lived contemporaneously for 58 years.
Ten generations of patriarchs, from Noah to Terah, were alive at his birth:
Noah, Shem, Arpachshad, Shelah, Eber, Peleg, Reu, Serug, Nahor, Terah
(Gen 10:21–25; 11:10–26).

Abraham lived about 2,000 years after Adam, and Jesus Christ was born as a descendant of Abraham approximately 2,000 years after him (Matt 1:1). Thus, Abraham lived during the junction in the work of salvation between the first man, Adam, and Jesus Christ.

Abraham was born as a descendant of Shem in 2166 BC in the fertile land of Ur of Chaldeans located southeast of what is now Baghdad, the capital of Iraq. By this time, it had been 292 years since the judgment of the flood, so the land enjoyed a period of great prosperity. Since Ur was especially fertile, even among the lands in the Mesopotamian region, it had flourished into an advanced civilization and enjoyed a luxurious material culture. According to archeological discoveries, Ur was a city in which the worship of objects found in nature, such as the moon and the stars, was widespread. Even Terah, Abraham's father, was influenced by the practices of the land, and he, too, worshiped idols (Josh 24:2–3, 14–15). Ur and Haran, where Abraham lived, were central places for the worship of a moon-god named "Sin." Thus, some of the names found in Abraham's household, such as Terah, Sarah, Milcah, and Laban, are associated to moon-worship.[12] When Abraham was called out from Ur of the Chaldeans, a place of splendid material civilization and idol-worship, he moved to Haran and dwelt there until he finally departed to the land of Canaan at the age of 75 (2091 BC) (Gen 12:1-4; Acts 7:2-4).

2. The Calling of Abraham (Gen 11:26–32; 12:1–5; Acts 7:2–4), 2091 BC

Abraham's age, 75.

According to the chronology of the patriarchs, Noah was still alive when Abraham was born, so they lived 58 years contemporaneously.[13]

Shem actually outlived Abraham. Abraham surely inherited the faith of his godly ancestors—Noah, Shem, and Eber—directly and indirectly through various channels. The faith of these godly ancestors was the light of salvation for Abraham during the dark times in which he lived. These ancestors helped kindle Abraham's faith as he grew up in an environment immersed in idol-worship.

God's calling of Abraham from an idol-worshiping pagan family was not just the calling and salvation of one individual. It was actually a fresh start in God's work—the work to establish one individual as the father of faith in order to advance His greater plan to save mankind.

There were two instances where Abraham had left his hometown. First, he left Ur of the Chaldeans along with his father Terah (Gen 11:31; Acts 7:2–3). Second, he departed from Haran at the age of 75, after quite some time of dwelling (Gen 12:4; Acts 7:4).

Hebrews 11:9 states, "By faith he lived as an alien in the land of promise," revealing that Abraham spent lonely days in a foreign land as a sojourner with no one in the land to warmly embrace him. In Acts 7:5, Stephen preached, "And He gave him no inheritance in it, not even a foot of ground." Abraham must have suffered greatly as a sojourner after leaving his father's house and his relatives. Because he was a stranger in a foreign land, he silently had to endure unfair treatment and persist through tear-filled days.

However, Abraham believed in God's promise, and he placed his hope in that promise. Wherever he went, he built an altar for God, and he lived according to God's commands (Gen 12:7–8; 13:4). He lived his life with God, Immanuel.

3. The Ratification of the Covenant of the Torch
(Gen 15:7–21), 2082 BC

Abraham's age, 84, ten years since his arrival at Canaan (Gen 16:3).

Among the covenants of God established in Genesis, there are three that were given with visual signs that have a strong impact. These are the "covenant of the rainbow" that God made with Noah and his sons after the judgment of the flood, the "covenant of the ladder" that God made with Jacob at Bethel, and the "covenant of the torch" that God made with Abraham in Genesis 15.

Among these three covenants, only the covenant of the torch involved a sacrifice offering as proof of the covenant (Gen 15:8–10). This offering is a foreshadowing of the redemptive work of Jesus Christ who would come in human form to be offered as a sacrifice for the salvation of the chosen people (John 1:29; 1 Cor 5:7).

An important characteristic of the covenant of the torch is the flaming torch representing God's presence that passed between the pieces of the offering (Gen 15:17). According to the customs of those times, both parties involved in a contract would pass between the pieces of the offering. However, God was the only One to pass between the pieces in this covenant. The reason is that man has fallen and become totally inept and incapable of entering into a covenant with the almighty and holy God. Thus, in His boundless compassion, mercy, and love, God entered into a unilateral covenant with His people. This is evidence of God's love and grace because He loved us first (1 John 4:10, 19). Our salvation today rests upon God's unilateral love and grace, not upon our deeds, achievements, or merit (Eph 2:8–10).

4. Abraham Takes Sarah's Maidservant Hagar (Gen 16:1–3), 2081 BC, First Year of the Covenant of the Torch

Abraham's age, 85.

Abraham was about 85 years old when he took Hagar, Sarah's Egyptian maidservant, as his concubine in 2081 BC (Gen 16:3).

There was a time when Abraham and Sarah went down to Egypt because of a famine. There, Abraham deceived people by claiming that Sarah was his sister, and Pharaoh almost took her (Gen 12:10–20). As a result of this episode, Pharaoh gave Abraham gifts of sheep, oxen, donkeys, male and female servants, and female donkeys and camels. Hagar is thought to have been one of these female servants.

Before departing from Haran at the age of 75, Abraham received a promise from God: "I will make you a great nation" (Gen 12:1–4). He then waited ten years. When he was 84 years old, before God initiated the covenant of the torch, God showed him the stars in the heavens and said, "So shall your descendants be" (Gen 15:5). However, less than one year after receiving this promise, he listened to his wife Sarah rather than God. He committed the grave mistake of taking Hagar as his concubine (Gen 16:2). There was much discord in Abraham's family as a consequence of this action. As soon as Hagar had conceived Abraham's son, she despised her mistress, Sarah (Gen 16:4), and in return, Sarah treated her harshly (Gen 16:6).

Likewise, those who do not have faith in God's promise and listen to other people's words, make their own paths in life more difficult and painful.

5. The Birth of Ishmael through Hagar (Gen 16:1–16), 2080 BC, Second Year of the Covenant of the Torch
Abraham's age, 86.

Abraham was 86 years old when Ishmael was born to him through Hagar in 2080 BC (Gen 16:16). Abraham had foolishly attempted to fulfill God's promise regarding his descendants, "… but one who shall come forth from your own body, he shall be your heir" (Gen 15:4), through Sarah's maidservant, Hagar. At one time, even before the covenant was made, Abraham foolishly considered making his servant, Eliezer of Damascus, his heir (Gen 15:3). We must not attempt to fulfill God's promise through human means. God's promises are only fulfilled through His ways (Isa 55:8–9).

Abraham and Sarah's unbelief led to Ishmael's conception through Hagar, an event that ignited family discord. After Hagar conceived, she despised her mistress in her sight (Gen 16:4). Sarah, realizing this, complained against her husband and treated Hagar harshly (Gen 16:6). In Hebrew, "to treat harshly" (Gen 16:6) is in the Piel form of עָנָה ('ānâ). This word was also used to describe the oppression that the Israelites were to endure in Egypt (Gen 15:13). Sarah was so severe with Hagar that Hagar fled from the presence of her mistress (Gen 16:6).

Abraham's impatient and imprudent action brought great strife to the family—a hostility that did not end in his lifetime, but continues to affect his descendants even today. Both Jews, the descendants of Isaac, and Arabs, the descendants of Ishmael, trace their ancestry back to Abraham. Hagar's son, Ishmael, is the ancestor of today's Arabs. Thus, the ongoing war in the Middle East is a continuation of the conflict between the Jews and the Arabs dating back to Abraham's time. In reality, the war in the Middle East is the result of Abraham's lack of patience regarding God's promised descendant and his attempt to fulfill the promise by human design. His human thoughts, ways, and actions became a great thorn for himself and his descendants.

6. Abram and Sarai Renamed (Gen 17:5, 15–16); The Covenant of Circumcision (Gen 17:9–14), 2067 BC, Fifteenth Year of the Covenant of the Torch

Abraham's age, 99; Sarah's age, 89.

God kept His silence and did not appear to Abraham for 13 years after Abraham became Ishmael's father at the age of 86. This can be understood as God's response to Abraham's unbelief.

At last, when Abraham was 99 years old, God appeared to him and proclaimed, "I am God Almighty" (Gen 17:1), אֲנִי־אֵל שַׁדַּי (*'ănî-'ēl šadday*) in Hebrew. This was a reminder that although Abraham did not believe, God would still fulfill His promise, even in the most improbable circumstances.

God Almighty appeared to Abraham when he was 99 years old and gave him a new name before entering into the covenant of circumcision (Gen 17:9–14). God changed his name from *Abram* to *Abraham*, which means "father of a multitude of nations" (Gen 17:5). The name *Abram* has a meaning of "exalted father" with a narrow significance of an individual father. However, the name *Abraham*, which means "father of a multitude of nations," is more embracing and universal. This foreshadows how Abraham will become the father of all who believe in Jesus Christ without regard to their blood lineage (Rom 4:16; Gal 3:7, 29).

Then, God commanded the covenant of circumcision to Abraham. The word *circumcision* is מוּלָה (*mûlâ*) in Hebrew and περιτομή (*peritomē*) in Greek. It refers to the Israelite practice of cutting off a male child's foreskin eight days after birth (Gen 17:12; Lev 12:3; Luke 2:21).

In Genesis 17:10 God commanded, "This is My covenant, which you shall keep, between Me and you and your descendants after you: every male among you shall be circumcised." Thus, circumcision was a sign of becoming God's people (Gen 17:4) and their promise that they would adhere to the covenant. As proof of the covenant between God and the Israelites (Gen 17:11), the physical mark on the flesh was to serve as a constant reminder of the everlasting covenant with God (Gen 17:13).

After God renamed Abraham and instituted the covenant of circumcision, He renamed Sarai and said that she would have a son (Gen 17:16). Abraham's wife, whose original name was *Sarai*, was given a new name *Sarah* (Gen 17:15-16). The name *Sarai* means "a woman of high rank" or "my princess," which pertained only to herself. However, the name *Sarah*, which means "mother of nations," is more embracing of others. This act of renaming Sarai also foreshows God's redemptive plan to have Jesus Christ come in the line of Isaac, who will be born of Sarah, and that there will be many nations which will come to believe in Jesus Christ (Gal 4:26).

Although God Himself gave Abraham the promise of descendants through the covenant of circumcision, Abraham did not believe that he could have a son, and he confessed his wish for Ishmael to live before God (Gen 17:17-18). However, God clearly said, "No, but Sarah your wife shall bear you a son, and you shall call his name Isaac; and I will establish My covenant with him for an everlasting covenant for his descendants after him" (Gen 17:19). He reconfirmed that He would fulfill His covenant only through Isaac and not through Ishmael.

7. The Birth of Isaac, the Covenantal Son (Gen 21:1–5), 2066 BC, Sixteenth Year of the Covenant of the Torch

Abraham's age, 100; Sarah's age, 90.
Ages of the godly ancestors at the time: Shem, 490; Arpachshad, 390; Shelah, 355; Eber, 325.

Twenty-five years after God first made His covenant with Abraham, He took note of Sarah and, in accordance with His promise, did for her as

He had spoken. At last, when Abraham was 100 years old, God gave to him Isaac, the son of the promise (Gen 21:1–7; Matt 1:2). The phrase "took note" in Genesis 21:1 means that God "looked after," "cared for," and "had affection" for her. The Hebrew word for "took note" is פָּקַד (pāqad) and is used 285 times in the Old Testament alone. However, it is used for the first time in Genesis 21:1 and indicates that God visited Sarah, and looked after her. At the age of 90, Sarah was well advanced in years and beyond the age of childbearing, but God remembered His covenant, visited her, and looked after her so that she experienced the miracle of giving birth to Isaac. Abraham waited for 25 years after he first received the promise and blessing of פָּקַד (pāqad). Today, miraculous blessings also await those who believe in God's promise and wait patiently until the end.

There were a few occasions when Abraham did not completely believe in God's promise. However, Romans 4 praises Abraham's faith. Romans 4:20–22 states, "Yet, with respect to the promise of God, he did not waver in unbelief, but grew strong in faith, giving glory to God, and being fully assured that what He had promised, He was able also to perform. Therefore also it was reckoned to him as righteousness."

Here, the phrase "grew strong in faith" seems to contradict the accounts of Abraham's unbelief. However, the phrase "grew strong in faith" in Greek is ἐνεδυναμώθη (enedynamōthē), an indicative aorist passive rendering of ἐνδυναμόω (endynamaō), which shows that it is God, not man, who made Abraham's faith strong. By the work of God, Abraham's faith grew increasingly strong so that at last he possessed the kind of faith that God had desired. Although there were times in Abraham's life when he did not believe, his life ultimately concluded in faith.

Although we may have a past marred by unbelief, if that past is concluded in faith by the grace of God, then God will acknowledge our lives as lives of faith.

CHAPTER 8

The History of Isaac

1. Hagar and Ishmael Are Cast Out to the Wilderness of Paran (Gen 21:8–21), 2063 BC, Nineteenth Year of the Covenant of the Torch

Abraham's age, 103; Ishmael's age, 17; Isaac's age, 3.

Abraham drove out Hagar and Ishmael after Isaac was weaned (Gen 21:8–14). According to the Hebrew custom, children normally were weaned at 3 years of age (Exod 2:9–10; 1 Sam 1:22). Thus, presumably Hagar and Ishmael were driven out three years after Isaac had been born (Gen 21:8). Since Ishmael was 14 years older than Isaac, he was most likely driven out around the age of 17 (Gen 16:16; 21:5).[14] Although Ishmael was the son of a maidservant, Abraham had loved and cared for him for 17 years. Thus, their expulsion caused him much agony.

Hagar and Ishmael were driven out because Ishmael had mocked Isaac (Gen 21:9). In Genesis 21:9, the Hebrew word צָחַק (ṣāḥaq) means "to laugh" or "to mock." When Isaac was weaned and a great feast thrown for him, Ishmael mocked Isaac, most likely out of fear that Isaac might become the rightful heir of their father Abraham's inheritance.

Later, the apostle Paul applied this episode to the situation in the church during his time.

> **Galatians 4:29** But as at that time he who was born according to the flesh persecuted him who was born according to the Spirit, so it is now also.

Here, he who was "born according to the flesh" refers to Ishmael, and he who was "born according to the spirit" refers to Isaac. During Paul's time, those who were born according to the flesh (i.e., the followers of Moses' law) rejected the gospel and persecuted those who were born of the Spirit through the gospel.

This conflict will continue until the end of this world. The word *persecuted* in Galatians 4:29 is an imperfect active indicative form of the Greek verb διώκω (*diōkō*), signifying that Ishmael's persecution did not end at once, but would continue until the end of time. Likewise, the persecution of the believers, the descendants of the promise, by those born of the flesh will also continue. History proves that the Arabs, the descendants of Ishmael, have continued to cause suffering for the Jews, the descendants of Isaac. However, in the end, those born of the flesh will be driven out, and the descendants of the promise will triumph and receive the kingdom of God as an inheritance (Gal 4:30).

2. Isaac Is Given as a Burnt Offering on a Mount in Moriah (Gen 22:1–18), 2041–2030 BC (Estimated), Forty-first through Fifty-second Year of the Covenant of the Torch
Abraham's age, 125–136; Isaac's age, 25–36.

Abraham received the final confirmation of the covenant after he obeyed God's command to offer up Isaac as a burnt offering on a mount in Moriah (Gen 22:1–18). This same mount in Moriah would later become the place where King David built an altar for the Lord and where King Solomon built the house of the Lord (2 Chr 3:1).

Abraham offered up Isaac when Isaac was younger than 37 years old (somewhere between the ages of 25 and 36). After the incident in Genesis 22, Sarah died at the age of 127 when Isaac was 37 years old (Gen 23:1). Since Sarah was still alive when Abraham offered Isaac in Genesis 22, Isaac must have been between the ages of 25 and 36 when this event occurred.

It must have been difficult for Abraham to have offered up Isaac since Isaac was a grown man strong enough to carry the wood for the sacrifice up the mount. The offering was possible because of Isaac's complete trust in the faith of his father, and his personal faith in the God he served. In Genesis 22:6–8, the Bible twice reports that "the two of them walked on together," suggesting that the two men had become one in faith regarding this offering.

The scene of Isaac carrying up the wood for the sacrifice in total obedience foreshadows Jesus Christ's act of carrying His own cross up to Golgotha to be offered as a sacrifice for all mankind in total obedience (Matt 20:28; John 1:29). Just as Abraham received the confirmation of the covenant by offering up his only son on a mount in Moriah (Gen 22:16–18; Heb 11:17–19), so too, did God demonstrate His love for sinners by allowing His only begotten Son to be nailed to the cross in Golgotha (Rom 5:8).

In Genesis 22:12, God acknowledged Abraham's faith when He said, "Do not stretch out your hand against the lad, and do nothing to him; for now I know that you fear God, since you have not withheld your son, your only son, from Me." Then He gave Abraham the blessing of Jehovah Jireh (Gen 22:14), the blessing of great blessings (Gen 22:17), the blessing of his seed multiplying greatly, the possession of the gate of their enemies (Gen 22:17), and the blessing that all nations of the earth will be blessed in his seed (Gen 22:18).

Even today, we may face the trial of having to offer up what is most important to us: "Take now your son, your only son, whom you love, Isaac" (Gen 22:2). If we have the faith to offer up what is most important to us without holding anything back in times like this, our trials will turn into great blessings.

3. The Death of Sarah (Age 127) and Purchase of the Cave of Machpelah (Gen 23:1–2), 2029 BC, Fifty-third Year of the Covenant of the Torch

Abraham's age, 137; Isaac's age, 37.

Genesis 23:1 states, "Now Sarah lived one hundred and twenty-seven years; these were the years of the life of Sarah." Adam died at the age of 930, but there is no record of when Eve died. Likewise, there are no records of the death of any other patriarchs' wives; thus, Sarah's death was the exception. Genesis 23 is entirely dedicated to the account of Sarah's death and burial. This serves as an attestation to the greatness of her faith. Ever since Abraham set out from Ur of the Chaldeans, their lives together was a continuous sojourn. Yet, she faithfully stayed by him regardless of the circumstances (Gen 17:16; Heb 11:11–12).

Sarah was Abraham's most faithful companion in his journey as a wanderer (1 Pet 3:6). She was with Abraham for 62 years after she departed from Ur of the Chaldeans with Abraham at the age of 65. She ended her life as his companion at the age of 127 and was buried in the cave of Machpelah (Gen 23:19). Her life was neither easy nor void of mistakes. Yet, she believed in God and considered Him faithful (Heb 11:11). She lived her life to fulfill the work of salvation and became a good example for all believers.

Abraham buried his wife in the cave of Machpelah (Gen 23:18–19). When Abraham first entered Canaan, he was called a "Hebrew" (Gen 14:13), meaning "to cross over," because he had crossed over the Euphrates River from Ur of the Chaldeans. Abraham, who had been treated like a foreigner by the Canaanites, said of himself, "I am a stranger and a sojourner among you" (Gen 23:4). Thus, it is possible to imagine the difficulty when Abraham tried to purchase a tract of Canaanite land. However, upon Sarah's death, Abraham proposed buying land for his wife's burial from the sons of Heth (Gen 23:3). To his surprise, Ephron, a leader among the sons of Heth, offered to give the cave to Abraham at no cost (Gen 23:11), but he declined the offer and bought the land from Ephron for 400 shekels of silver.

This was an act of faith based on the covenant of the torch. He placed a seal on the land of Canaan as a sign that it belonged to the Israelites, thus establishing the first step toward ownership of the land that God had promised to them.

Faith is having a firm trust in God's promise, looking toward it, and actually working to fulfilling it (Heb 11:1). Through the small cave of Machpelah, Abraham looked upon the enormous land of Canaan, which God had promised to him. The name *Machpelah* means "double cave," and it became a family burial place for Abraham's family. Besides Sarah, other people of faith—Abraham (Gen 25:9), Isaac (Gen 49:31), Rebekah (Gen 49:31), Leah (Gen 49:31), and Jacob (Gen 49:29–33; 50:13)— were buried there. Jacob, the last one to be buried at Machpelah, had died in Egypt, but his body was carried all the way to Canaan to be buried in the same cave. Years later, Moses used this same cave located in the Promised Land where their forebears of the covenant were buried, to justify leading the Israelites out of Egypt.

God's promise regarding the land of Canaan began to bear fruit with the purchase of Sarah's burial place. The burial of the ancestors' bones in Canaan was like a seed of faith that was planted into the minds of Abraham's descendants and allowed them to believe that the land of Canaan is their Promised Land where they must return.

4. The Marriage of Isaac and Rebekah (Gen 24; 25:20), 2026 BC, Fifty-sixth Year of the Covenant of the Torch

Abraham's age, 140; Isaac's age, 40.

When Abraham became old and well advanced in years, he sent his servant Eliezer to find a wife for Isaac, who was to inherit the covenant. By God's providence, Eliezer met Rebekah, who was the daughter of Bethuel the Aramean of Paddan-aram and the sister of Laban (Gen 25:20). Bethuel was the son of Nahor and Milcah (Gen 22:20–23) (see Reference 1: "Abraham's Genealogy").

Laban and Bethuel realized that this marriage had come from God and consented to the marriage (Gen 24:50–51). Rebekah also consented to leave right away with Eliezer, although leaving her homeland for the distant land of Canaan must have been a difficult decision. She was essentially obeying God's will in saying, "I will go" (Gen 24:58). She departed immediately, rejecting her family's suggestion that she stay another ten days (Gen 24:55).

Isaac was meditating when Eliezer brought Rebekah (Gen 24:63). He was praying that his marriage would be established according to God's will. When Rebekah came, Isaac married her, and he was comforted after his mother's death (Gen 24:67).

CHAPTER 9

The History of Jacob and Esau

1. The Birth of Jacob and Esau (Gen 25:19–26), 2006 BC, Seventy-sixth Year of the Covenant of the Torch

Abraham's age, 160; Isaac's age, 60.
Ages of the godly ancestors at the time: Shem, 550; Shelah, 415; Eber, 385.

Isaac married Rebekah at the age of 40, and he had no children for the first 20 years of his marriage to her (Gen 25:20, 26). Isaac was probably deeply distressed that he did not have a son to fulfill God's covenant. He earnestly prayed that his wife would conceive a child (Gen 25:21). The word used for "to pray" in Genesis 25:21 is עָתַר ('ātar) in Hebrew, meaning "to burn incense." It shares the same root as the word for "fragrance" or "incense" (עָתָר, 'ātār). It can be understood that sincere prayers become a holy incense that rises to be an offering before God (Rev 5:8; 8:3–4).

Isaac persevered in prayer for 20 years, and at last God heard his prayer, and Rebekah bore him twin sons, Esau and Jacob, when he was 60 years old (Gen 25:21–22). While Isaac was praying, Abraham must have sympathized with him and prayed together with him for the fulfillment of God's covenant. In the past, God said to Abraham, "No, but Sarah your wife shall bear you a son, and you shall call his name Isaac; and I will establish My covenant with him for an everlasting covenant for his descendants after him" (Gen 17:19). Abraham most likely prayed with Isaac and consoled him, since he was once in the same situation when his wife was barren.

Abraham had Isaac at the age of 100, and Isaac had Jacob at the age of 60. Since Abraham lived 175 years, three generations—Abraham, Isaac, and Jacob—lived contemporaneously for 15 years (Heb 11:9). While dwelling in the tents together, Abraham taught Isaac and Jacob the Word of God. Passing down his faith to his descendants was the duty for which Abraham was called and part of his holy obligation to fulfill the covenant (Gen 18:18–19).

Because Jacob spent much time in the tents being educated about the faith by his grandfather Abraham, he yearned to complete the work of God's eternal inheritance (Gen 25:27).

Today, the church is God's tent. Mary enjoyed sitting at the foot of Jesus to listen to His Word, and Jesus acknowledged her by saying, "For Mary has chosen the good part, which shall not be taken away from her" (Luke 10:42). Like Jacob and Mary, we too must choose to listen to the Word and yearn after it so that "the good part" we choose may not be taken away as in Luke 10:39, "And she had a sister called Mary, who moreover was listening to the Lord's word, seated at His feet."

2. The Death of Abraham (Age 175) (Gen 25:7–8), 1991 BC, Ninety-first Year of the Covenant of the Torch

Abraham's age, 175; Isaac's age, 75; Ishmael's age, 89, Esau and Jacob's age, 15. Ages of the godly ancestors at the time: Shem, 565; Shelah, 430; Eber, 400 [the ages of the descendants in relation to their respective ancestors]. Shem–Isaac's age, 110; Jacob's age, 50; Shelah–Isaac's age, 78; Jacob's age, 18; Eber–Isaac's age, 139; Jacob's age, 79.

Ever since Abraham was called at the age of 75 (Isa 51:2), God blessed him in every way so that he was greatly multiplied (Gen 24:1, 35). Furthermore, God blessed him with good health so that even after he was 140 years old, he took Keturah as his wife and had six more children (Gen 25:1–2). After this, in accordance with the prophecy in Genesis 15:15, Abraham lived until the ripe old age of 175 and was gathered to his people (Gen 25:7–8).

Abraham died 38 years after his wife Sarah. Although Abraham had driven him out, Ishmael came to see his father after learning about his death and was with Isaac to bury him in the cave of Machpelah (Gen 25:9).

If there is one special characteristic about Abraham's 175-year life, it is that he lived the life of a sojourner (Gen 23:4). He dwelt in tent homes and never built a permanent home to live in, for he "desired a better country, that is a heavenly one," a city that God had prepared for him (Heb 11:9–16).

The Bible records the account of Isaac, the second person to inherit the covenant after the death of Abraham. It was at this time, while he was living in Beer-lahai-roi, that a second great famine struck the land.

Isaac sought to go down to Egypt, but because God confirmed the covenant that He made with Abraham regarding the land and the descendants, Isaac decided to stay in Canaan (Gen 26:1–5). Because Isaac obeyed God and stayed in the land, he sowed in the land and in the same year reaped a hundredfold, even during the famine when there was no rain (Gen 26:12). The Lord blessed him so that he "became rich, and continued to grow richer until he became very wealthy . . . so that the Philistines envied him" (Gen 26:13–14).

From then on, Isaac expanded his territory, which was to become a home for the descendants of the promise in the future. He also began to dig wells and became prosperous (Gen 26:17–22). Then he went back to Beersheba, where he received God's promise regarding the multiplication of his descendants. He built an altar and continued to dwell there (Gen 26:23–25).

3. The Marriage of Esau (Age 40) (Gen 26:34), 1966 BC, 116th Year of the Covenant of the Torch

Isaac's age, 100; Jacob's age, 40.

Esau lived with his grandfather, Abraham, and his father, Isaac, so he probably knew very well that he was not to marry a Canaanite woman. However, he followed the lusts of his flesh and chose for himself women pleasing to him from among the daughters of Heth. He married Judith, the daughter of Beeri the Hittite and Basemath, the daughter of Elon the Hittite (Gen 26:34), causing grief to Isaac and Rebekah (Gen 26:35).

After Jacob fled to Laban's house, Esau learned that his marriage to these Canaanite women had displeased his father, and so he married Mahalath the daughter of Ishmael (Gen 28:6–9). His action, however, was led not by the will of God, but by his human desire to appease his father.

Esau did not follow the faith of his parents, and he engaged in bigamy according to human desires and wit, positioning himself even further from God's will. Today, those who indulge in the world and commit spiritual adultery will move further and further from God's will and bring grief to God (Ps 95:10; Isa 63:10; Eph 4:30; Jas 4:4).

4. Jacob Receives the Blessing of the Firstborn, 1930 BC, 152nd Year of the Covenant of the Torch

Isaac's age, 136; Jacob's age, 76.

Esau, Jacob's older brother, despised his birthright and sold it to Jacob for a bowl of lentil stew (Gen 25:28–34). Esau loved worldly things more than spiritual things. The word for "despised" in Genesis 25:34 is בָּזָה (bāzâ) in Hebrew and also means "to disdain" and "to hold in contempt."

Unlike Esau, Jacob yearned greatly for the birthright of the firstborn. From deep within his heart, he wanted to inherit the blessing of his grandfather, Abraham, and become the spiritual firstborn. This is why the first thing Jacob requested of his brother when he asked for the stew was the birthright for which he had yearned (Gen 25:31).

Genesis 25:27 sheds some light on the characters of Esau and Jacob: "When the boys grew up, Esau became a skillful hunter, a man of the field; but Jacob was a peaceful man, living in tents." Jacob enjoyed dwelling in tents because it was there that he heard the Word of God from Abraham, Isaac, and Rebekah. In Hebrew, the word *peaceful* in verse 27 is תָּם (tām), meaning "perfect" (cf. Job 1:8; Ps 37:37), demonstrating that Jacob's everyday life had been a life of faith. Esau, on the other hand, disliked listening to the Word of God and enjoyed going out into the field.

Hebrews 12:16 describes Esau, who had his birthright taken away by Jacob, as "godless" (βέβηλος, bebēlos). The Bible shows that Esau cried out in tears afterwards for the birthright he had lost, but found no place for repentance (Gen 27:34, 36, 38; Heb 12:17), for he had despised and mocked the most precious opportunity that God had given to him in his life and sold it for a cheap price.

Eventually, God led Isaac to bless Jacob, not Esau, as the firstborn in faith (Gen 27:27–29, 39–40; Heb 11:20) (see Reference 2: "A Single Blessing of the Firstborn").

5. Jacob Flees from His Brother Esau (Gen 27:41–28:5), 1930 BC (Estimated), 152nd Year of the Covenant of the Torch

Isaac's age, 136; Jacob's age, 76.

(1) The flight of Jacob

Esau, angry that Jacob had taken his birthright, sought to kill him (Gen 27:41). Knowing what was in Esau's heart, Rebekah helped Jacob to flee from Esau. She remembered what God had revealed to her while her sons were still in her womb: "And the older shall serve the younger" (Gen 25:23).

She had conviction in this revelation and was determined to make sure that Jacob, not Esau, received the blessings, even if a curse might fall upon her (Gen 27:13). Rebekah was a mother who did not forget what God had once revealed to her, and she took action until the Word was fulfilled. Isaac's age at this time is uncertain, but since Jacob fled when he was about 76 years old, it can be presumed that Isaac was about 136 years old.

As Jacob was leaving, Isaac blessed him, saying, "And may God Almighty bless you and make you fruitful and multiply you, that you may become a company of peoples. May He also give you the blessing of Abraham, to you and to your descendants with you; that you may possess the land of your sojournings, which God gave to Abraham" (Gen 28:3–4). Since Esau's marriage to Gentile women had grieved them so much (Gen 26:34–35; 27:46), Isaac and Rebekah charged Jacob to choose a wife among the daughters of Laban and sent him to Paddan-aram (Gen 28:1–5).

(2) The vision of the ladder in Luz (Gen 28:10–19)

As he was fleeing to Haran, Jacob came to a place called Luz. There, he took one of the stones, put it under his head, and fell asleep. In a vision, he saw a ladder set between heaven and earth, and he felt the glorious presence of God.

Through this vision, God initiated a covenant of hope with Jacob, saying, "And behold, I am with you, and will keep you wherever you go, and will bring you back to this land; for I will not leave you until I have done what I have promised you" (Gen 28:15). In Genesis 28:13–15, God revealed Himself as the "God of your father Abraham and the God of Isaac" and promised to lead him back to the land of Canaan. After experiencing the presence of God, he called this place *Bethel*, meaning "house of God," to commemorate the event (Gen 28:19).

Jacob's vision of the ladder represents Jesus Christ, who would come as the spiritual ladder connecting heaven and earth. The great reformers John Calvin and Martin Luther also interpret the vision of the ladder as a foreshadowing of Jesus Christ, the mediator between God and sinners. In John 1:51, Jesus Himself said, "Truly, truly, I say to you, you shall see the heavens opened, and the angels of God ascending and descending on the Son of Man." Jesus Christ is the spiritual ladder, the sole mediator between God and sinners, the only path through which sinners can meet the holy God (John 14:6; Gal 3:19–20; 1 Tim 2:5; Heb 7:15–28; 8:6; 9:11–15; 12:24).

6. Jacob's Twenty Years of Refuge (Gen 29–31), 1930–1910 BC, 152nd through 172nd Year of the Covenant of the Torch

Isaac's age, 136–156; Jacob's age, 76–96.

Jacob was full of expectation after he had received the great blessing and the covenant at Luz. However, contrary to his expectations, he was treated worse than a servant in his uncle Laban's house. He entered Laban's house at the age of 76, labored for Laban for seven years, and was given Leah as wife. Jacob also took Rachel, whom he loved, as wife with the condition that he would work an additional seven years for Laban (Gen 29:18, 27).

Jacob was 83 years old when he married in 1923 BC, the one hundred and fifty-ninth year of the covenant of the torch (Gen 31:41; 29–30). According to these calculations, Jacob was married at an old age—after much of his youth had past—forty-three years later than his brother Esau. Both Isaac and Esau were married at the age of 40 (Gen 25:20; 26:34).

During the seven years of additional labor, Jacob obtained 11 sons (excluding Benjamin) and one daughter through his wives Leah, Rachel, Bilhah, and Zilpah. During the seven years, Leah gave birth to six sons and one daughter. Thus, assuming that she gave birth to one child each year, she had Dinah on the fourteenth year of Jacob's stay in Haran (first seven years + second seven years). Since it was not too long after this time that Rachel gave birth to Joseph, it is highly possible that Dinah and Joseph were the same age (Gen 30:21–24).

Even after the birth of his eleventh son, Joseph, Jacob labored another six years for his uncle Laban's flock (Gen 30:25–31; 31:41). Genesis 31:40 states, "Thus I was: by day the heat consumed me, and the frost by night, and my sleep fled from my eyes." The Hebrew word for "heat" in this verse is חֹרֶב (ḥōreb), which refers to the ground-cracking heat of a drought, and the word for "frost" is קֶרַח (qeraḥ), which refers to water-freezing coldness. Jacob endured such heat and cold without rest in order to watch over Laban's flock. Yet, Laban, his uncle and father-in-law, changed his wages ten times (Gen 31:7, 41).

Even at an old age (from the age of 76 to 96), Jacob lived for 20 years in Laban's house, where he was treated as if he were less than a human being and suffered indignity (Gen 31:40–42). He endured the trials of "the rod of men and the strokes of the sons of men" (2 Sam 7:14). It was the Word of God that gave him the strength to endure the 20 years of affliction: "And behold, I am with you, and will keep you wherever you go, and will bring you back to this land; for I will not leave you until I have done what I have promised you" (Gen 28:15).

The angel of the Lord appeared to Jacob to comfort him and to fill him with hope, saying, "For I have seen all that Laban has been doing to you. I am the God of Bethel, where you anointed a pillar, where you made a vow to Me; now arise, leave this land, and return to the land of your birth" (Gen 31:12–13).

The God of Jacob is our God today. He sees all of our suffering and keeps an account to wipe away our tears and repay us according to our labor.

Here, God revealed Himself to Jacob as the God of Bethel (Gen 31:13), the same God who initiated the covenant of the ladder 20 years before, promising him descendants like the dust of the earth and guaranteeing his return to Canaan (Gen 28:13–15).

Through the God of Bethel, Jacob came to realize that the misunderstandings and injustice that he suffered under the hands of Laban and even the length of the period of suffering were part of God's sovereign will. He realized that the time had come for him to return to the land of Canaan.

When Jacob left Canaan at the age of 76, he was like a fugitive on the run, but now at the age of 96, he was returning as the head of a large clan that included four wives, 12 sons, and exceedingly great wealth (Gen 30:43; 31:1).

The flow of God's work of salvation, which had been passed down from Abraham to Isaac, appeared to have halted with Jacob's departure from the Promised Land, but this was not the case. In fact, not only did God give Jacob 12 sons so that they might become the foundation for the twelve tribes of the nation of Israel, but He also called Jacob back to Canaan so that the flow of the work of salvation would continue ever so vigorously.

7. The Birth of Joseph (Gen 30:22–24), 1916 BC, 166th Year of the Covenant of the Torch

Isaac's age, 150; Jacob's age, 90.

Rachel was able to give birth to Joseph wholly because God remembered her. Genesis 30:22 states, "Then God remembered Rachel, and God gave heed to her and opened her womb." Here, the Hebrew word for "remembered," זָכַר (zakar), refers not to the mere act of remembering, but to a deep understanding and care (cf. Gen 8:1; 1 Sam 1:19). In Egypt, Joseph became second-in-command at the age of 30 and reunited with his father after the seven years of abundance had passed, on the third year of the famine. Since Joseph was 40 years old at this time and Jacob was 130 years old, we can deduce that Joseph was born to Jacob when he was 90 years old (Gen 45:6, 11; 46–47; 47:9, 28).

Rachel's womb, which had been closed for seven years, miraculously opened when God remembered her; all it took was His remembrance. When God remembered Samuel's mother, Hannah, she gave birth to three sons and two daughters.

> **1 Samuel 1:19** Then they arose early in the morning and worshiped before the LORD, and returned again to their house in Ramah. And Elkanah had relations with Hannah his wife, and the LORD remembered her.
>
> **1 Samuel 2:21** And the LORD visited Hannah; and she conceived and gave birth to three sons and two daughters. And the boy Samuel grew before the LORD.

The precious blessing of God's remembrance awaits those who believe and wait until the end (Ps 40:1; Isa 30:18; Lam 3:25–26; Heb 3:14).

8. Jacob Returns to Canaan (Gen 33:18–20), 1910 BC, 172nd Year of the Covenant of the Torch

Isaac's age, 156; Jacob's age, 96; Joseph's age, 6 (estimated).[15]

(1) Israel—Jacob's new name

Mahanaim (מַחֲנַיִם, *maḥănayim*) was the first encampment for Jacob's clan as he was returning to Canaan after fleeing from Esau 20 years earlier (Gen 32:1–2). The name *Mahanaim* means "two camps"; two armies of the angels of God met Jacob and surrounded his groups on all four sides (Ps 34:7; 91:11).

Because Jacob feared greatly the revenge that he might suffer at the hands of his brother Esau, the sight of the angels of God surrounding his family brought great comfort so that he could boldly continue his journey back to Canaan. He was now sure that God would lead him safely to the land of Canaan, and that He would continue to protect him in that land.

Then, messengers told Jacob that his brother Esau was coming to meet him with 400 men (Gen 32:6; 33:1). If Esau had no intention of taking revenge, he would not have needed 400 men.

Realizing the desperate situation he was in and knowing that he could do nothing by his own strength, Jacob remained behind alone, risking his life. He began to pray at the ford of the Jabbok (Gen 32:24). The name *Jabbok* (Gen 32:22) in Hebrew is יַבֹּק (*yabbōq*), meaning "to flow." While Jacob was experiencing great fear and distress (Gen 32:7), he keenly realized that all of the worldly merits and advantages, on which he depended all along, were useless. He must have prayed with all his trust in God alone, giving up all the human-centered abilities, tactics, and wit that belonged to his old self.

He prayed with his life on the line until the socket of his thigh became dislocated. He said to the angel of God, "I will not let you go unless you bless me," and at last, through his prayer, he received the new name *Israel* (Gen 32:26–28). The name *Israel* also became the name of the nation that his descendants would establish, demonstrating that the spiritual root of the nation had come through Jacob.

(2) Jacob protects Rachel and Joseph

When Jacob saw that Esau was coming to meet him with his army of men, he placed Rachel and Joseph in the very end of the caravan in order to protect them from Esau (Gen 33:1–3). He did this because Rachel is the one whom God remembered and opened her womb to give birth to Joseph (Gen 30:22). Jacob promised Laban to work seven years for him in order to get married to Rachel (Gen 29:18, 20, 25). It was also for Rachel that he worked another seven years (Gen 29:27–28, 30). In total, he worked for 14 years to take Rachel as his wife.

The "wife" to whom the prophet Hosea refers in Hosea 12:12 was Rachel: "Now Jacob fled to the land of Aram, and Israel worked for a wife, and for a wife he kept sheep." Among his four wives (Leah, Rachel, Bilhah, and Zilpah), Rachel was the only true wife in his eyes. H. C. Leupold says, "Now Jacob had naturally destined Rachel to be his only wife. Her sons should have been the firstborn."[16]

(3) Jacob and Esau reconcile
Jacob bowed down to the ground seven times until he came near to Esau (Gen 33:3). Jacob was already 96 years old at the time. Bowing down to the ground was the most respectful way to greet another person. Thus, Jacob bowed down to the ground to demonstrate that he had deeply repented of all the things he had done to his brother in the past.

Esau, seeing Jacob bowing to him with great difficulty from a dislocated thigh, ran to meet him and embraced him. He fell on Jacob's neck and kissed him, and they both wept (Gen 33:4). All the feelings of hatred, conflict, and anger melted away instantly.

All of this was through the work of God. Once Jacob reconciled his relationship with God through prayer at Jabbok, God reconciled Jacob's relationship with his brother Esau. If we reconcile our relationship with God and please Him, then He will help us resolve the issues that are too great for us to handle. He helps us make peace with our enemies.

> **Job 22:21** Yield now and be at peace with Him; thereby good will come to you.
>
> **Proverbs 16:7** When a man's ways are pleasing to the LORD, He makes even his enemies to be at peace with him.

9. Leah's Daughter Dinah Is Disgraced (Gen 34), 1900 BC (Estimated), 182nd Year of the Covenant of the Torch

Isaac's age, 166; Jacob's age, 106; Joseph's age, 16.

By God's providence, Jacob returned to the land of Canaan after 20 years. He dwelt in the city of Shechem, camping before the city. He bought the land where he pitched his tent for 100 pieces of silver (Gen 33:18–20). Jacob remembered God's promise to Abraham when he passed through the land of Shechem. God said, "To your descendants I will give this land" (Gen 12:7). Jacob probably bought the land as a guarantee that the Israelites would possess this land rooted in God's promise.

Jacob experienced many unfortunate events while he was dwelling in Shechem. Dinah, his only daughter, was disgraced and humiliated by the son of Hamor the Hivite who raped her (Gen 34:1–2). Given the fact that Hamor had suggested marriage, Dinah must have been around 16 years of age (Gen 34:8).[17]

Simeon and Levi, along with the other sons of Jacob, became enraged at how their sister had been defiled. They deceitfully proposed to Hamor and his son that the Israelites would allow intermarriage with them as long as all the Hivite men are circumcised. While the Hivite men were incapacitated from the pain of circumcision, Simeon and Levi took their swords and killed every male (Gen 34:24–27).

Why did such disgrace fall upon Jacob? Jacob had not kept his oath to God. After the vision of the ladder he saw in Bethel while he was fleeing from Esau, he vowed that if God allowed him to return safely to Canaan, he would return to Bethel and build an altar of thanksgiving before God.

> **Genesis 28:20–22** Then Jacob made a vow, saying, "If God will be with me and will keep me on this journey that I take, and will give me food to eat and garments to wear, [21]and I return to my father's house in safety, then the LORD will be my God. [22]And this stone, which I have set up as a pillar, will be God's house; and of all that Thou dost give me I will surely give a tenth to Thee."

Jacob should have kept his vow and returned to Bethel soon after he bought the land in Shechem. Nevertheless, he became oblivious about his vow and stayed in Shechem for about ten years since he had returned to Canaan from Paddan-aram.[18] All the tragic and unfortunate events that Jacob experienced in Shechem were a result of his negligence and unfaithfulness in keeping his vow.

God appeared to Jacob after Dinah had been disgraced and after his sons had shed the blood of revenge. God said to Jacob, "Arise, go up to Bethel, and live there; and make an altar there to God, who appeared to you when you fled from your brother Esau" (Gen 35:1). Jacob obeyed God's command and built an altar for the Lord in Bethel and named the place *El-bethel* (Gen 35:6–7). God's persistence in making Jacob keep his vow and establishing Jacob as a worthy successor to the covenant was part of His plan of salvation.

10. Birth of Benjamin and Death of Rachel (Gen 35:16–20); Reunion with Isaac (Gen 35:27), 1900 BC (Estimated), 182nd Year of the Covenant of the Torch

Isaac's age, 166; Jacob's age, 106; Joseph's age, 16.

After the Dinah episode, Jacob arrived at Bethel and built an altar there. Afterwards, he departed from Bethel again and journeyed toward Ephrath (Gen 35:15–18). Rachel had dearly longed for a second son after Joseph was born (Gen 30:24). Her wish was fulfilled when she gave birth to Benjamin on the way to Ephrath, but she died after a hard labor.

Her hard labor was presumably due to the fact that it was in the middle of a journey and she was 16 years older than when she had Joseph. These factors could have contributed to her death. Rachel was buried on the way to Ephrath (i.e., Bethlehem), and Jacob set up a pillar over her grave (Gen 35:19–20).

Even before Jacob could be consoled after losing his most beloved wife, as he journeyed from Ephrath and pitched his tent beyond the tower of Eder, he had heard that his son Reuben had relations with Bilhah, his concubine (Gen 35:21–22).

After leaving Laban's house, Jacob dwelt in the land of Shechem (Gen 33:18) and passed through Bethel and Ephrath (i.e., Bethlehem). It took him about ten years since he left Laban's house until he finally arrived in Hebron where Abraham and Isaac had dwelt together (Gen 35:27; 37:1). He had an emotional reunion with his father, Isaac, after about 30 years since he had fled from Esau to Paddan-aram (Gen 28) (see Reference 3: "The Number of Years that Abraham, Isaac, Jacob, and Joseph Lived Together"). The 30 years is a sum of the 20 years of his stay at his uncle Laban's house and about ten years of his stay in Shechem after his departure from Laban's house.[20] Isaac was now about 166 years old, and Jacob was 106 years old, so it is estimated that Jacob had lived 14 years with Isaac until Isaac died.

Joseph was 16 years old when Jacob returned to Hebron and reunited with Isaac. This was not long after Joseph lost his mother, Rachel. After this, at the age of 17, Joseph was sold into slavery in Egypt as a result of his brothers' jealousy, so he spent about one year with his grandfather Isaac. Joseph was probably greatly influenced by Isaac during this year. One year was a short period of time, but it was the precious time needed to inherit the covenant and to establish deeply the root and foundation for his faith.

CHAPTER 10

The History of Joseph

1. Two Dreams that God Gave to Joseph and the 13 Years of Trial (Gen 37; 39; 40), 1899 BC, 183rd Year of the Covenant of the Torch

Isaac's age, 167; Jacob's age, 107; Joseph's age 17.

Jacob had Joseph through Rachel at the age of 90 (1916 BC, 166th year of the covenant). Joseph had two dreams at the age of 17, but his dreams were different from the dreams of other people. His dreams were revelations. In the first dream, 11 bound sheaves bowed down to Joseph's sheaf. In the second dream, the sun, moon, and 11 stars bowed down to Joseph (Gen 37:6–11). The fact that he had two such dreams indicates that it was not a coincidence, but something that God plans and will fulfill.

The Hebrew word for "bowing" (Gen 37:7, 9) that appears in the account of these two dreams is שָׁחָה (šāḥâ), a Hishtapel form of חָוָה (ḥāwâ), referring to the act of bowing voluntarily. A dream about receiving a bow is not ordinary. The act of bowing symbolizes complete admiration and submission. People tend to bow to the ones they consider greatly superior in personality, beliefs, and/or achievements. People bow to the rulers who reign wisely and bring inspiration to the nation. Also, the defeated bows to his conqueror.

Joseph's dream meant that there would come a time when his brothers would voluntarily respect and obey him. It meant that Joseph was the firstborn among his brothers. Moreover, it foretold that he would become a world leader. All the Egyptians actually bowed down to him after he assumed the second-in-command position in Egypt (Gen 41:43). His brothers bowed down to him when they came to Egypt to obtain food (Gen 42:6; 43:26, 28; 44:14), and people from all of the earth also came to buy food from Joseph because the famine was so severe (Gen 41:54–57). Thus, one aspect of the dream was fulfilled.

Furthermore, the dream was also a foretelling of how God's plan to move Jacob's family to Egypt to fulfill the covenant of the torch would be accomplished through Joseph. Joseph had monopolized his father's love and was hated by his brothers (Gen 37:3–4). After the dream, he was almost killed by his brothers (Gen 37:20), and he experienced the adversity of being sold into Egypt (Gen 37:12–36).

Presumably, Benjamin was about one year old around this time. Joseph suffered the heartache of the early loss of his mother, but it must have pained him even more to leave his infant brother behind. Isaac was 167 years old and still alive and Jacob was 107 years old when Joseph was sold at age of 17.[21] Since Isaac lived until the age of 180, he "shared the grief of Jacob over the loss of his son for 13 years." Isaac probably comforted Jacob, as he "could see in these sorrows of Jacob the hand of God."[22]

Joseph's brothers sold him to the Midianite merchants, who then resold him in Egypt to Potiphar, who put Joseph in charge of his household (Gen 39:1–6). When it had been about ten years since Joseph was sold into Egypt, he was unjustly imprisoned for a baseless accusation of rape because he had rejected the sexual advances of Potiphar's wife (Gen 39:7–23).

It is only natural for a person who is unjustly accused and imprisoned to try to prove his innocence. However, Joseph was just a slave in a foreign land and had no power to do so. Consequently, Joseph endured his wretched state in prison for over two years (nearly three years [Gen 41:1]). Regarding Joseph's trial and suffering, the psalmists wrote, "They afflicted his feet with fetters, he himself was laid in irons; until the time that his word came to pass, the word of the Lord tested him" (Ps 105:18–19). Severe affliction upon Joseph was part of God's administration to fulfill the covenant of the torch, which He made with Abraham.

2. The Death of Isaac (Gen 35:28–29) and the Ascension of Joseph to Second-in-Command (Gen 41:1–46), 1886 BC, 196th Year of the Covenant of the Torch

Isaac's age at death, 180; Jacob's age, 120; Joseph's age, 30.

When he obeyed God's command for his father to offer him on a mount in Moriah, Isaac became the model of obedience. After this, he spent his whole life achieving God's plan for salvation until he died at the age of 180 and returned to his ancestors (Gen 35:28–29). Ishmael, who was 14 years older than Isaac, died 57 years before Isaac at the age of 137 in 1943 BC (Gen 25:17). Joseph was 30 years old and in Egypt at the time when his grandfather, Isaac, died.

While Joseph was in prison, he interpreted the dreams of Pharaoh's two officials (Gen 40:1–23). As a result of this incident, he was invited to interpret Pharaoh's dreams, which ultimately led to his ascension as second-in-command in Egypt.

Pharaoh's appointment of Joseph as second-in-command after hearing Joseph's interpretation of his dreams occurred immediately because during this short period of time, God had worked to move Pharaoh's heart (Ps 105:20–22). In Genesis 41:39, Pharaoh said to Joseph, "Since God has informed you of all this, there is no one so discerning and wise as you are." Pharaoh had a conviction that Joseph's wisdom and intelligence came from God, not man, and thus he did not hesitate to appoint Joseph as his second-in-command.

Joseph was about 6 years old when Jacob departed from Laban's house. He must have lived about ten years in Succoth and Shechem with Jacob before he came to Hebron where Isaac was living.[23] Since Joseph was sold to Egypt when he was about 17 years old, he spent about one year with his grandfather, Isaac (Gen 35:27). During this short time, Isaac most likely concentrated on teaching young Joseph about the Word of God, which was originally given to Abraham, passed down to Isaac and then to Jacob. As a result, Joseph received dreams from God and became a man of great faith with a deep understanding of God's plan. Isaac's teachings in all likelihood greatly influenced Joseph.

3. The Seven Years of Plenty (Gen 41:47–53), 1885–1879 BC, 197th through 203rd Year of the Covenant of the Torch

Seven Years of Famine (Gen 41:54–57), 1878–1872 BC, 204th through 210th Year of the Covenant of the Torch

Pharaoh, the Egyptian king at that time, had two dreams (Gen 41:1–7). In the first dream, there were seven sleek, fat cows, but then seven ugly, gaunt cows appeared and devoured the seven sleek and fat cows. When he slept again and had a second dream, there were now seven ears of grain on a single stalk, plump and good. Then, seven ears, thin and scorched by the east wind, sprouted up after them, and these thin ears swallowed up the seven plump and full ears. Having two dreams like this meant that God planned it, and that it would be fulfilled (Gen 41:32).

However, none of the magicians or wise men in Egypt could interpret the meaning of this dream except for Joseph (Gen 41:24–36). The seven sleek and fat cows and seven plump ears prophesied seven years of plenty, while the seven lean and ugly cows and seven thin ears prophesied seven years of famine, so great that it would swallow up the years of plenty. Historically, the events occurred according to Joseph's interpretation of the dreams.

Famines are among the signs of the end time (Matt 24:7; Mark 13:8; Luke 21:11), but the famine of the Word of God will also come. Amos 8:11–12 states, "'Behold, days are coming,' declares the LORD God, 'When I will send a famine on the land, not a famine for bread or a thirst for water, but rather for hearing the words of the LORD. And people will stagger from sea to sea, and from the north even to the east; they will go to and fro to seek the word of the LORD, but they will not find it.'"

This period of famine is part of the tribulation that will come upon the believers in the last days (Amos 4:6–11). We will be unable to hear the Word of God during the times of tribulation because teaching and hearing the Word of God will be prohibited.

Just as God forewarned Joseph regarding the years of famine before the years of plenty, God will also give us years of plenty for the Word of God before the famine strikes (Isa 2:2–3; Mic 4:1–2). While the Word of God is abundant, it is "the acceptable time" (2 Cor 6:2) and the time when the Lord may be found (Isa 55:6). The times are becoming increasingly evil; we will need wisdom to make the most of our time (Eph 5:16) and the wisdom to prepare with the Word of God for the famine ahead.

4. Jacob and 70 Members of His Family Migrate to Egypt
(Gen 46:1–27), 1876 BC, 206th Year of the Covenant of the Torch, Third Year of the Great Famine

Jacob's age, 130; Joseph's age, 40.

God advanced His plan to protect the Israelites by sending Joseph to Egypt in advance and establishing him as second-in-command. Jacob's family moved to Egypt after the seven years of plenty, in the third year of the famine, ten years after Joseph assumed his lofty position.

> **Genesis 45:6** For the famine has been in the land these two years, and there are still five years in which there will be neither plowing nor harvesting.

> **Genesis 45:11** There I will also provide for you, for there are still five years of famine to come, lest you and your household and all that you have be impoverished.

(1) The lonely 23 years of Jacob until he reunites with Joseph

Jacob fell into a state of deep sorrow after he lost his most beloved Joseph. Genesis 37:34 states, "So Jacob tore his clothes, and put sackcloth on his loins, and mourned for his son many days. Then all his sons and all his daughters arose to comfort him, but he refused to be comforted. And he said, 'Surely I will go down to Sheol in mourning for my son.' So his father wept for him."

At the age of 120, thirteen years after Jacob had lost Joseph, he also lost his father, Isaac, who had been the cornerstone of his faith and his greatest comforter. Not too long afterwards, a severe famine struck the land. When Jacob sent his sons to Egypt to buy some food, Simeon was taken captive (Gen 42:36). Thus, tragedy continued for Jacob for 23 years after he had parted with Joseph until they were reunited.

It is evident that Jacob had a special affection for Benjamin, born to him by his beloved Rachel. He probably saw in Benjamin the face of Rachel, dying in the midst of labor pains, and the face of Joseph, whom he loved so dearly. Thus, Benjamin was Jacob's sole comfort in his old age. When his sons sought to take Benjamin with them on their second trip to Egypt for food, Jacob said, "My son shall not go down with you; for his brother is dead, and he alone is left. If harm should befall him on the journey you are taking, then you will bring my gray hair down to Sheol in sorrow" (Gen 42:38).

However, at last, after 23 years, at the age of 130, Jacob reunited with his son Joseph whom he thought was dead. At first, Jacob was stunned (i.e., great excitement causing difficulty in breathing) to learn that Joseph was alive, but his spirit revived (Gen 45:27–28) when he saw the "ten donkeys loaded with the best things of Egypt, and ten female donkeys loaded with grain and bread and sustenance" that Joseph had sent (Gen 45:23). The account that Jacob's spirit revived and his own words, "It is enough; my son Joseph is still alive. I will go and see him before I die," hint at the long years of loneliness and despair. The 54 years of life between the time he fled from Esau at the age of 76 until he moved to Egypt at the age of 130 were years of continuous affliction. For this reason, when Jacob stood before Pharaoh, he confessed, "The years of my sojourning are one hundred and thirty; few and unpleasant have been the years of my life, nor have they attained the years that my fathers lived during the days of their sojourning" (Gen 47:9). Nevertheless, through Jacob's sojourning life, God continued to advance and fulfill His covenant.

We must give thanks even when we face difficulties in our lives today. We must have the eyes to see that God has plans to change our lives and cause all things to work together for good.

(2) Jacob hesitates to depart for Egypt

Jacob received the new name *Israel* and a reconfirmation of God's promise regarding the land and the descendants (Gen 35:1–15) when he built an altar in Bethel at the age of about 106. It was 24 years after this that the God of the covenant reappeared to Jacob in Beersheba. Jacob took all his possessions to leave at the age of 130 and made an offering to the God of his father, Isaac in Beersheba. He hesitated at first because of the thought that he was giving up on the land that Abraham and Isaac had protected until then. The land of Egypt was a land that had nothing to do with the promise. It was a land of idol worship where keeping the pure faith would be difficult, but Jacob received four promises while he built an altar in Beersheba and offered up a sacrifice offering to God.

First, "Do not be afraid to go down to Egypt, for I will make you a great nation there" (Gen 46:3).

Second, "I will go down with you to Egypt" (Gen 46:4).

Third, "I will also surely bring you up again" (Gen 46:4).

Fourth, "Joseph will close your eyes" (Gen 46:4).

After receiving these four amazing promises, Jacob took all that he had and left Beersheba for Egypt (Gen 46:5–6). This was the beginning of the fulfillment of God's prophecy, "Your descendants will be strangers in a land that is not theirs" (Gen 15:13). Furthermore, the foundation was being laid for the fulfillment of the prophecy that Israel would come out of Egypt as a great nation and return to Canaan.

It was not God's plan to allow the Israelites to become a great nation with ease. His plan was to raise them into a great nation through affliction and trial in the iron furnace of Egypt (Deut 4:20; 1 Kgs 8:51; Jer 11:4). It is certain even now that we will pass through Egypt's iron furnace before entering God's kingdom (Acts 14:22; Rom 8:17; 1 Pet 4:12–16).

(3) Seventy members of Jacob's family move to Egypt (Gen 46:8–27)

The number of people who entered Egypt was 70 if we count Jacob, Joseph, Manasseh, and Ephraim, but 66 if we exclude them (Gen 46:26–27). Careful examination of the list of people who entered Egypt shows that the list includes not only people who entered Egypt, but also people who were later born in Egypt. Benjamin was about 24 years old during the move, but Genesis 46:21 lists ten of Benjamin's sons as having moved to Egypt: Bela, Becher, Ashbel, Gera, Naaman, Ehi, Rosh, Muppim, Huppim, and Ard. In addition, Numbers 26:40 records Ard and Naaman as sons of Bela, indicating that they were Benjamin's grandchildren.

God recorded this list of 70 that included descendants not yet born for a specific reason. In the Bible, the number *seven* is the number of perfection and completion, while the number *ten* signifies the end of the basic counting numbers and the fullness of the numbers. Thus, seventy, the multiplication of seven and ten, represents complete perfection and fullness. This demonstrates that all of Jacob's family, without exception, moved to Egypt according to God's providence and symbolizes the fullness of their prosperity and their complete salvation.

5. Israel Dwells in the Land of Goshen and Raises Livestock (Gen 46:28–34; 47:1–12), 1876 BC, 206th Year of the Covenant of the Torch

The move of the 70 to Egypt and their dwelling place in Goshen were part of God's administration. Joseph did not choose a comfortable or a well-known city in Egypt for his family; he chose Goshen. Joseph chose five men among his brothers and presented them to Pharaoh. They spoke to him, saying, "We have come to sojourn in the land…. Now, therefore, please let your servants live in the land of Goshen" (Gen 47:4). The word *sojourn* means a temporary stay (in a foreign land). In Hebrew it is גּוּר (*gûr*), meaning "to live temporarily" (Gen 12:10; 35:27). Thus, Egypt was not to be their permanent dwelling place.

Why did Joseph choose Goshen as Israel's temporary dwelling place?

(1) In order to protect the purity of faith
The land of Goshen was geographically distant from the population centers of Egypt, enabling the Israelites to keep their faith in the Lord pure without being influenced by the idol-worshiping Egyptian culture. If the Israelites had dwelt in one of the comfortable cities in Egypt, the purity of their faith would have become rapidly tainted by Egypt's polytheistic, idol-worshiping culture.

Joseph coached his father and his brothers in advance. If Pharaoh asked about their occupation, they were to answer, "Your servants have been keepers of livestock from our youth even until now, both we and our fathers" (Gen 46:33–34). Genesis 46:34 tells us this was because shepherds were loathsome to the Egyptians.

In Hebrew, the word *loathsome* is תּוֹעֵבָה (*tôʿēbâ*), meaning "disgusting," "abominable," and "detestable." The Egyptians had great contempt for livestock keeping, and the Israelites who engaged in the occupation were known as a lowly nation. The Egyptians probably shunned the Israelites and refused to intermarry with them or travel within the region of Goshen. As a consequence, the Israelites were naturally sheltered in the land of Goshen and were able to protect their purity as a nation of God.

(2) For the growth and advancement of the nation

Since Joseph was second-in-command in Egypt, he could have helped the Israelites change from keeping livestock to a more respectable occupation. However, if they had received such special treatment, the Egyptians would have looked upon them with jealousy or become suspicious of their intentions.

Thus, Joseph used the fact that livestock keepers were detestable to the Egyptians to his advantage, emphasizing that the Israelites had engaged in that occupation since the time of their ancestors so that the Israelites would not become a thorn in the side of the Egyptians. He made the Israelites look like a weak and small nation in the eyes of the Egyptians.

It was Joseph's wise dealings that allowed the Israelites to live in a foreign land for 430 years. In this "consecrated" land the Israelites grew and prospered, so Genesis 47:27 testifies, "Now Israel lived in the land of Egypt, in Goshen, and they acquired property in it and were fruitful and became very numerous." In reality, Goshen was an especially protected land; it was part of God's administration to allow the Israelites to grow into a large nation.

(3) Because it is located close to the border

The land of Goshen was located on the border of Egypt and was geographically closest to Canaan. Goshen was a strategic location, given that the Israelites would have to leave Egypt later in time. Joseph had the conviction that the Israelites would return to Canaan according to the covenant, although they had entered Egypt to dwell there temporarily (Gen 15:13–16).

Keeping livestock required the people to migrate from one place to another. For generations, the Egyptians farmed around the fertile land by the Nile River, where water was plentiful. It was their main occupation, and they regarded it sacred. Whereas farmers could not easily move away from their land, keepers of livestock easily migrated from place to place looking for grazing fields. By engaging the Israelites in keeping livestock, Joseph effectually trained them to be able to move at any time.

6. Death of Jacob (Age 147) and His Funeral (Gen 47:28–31; 49:29–33; 50:1–14), 1859 BC, 223rd Year of the Covenant of the Torch

Joseph's age, 57.

There are very few people whose life journey is as difficult as Jacob's (Gen 47:9). His was especially difficult because he was laying the foundational work for the fulfillment of the covenant. However, after Jacob reunited with Joseph, he enjoyed delightful fruit at the end of the wretched journey (Gen 46:30). At the end of his life he was praised by the king and enjoyed the abundance of Goshen surrounded by his sons. He was able to come this far because God's covenant was the center of his life. In reality, Jacob's life progressed according to God's administration for salvation; he had given up his life in total obedience for this purpose.

Jacob lived 17 years in Egypt and returned to his ancestors. Jacob remembered God's words in Beersheba, "Joseph will close your eyes" (Gen 46:4), and specifically called Joseph among all his sons and said, "Place now your hand under my thigh and deal with me in kindness and faithfulness. Please do not bury me in Egypt, but when I lie down with my fathers, you shall carry me out of Egypt and bury me in their burial place" (Gen 47:29–30).

(1) Jacob's last words for the fulfillment of the covenant

Genesis 47:28–31 And Jacob lived in the land of Egypt seventeen years; so the length of Jacob's life was one hundred and forty-seven years. [29]When the time for Israel to die drew near, he called his son Joseph and said to him, "Please, if I have found favor in your sight, place now your hand under my thigh and deal with me in kindness and faithfulness. Please do not bury me in Egypt, [30]but when I lie down with my fathers, you shall carry me out of Egypt and bury me in their burial place." And he said, "I will do as you have said." [31]And he said, "Swear to me." So he swore to him. Then Israel bowed in worship at the head of the bed.

In Genesis 47, when the time for Jacob to die drew near, he specifically called Joseph (v. 29) and pleaded with him to bury his body in Canaan, in the land his fathers bought, in their burial place (v. 30). Jacob made Joseph swear to him repeatedly (v. 31).

The burial place in Canaan is the cave of Machpelah in Hebron that Abraham bought from the Hittites for 400 shekels of silver (Gen 23:16–18). Sarah (Gen 23:19–20), Abraham (Gen 25:7–10), Isaac (Gen 49:31), Jacob (Gen 50:13), Rebekah, and Leah were buried there (Gen 49:31).

The request that Jacob made on his deathbed was founded upon the promise he had received from God before he moved to Egypt, "I will also surely bring you up again" (Gen 46:4), and from his conviction in the fulfillment of God's covenant of the torch with his grandfather, Abraham, 223 years earlier (Gen 15:13–16). By asking Joseph to bury him in Canaan just before his death, Jacob reconfirmed that Canaan was the rightful home of the Israelites for permanent dwelling. Furthermore, he taught his descendants that God will lead them out of Egypt, and that they will return to Canaan, where they will permanently settle.

As Jacob was making his request, he required Joseph to place his hand under his (Jacob's) thigh and swear to him. In the Ancient Near East, the hand was placed under the thigh when a solemn vow was being made.

In Hebrew, the word *thigh* is יָרֵךְ (*yārēk*), referring to the bone between the pelvis and the thighbone below the waist. The New International Version (NIV) renders it as "side" also (Exod 32:27, Ps 45:3). In the regions of the Ancient Near East, the thigh was related to a man's reproductive organs (Judg 3:16, 21), so the word represented the origin of life. Thus, a vow with a hand on the thigh of the other person was a solemn vow made with one's life on the line. One would be pledging total obedience and trust in the other person's authority. Furthermore, it was an act that guarantees that effectiveness and responsibility of the vow continue to be valid even to their descendants (Gen 24:2, 9). Thus, Jacob's request for Joseph to place his hand on his thigh demonstrates Jacob's unwavering belief that it is God's will for his bones to be buried in Canaan, and that the vow will be effective throughout the generations.

(2) Jacob worships at the head of the bed

Jacob bowed in worship at the head of the bed after he made his last request to have his bones buried in Canaan. In Genesis 47:31, Jacob said, "'Swear to me.' So he swore to him. Then Israel bowed in worship at the head of the bed." Genesis 48 records the account of the blessing of Joseph's two sons. He had gathered his strength to sit up on his bed to speak to Joseph and to bless his sons.

The phrase "now it came about after these things" in Genesis 48:1 was written in the *waw*-consecutive, indicating a close relationship between Jacob's request to have his bones buried in Canaan in Genesis 47 and the blessing of Joseph's sons in Genesis 48. It appears that there is no chronological gap between the two episodes, and that they were continuous events.

Hebrews 11:21 states, "By faith Jacob, as he was dying, blessed each of the sons of Joseph, and worshiped, leaning on the top of his staff." As Jacob was dying, he blessed his children and also worshiped leaning on top of his staff. There is, however, a significant difference in the record in Genesis compared to the record in Hebrews. In Genesis, it is written that Jacob worshiped at the head of the bed (Gen 47:31), but in Hebrews, it is written that he leaned on top of his staff (Heb 11:21). At first reading, these two verses do not seem to agree.

First, why did Jacob worship at the head of the bed at this moment? An examination of 1 Kings 1:47–48 may help our understanding. When King David was old and advanced in age (1 Kgs 1:1, 15), he was so thankful upon hearing that his son Solomon had acceded to the throne that he "bowed himself on the bed" and praised God (1 Kgs 1:47). The word *bowed* used in this verse is the same word in Hebrew, שָׁחָה (*šāḥâ*), from חָוָה (*hāwâ*) as the word *worshiped* used to describe how Jacob worshiped at the head of the bed. Jacob worshiped God as he saw through faith that Joseph would successfully continue the inheritance of the covenant just as David bowed on his bed when he heard that his kingdom has been securely passed to Solomon.[24]

Second, what is the difference between "the head of the bed" and the "top of the staff"? Jacob could barely move about when he spoke his last words to his children. Genesis 47:29 states, "The time for Israel to die drew near," and Genesis 48:1 states, "Now it came about after these things that Joseph was told, 'Behold, your father is sick.'" He was so frail that he had to collect his strength to sit up on the bed (Gen 48:2). Thus, the scene of Jacob worshiping at the head of the bed shows that although his flesh had become old and weak, his faith had grown stronger so that he trusted only in God and worshiped Him. It was the conclusion of one whose faith was never disorderly.

Jacob's faith in Hebrews 11 is demonstrated through the act of resting "his head on top of his staff." Even in the last hour before death he worshiped with all his strength. This was his faith toward God, and the author of Hebrews expressed this faith as "he rested his head on top of the staff."

In the Bible, the staff has a significant meaning in reference to the work of salvation. The staff had three functions: first, it was a tool used to tend the sheep (Heb 11:21); second, it was used as a tool of protection from unrighteousness (Ps 89:32; Isa 11:4;); and third, it was a tool to lead the way (Ps 23:4).

Jesus is the staff that we must rely on during our life journey. He is the staff of protection and guidance (Ps 71:5; 23:4; Isa 11:4; John 14:6). Only Jesus is the staff that helps us conquer a corrupt world and leads us to the Promised Land in heaven.

One interesting fact is that in the Hebrew language, the same consonants are used for the "head of the bed" and the "top of the staff." The word *bed* is מִטָּה (*miṭṭâ*), and *staff* is מַטֶּה (*maṭṭeh*). Thus, if the Hebrew word מטה is read as *miṭṭâ*, it becomes "bed"; and if the same word is read as *maṭṭeh*, it becomes "staff." Around 250–150 BC, the people recording the Septuagint translated מטה as ῥάβδος (*rhabdos*) in Genesis 47:31 by rendering it as *maṭṭeh* ("staff"), which the author of Hebrews followed in Hebrews 11:21. However, in around 500–950 AD, the Masoretic Text started to render מטה as *miṭṭâ* ("bed"). Thus, the words *bed* and *staff* were originally the same word with different vowels. This demonstrated that although Jacob's body was old and weak, at the head of the bed, he rested on God, the spiritual staff, and worshiped Him.

As Jacob spoke his last words, he called God, "the God who has been my shepherd all my life to this day" (Gen 48:15). This is a confession that God had been his staff all his life. It was the scene of a moving closure to his difficult 147-year life journey; he trusted and worshiped only God at the head of his bed. Likewise, the end of the journey for the saints must be just as beautiful so that the scene of the death of the godly may be precious in God's sight (Ps 116:15).

If there is just one thing necessary during a believer's journey in life, it is a staff. Even in Mark 6:8, Jesus instructed, "They should take nothing for their journey, except a mere staff."[25] Believers must not rely on their past experiences, their surroundings, the powers of this world, or material wealth. They must not be tangled up in worries regarding their future. When we live with Jesus Christ and His Word as our staff, we can also conclude our lives as beautifully as Jacob did.

(3) Jacob takes Ephraim and Manasseh, his grandsons through Joseph, as his own sons

As Jacob was putting closure to his life, he gathered his last strength to pass down the covenant to his descendants. As the one who had inherited the covenant, he felt that it was his final obligation to pass down the covenant. Hence, it was his last battle.

There are many records of Jacob's acts of faith, but God selected two of them to be recorded in the Book of Hebrews. First was his blessing of Joseph's two sons, and second was his act of worship leaning on top of the staff. Both acts were carried out just before the end of his life.

> **Hebrews 11:21** By faith Jacob, as he was dying, blessed each of the sons of Joseph, and worshiped, leaning on the top of his staff.

When Joseph heard that Jacob was sick and was about to die (Gen 48:1), he brought his two sons to him. At this time, Jacob collected his strength and sat up in the bed (Gen 48:2). He was old and could not easily move about, but when his beloved Joseph and his two sons came to Jacob, life revived in him.

The first thing that Jacob said to Joseph as he thought back to God's blessings given at Luz was God's promise "I will give this land to your descendants after you for an everlasting possession" (Gen 48:4). Then Jacob pronounced that he would take Joseph's two sons, Ephraim and Manasseh, as his own sons, just as Reuben and Simeon were his (Gen 48:5). He added, "But your offspring that have been born after them shall be yours; they shall be called by the names of their brothers in their inheritance" (Gen 48:6). Jacob had just given Ephraim and Manasseh positions as patriarchs so that they might have equal rights to a portion of the Promised Land.

Next, Jacob did not follow the order of birth as he was blessing Ephraim and Manasseh. Instead, he crossed his arms, according to God's administration of salvation, and gave the greater blessing to the younger brother, Ephraim (Gen 48:13–19). Joseph attempted to uncross Jacob's arms and move his right arm from Ephraim's head to Manasseh's head, but Jacob refused, saying, "I know, my son, I know" (Gen 48:19), and blessed the younger with the blessing of the firstborn.

Then Jacob said, "Behold, I am about to die, but God will be with you, and bring you back to the land of your fathers" (Gen 48:21), emphasizing again how his descendants must return to the land of Canaan.

Until the very last moment of his life, Jacob planted the covenant faith into his grandsons: the land of Goshen was not a permanent location for the chosen people of Israel, for the land of Canaan was their Promised Land.

(4) Jacob gathers up his feet into the bed

✳ The following description of Jacob's death is exposited for the first time in history.

Jacob collected his strength to bless each of his children and to earnestly worship God at the head of his bed. What did Jacob do just before he breathed his last? "He gathered up his feet into the bed" (Gen 49:33).

> **Genesis 49:33** And when Jacob had made an end of commanding his sons, he gathered up his feet into the bed, and yielded up the ghost, and was gathered unto his people. (KJV)

The Hebrew text for Genesis 49:33 is as follows:

וַיְכַל יַעֲקֹב לְצַוֹּת אֶת־בָּנָיו וַיֶּאֱסֹף רַגְלָיו אֶל־הַמִּטָּה

'elhammiṭṭâ   raglāyw wayye'ĕsōp 'etbānāyw   lĕṣawwōt ya'ăqōb wayĕkal

וַיִּגְוַע וַיֵּאָסֶף אֶל־עַמָּיו

'el'ammāyw   wayyē'āsep wayyigwa'

Here, the Hebrew expression for Jacob's act is וַיֶּאֱסֹף (wayye'ĕsōp), the waw-consecutive of אָסַף ('āsap), meaning "to gather." Jacob sat up on the bed to bless his sons and continued to gather his feet into the bed so that he lay in an orderly style.

Jacob did not waver before death; he was calm and godly. He gathered up his feet, meaning that he focused his heart. His posture demonstrated his sincerity. Even in this world, we gather our hands and feet together when we are standing before an elder. Hence, Jacob's act of drawing (gathering) his feet before being gathered to his people is representative of his life's unwavering walk according to the Word of God. Jacob was gathering and presenting to God all the footsteps he has taken in the sojourning life that God had allowed him. They were truly steps taken in faith. Now by gathering his feet, Jacob was summing up his life. This was the culmination of his life's final account.

Only those who fulfilled the tasks entrusted to them can gather up their feet the way Jacob had done. Although his 147-year life journey was a difficult one, he completed all the duties that were entrusted to him with regard to the plan for salvation and was now gathering his feet with which he had walked with God so that he might return to his true homeland. The scene of the last moment of Jacob's life is a model of a most beautiful and blessed closure to life on this earth.

At the end of our lives, we must also be able to give thanks and confess "the God who has been my shepherd all my life to this day" (Gen 48:15). There are so many people who cannot "gather up their feet" before they die, let alone worship at the head of the bed. There could be no greater blessing for us than to be able to give thanks to God for fulfilling every part of His promise without fail before we gather up our feet to enter the kingdom of God.

(5) Jacob's great funeral procession

As he had sworn to Jacob (Gen 47:30–31), Joseph carried Jacob's body to the land of Canaan and buried him in the cave of the field of Machpelah (Gen 50:12–13). Jacob's body was embalmed for 40 days according to the Egyptian custom, and all the Egyptians wept before his body for 70 days (Gen 50:2–3).[27]

Jacob's funeral must have been a royal funeral since it was customary that people weep for kings for 72 days. It was only after the 40 days for the embalming and the 70 days of wailing that Joseph departed for Canaan according to Jacob's last wishes.

There was an expanse of about 200 miles (320 km) of wilderness between Goshen in Egypt and the cave of Machpelah. It is written that all of Pharaoh's servants, the elders of his household, and all the elders of the land of Egypt went along with Joseph on this long-distance journey (Gen 50:7). In addition, all of Joseph's household, his brothers, and his father's household (Gen 50:8), along with chariots and horsemen, went up with him (Gen 50:9). Jacob's funeral must have been extravagant, judging from the great company that went to the funeral. Martin Luther (1483–1546) noted that there was no other funeral in the Bible recorded with such respect and detail.

The inhabitants of the land of Canaan saw the funeral procession and were so moved by it that they renamed the threshing floor of Atad to "Abel-mizraim," which means "This is a grievous mourning for the Egyptians" (Gen 50:11). The funeral was carried out with extravagance and in accordance with Jacob's wishes to demonstrate that his descendants would return to Canaan as God had promised through the covenant of the torch.

What does the scene of Jacob's funeral procession toward the burial place bring to mind? It is a foreshadowing of the exodus procession; Israel's triumphant procession out of Egypt about 413 years later. Jacob's burial in Canaan in the cave of Machpelah is another symbolic gesture to demonstrate ownership of the land. At the same time, it is the fulfillment of the covenant at Beersheba (Gen 46:4), where God promised that He would call Jacob back to Canaan.

Even as Jacob was breathing his last, he had total conviction in the fulfillment of the covenant; in faith he embraced the land of Canaan in his heart. The end of his life was as peaceful as the glow of the setting sun upon the sea after a storm. In this manner, conviction in God's covenant of the torch only grew stronger with each fulfillment as it passed through Abraham to Isaac and now to Jacob.

7. The Death of Joseph (Age 110) (Gen 50:22–26), 1806 BC, 276th Year of the Covenant of the Torch

(1) The 400 years of suffering

The Israelites who moved to Egypt during Jacob's time lived a relatively abundant and peaceful life thanks to the solid foundation that Joseph had established for them. However, the fulfillment of God's Word that they would be strangers in a foreign land and be enslaved for 400 years was at hand (Gen 15:13). The difficulties of living in a foreign nation probably began to surface as Joseph's reign as second-in-command came to an end.

The Israelites actually lived in Egypt for 430 years, but God said that they would suffer for 400 years in a foreign land, excluding the 30 years of peace they enjoyed while Joseph was in charge.[27] For this reason, the Bible records Israel's time in Egypt as 430 years (Gen 12:40–41; Gal 3:17) and as 400 years (Acts 7:6).

(4) Joseph's last words for the fulfillment of the covenant

Joseph lived another 53 years in Egypt after Jacob's death until the age of 110 (Gen 50:26). The age of the patriarchs came to a close upon his death. Unlike Jacob's extravagant funeral and burial in Canaan, Joseph's funeral consisted of his body being embalmed (mummified) and placed in a coffin in Egypt (Gen 50:22–26).

In 1806 BC, 276 years after the covenant of the torch was made, with death before him, Joseph made his descendants swear that they would carry his bones with them to Canaan when they left Egypt and bury them there (Gen 50:25). Joseph had no doubt about God's promise regarding the land of Canaan.

> **Genesis 50:24** And Joseph said to his brothers, "I am about to die, but God will surely take care of you, and bring you up from this land to the land which He promised on oath to Abraham, to Isaac and to Jacob."

As Joseph was speaking his last words, he first said that God would lead the Israelites out of Egypt and into Canaan (Gen 50:24). He was prophesying about the exodus in fulfillment of God's covenant (Gen 15:14). Regarding this, Hebrews 11:22 states, "By faith Joseph, when he was dying, made mention of the exodus of the sons of Israel, and gave orders concerning his bones."

Next, he gave orders concerning his bones (Gen 50:25; Heb 11:22). Unlike his father, Jacob, who asked that his body be immediately buried in Canaan, Joseph commanded that his bones be carried out of Egypt when God comes to Israel's aid. Joseph did not want the Israelites simply to take his body out to be buried in Canaan; he earnestly wanted to take part in Israel's exodus and enter Canaan together with his people.

As his life was coming to a close, Joseph remembered God's Word—God's covenant of the torch with Abraham. It had been 276 years since the covenant was made, but even in his last hour Joseph held on faithfully to the covenant. For this reason, Hebrews 11:22 regarded Joseph's act as an act of faith and recorded, "By faith Joseph, when he was dying… gave orders concerning his bones."

(3) Joseph's funeral

Unlike the account of Jacob's funeral, the Bible only states that Joseph was embalmed and placed in a coffin.

> **Genesis 50:26** So Joseph died at the age of one hundred and ten years; and he was embalmed and placed in a coffin in Egypt.

וַיָּמָת יוֹסֵף בֶּן־מֵאָה וָעֶשֶׂר שָׁנִים וַיַּחַנְטוּ אֹתוֹ וַיִּישֶׂם

wayyîsem *'ōtô* *wayyaḥanṭû šānîm* *wā'eśer* *benmē'â* *yôsēp wayyāmot*

בָּאָרוֹן בְּמִצְרָיִם

bĕmiṣrāyim *bā'ārôn*

This is the whole account of Joseph's funeral. There are no details provided on how they buried the body or how long they mourned. They just placed his body temporarily in a coffin. If they had immediately buried his body, for certain, he would have had a grand state funeral. However, in accordance with Joseph's earnest wishes, he had a funeral unbecoming of his high position; his body was just mummified. His funeral would be complete many years later when his body was buried in Shechem in the land of Canaan (Josh 24:32).

Joseph's body was embalmed according to the Egyptian custom and made into a mummy and placed in an אֲרוֹן (*'ărôn*) (Hebrew word for "coffin" meaning "chest" or "ark"). At the time, kings (pharaohs) and high government officials used coffins with two to three layers that were then placed again in a stone coffin (usually weighing many tons).[28]

The sentence "He was embalmed" (וַיַּחַנְטוּ אֹתוֹ, *wayyaḥanṭû 'ōtô*) refers to an elaborate mummification process. Thomas Leale suggests, "The Egyptians had a kind of feeling, that while the mummy lasted, the man had not yet perished from earth."[29] His preserved body acted as a symbol that God's covenant was alive and active under His sovereignty.

Joseph wanted to be treated not as a ruler of Egypt, but as one of God's people. He did not allow his achievements in Egypt to be commended or his death to be mourned. He wanted only to return to Canaan, and he ended his life encouraging his descendants to wait for the fulfillment of the covenant. His death was not the end, but the beginning of the nation's great anticipation of the day when the Lord would come to their aid (Gen 50:24–25; Exod 2:25; 3:7–10; 4:31; Acts 7:34).

(4) The meaning of Joseph's mummy being placed in a coffin in Egypt

Joseph's mummy was with the Israelites in Egypt for 360 years from the time of his death until the exodus, acting as the symbol of the Immanuel God—the God of the covenant was with them. The presence of Joseph's body in Egypt was an invisible source of comfort and hope for a people suffering in a foreign land. Furthermore, it was the invisible bond that kept the 12 tribes together in solidarity until they could completely possess the land of Canaan.

Today, Joseph's bones are the model of the Immanuel God for those who are suffering in the sinful world and waiting in anticipation for their entry into the kingdom of God. Even today, God is pouring out the grace of Immanuel by proclaiming His Word through His servants. Just as the Israelites carried Joseph's bones out of Egypt into the wilderness ahead of their procession (Exod 13:19), we must firmly believe in God's Word and proceed with the Word in front of us.

PART FOUR

The History of the Exodus Until the Conquest of Canaan

In 1876 BC, 206 years after the ratification of the covenant of the torch, Jacob took his 70-member family and moved to Egypt. Joseph, who was second-in-command of Egypt, was 40 years old, and Jacob was 130 years old. After allowing the Israelites to live under slavery and affliction as strangers in the land of Egypt for 400 years, God finally executed the great work of the exodus in 1446 BC (Gen 15:13-14). After the exodus, the Israelites camped 42 times (Gilgal included) in the wilderness over a 40-year period and finally entered Canaan.

Stephen's expression "the congregation/church [ἐκκλησία, *ekklēsia*] in the wilderness" (Acts 7:38) in his sermon before he was martyred, implies that the congregation of the Israelites who wandered in the wilderness foreshadows the church in the New Testament era. In the wilderness, Israelites were punished for their grumblings and disbelief and were trained to become a godly and holy people who could take possession of the Canaan land. This process depicts clearly the journey of faith that Christians are taking today in order to become people of the heavenly kingdom.

This chapter will specifically examine the fulfillment process of God's covenant of the torch through the exodus, 40 years of the wilderness journey, and the conquest of Canaan.

Chart: The Chronology of the Exodus Until the Conquest of Canaan

(149 years, from 1539 BC to 1390 BC)

Year (BC)	Main Event	Content
1539	543RD YEAR OF THE CONVENANT Rise of a new king who did not know Joseph	① "The new king who did not know Joseph" (Exod 1:8; Acts 7:18) is believed to be Thutmose (1539–1514 BC), the third king from the 18th Dynasty that had newly risen up by destroying the Hyksos Dynasty (the 15th, 16th, and 17th Dynasties), which was from the Shemite lineage during the time when Joseph was second-in-command of Egypt. ② He had intentionally ignored Joseph's achievements and oppressed the Israelites by the method of forced labor because he feared the Israelites' population growth (Exod 1:11; Acts 7:17–19).
1526	556TH YEAR OF THE CONVENANT Birth of Moses	① Moses' mother was Jochebed from the tribe of Levi, and his father was Amram from the tribe of Levi. Moses was the youngest of his siblings, which included an older brother and sister (Exod 2:1–10; 6:16–20; 7:7; Num 26:57–59; 1 Chr 23:12–13). ② Moses was beautiful from birth (Exod 2:2). "Beautiful" signifies favorable and best in action, intelligence, and looks. Moses was a lovely child in the sight of God (Acts 7:20), and his parents saw that the child was beautiful by faith and nurtured him for three months in hiding (Heb 11:23).
1486	596TH YEAR OF THE CONVENANT Moses flees to Midian	① When Moses turned 40 years old, he remembered his fellow Israelites and came out to visit them (Acts 7:23). There, he saw an offensive scene of an Egyptian striking an Israelite, and he fatally struck the Egyptian (Exod 2:11–12; Acts 7:22–27). ② The next day, Moses found out that his deed of killing the Egyptian had been exposed. He fled to Midian away from the presence of Pharaoh, who wanted to kill him (Exod 2:13–15; Acts 7:28–29).
1446	636TH YEAR OF THE CONVENANT Calling of Moses and Israel's exodus	① God trained Moses in Midian for 40 years and eventually called to him from a burning bush at Mount Horeb for the great work of the exodus (Exod 3:1–10; Acts 7:30–34). ② The Israelites departed from Rameses in the great exodus on the fifteenth day of the first month in the first year, 430 years after their migration to Egypt and 360 years after the death of Joseph (Exod 12:37–41; Num 33:3).

Year (BC)	Main Event	Content
		③ They marched out courageously in martial array (Exod 13:18; Num 33:1) as the army of the Lord (Exod 12:41; 7:4).
		④ God allowed them to bring out great wealth in the exodus (Exod 3:21–22; 11:2–3; 12:35–36; Ps 105:37–38). This is the fulfillment of God's promise in the covenant of the torch (Gen 15:14).
		⑤ Moses recalled Joseph's will and took Joseph's bones in the exodus (Exod 13:19). Joseph's bones most likely were preserved in a coffin covered with one layer of sycamore wood (from a large sycamore tree or sycamore fig) or a double-layered coffin covered with an exterior sarcophagus.
1446–1407	636TH–675TH YEAR OF THE CONVENANT 40 years in the wilderness	① The 40 years in the wilderness were a period of punishment imposed as the result of disbelief. It was a time of sorrow and trouble for God because of their disbelief and disobedience (Ps 78:40–41; 95:10).
		② Because of the grumbling and rebellion caused by the ten spies' unfaithfulness in Kadesh-barnea during the early days of the wilderness (Num 13:25–14:4), God declared that the Israelites would have to spend 40 years, (one year for each day of spying on the land, which was 40 in total) wandering in the wilderness (Num 14:34). It took 40 years until all 603,550, except Joshua and Caleb, died in the wilderness (Num 32:13; Josh 5:6; Heb 3:17).
		③ The Israelites repeated the work of moving and camping 42 times over 40 years (Num 33) in the wilderness until they reached their final destination in Gilgal in the land of Canaan (Josh 4:19).
1407	675TH YEAR OF THE CONVENANT (40TH YEAR OF THE EXODUS) Death of three leaders: Miriam (1st month) Aaron (1st day of 5th month) Moses (11th month)	① Miriam died in Kadesh approximately one year prior to the Israelites entering Canaan (Num 20:1).
		② Aaron died at the age of 123, approximately eight months prior to the Israelites entering Canaan (Num 20:12). He died as God had proclaimed, about four months after he was sentenced to death in Numbers 20:12, 24 (Num 20:28; 33:38).
		③ Moses, who was forbidden from entering Canaan (Num 20:8–13), pleaded earnestly for God to allow him to enter Canaan, but God did not permit it (Deut 3:23–28).
		④ Approximately two months prior to entering Canaan, Moses climbed up Mount Nebo (aka, the mountains of Abarim, Mount Pisgah), gazed upon the land of Canaan, and then died at the age of 120 (Num 27:12–14; Deut 32:48–52; 34:1–8).

Year (BC)	Main Event	Content
1407	**675TH YEAR OF THE CONVENANT** Death of 603,548 soldiers numbered in the first census (before crossing the brook Zered)	① During the 38-year journey from Kadesh-barnea to the crossing of the brook Zered (Deut 2:13–16), the 603,548 from the first census of soldiers died (Num 1:46; 32:11–13). ② The prophecy in Numbers 14:26–35 was fulfilled, and thus Joshua and Caleb were the only persons from the first generation of the wilderness that survived to be counted again in the second census (Num 26:63–65). ③ The extermination of the soldiers at the brook Zered was not from natural causes, but from sudden death that God had caused (Num 32:14–15), just as God had sworn, "In the end all had been perished" (Deut 2:15) and "In the end all had been destroyed" (Num 32:13).
1407	**675TH YEAR OF THE CONVENANT** Death of 24,000 people in Moab (Shittim)	① The Plains of Moab was the last camp prior to the entry into the land of Canaan (Num 33:48–49). While staying here, the Israelites participated in worshiping Baal of Peor and committed adultery. As a result, 24,000 died by the plague (Num 25:1–9). ② This event occurred after the death of the soldiers numbered in the first census taken before crossing the brook Zered (Deut 2:13–16). Thus, the people who died at this place were the second generation of the wilderness.
1407	**675TH YEAR OF THE CONVENANT** Second census of soldiers	① The second census of soldiers was taken "after the plague" at Moab Shittim, where 24,000 died due to idolatry and adultery (Num 26). ② The purpose of the second census of soldiers was to number those who would experience the fulfillment of the covenant of the torch, to number those who would enter the Promised Land and fight, and to divide the Promised Land fairly among all the tribes.
1407	**675TH YEAR OF THE CONVENANT** Reiteration of the law	① Two months prior to entering into Canaan, on the first day of the eleventh month in the fortieth year (Deut 1:3), Moses reiterated the law to prepare the people for new life in the land of Canaan and to have them reflect upon the past history and repent (Deut 1–30).
1407	**675TH YEAR OF THE CONVENANT** Commissioning of Joshua as new leader	① According to the command of the Lord, Moses laid his hand upon Joshua and commissioned him before Eliezer the priest and the whole assembly (Num 27:18–23). ② Now Joshua was filled with the spirit of wisdom, since Moses had laid his hands on him (Deut 34:9), and the Israelites listened to him in obedience to the command of the Lord (Deut 34:9).

Year (BC)	Main Event	Content
1406	676TH YEAR OF THE CONVENANT Entry into Canaan, the Promised Land	① The Israelites arrived at the land of Canaan under the new leadership of Joshua on the tenth day of the first month in the forty-first year of the exodus (Josh 4:19). ② Since the Israelites set out from Rameses on the fifteenth day of the first month in the first year (Num 33:3), the time in the wilderness was five days short of 40 years. ③ They entered Canaan 400 years after the death of Joseph, 40 years after they carried out Joseph's bones out of Egypt during the exodus.
1406–1390	676TH–692ND YEAR OF THE CONVENANT Conquest of Canaan (after six years) and allocation of land among 12 tribes (after ten years)	① The battle to conquer key positions in the land of Canaan presumably ended in approximately six years (Josh 11:23; 14:15). Joshua conquered the entire land (Josh 10:40), took the entire land (Josh 11:16), and at last the land of Canaan became Israel's possession and inheritance (Josh 12:7–8). ② It took approximately ten years to distribute the conquered and unconquered areas equally among the 12 tribes. All of God's Word was fulfilled without fail (Josh 23:14) "according to all that He had sworn to their fathers" (Josh 21:44). This was the historical fulfillment of the "land" that God had promised in the covenant of the torch (Gen 15:18–21; Ps 105:44).
1390	692ND YEAR OF THE CONVENANT Death of Joshua and burial of Joseph's bones in Shechem	① As the leader succeeding Moses, Joshua conquered the land of Canaan for 16 years and died at the age of 110. He was buried in the land of his inheritance at Timnath-serah (Josh 24:29–30). ② Joseph's bones, which Moses took with him at the time of exodus (Exod 13:19), were buried in Shechem, in the heart of the land of Canaan (Josh 24:32). Joseph's bones were buried approximately 56 years after the start of the exodus (40 years of the wilderness journey and approximately 16 years of Canaan conquest). ③ With the burial of Joseph's bones in Shechem, the promise that "in the fourth generation they shall return here" was fulfilled (Gen 15:16). Likewise, every promise in the covenant of the torch was completely fulfilled in accordance with the Word (Josh 21:45; 23:14; Ps 105:42–45).

CHAPTER 11

The Emergence of Moses

1. The New Pharaoh Who Did Not Know Joseph (Exod 1:8), 1539 BC, 543rd Year of the Covenant of the Torch

(1) The exponential growth in the number of the Israelites

God made the 70 members of Israel's family powerful and numerous in the land of Egypt.

> **Genesis 47:27** Now Israel lived in the land of Egypt, in Goshen, and they acquired property in it and were fruitful and became very numerous.

This was the fulfillment of the promise that God had previously repeated from the time he had called Abraham, a promise that God also had reiterated to Jacob (Gen 12:2; 13:16; 15:5; 22:17; 32:12; 46:3; 48:16).

> **Exodus 1:7** (NASB) But the sons of Israel were fruitful and increased greatly, and multiplied, and became exceedingly mighty, so that the land was filled with them.

> **Exodus 1:7** (NLT) But their descendants, the Israelites, had many children and grandchildren. In fact, they multiplied so greatly that they became extremely powerful and filled the land.

The passage emphasizes the exponential increase of the Israelites through five consecutive descriptions: "were fruitful," "increased greatly," "multiplied," "became exceedingly mighty," and "the land was filled with them."

To be fruitful is פָּרָה (*pārâ*) in Hebrew, meaning "to bear fruits in abundance like a healthy tree." This is the same word for *fruitful* in Genesis 1:28.

To increase greatly is שָׁרַץ (*šāraṣ*) in Hebrew, meaning "to swarm" or "to teem" like fish. This word means "to grow and increase continuously and with vitality" (Gen 1:20).

To multiply is רָבָה (*rābâ*) in Hebrew, meaning "to grow exponentially." This expresses the fact that the promise of many descendants that God had given to Abraham (Gen 13:14–16; 15:15) was certainly being fulfilled. This is the same word used in Genesis 1:28.

To become mighty is עָצַם (*ʿāṣam*) in Hebrew, meaning "to become immeasurably mighty."

To fill is מָלֵא (*mālēʾ*) in Hebrew, meaning "to fill" or "to replete." This word is used in Genesis 1:28: "fill the earth." It signifies that the land of Goshen was full to the extent that a normal existence became strenuous. This implies that the time had come for God to lead His people into the new land, Canaan.

Especially notable among the five descriptions are "fruitful" (פָּרָה, *pārâ*), "multiply" (רָבָה, *rābâ*), and "fill" (מָלֵא, *mālēʾ*) because they are the same Hebrew verbs used in Genesis 1:28 in the commands to the man and woman: "Be fruitful and multiply, and fill the earth." This command is again proclaimed in the covenant of the flaming torch, "Your descendants shall be as many as the stars of the heavens" (Gen 15:5), and fulfilled through the exponential increase in the number of the Israelites in Egypt.

They were 70 people when they first entered Egypt (Gen 46:27). At the first census, taken 430 years later, which counted only soldiers over 20 years of age, their number had increased to 603,550 (Num 1:46; 2:32; cf. Exod 38:26). The number of male adults (603,550) was about 8,622 times larger than the original 70 who existed 430 years earlier. Including women, children, and the elderly, an estimated two million people existed at that time—a figure about 28,600 times larger than the original 70.

Numbers 23:10 depicts the Israelites as a people so great in number that they are difficult to count: "Who can count the dust of Jacob, or number the fourth part of Israel?" They existed in such great numbers that Pharaoh felt threatened, fearing that they would "fight against us, and depart from the land" (Exod 1:10).

Having such a growth rate is powerful evidence that virtually no obstacles were present to suppress the Israelite population growth, such as various diseases, plagues, wars, and natural disasters. Even while they were enslaved in Egypt, God had completely protected them and granted them physical health. Therefore, such an exponential population growth became possible.

(2) The emergence of a new king

Truly, the 430 years in Egypt were a "scheduled" period of time through which God specifically blessed the Israelites. Henceforth, the fulfillment of the covenant that God had promised was rapidly progressing in accordance with His divine plan. However, a time of extreme affliction began with the emergence of a new king who did not know Joseph.

Exodus 1:8 Now a new king arose over Egypt, who did not know Joseph.

The "new king ... who did not know Joseph" refers to the king of the 18th Dynasty in Egypt. The dynasty that had previously reigned over Egypt was the Hyksos Dynasty (the fifteenth, sixteenth, and seventeenth kings) from the Shemite lineage in the northeast part of Egypt.

The Hyksos Dynasty was destroyed by Ahmose I (1584–1560 BC) of the 18th Dynasty around 1580 BC, about 300 years after the Israelites had moved to Egypt. The 18th Dynasty, composed of pure, native Egyptians, destroyed the government of the Hyksos (who were foreigners) and established an indigenous throne. In the process, they obliterated all of Joseph's accomplishments.

The *new king* in Exodus 1:8 is מֶלֶךְ־חָדָשׁ (*melek-ḥādāš*), which in Hebrew means "different king." This shows that the dynasty of Egypt had changed from the Hyksos Dynasty to the 18th Dynasty. Also, the word *arose* is קוּם (*qûm*) in Hebrew, meaning not simply to "get up," but also to "arise for war" (Ps 3:7), which further testifies to the fact that the 18th Dynasty rose to overthrow the Hyksos Dynasty.

So who specifically was the "new king ... who did not know Joseph?" He was Thutmose I, the third king of the new 18th Dynasty. The year of Moses' birth is 1526 BC, and it is well known that Thutmose I reigned over Egypt from 1539 BC to 1514 BC.

(3) A new dynasty and its policy

The 18th Dynasty perceived the Israelites as remnants of the Hyksos Dynasty and enforced extreme measures to oppress them. They not only disregarded the promise and the relationship that the previous pharaoh had with Joseph, but also obliterated Joseph's accomplishments altogether. The new dynasty enslaved the Israelites and gave them harsh, laborious work. In order to boast of Pharaoh's majesty, Egypt began to construct a great pyramid and two cities, Pithom and Raamses (Exod 1:9–11). They assembled the Israelites, who for generations lived as nomads and raised livestock; now, however, they were lashed and forced to mash dirt, burn and transport bricks, and dig waterways. The oppression and affliction were so great and unbearable that their descendants later described the experience as "the iron furnace" (Deut 4:20), "the midst of the iron furnace" (1 Kgs 8:51), and "Egypt … the iron furnace" (Jer 11:4) as they looked back and remembered Egypt.

(4) The time of the new dynasty

Regarding the time of the new king who did not know Joseph, Acts 7:17–18 states, "But as the time of the promise was approaching which God had assured to Abraham, the people increased and multiplied in Egypt, until there arose another king over Egypt who knew nothing about Joseph." Here, the "time of the promise … which God had assured to Abraham" is referring specifically to the time of the fulfillment of the prophecy of Genesis 15:13 when slavery comes to an end and the Israelites come out of Egypt.

If the Egyptian dynasties had continued to treat the Hebrews hospitably, the Israelites would have accepted the religion, culture, and tradition of the Egyptians and fallen astray in corruption. However, God saw in His administration in the history of redemption that the time of the exodus was imminent, and He raised up a "new king who did not know Joseph." Through harsh oppression against the chosen people, God began the work of completely separating the Israelites from Egypt. God intervened to make them realize that Egypt was a foreign land that they must eventually leave, to remember God's words that were passed down from their forebears, and to cry out to God in prayer (Exod 2:23).

2. The Birth of Moses (Exod 2:1–22), 1526 BC, 556th Year of the Covenant of the Torch

(1) The background of the times at Moses' birth

Thutmose I imposed cruel and oppressive policies on the Hebrews and taxed them with unbearable, laborious work. He also enforced a policy to have all the newborn male Hebrews cast into the Nile River in an attempt to blot out the nation (Exod 1:15–22).

It was at this time that Moses was born to Amram and Jochebed. Moses' mother, Jochebed, was a daughter of Levi, and thus she was born to a very godly family (Exod 2:1; 6:20; Num 26:57–59). Moses' father, Amram, was also from the tribe of Levi (Exod 2:1). Moses' parents raised him in hiding for three months (Exod 2:1–2). When they could hide Moses no longer, they put him in a wicker basket covered with tar and pitch and set it among the reeds by the bank of the Nile (Exod 2:3). Moses was discovered by Pharaoh's daughter, who drew him out of the water (Exod 2:5–6). Thus, Moses' name means "drawn out of the water" (Exod 2:10).

Pharaoh's daughter who drew Moses out of the Nile River is Hatshepsut, daughter of Thutmose I. She had married Thutmose II, but he died young (1514–1504 BC). At that point, Thutmose III, the son born to Thutmose II through his concubine, succeeded the throne, and Hatshepsut reigned as regent. Later, she herself took the throne of the pharaoh and reigned for 22 years (1504–1482 BC).

(2) The faith of the parents (Amram and Jochebed) who saw that Moses was beautiful

Exodus 2:2 And the woman conceived and bore a son; and when she saw that he was beautiful, she hid him for three months.

Despite the harsh life of slavery in Egypt, Moses' parents did not let their lamp of faith go out, and they passed down their faith in Jehovah to Moses.

Amram and Jochebed saw that Moses was beautiful. Here, definitions of "beautiful" are "very pleasing to the senses or mind aesthetically," "of a very high standard," and "excellent." In Hebrew, it is טוֹב (ṭôb), meaning "fair" or "good." Thus, Acts 7:20 describes baby Moses as "exceeding fair in the sight of God" (KJV).

That "Amram and Jochebed saw that Moses was beautiful" signifies that they saw their child through God's eyes. Since they had the eyes of God, they came to discover His administration hidden in Moses, and from that instant, they did not fear Pharaoh's command and could bravely hide the baby for three months. Concerning this, the author of Hebrews stated what they did was "done by faith," placing Moses' parents, Amram and Jochebed, onto the list of the forebears of faith (Heb 11:23).

Today, when we look upon our children, we must raise them by faith just as Moses' parents did, looking upon them not from the world's perspective, but from God's. We must not neglect the precious work of passing down our faith to our children (Gen 18:18–19; Joel 1:3; 2 Tim 1:5).

3. Moses Flees to the Land of Midian at the Age of 40 (Exod 2:11–15)

1486 BC, 596th Year of the Covenant of the Torch

(1) His preparation as a leader

> **Acts 7:22** "And Moses was educated in all the learning of the Egyptians, and he was a man of power in words and deeds."

After Moses' parents placed him in a reed wicker basket, setting it down on the Nile River, Pharaoh's daughter soon discovered Moses when she came out to bathe, and she took him and raised him as her own son.

Moses' biological mother, Jochebed, who had become his nurse by God's amazing providence, nurtured Moses solely by faith in accordance with God's ordinance and law, instilling in him a strong awareness of his ethnic heritage and his place with the chosen people. Although he originated from parents who were slaves, he received the same treatment as any other Egyptian prince and enjoyed the privileges of receiving the highest education of Egypt, which included academics, technology, military, architecture, religion, and other subjects. He was well equipped to become a leader—a "man of power in words and deeds" (Acts 7:22).

Although Moses grew up as the stepson of Hatshepsut, who was an enormously powerful princess in Egypt, he was still a foreigner to the Egyptians. Concern and anguish regarding the future of his people grew day by day as his status rose and as his power grew.

When Moses reached manhood, he awoke to the realization that he was a leader who would liberate the Hebrew people from slavery in Egypt. This is clearly apparent in passages such as "Now it came about in those days, when Moses had grown up, that he went out to his brethren and looked on their hard labors" (Exod 2:11), and "But when he was approaching the age of 40, it entered his mind to visit his brethren.... And he supposed that his brethren understood that God was granting them deliverance through him" (Acts 7:23–25). Judging from that fact that Moses addressed the Israelites who had been suffering under bondage as "his brethren" (Exod 2:11) and understood them to be "companions" (Exod 2:13), it is apparent that he had a strong determination to save them.

Moses' affection for his suffering brethren grew from the time that he was nursed and taught about faith in God at the bosom of his mother, Jochebed. When Moses turned 40 years old, he desired to begin the active work of saving his people.

(2) Moses attempts to save God's people

When Moses was 40 years old and a prince of Egypt, he inspected the condition of his people. On one occasion, he came upon one of the Hebrew slaves who was being treated unjustly and was being oppressed (Acts 7:24). Here, the word for "oppress" is καταπονέω (*kataponeō*) in Greek, meaning "to be severely beaten and persecuted" or "to be oppressed by evil deeds." The bondage was already too heavy for them, and yet they were being severely beaten and persecuted as well. Moses witnessed the entire scene, and no longer able to withstand it, he killed the Egyptian officer who had been afflicting one of his brothers (Exod 2:11–12; Acts 7:24).

Moses "supposed that his brethren understood that God was granting them deliverance through him" from his action (Acts 7:25). However, the betrayal by his own people forced him to flee from Pharaoh (Thutmose III)—who wanted to kill him—and go to Midian (Exod 2:14–15).

By an act of faith, Moses refused to be called the son of Pharaoh's daughter.

> **Hebrews 11:24** By faith Moses, when he had grown up, refused to be called the son of Pharaoh's daughter;

If Moses had chosen to stay as the son of Pharaoh's daughter, he would have lived in the splendor of wealth and honor in Egypt. Nevertheless, having realized that it was only the "passing pleasures of sin" (Heb 11:25), at once Moses rejected the glory secured and guaranteed for him and chose to endure ill treatment with the people of God. Hebrews 11:26 interpreted the sufferings that Moses received with the stubborn people after leaving Pharaoh's palace as "the reproach of Christ."

Rather than settling for the "passing pleasures of sin," we must look to the rewards of heaven (Heb 11:6). Even if the world rejects us and does not welcome us, may we become people of faith who will be conformed to Christ's death and fill up that which is lacking in Christ's afflictions (Phil 3:10; Col 1:24).

4. Moses Trained for 40 Years in the Land of Midian
(Exod 2:16–22), 1486–1446 BC, 596th through 636th Year of the Covenant of the Torch

When Moses was reported as a murderer, Thutmose III saw it as a good opportunity to eliminate him, for Moses was his political rival. He plotted to kill Moses by portraying Moses' murder of an Egyptian (Exod 2:11–12) as a revolt of the Hebrews against the Egyptians and treating it as treason against the state (Exod 2:15). However, God led Moses to the wilderness of Midian and put him through demanding training to inwardly prepare him to become a leader of the exodus.

God's administration through Moses was a depiction of God's future providence of salvation for mankind through Jesus Christ.[30] Deuteronomy 18:15 states, "The Lord your God will raise up for you a prophet like me from among you, from your countrymen, you shall listen to him." God was prophesying that He would raise up a prophet like Moses, and that through the Christ (i.e., the Messiah) many people will receive salvation (Deut 18:18–20; 34:10; Acts 3:20–24; 7:37; see also Matt 5:17; John 1:45; 6:14; 7:40). The relationship between God and Moses was very intimate, "face to face" (פָּנִים אֶל־פָּנִים, *pānîm el-pānîm*), just like two people who confide in each other as close friends (Exod 33:11; Deut 34:10; see also Ps 25:14). Numbers 12:8 emphasizes this closeness even more by using the words, פֶּה אֶל־פֶּה (*peh el-peh*), meaning "mouth to mouth." This shows that God's Word which Moses delivers is accurate and authoritative enough for God to stand as a guarantee.

Although Moses cannot be compared to Jesus, for Jesus Christ is far more superior and more perfect than Moses (2 Cor 3:13–18; Heb 3:1–6), the betrayal and rejection that Moses experienced from his own people foreshadows Jesus' crucifixion, the betrayal and envy of His own people (Matt 27:18; Mark 15:10). The *Oxford Bible Interpreter* explains, "God has fulfilled the salvation of mankind through the Christ that men betrayed. In other words, God used men's betrayal as a method to fulfill His will for the redemption of mankind."[31] Men persecuted

Jesus Christ out of their ignorance; nevertheless, God has perfectly fulfilled His great will for the redemption of mankind and gained victory through the cross.

No power can stop God's redemptive providence through the cross of Jesus Christ, which was absolutely predestined before the ages to save His chosen ones (Matt 26:24; Luke 22:22). Just as Jesus Christ triumphed by breaking the power of death and rising on the third day, so too will the saints who follow Him, in whatever they may face, be more than conquerors through Him who loved us (Rom 8:35–39). Hallelujah!

5. Moses Calls for the Great Exodus (Exod 3:1–10), 1446 BC, 636th Year of the Covenant of the Torch

Thutmose III, the ruthless Pharaoh of Egypt who wanted to kill Moses, died (Exod 2:23). After his death, Amenhotep II (1450 BC–?) succeeded the throne. This indicates that the time of the exodus, which God had promised to Abraham through the covenant of the flaming torch, had arrived. God called Moses at Mount Horeb. By that time, he had been trained in the wilderness of Midian for 40 years (Exod 3:1–10; Acts 7:30–34).

What kind of place is Mount Horeb? Mount Horeb is a completely dry, parched mountain. The "bush" in Exodus 3:2–4 refers to a thorn bush, a short shrub that grows in such dry areas. This unsightly, stripped bush mirrored the withered Israelites who had been driven to Egypt and forced into a miserable life of bondage, slavery, and affliction for 400 years (Exod 1:12–14). The flaming thorn bush represented the Israelites who were in the midst of fiery suffering in Egypt, as though they were in a furnace (Deut 4:20; 1 Kgs 8:51; Jer 11:4). The fact that the bush was on fire but not consumed reveals that although the Israelites were in midst of great suffering, they did not perish.

This event signaled that the time had come for God to deliver them from Egypt, just as He had promised Abraham through the covenant of the torch. Especially, the appearance of an angel of the Lord in the flame of a burning thorn bush was God's clear revelation that He had heard the groaning of His people and would deliver them (Acts 7:30–32). With this revelation, the great exodus would finally unfold.

CHAPTER 12

The Exodus of the Israelites

1446 BC, 636th Year of the Covenant of the Torch
Moses' age, 80.

Exodus 2:23–25 Now it came about in the course of those many days that the king of Egypt died. And the sons of Israel sighed because of the bondage, and they cried out; and their cry for help because of their bondage rose up to God. ²⁴So God heard their groaning; and God remembered His covenant with Abraham, Isaac, and Jacob. ²⁵And God saw the sons of Israel, and God took notice of them.

On the fifteenth day of the first month of the year 1446 BC, the Israelites finally were released from slavery in Egypt and embarked on the exodus to enter the Promised Land (Exod 12; Num 33:3). If only the young men are counted, the people who came out of Egypt numbered 603,550 (Exod 38:26; Num 1:46); if the children, women, and elderly are included, there were over two million people. It was a mass migration of a nation. The fullness of time had come, and God was fulfilling the covenant of the torch, which He had made with Abraham 636 years earlier. He acknowledged Israel and delivered them out of Egypt.

1. God's Remembrance and the Exodus (Exod 2:23–25; 3:7–9, 16)

What made the exodus possible was, above all, the fact that God saw and acknowledged Israel. Exodus 2:25 states, "God looked upon the children of Israel, and God acknowledged them" (NKJV). The Hebrew verbs in this sentence are רָאָה (*rāʾâ*) and יָדַע (*yādaʿ*). The verb רָאָה (*rāʾâ*) means "to see (closely)," and יָדַע (*yādaʿ*) means "to know (by experience)." Thus, God had been seeing, hearing, and acknowledging all of the excruciating reality of the Israelites' oppression in Egypt (Exod 3:7–10). God, who is faithful in His covenants, remembered the covenant with Abraham, Isaac, and Jacob and looked upon and acknowledged the children of Israel (Exod 2:23–25; cf. Gen 15:14; 46:4; Ps 105:8–10, 42; 106:45).

God's act of seeing and acknowledging the plight of the Israelites was indeed what Joseph had prophesied about 360 years ago—the act of visitation (Gen 50:24–25). In a similar context as in "see and acknowledge," the word *visit* (NKJV)/*take care* (NASB)(פָּקַד, *pāqad*) means "to look after, to go to anyone." Especially in Genesis 50:24 and Genesis 50:25, the phrase "surely visit you" (NKJV) or "surely take care of you" (NASB), is פָּקֹד יִפְקֹד (*pāqōd yipqōd*), an infinitive absolute construction that repeats the verb for emphasis. It means that God will visit, and He is sure to visit. Certainly, God's visit and care (also as mentioned above, His act of "seeing" and "acknowledging") was the fundamental driving force of the exodus.

2. The Sins of the Egyptians against the Chosen People

Pharaoh and the Egyptians received God's judgment on the day of the Israelites' exodus. What were the actual sins of the Egyptians?

(1) The sin of craftily oppressing the chosen people (Exod 2:23; 3:7, 9; 6:9; Acts 7:6)

Psalm 105:25 (NASB) He turned their heart to hate His people, to deal craftily with His servants.

Acts 7:19 (NASB) "It was he who took shrewd advantage of our race, and mistreated our fathers so that they would expose their infants and they would not survive."

Acts 7:19 (NIV) "He dealt treacherously with our people and oppressed our forefathers by forcing them to throw out their newborn babies so that they would die."

The word *craftily* means "to adept." The word is used to depict "Satan's activities" in the Bible. In Psalm 105:25, this word in its original text means "to conspire against." God judged the Egyptians for the sin of afflicting His people through crafty deceit and for using policies in an attempt to wipe them out.

Exodus 18:11 refers to the Egyptians as "those who had treated Israel proudly. The word *proud* (זוד, *zūd*) means "to act contemptuously as one pleases." Since the Egyptians afflicted the Israelites as they pleased and attempted to wipe out the race, God charged them for their sins.

(2) The sin of treating the chosen people with insolence and contempt

Exodus 18:11 "Now I know that the LORD is greater than all the gods; indeed, it was proven when they dealt proudly against the people."

Nehemiah 9:10 "Then You performed signs and wonders against Pharaoh, against all his servants and all the people of his land; For You knew that they acted arrogantly toward them, and made a name for Yourself as it is this day."

The NRSV of Nehemiah 9:10 states, "For you knew that they acted insolently against our ancestors." Those who are too arrogant commit the sin of pride by treating others with insolence and contempt. In the Bible, all those who were arrogant, regardless of their position or who they were, could not avoid God's wrath and judgment. King Nebuchadnezzar (Dan 4:28–33), King Uzziah (2 Chr 26:16), King Amaziah (2 Chr 25:19), King Hezekiah (2 Chr 32:25), and Haman (Esth 5:11–12; 7:5–10) were people who received God's wrath because of their arrogance.

God certainly judges those who are arrogant today (2 Chr 14:10; Ezek 28:2, 5, 17; 31:10–11; Dan 4:30–31, 37; 5:20).

3. The Ten Plagues in Egypt

God delivered His people after judging the Egyptians through the ten plagues for the ill treatment of His chosen people. Formerly, God had spoken in the covenant of the torch, "I will also judge the nation whom they will serve" (Gen 15:14). The word *judge* means "to punish and rule" and also has the connotation "to condemn" (Ps 94:10, 12; Jer 26:18). The condemnation on the Tower of Babel (Gen 11:1–9) and Sodom and Gomorrah (Gen 19:24–25) resulted from God's judgment.

(1) The ten plagues

God's judgment on Egypt, "the nation whom the Israelites served," was fulfilled through the ten plagues.

The first plague was the plague of turning water into blood (Exod 7:19–25); the second was the plague of frogs (Exod 8:1–15); and the third was the plague of gnats (Exod 8:16–19). The magicians of Egypt had imitated Moses with the first and second plagues (Exod 7:22; 8:7), but starting from the third plague of gnats, Pharaoh's magicians could no longer do so (Exod 8:18).

The fourth plague was the plague of flies (Exod 8:20–24); the fifth was the plague of pestilence (Exod 9:1–7); the sixth was the plague of boils (Exod 9:8–12); the seventh was the plague of hail (Exod 9:18–35); the eighth was the plague of locusts (Exod 10:4–20); the ninth was the plague of darkness (Exod 10:21–29); and the tenth was the plague of (striking) the firstborn (Exod 12:1–36). In the background of the continuing plagues was God's work of hardening Pharaoh's heart (Exod 4:21; 7:3; 8:19; 9:12; 10:1, 20; 11:10; 14:4, 8, 17).

Why did God successively pour out the ten plagues upon Egypt?

First, it was intended to gain honor by showing God's authority and power to Pharaoh, his servants, and the Israelites (Exod 10:1; 14:17–18).

> **Exodus 14:4** "Then I will harden Pharaoh's heart, so that he will pursue them, and I will gain honor over Pharaoh and over all his army, that the Egyptians may know that I am the Lord," And they did so.

The NLT of Exodus 10:1 states, "Then the Lord said to Moses, 'Return to Pharaoh and make your demands again. I have made him and his officials stubborn so I can display my miraculous signs among them.'"

The amazing fact is that even in midst of these frightful plagues the land of Goshen, where the Israelites lived, was protected. During the plague of flies, the plague of hail, and the final plague of darkness, God distinguished the land of Goshen, and protected it from the plagues (Exod 8:22–23; 9:26; 10:23).

The word for *put a division* in Exodus 8:23 is פְּדֻת (*pĕdūt*) in Hebrew, connoting "redemption, set a ransom" (see Ps 111:9; 130:7). Hence, God's putting a division between the Israelites and the Egyptians during the plagues manifested the fact that He would surely deliver them from the sufferings in Egypt.

Second, the ten plagues were intended to execute judgments on all of the idols that the Egyptians served.

> **Exodus 12:12** "For I will go through the land of Egypt on that night, and will strike down all the first-born in the land of Egypt, both man and beast; and against all the gods of Egypt I will execute judgments—I am the LORD."
>
> **Numbers 33:4** … while the Egyptians were burying all their first-born whom the LORD had struck down among them. The LORD had also executed judgments on their gods.

The phrase "all the gods" in Exodus 12:12 has the connotation of "omitting not a single one among the gods of Egypt."

During that time, Egyptians not only worshiped the images of men or beasts, but also served countless numbers of idols throughout nature, such as sky, earth, sun, rivers, and waterfalls, to all sorts of living creatures, such as snakes, eagles, geese, alligators, beetles, and frogs. By completely destroying their idols, God showed them not only that such idols are useless and vain, but that their ends are also tragic (1 Sam 5:3; Jer 43:12; 50:2). Thus, although the ten plagues that fell upon Egypt were a means for the exodus, it is fundamentally significant in showing that God is the only Lord over this earth, and that all other gods that mankind believes in and worships are impotent and worthless (Ps 135:15–18).

God wanted the Israelites to explain and pass on to their descendants their testimony of the plagues that God poured out upon Egypt (Exod 12:25–27; Deut 6:20–25). God wanted all the Israelites throughout the generations to know His power and realize that He is their Jehovah.

> **Exodus 10:2** "… and that you may tell in the hearing of your son, and of your grandson, how I made a mockery of the Egyptians, and how I performed My signs among them; that you may know that I am the LORD."

(2) The implication of the tenth plague, the plague of the firstborn
God revealed to Moses in advance regarding the plague of the firstborn, the tenth plague that He would send upon Egypt (Exod 11:4–6; 12:12) and a judgment rendered by God Himself (Exod 12:29; Ps 135:8).

The reason why God struck the firstborn of Egypt was that the firstborn signifies "the beginning of strength" (Gen 49:3; Deut 21:17; Ps 78:51; 105:36). "The beginning of strength" also means the "first fruit of strength," referring to the eldest son for human beings and the first birth for animals.

The plague of the firstborn was not carried out through Moses or Aaron. God Himself came down to the land of Egypt at night and executed His judgment. From men to beasts, all the firstborn in Egypt became the target (Exod 11:4–5; 12:29; Ps 136:10). This was a work that God had administered to save Israel, His firstborn.

> **Exodus 4:22–23** "Then you shall say to Pharaoh, 'Thus says the LORD, "Israel is My son, My first-born. ²³So I said to you, 'Let My son go, that he may serve Me'; but you have refused to let him go. Behold, I will kill your son, your first-born.""""

In the same way that the first son is most precious to the father of a family for the continuation of the family lineage, from God's perspective, Israel is His firstborn. Israel is a special race that God chose from all the nations on earth to be a people for His own possession out of all the peoples who are on the face of the earth and under heaven (Deut 7:6; 14:2; 32:9; Ps 135:4).

Concerning the history of the exodus, Hosea 11:1 states, "When Israel was a youth I loved him, and out of Egypt I called My son." But what is mysterious is that Matthew 2:14–15 depicts the calling of Jesus from Egypt as fulfillment of Hosea 11:1. The exodus primarily discloses the historical events related to the deliverance of Israel, but furthermore, it unveils the amazing divine administration in the history of redemption, through which Jesus Christ will later come and deliver God's firstborn, the saints, from this world.

4. The Chosen People Leave Egypt in Martial Array

> **Exodus 13:18** Hence God led the people around by the way of the wilderness to the Red Sea; and the sons of Israel went up in martial array from the land of Egypt.

> **Numbers 33:1** These are the journeys of the sons of Israel, by which they came out from the land of Egypt by their armies, under the leadership of Moses and Aaron.

The Israelites came out of Egypt in martial array. This "martial array" conjures up images of rank-and-file formation, thus indicating that when the Israelites came out of Egypt, they did not crowd and flee in chaos as if they were a mob of escaping slaves; instead, they marched out in orderly ranks. They were not fugitives, but rather an army of God that believed in God's promise and marched out with dignity.

> **Isaiah 52:12** But you will not go out in haste, nor will you go as fugitives; For the LORD will go before you, and the God of Israel will be your rear guard.

This was a display of dignity and boldness resulting from God's grace (Exod 14:8). The Bible refers to the Israelites in martial array as "the armies of the LORD" (Exod 12:41 NKJV) and states, "Bring out the children of Israel out of the land of Egypt according to their armies" (Exod 6:26 NKJV; cf. 12:51). God also called Israel "My armies and My people, the children of Israel" (Exod 7:4 NKJV).

When the Israelites marched out of Egypt in martial array, God had the Israelites bring out great wealth along with them (Exod 3:21–22; 11:2–3; 12:35–36). The Israelites openly requested great wealth like a victorious army plundering the spoils; they took all that the Egyptians gave and marched out. When the Israelites requested articles of silver, gold, and clothing from the Egyptians, the Egyptians gave up their possessions without another thought, hoping that the Israelites would leave quickly, for they were terrified that even greater plagues might strike them.

Indeed, it was a miraculous work in which the Lord gave the Israelites favor in the sight of the Egyptians so that they seemed exceedingly great (Exod 12:35–36). Thus, Numbers 33:3 says, "The sons of Israel started out boldly in the sight of all the Egyptians." The slaves who were oppressed under unspeakable humiliation, sorrow, and contempt for 400 years were now marching with dignity like the armies lined up in ranks and files. The moment that the Egyptians saw the army, they could not help but be completely overwhelmed.

> **Leviticus 26:13** "I am the LORD your God, who brought you out of the land of Egypt so that you should not be their slaves, and I broke the bars of your yoke and made you walk erect."

This was a fulfillment of the covenant of the torch which God had formerly entered with Abraham: "And afterward they will come out with many possessions" (Gen 15:14).

5. Moses Carries Joseph's Bones Out of Egypt

Exodus 13:19 (NKJV) And Moses took the bones of Joseph with him, for he had placed the children under solemn oath, saying, "God will surely visit you; and you shall carry up my bones from here with you."

Just as Joseph willed through his last words (Gen 50:25), Moses took Joseph's bones with him during the exodus. This was the moment of fulfillment, 360 years after Joseph gave the command to take his bones with them from Egypt.

Moses taking the bones of Joseph himself was more than just a commitment to carry out Joseph's request. It was a result of his own faith and his sense of duty regarding the fulfillment of the covenant. Moses understood that the exodus was not a mere emancipation from slavery, but the profound historical event of fulfilling the covenant of the torch, which God entered with Abraham in the divine administration of the redemptive history. Hence, Moses did not forget to take Joseph's bones.

Joseph's bones had been preserved as a mummy. In Genesis 50:26 the Hebrew word for "coffin" is אָרוֹן ('ărôn), meaning "chest (ark)." In those days in Egypt, a chest (coffin) used to keep mummies was usually made of long-lasting sycamore wood (tall maple tree or sycamore figs).[32] Sycamore wood was a very suitable material for the coffins of mummies 3,000 years ago because it is smooth yet very durable and resists humidity and decomposition.

Since Joseph was a high official, it is presumed that the inside of his coffin was made of nondecaying sycamore wood, and its outside was layered with stone covering (sarcophagus), according to the Egyptian funeral customs in those days.[33] Even without the sarcophagus, Joseph's coffin probably weighed a lot, requiring many people to carry it with extreme care. The *Encyclopaedia Judaica* states, "During the 40 years' wandering in the wilderness the coffin was carried next to the Ark of the Covenant."[34]

The Israelites embarked alongside Moses during the great exodus by carrying the "coffin of Joseph." This was a reminder that the Israelites were completely saved from the slavery in Egypt just as Joseph prophesied, and the historical moment when the covenant of the torch that God had made with Abraham was being fulfilled.

6. God's Providence Leads the Israelites to the Red Sea

After the plague of the firstborn, the Israelites embarked on the exodus from Rameses (Num 33:3). There were three main roads to get to Canaan from Egypt in those days (see endpapers: "Map of The Exodus and Wilderness Journey").

The first route is called "the Sea Road." In the Bible, this route is called the "way of the land of the Philistines" (Exod 13:17). This road follows the coastline of the Mediterranean Sea, through the cities of the Philistines, such as Gaza; it is the shortest route to Canaan, only about a ten-day journey. God, however, led the Israelites, who had journeyed from Rameses, around by the way of the wilderness to the Red Sea, preventing them from taking the "way of the land of the Philistines."

> **Exodus 13:18** Hence God led the people around by the way of the wilderness to the Red Sea; and the sons of Israel went up in martial array from the land of Egypt.

The word for "led around" in this verse is סָבַב (sābab) in Hebrew, meaning "to turn about," "to go around," and "to surround." From the start, God did not lead them to the nearest "way of the land of the Philistines," but led them around by the "way of the wilderness to the Red Sea" (Exod 13:18).

The second route is the "Way to Shur." This route starts from the Goshen area, passes Succoth and through the heart of the wilderness of Shur, leading to the center of southern Canaan. The Israelites, who left Rameses and camped for the first time in Succoth, could have taken this route. However, God again led them down to Etham and did not let them take the way through Shur.

> **Exodus 13:20–21** Then they set out from Succoth and camped in Etham on the edge of the wilderness. ²¹And the LORD was going before them in a pillar of cloud by day to lead them on the way, and in a pillar of fire by night to give them light, that they might travel by day and by night.

The third route is the "Way through Mount Seir." This road starts from On of Egypt through the northern part of the Gulf of Suez across the central area of the Sinai Peninsula, ending at Ezion-geber at the northern tip of the Gulf of Aqaba. From there, the Israelites could have continued on northward to the King's Highway by the east side of the Jordan River, passing through the Plains of Moab, and crossing the Jordan River into Canaan (Num 20:17; 21:22).[35]

After departing from Rameses the Israelites arrived at Succoth, camped there (Exod 12:37; Num 33:5), and then moved on to the edge of the wilderness, at Etham, and camped (Exod 13:20; Num 33:6). Setting off from Etham, as they descended down toward the Red Sea, the Israelites could have followed this path into Canaan. However, God changed their direction again and let them camp before Migdol, by the Red Sea (Num 33:7).

> **Exodus 14:2** And all the sons of Israel grumbled against Moses and Aaron; and the whole congregation said to them, "Would that we had died in the land of Egypt! Or would that we had died in this wilderness!"

"To turn back" is שׁוּב (*šûb*) in Hebrew, meaning "to circle around," and "to return." God commanded the Israelites to turn to a direction opposite from where they were headed. God had them change their direction to head toward the Red Sea. This direction, however, lead them to a dead end with no way out. Having heard of this situation, Pharaoh thought, "They are wandering aimlessly in the land; the wilderness has shut them in," and he started chasing after them with his chariots (Exod 14:4–7).

Why, then, did God not choose the shorter routes to Canaan, but instead continue to change their course or even turn them around, ultimately leading them through the longest route of crossing—across the Red Sea and toward the southern part of the Sinai Peninsula? There are two reasons.

First, God was concerned that the people may "change their minds when they see war and return to Egypt."

> **Exodus 13:17** Now it came about when Pharaoh had let the people go, that God did not lead them by the way of the land of the Philistines, even though it was near; for God said, "Lest the people change their minds when they see war, and they return to Egypt."

At that time, "the way of the land of the Philistines" was the shortest course to Canaan, but God did not lead them through that route.

Since the "way of the land of the Philistines" was a major trade route in those days, that route was guarded by the Egyptian border patrols, and in order to enter Canaan, they must pass through Gaza, where belligerent Philistines were posted. Thus, had the Israelites taken this route, an all-out war would have been inevitable. Other routes also posed a great danger of war.

Second, God had a strategy to destroy Pharaoh and the Egyptian army (Exod 14:4).

> **Exodus 14:17–18** "And as for Me, behold, I will harden the hearts of the Egyptians so that they will go in after them; and I will be honored through Pharaoh and all his army, through his chariots and his horsemen. [18]Then the Egyptians will know that I am the LORD, when I am honored through Pharaoh, through his chariots and his horsemen."

God led the Israelites to the Red Sea in order to judge the sins of Egypt, the sins of cruelly killing the Israelite baby boys by casting them into the Nile and afflicting the chosen people of Israel for 400 years (Exod 1:22). When the Israelites camped before Migdol, near the Red Sea, Pharaoh determined that they were shut in by the wilderness, changed his mind, and began to chase after them with his army (Exod 14:3–7). This, however, was God's superb strategy of leading Pharaoh of Egypt and his army to the Red Sea by intentionally making it seem like the Israelites had been shut in by the wilderness.

Pharaoh, just as God had planned, chased the Israelites all the way to where they camped by the sea, beside Pi-hahiroth, in front of Baal-zephon (Exod 14:9), and "the Egyptians took up the pursuit, and all Pharaoh's horses, his chariots and his horsemen went in after them into the midst of the sea" (Exod 14:23). God had confused Pharaoh and his army so that the soldiers trembled in great terror. They were disoriented and did not even know what to do. The wheels of the chariots came off and broke so that they could move no farther (Exod 14:24–25). In the end, God restored the flow of the sea at daybreak and returned the Red Sea back to its orginal state, thereby letting no one escape and destroying them all.

As given in God's Word that He would be honored through Pharaoh, all Pharaoh's chariots and horsemen—his entire army—ended up buried in the Red Sea.[36] There are numerous references to this event in the Bible (Exod 14:27–28; 15:4–5, 10, 21; Ps 78:53; 106:11).

> **Exodus 14:30** Thus the LORD saved Israel that day from the hand of the Egyptians, and Israel saw the Egyptians dead on the seashore.

Exodus 15:19 For the horses of Pharaoh with his chariots and his horsemen went into the sea, and the LORD brought back the waters of the sea on them; but the sons of Israel walked on dry land through the midst of the sea.

Psalm 136:15 But He overthrew Pharaoh and his army in the Red Sea, for His lovingkindness is everlasting.

The Israelites were no longer slaves of Egypt; they found their freedom as the chosen people to fulfill God's administration in the history of redemption.

7. Dry Land Appears in the Midst of the Red Sea

God dried up the land and allowed His people to walk through the midst of the sea as on land (Josh 2:10; 4:23; Neh 9:11; Ps 74:15; Isa 51:10).

Exodus 14:21-22 Then Moses stretched out his hand over the sea; and the LORD caused the sea to go back by a strong east wind all that night, and made the sea into dry land, and the waters were divided. ²²So the children of Israel went into the midst of the sea on the dry ground, and the waters were a wall to them on their right hand and on their left.

Regretting that he had let the Israelites go, Pharaoh chased after them with his chariots, horsemen, and army (Exod 14:9–10). However, God moved His angel and the pillar of cloud behind, placing them between the camp of the Egyptians and the camp of the Israelites. Over the Egyptian camp was cloud and darkness, yet there was light for the Israelites. Thus, the Egyptians could not come near the Israelites all night (Exod 14:19–20).

Then, God had Moses stretch out his staff over the Red Sea and divide the waters (Exod 14:21–22; Ps 78:13; 136:13). When Moses stretched out the staff, God's amazing power caused the waters to become walls on both sides, and the sea turned into dry land (Exod 14:21; Ps 106:9). According to scientists today, the wind speed needs to be at least 240 miles (384 km) per hour in order for the Red Sea to divide and the water to stand as walls on right and left sides (Exod 14:22).

However, the Bible testifies that it was a blast of breath from God's nostrils (Exod 15:8; 2 Sam 22:16; Job 4:9; Ps 18:15) and His rebuke (Ps 106:9; Isa 50:2; Nah 1:4) that divided the Red Sea. Even though the ground beneath the Red Sea had been wet for thousands of years, it dried up immediately when God caused a strong east wind by the blast of His nostrils and His rebuke. Thus, the Israelites were able to walk on "dry land" through the divided sea—that is, the earth in midst of the sea (Exod 14:21–22, 29). Truly, this scene of over two million people passing through on dry land in the midst of a parted sea must have been a spectacular sight.

As the Israelites escaped from Egypt, crossed the Red Sea, and were liberated from the slavery in Egypt, saints, too, can escape from the sinful world like Egypt and find liberation from the bondage of sin only through the baptism of Jesus Christ (1 Cor 10:1-2).

CHAPTER 13

The 40 Years in the Wilderness

1446–1406 BC, 636th–676th Year of the Covenant of the Torch
Moses' age from 80 to 120

The day after the Passover in the year 1446 BC, in the fifteenth day of the first month, the Israelites marched out of Egypt "with an high hand in the sight of all the Egyptians" while the Egyptians mourned in terrible grief as they buried their firstborn (Num 33:3 KJV).

The forty years of the wilderness that followed the exodus were, by the great authority of God, a period of punishment for Israel's sin of grumbling against God and refusing to enter into Canaan because of their disbelief in God's mighty power. Furthermore, it was a period of discipline as well, so that they would be able to live as God's own people by the time they conquer Canaan.

Throughout the forty years, countless numbers of Israelites endlessly rebelled against God, continuously grumbling and betraying His grace. They troubled His heart and deeply grieved Him (Deut 9:7, 24; Ps 78:40–41; 95:10). Nonetheless, God showed endless mercy and compassion even in the midst of His great wrath. He carried them, just as a man carries his son, guiding them all the way to the land of Canaan (Deut 1:31) because He remembered His holy covenantal Word with Abraham (Ps 105:42). The Israelites' 40-year journey in the wilderness is a true example and warning (1 Cor 10:1–11) for the journey of faith by today's saints in the church in the wilderness (Acts 7:38) KJV.

1. The 40-Year Wilderness Journey Condensed into Numbers 33

Bringing closure to the forty years in the wilderness, Numbers 33–36 reflects on the history of the exodus and the wilderness journey, reiterates the law, and delivers God's commands concerning the subsequent undertaking to conquer the land of Canaan. In particular, Numbers 33 records how the Israelites camped forty-one times during the forty years in the wilderness by compressing the vast journey in chronological order.

(1) Recorded by the "command of the LORD"

Moses emphasized in Numbers 33 that the forty-one camp sites were recorded by the "command of the LORD."

> **Numbers 33:2** (NASB) And Moses recorded their starting places according to their journeys by the command of the LORD, and these are their journeys according to their starting places.

> **Numbers 33:2** (KJV) And Moses wrote their goings out according to their journeys by the commandment of the LORD: and these are their journeys according to their goings out.

As Moses wrote about the wilderness journey and each of the camp sites, he must have vividly recalled the endless grace of Immanuel that God had bestowed upon His people even in the midst of their disobedience, the due wrath and judgment, his conflicts with the people, the tears he had to shed, and continuous betrayals and rebellions. Those camp sites were truly places of unforgettable and everlasting memories to Moses and the people. They were places that God went ahead and found for them.

Thus, Numbers 10:33 explains that the ark of the covenant of the Lord, which symbolizes God's presence, journeyed in front of the people for three days to seek out a resting place for them. The names of the places that God Himself had selected for them may certainly imply the events that occurred in that specific place and its redemptive significance (1 Cor 14:10).

(2) Recorded "according to their journeys"

> **Numbers 33:2** And Moses recorded their starting places according to their journeys by the command of the LORD, and these are their journeys according to their starting places.

Numbers 33 has 41 accounts of the phrase וַיִּסְעוּ ... וַיַּחֲנוּ (wayyisʿû ... wayyaḥănû), meaning "They journeyed from ... and camped by...." They had repeated the act of camping, packing, and marching 41 times in the wilderness. Moses recorded the places of their camps, and there are three reasons for recording in detail even the unfamiliar places that were never mentioned in parts of the Bible.

First, it was to prove that the 40 years of marching in the wilderness was a historical fact. Later, the Israelites would observe the Feast of Booths in the land of Canaan, which they had conquered during the time of Joshua, in remembrance of the times when they had lived in booths (tents). Even after the Israelites returned from their captivity in Babylon, they observed the Feast of Booths by making booths and living in them (Lev 23:34–43; Num 29:12–38, Neh 8:17).

Second, it was to remind the Israelites of God's never-ending fervent love—a love that saves His people, whom He had chosen, despite their numerous failures and sins. Although they were in the wilderness, a land of death unfit for mankind to survive, God's care and protection at each and every place during those 40 years allowed them to lack no necessities (Deut 2:7; 8:4; 29:5). Indeed, this was another demonstration of God's faithful love, which fulfills what He had promised (Ps 105:8–10, 42).

Third, it showed that the first generation in the wilderness could not enter Canaan because of their disbelief, thereby teaching the second generation in the wilderness that the conquest of Canaan and settlement in the land were possible only when they completely put their trust in God.

> **Psalm 78:8** And not be like their fathers, a stubborn and rebellious generation, a generation that did not prepare its heart, and whose spirit was not faithful to God.

(3) The camps of Israel centered around the tabernacle

The Israelites had been enslaved in Egypt for 400 years, but God allowed them to be born again as the hosts of God (Exod 7:4; 12:41). Thus, the exodus was not a disorderly escape, but rather an orderly march carried out in martial array like an army (Exod 13:18–19; Num 33:1). They also camped according to their divisions and marched according to their own camp (Num 1:52).

According to *Webster's Revised Unabridged Dictionary*, the word *camp* means "temporary living quarters specially built by the army for soldiers." In Hebrew, it is מַחֲנֶה (*maḥăneh*), meaning "encampment" or "camp."

In the very center of the camp was God's tent of meeting (Num 2:2, 17). The Levites camped around the tent of meeting on all four sides (Num 3:21–39). On the east side, the sons of Moses and Aaron camped

(Num 3:38); on the west side, the families of the Gershonites (Num 3:23); on the south side, the families of the sons of Kohath (Num 3:29); and on the north side, the families of Merari (Num 3:35). Around them were the 12 tribes of Israel, three tribes on each side according to their armies and standard (Num 2:1–31). Thus, the Israelites camped around God's Tent of Meeting, marched, and pitched tents again according to God's command to Moses (Num 2:34).

(4) The number of camps: 42

The Israelites camped 42 times from Succoth, the first camp since the exodus, until Gilgal, the last camp. The wilderness route through the 42 camp sites can be divided into five general sections.

(i)   **The journey from Rameses to the Wilderness of Sinai**
(Route indicated in yellow on the map of the wilderness journey)
The Israelites camped ten times in this section. They departed from Rameses on the fifteenth day of the first month in the first year of the exodus (Num 33:3) and arrived in the Wilderness of Sinai on the third month of the first year of the exodus (Exod 19:1).

(ii)   **The journey from the Wilderness of Sinai to Rithmah (Kadesh-barnea)**
(Route indicated in orange on the map of the wilderness journey)
The Israelites camped three times in this section. They stayed at Mount Sinai about one year and departed from the Wilderness of Sinai on the twentieth day of the second month in the second year of the exodus (Num 10:11–12). It is an 11-day journey from Mount Sinai to Kadesh-barnea (Deut 1:2); however, taking into account all the things that took place at Taberah, Kibroth-hattaavah, and Hazeroth, it probably would have taken much longer than 11 days for over two million Israelites.

(iii) **The journey from Rithmah (Kadesh-barnea) around and back to Kadesh**
(Route indicated in red on the map of the wilderness journey)
The Israelites camped 18 times in this section. According to Numbers 20:1, they arrived back in Kadesh on the first month of the fortieth year of the exodus. The Israelites departed from Rithmah, which is adjacent to Kadesh, and returned to Kadesh after 38 years (Deut 2:14).

(iv) The journey from Kadesh to the Brook Zered

(Route indicated in green on the map of the wilderness journey)

The Israelites camped six times in this section. Aaron died on Mount Hor on the first day of the fifth month in the fortieth year of the exodus during this section of the journey (Num 33:38). Brook Zered is a turning point in the wilderness because all those who were counted among the 603,550 people in the first census (Num 1:46), except Joshua and Caleb, were struck to death and perished by God's judging hands (Deut 2:13-16).

(v) The journey from Crossing the Brook Zered to Gilgal

(Route indicated in purple on the map of the wilderness journey)

The Israelites camped five times in this section. The second generation of Israelites in the wilderness victoriously pressed on across the Jordan River into Canaan and pitched the final, forty-second camp in Gilgal.

2. The 42 Camps

✳ These camp sites are organized and exposited in connection to the journey routes for the first time in history.

(1) Journey from Rameses (1446 BC, 1st month, 15th day) to the Wilderness of Sinai (1446 BC, 3rd month)—ten camps

(Route indicated in yellow on the map of the wilderness journey)

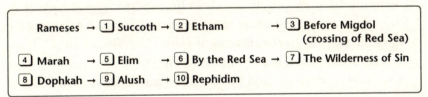

Rameses → ① Succoth → ② Etham → ③ Before Migdol (crossing of Red Sea)
④ Marah → ⑤ Elim → ⑥ By the Red Sea → ⑦ The Wilderness of Sin
⑧ Dophkah → ⑨ Alush → ⑩ Rephidim

After departing from Rameses the Israelites crossed the Red Sea (1446 BC, first month, twenty-first day; six days since the exodus).[37] They passed through the Wilderness of Sin (1446 BC, second month, fifteenth day) and arrived in the Wilderness of Sinai. The name *Rameses* (רַעְמְסֵס, *raʿamsēs*) means "Ra [the sun god of Egypt] created it." It was located on the northeastern region of the Nile Delta, in the region of Goshen where the Israelites lived. Rameses, also known today as Tanis, was a storage city that was built by the forced labor of the Israelites (Exod 1:11).[38]

| 1 | Succoth | סֻכֹּת / Numbers 33:5 |

Succoth is the first camp site.

Meaning *Succoth* means "booths" or "shelter." This name is derived from סָכַךְ (*sākak*), meaning "to block" with a fence or "to cover."

Location Succoth is located between Egypt and the Sinai Peninsula, a rest stop for those passing through Egypt. It is located 32 miles (52 km) southeast of Rameses. This is not the same place as Succoth located by the Jabbok River on the east side of the Jordan River (Gen 33:17; Josh 13:27). Today, this place is known as Tell el-Maskutah in Wadi Tumeilat.

Event The Israelites departed from Rameses on the fifteenth day of the first month (the day after the Passover [Num 33:3]). Since Succoth is 32 miles (52 km) from Rameses, it probably took more than two days for over two million Israelites to travel.

Lesson Although the Israelites decisively departed from Rameses in the exodus, they moved toward Succoth with fear and uncertainty about what lay before them. God led the Israelites to Succoth and provided safety and protection as if they were in a shelter. Saints who are redeemed through the blood of Jesus shed on the cross can also find absolute protection in their journey toward heaven, as long as they dwell in Jesus only (John 10:1, 9–10).

The Israelites ate unleavened bread in Succoth (Exod 12:37–39). Not mixed with leaven (yeast), unleavened bread was the food that people were able to make quickly and eat in times of emergency (Gen 18:6; 1 Sam 28:24). Leavened bread is easier to eat because it ferments the dough and causes it to rise, making it softer. Unleavened bread, however, is hard and thus difficult to eat and digest.

Jesus said, "Watch out and beware of the leaven of the Pharisees and Sadducees" (Matt 16:6; Mark 8:15; Luke 12:1) and taught that the teaching and hypocrisy of the Pharisees and Sadducees are the leaven (Matt 16:12; Luke 12:1). Therefore, unleavened bread signifies the pure Word of God, uncorrupted by human teaching or customs, and it denotes the integrity of the saints who have received that Word.

Having the Israelites eat unleavened bread in Succoth teaches Christians today, who have come out of the sinful world and begun their march toward heaven, to cast out the worldly teachings (Matt 16:12) and hypocrisy (Luke 12:1) like "the old leaven" and "the leaven of malice and wickedness" (1 Cor 5:7–8). We must guard the integrity of our faith by receiving only the pure and true Word of God.

| 2 | Etham | אֵתָם / Numbers 33:6 |

Etham is the second camp site.

Meaning ▶ *Etham* means "fort" or "defense wall." This is a name derived from an Egyptian word that means "with them." The name *Etham* was used with a broader meaning, referring to the entire Wilderness of Shur (Exod 15:22; Num 33:8).

Location ▶ Etham is located on the eastern border of Egypt. It is about a one-day journey from Succoth. Etham was called "the edge of the wilderness" (Exod 13:20; Num 33:6) because it was also the departure point for the 40-year wilderness journey. It is located at the eastern edge of Wadi Tumilat today.

Event ▶ The pillars of cloud and fire appeared for the first time here at Etham (Exod 13:20–22).

Lesson ▶ True to the meaning of *Etham*, God became the fort and defense wall of Israel by sending the pillars of cloud and fire throughout their forty years in the wilderness.

The wilderness through which the Israelites marched underwent the scorching heat of the sun in the day and piercing cold at night. However, the pillars of cloud created a cool shade by day, and the pillars of fire gave warmth, providing the Israelites with the best environment and consistent weather that was neither too hot nor too cold. Moreover, the pillars of fire brightened the path of the Israelites at night as though it were day and kept them from falling into pits. This was truly the blessed protection and love of God, Immanuel.

How long did the pillars of cloud and fire guide the Israelites? The entire journey of the wilderness was five days short of 40 years (Num 33:3; Josh 4:19). Given that the journey from the exodus to Etham was four days,[39] the time that the pillars of cloud and fire led the Israelites is about nine days short of 40 years—that is, 39 years, 11 months, and 21 days.

What kinds of protection did the pillars of cloud and fire provide for the Israelites?

First, the pillars were the protection of God's lead. All that the Israelites had to do was to follow God's lead as He went forth before them with the pillar of cloud, just as Numbers 9:17–18 testifies: "And whenever the cloud was lifted from over the tent, afterward the sons of Israel would then set out; and in the place where the cloud settled down, there the sons of Israel would camp. At the command of the LORD the sons of Israel would set out, and at the command of the LORD they would camp; as long as the cloud settled over the tabernacle, they remained camped."

Second, they were the protection that was never removed. Exodus 13:22 states, "He did not take away the pillar of cloud by day, nor the pillar of fire by night, from before the people." In Hebrew, the phrase "did not take away" (לֹא־יָמִישׁ, *lōʾ-yāmîš*) uses an imperfect form of מוּשׁ (*mûš*) with the negative particle לֹא (*lōʾ*), signifying that the pillars continuously protected the Israelites, never leaving them.

Third, they were the protection of absolute safety. The pillars of fire and cloud created a strong defense wall that protected Israel from the forces of their enemies (Exod 14:19–20; Num 10:33–34). Psalm 105:39 explains, "He spreads a cloud for a covering, and fire to illumine by night." Here, the Hebrew word for "covering" is מָסָךְ (*māsāk*), referring to a covering or veil that completely conceals without an opening. God had completely eliminated and blocked all attacks from Israel's enemies with the pillars of cloud and fire. Thus, wherever the pillars of cloud and fire were present, a perfect fort and a perfect city wall were present.

3	Before Migdol	לִפְנֵי מִגְדֹּל / Numbers 33:7

Before Migdol is the third camp site.

Meaning *Migdol* means "fortress" (military defense facility) or "tower" (a lookout). This name is derived from גָּדַל (*gādal*), meaning "to make great or important" or "to make powerful."

Location Migdol was a town located on the northern end of the Red Sea. Exodus 14:2 describes its location as by the sea, before Pi-hahiroth, and in front of Baal-zephon. It was a flat area of seashore large enough for the two million people of Israel to camp.

The southern end of the Migdol coastline is mountainous. These mountains were very useful as lookout points to detect the movements of the Egyptian army, which is how the name *Migdol* was derived.

Event Immediately before they crossed the Red Sea, God led the Israelites to Migdol by telling them to "turn back" (change of direction [Exod 14:2]).

The Egyptian army had "six hundred select chariots and all the other chariots of Egypt with officers over all of them" (Exod 14:7). The Egyptian army that followed Israel was an elite unit with an organized command structure. Conversely, the Israelites had not received any kind of military training, nor were they armed. Thus, it was simply impossible for Israel to defeat the Egyptians by military force.

Lesson Through the great miracle of parting the Red Sea, however, God saved the Israelites from the hands of the Egyptian army.

First, God moved a pillar of cloud to stand behind the Israelite camp. According to Exodus 14:19–20, "And the angel of God, who had been going before the camp of Israel, moved and went behind them; and the pillar of cloud moved from before them and stood behind them. So it came between the camp of Egypt and the camp of Israel; and there was the cloud along with the darkness, yet it gave light at night. Thus one did not come near the other all night." God caused darkness before the Egyptian camp and it became a fortress, so that they could not attack Israel while the Red Sea parted and the dry land appeared.

Second, God parted the Red Sea with a strong east wind. When Moses stretched out the staff in his hand over the sea, God swept the sea back with a strong east wind all night (Exod 14:21). According to a study by modern scientists, a wind of at least 240 miles (385 km) per hour would be needed to part the Red Sea. It was only by God's special help that the Israelites were able to safely cross through the divided sea in the midst of such a strong wind.

The parting of the Red Sea was a blast from God's nostrils as well as His rebuke. Exodus 15:8 says, "And at the blast of Thy nostrils the waters were piled up, the blowing waters stood up like a heap; the deeps were congealed in the heart of the sea" (cf. 2 Sam 22:16; Ps 18:15). According to Psalm 106:9, "He rebuked the Red Sea and it dried up; and He led them through the deeps, as through the wilderness" (cf. Isa 50:2; Nah 1:4).

Third, the sea waters became like a wall on the right and left sides, and the land in between the waters became dry. Exodus 14:21–22 says, "So the waters were divided; and the sons of Israel went through the midst of the sea on the dry land, and the waters were like a wall to them on their right hand and on their left." Thus, the Israelites walked on dry land through the midst of the sea (Exod 14:29). It is surely an amazing miracle for the land that was underwater for thousands of years to become suddenly dry.

The waters became like walls on the right and left side (Exod 14:29). The word *wall* in this verse is חוֹמָה (ḥômâ) in Hebrew, referring to a big "city wall" (Nah 3:8). God turned water into a city wall to protect Israel. Psalm 78:13 states, "He divided the sea, and caused them to pass through."

Fourth, God buried Pharaoh and his army in the Red Sea. After the Israelites crossed the sea on dry land, the Egyptian army followed them into the sea (Exod 14:23). God looked down on the army of the Egyptians and brought them into confusion (Exod 14:24). The word for "confuse" in this verse is הָמַם (hāmam) in Hebrew, which means "to throw into confusion" or "to trouble." The NRSV renders it as "and threw the Egyptian army into panic."

Furthermore, God caused the chariot wheels to swerve and made them drive with such difficulty that the Egyptians could not chase after the Israelites or flee (Exod 14:25). When God gathered the waters together again, the waters started flowing and covered Pharaoh and his army (Exod 15:10). All of the Egyptian army who pursued Israel were buried under the Red Sea (Exod 14:27–28, 30; 15:1–5, 10, 19, 21; Ps 78:53; 106:11; 136:15).

Even Pharaoh's choicest officers were drowned in the Red Sea (Exod 15:4). The choicest of his officers are the "finest of Pharaoh's officers" (NLT), the "best of Pharaoh's officers" (NIV).

Moses and the Israelites highly exalted God for this amazing grace (Exod 15:1–18), and Miriam and all the women responded with timbrels and dancing (Exod 15:20–21). Just as He had said, God was honored through Pharaoh and all his army and through his chariots and his horsemen (Exod 14:4, 17–18).

The events that took place before Migdol—the crossing of the Red Sea and the burial of the Egyptian army in the Red Sea—were a dramatic triumph of God who alone planned and carried them out by His sovereign authority.

The Bible testifies that the Israelites finally began to fear the Lord and believed in the Lord and in His servant Moses after they witnessed this great power of God (Exod 14:31). It was much the same in the time of Joshua. From the day that they crossed the Jordan River on dry land, the Israelites revered Joshua just as they had revered Moses (Josh 3:7; 4:14).

Just as the meaning of *Migdol* implies, there were great events of salvation that proclaimed to all the heavens and the earth that God is our only tower of refuge and a strong fortress on which we can depend (2 Sam 22:3–4; Ps 11:1; 17:8; 18:2; 57:1; 61:3;).

4	Marah	מָרָה / Numbers 33:8

Marah is the fourth camp site.

Meaning *Marah* means "bitterness" or "a bitter taste." The word is derived from מָרַר (*mārar*), meaning "to be bitter," "to be despairing," or "to be afflicted."

Location Marah is located about 45 miles (72 km) southeast of Suez, on the coastline of the Red Sea. They camped about three days into the Wilderness of Shur after crossing the Red Sea (Exod 15:22). It is known as Ain Hawarah today.

Event The Israelites were suffering from thirst because they had no water during their three days of marching in the wilderness. After walking without a drop of water for three days, they finally found a pool of water. However, when they discovered that the water was too bitter to drink, the Israelites began to grumble against Moses (Exod 15:22–24).

Lesson When Moses cried out to God in prayer because of the bitter water at Marah, God showed him a tree (Exod 15:25), and the waters became sweet when Moses threw it into the waters.

After solving the problem of the potable water, God gave His statute (חֹק, *ḥōq*, "general law") and regulation (מִשְׁפָּט, *mišpāṭ*, "legal ordinance") for the first time since the exodus and tested them to see if they would obey (Exod 15:25–26). He promised them that He would be their Jehovah Rapha (יְהֹוָה רָפֵא, *yhwh rāpā'*), the "Lord who heals," to those who dispose of all their sinful habits from their life of slavery in Egypt and earnestly heed and obey the statutes and regulations that God commands (Exod 15:26).

The bitter water, like the sufferings, pains, and trials that we encounter on our journey in life can be turned into sweet water only through Jesus, who is the Tree of Life (Luke 23:31).

| 5 | Elim | אֵילִם / Numbers 33:9 |

Elim is the fifth camp site.

Meaning ▶ *Elim* is a plural form of אַיִל (*'ayîl*), which means "strength," "tree," or "terebinth." Thus, *Elim* means "trees" or "large trees."

Location ▶ It was an oasis around a wadi that flows along a main road between Marah and the Wilderness of Sin. It was the first region found with spring water. It is located about 6 miles (10 km) south of Marah, and is known as Wadi Gharandel today.[40]

Event ▶ Elim was an oasis with many streams and springs. There were 12 springs of water and 70 date palms (Exod 15:27). Date palms reach over 85 feet (25 m) in height with featherlike leaves on top that grow to about ten feet (3 m) in span.

After having walked through dry wilderness without a drop of water or any type of plant, the Israelites probably quenched their thirst with great excitement when they arrived at Elim. It was a place where the Israelites were able to relax and rest for the first time since the exodus.

Lesson ▶ After giving them the grace of turning bitter water into sweet water, God led the Israelites to Elim, a place where they could sufficiently rest.

This gives us the hope that the Elim of blessings awaits us as long as we can find the Lord, even in the midst of life's sufferings. The 12 springs of water and 70 date palms are reminiscent of the 12 tribes and 70 elders that Moses was leading (Num 11:16–17), and also of the 12 disciples and 70 followers of Jesus (Matt 10:1; Luke 10:1).

A true church where Jesus dwells is a church with 12 springs of water and 70 date palms, an oasis and resting place that provides the water of life to many people.

| 6 | By the Red Sea | עַל־יַם־סוּף / Numbers 33:9 |

By the Red Sea is the sixth camp site.

Meaning *Red Sea* means "sea of reeds."

Location The camp was by the Red Sea, located between Elim and the Wilderness of Sin.

Event The book of Exodus does not mention anything about camping by the Red Sea (Exod 16:1), but Numbers 33:10 clearly states, "And they journeyed from Elim, and camped by the Red Sea." It seems that this place is so named because the Israelites crossed through a stream of water that flows into the Red Sea and camped by the Red Sea.

Lesson By this time, the Israelites had begun to run out of food. They had already begun grumbling that they were about to die of hunger in the Wilderness of Sin (Exod 16:1–3), so they had even less food by the time they were camping by the Red Sea. As disbelief began to sprout from their worries and concerns about food, their hearts began to waver like reeds.

A reed grows in swampy land or by water to about six to ten feet (2–3 m) in height. Its stem is hollow and has joints, but it is firm and straight. However, a reed usually symbolizes weakness because it sways easily in the wind and is not strong enough to be used as a stick or staff.

God told the Israelites not to "rely on the staff of this crushed reed, even on Egypt" (2 Kgs 18:21; Isa 36:6; Ezek 29:6). Although Egypt may have seemed strong, in the eyes of God it was only a crushed reed.

There is no gain in depending on the powers of the visible world; rather, there comes only great shame and distress (Isa 30:1–7). The strength of the living God is a strength that does not break (Ps 18:1; Isa 40:31). Blessed is the person whose strength is in the Lord (Ps 84:5).

| 7 | The Wilderness of Sin | מִדְבַּר־סִין / Numbers 33:11 |

The Wilderness of Sin is the seventh camp site (Exod 16:1–36).

Meaning *Sin* (סִין, *sîn*) means "thorny bush," "swampy land," or "clay."

Location It is located southeast of the Wilderness of Shur, between Elim and Mount Sinai (Exod 16:1). It is the eastern border district of Egypt.

Event ▶ The Israelites arrived in the Wilderness of Sin one month after the exodus—the first year, second month, fifteenth day (Exod 16:1). Although the Israelites experienced the miraculous exodus, they turned right around and grumbled against the men of God, Moses and Aaron (Exod 16:2). Here, God began to provide them with manna, food from heaven. The amount that each person was to gather was one omer (Exod 16:16).[42] Manna came down for 39 years and 11 months; from one month after the exodus (first year, second month, fifteenth day) until the forty-first year, first month, fifteenth day (Josh 5:10–12).

Lesson ▶ When their earthly food ran out, the Israelites began to speak against God, and their words were like the meaning of the place, "thorns" (סִין, *sîn*). They spoke against God, saying, "Can God prepare a table in the wilderness?" (Ps 78:19) and "Can He give bread also?" (Ps 78:20). Having heard this, God was full of wrath, and He grieved. Then, He commanded the clouds above, opened the doors of heaven, and rained down manna upon them every single day for their food (Exod 16:4–36; Ps 78:21–25).

Thorns are needle-like sharp points on plants that inflict pain upon people and animals. Spiritually, thorns are people who are extremely arrogant and wicked, always standing against God and hurting others spiritually and physically (2 Sam 23:6).

Despite the thorny grumblings that pricked His heart (Exod 16:3), God was full of compassion and sent down manna to solve the issue of hunger and quiet the grumblings. Jesus Christ is the spiritual manna that solves the issue of hunger for the spirit and body (John 6:48–51).

8	Dophkah	דָּפְקָה / Numbers 33:12–13

Dophkah is the eighth camp site.

Meaning ▶ *Dophkah* is interpreted as "stone or metal (malachite)" or "drover." Malachite is a green-colored mineral, a class of gem used for decorative purposes and also as raw material for cosmetics. The word is derived from דָּפַק (*dāpaq*), meaning "to beat," "to knock," or "to drive (cattle) hard."

Location ▶ Dophkah is located about 50 miles (80 km) northwest of Mount Sinai. It is thought to be what is Serabit el-Khadim today.

Event This is the first camp after the Israelites' departure from the Wilderness of Sin, where manna came down. There was a well-known copper mine in this area, and the Egyptian dynasties mined their copper here.

Lesson It is estimated that the Israelites remained in the Wilderness of Sin for at least a week as they enjoyed eating the manna. They experienced how manna came down every day and twice on the sixth day; on that day, everyone gathered twice as much, and it did not become foul, nor was there any worm in it. On the seventh day, manna did not come down at all (Exod 16:22–24, 29). It was at this place that they were rebuked for their disbelief and disobedience, and they learned to keep the Sabbath on the seventh day (Exod 16:22–30).

The Israelites may have been complacent and wanted to settle down as they began to eat manna; they remained in the Wilderness of Sin for quite a long time. God probably had to drive them hard, as the meaning of *Dophkah* indicates, to move them to the next camp.

There was also a time when Jesus had to drive His disciples across a lake on a boat after He performed the miracle of feeding 5,000 people (Matt 14:22). Here, the Greek word used is ἀναγκάζω (*anankazō*), meaning "to necessitate" or "to compel." Perceiving that they were intending to make Him a worldly king and a political messiah by force (John 6:15), Jesus separated His disciples from the crowd so that they would not be swept away by it. Likewise, when God pushes and demands of us beyond our understanding, we must realize that the providence of God's love is at work.

9	Alush	אָלוּשׁ / Numbers 33:13

Alush is the ninth camp site.

Meaning *Alush* means "a crowd of people," "rugged land," or "I will knead dough."

Location Alush is located about 11 miles (18 km) from Dophkah, toward Rephidim. It is known as Wadi el-'Eshsh today.

Event Alush is topographically rugged as its name suggests. The hearts of the Israelites were probably becoming hard like the land of Alush because they had been eating the same manna in the same way every day.

Lesson ▶ Manna first came down in the Wilderness of Sin and continued to come down in the same manner around the camp site in Dophkah as well as in Alush. In the beginning, they ate manna without cooking it (Exod 16:15–16). It tasted like wafers with honey (Exod 16:31). However, six days after manna started coming down, God told them, "Bake what you will bake and boil what you will boil and all that is left over put aside to be kept until morning," teaching them how to prepare manna (Exod 16:23).

Numbers 11:8 states, "The people would go about and gather it and grind it between two millstones or beat it in the mortar, and boil it in the pot and make cakes with it; and its taste was as the taste of cakes baked with oil." The expression "with oil" is שֶׁמֶן (šemen) in Hebrew, referring to the olive oil used to knead dough.

This shows us a hint that the Israelites made cakes from manna by mixing and kneading it with oil. The word *make* in Numbers 11:8 is in the perfect tense, signifying that they have cooked manna from before Taberah, where the events of Numbers 11 take place. On the basis of the meaning of *Alush* ("I will knead dough"), it is estimated that they had begun to mix manna with oil and cooked it from the time they were camping at Alush.

Although the Israelites made the dough, it was God who sent down the manna and taught them how to cook it. All things in our lives are kneaded by the God's providential hands (1 Chr 29:11–12; Prov 21:1; Isa 64:8). Therefore, we must have a faith that humbly trusts in the Lord, confessing, "My times are in Thy hand" (Ps 31:15).

10	Rephidim	רְפִידִים / Numbers 33:14

Rephidim is the tenth camp site.

Meaning ▶ *Rephidim* means "plains," "a resting place," or "a place of Sabbath." The name is derived from רְפִדִם (rĕpîdîm), which means "lamp" or "torch."

Location ▶ Rephidim was a beautiful oasis located about 12 miles (20 km) northwest of Mount Sinai. It is located between the Wilderness of Sin and the Wilderness of Sinai (Exod 17:1; 19:2). It is known as Wadi Firan today.

Event Rephidim originally was abundant with water, but it was suffering from a severe drought when the Israelites arrived. There was water at Marah, but it was too bitter to drink. Adding to the disappointment of the Israelites, there was supposed to be plenty of water in Rephidim, but this was not the case. The grumblings of the people became worse because of this water problem. Eventually, they quarreled with Moses to the point where they almost stoned him (Exod 17:2–4). They even quarreled with God, asking, "Is the LORD among us, or not?" (Exod 17:7).

In such a desperate situation, Moses cried out to God and prayed. Then, God told Moses to "strike the rock" at Mount Horeb. Moses obeyed and did as God had commanded him, which resulted in a gush of water sufficient for two million people to drink from.

According to the description of this event in Isaiah 48:21, "God split the rock, and the water gushed forth." Psalm 105:41 states, "He opened the rock, and water flowed out," and Psalm 78:20 states, "He struck the rock, so that the waters gushed out, and streams were overflowing." Furthermore, Psalm 114:8 states that God "turned the rock into a pool of water, the flint into a fountain of water," and Deuteronomy 8:15 describes it as God "brought water for you out of the rock of flint."[42]

Moses called this place "Massah" and "Meribah" (Exod 17:7). *Massah* (מַסָּה, *massâ*) means "test" and Meribah (מְרִיבָה, *měrîbâ*) means "quarrel." Moses gave these two names to the sites so that throughout the generations people would not forget the Israelites' act of disbelief by quarreling with Moses and testing the existence of God over the problem of potable water (Ps 95:8–9).

Immediately after this appalling display of disbelief, Israel was attacked by the Amalekites. At that time, Moses prayed to God with his hands lifted up. Aaron and Hur helped him by supporting his arms, and God allowed them to gain victory in the battle against the Amalekites (Exod 17:8–16). There, Moses built an altar and gave it the name *Jehovah Nissi* ("the Lord is my banner").

Rephidim is also the place where Moses, with the advice of his father-in-law, Jethro, selected able men (i.e., men who fear God, men of truth, those who hate dishonest gain and the like) and put them in charge over the people, leaders of thousands, of hundreds, of fifties, and of tens.

As a result of the complaints against God, the beautiful land called "a resting place" and "a place of Sabbath" became a dark and gloomy place of testing and quarreling with God. There is no peace for the wicked who grumble against God (Isa 48:22; 57:21).

Although they tested and quarreled with God, God's abounding mercy allowed water to come forth from a rock in Mount Horeb, and He granted them the grace to gain victory in the battle against Amalek. This is evidence of God's everlasting lovingkindness, who shows compassion and mercy even in the midst of wrath (Isa 54:8).

(2) The Journey from the Wilderness of Sinai (1446 BC, 3rd month–1445 BC, 2nd month, 20th day) to Rithmah (Kadesh-barnea)—three camps
(Route indicated in orange on the map of the wilderness journey)

Two months after their departure from Rameses, the Israelites arrived at Mount Sinai on the third month in the first year of the exodus (Exod 19:1). They remained there about one year until the twentieth day of the second month in the second year of the exodus. Here, Moses received the law and built the tabernacle of the tent of meeting on the first day of the first month in the second year of the exodus (Exod 25–40; 40:2, 17). Then, right before their departure from Mount Sinai, on the first day of the second month in the second year of the exodus, they took a census of the soldiers (Num 1:1–3). The number of men from age 20 and up was 603,550 (Num 1:46). After the census was taken, they finally departed from the Wilderness of Sinai toward the Wilderness of Paran on the twentieth day of the second month in the second year of the exodus (Num 10:11–12).

According to Deuteronomy 1:2, "It is eleven days' journey from Horeb by the way of Mount Seir to Kadesh-barnea." Here, the "eleven days' journey" is the estimated travel time, not the actual time it took the Israelites. In distance, it is approximately 165 miles (265 km). This distance could be covered in 11 days if one walks 15 miles (24 km) each day. However, the Israelites rebelled three times since their departure from Mount Sinai until their arrival at Kadesh-barnea. Each time, their journey had to be stopped, and so it took much more time than eleven days to reach Kadesh-barnea.

The following are the places where the Israelites camped in the journey from the Wilderness of Sinai to Kadesh-barnea.

> [11] **The Wilderness of Sinai** → [12] **Kibroth-hattaavah** → [13] **Hazeroth**

11	The Wilderness of Sinai	מִדְבַּר סִינַי / Numbers 33:15

The Wilderness of Sinai is the eleventh camp site.

Meaning ▶ *Sinai* (סִינַי, *sînay*) means "forest of thorn bushes," and its other name is Horeb (חֹרֵב, *ḥōrēb*) meaning "dry land."

Location ▶ The Wilderness of Sinai is located approximately 6 miles (10 km) southeast of Mount Sinai. It is thought to be the region known as Jebel Musa today.

Event ▶ The Israelites received the law as they stayed at Mount Sinai for about one year (Exod 19:3–24:18), built the tabernacle (Exod 35–40), and took the first census of their soldiers (Num 1:1–3). Here, God allocated the camps of the tribes on all four sides of the tabernacle of the tent of meeting, provided the order of march by tribes, and prepared them with everything they would need (Num 2-10).

Lesson ▶ God gave His amazing grace to Moses upon Mount Sinai. He gave the Ten Commandments, the law, and the pattern of the tabernacle. Exodus 31:18 states, "And when he had finished speaking with him upon Mount Sinai, He gave Moses the two tablets of the testimony, tablets of stone, written by the finger of God."

God ratified a covenant at this place (Exod 19:3–25; 24:1–8). This covenant was to teach the Israelites, who would enter into Canaan to fulfill the covenant of the torch, how to go about living in the land of Canaan. Through the Ten Commandments and the law, God wanted them to live in that land as God's own possession, His kingdom of priests and a holy nation (Exod 19:5–6).

Furthermore, God gave them the pattern of the tabernacle because He wanted them to worship according to His appointed law in the tabernacle. When the work of building the tabernacle was completed according to His instructions, a cloud covered the tent of meeting, and the glory of the Lord filled the tabernacle (Exod 40:34–35). Ratifying the covenant at Mount Sinai was God's great work of declaring that the Israelites are God's chosen people who would possess the land of Canaan.

Contrary to God's great work, Aaron and the Israelites made an image of a calf in molten gold and worshiped it, saying, "This is your god, O Israel, who brought you up from the land of Egypt," as they ate, drank, and celebrated before it. Seeing this, the Lord was grieved and said to Moses, "I have seen this people, and behold, they are an obstinate people" (Exod 32:9). 2 Samuel 23:6 states, "But the worthless, every one of them will be thrust away like thorns, because they cannot be taken in hand." The Israelites who were below Mount Sinai had become worthless like a forest of thorn bushes, as the meaning of *Sinai* implies (Nah 1:10; Matt 7:16).

Do we currently have a faith that is "on Mount Sinai" or "below Mount Sinai?"

| 12 | Kibroth-hattaavah | קִבְרוֹת הַתַּאֲוָה / Numbers 33:16 |

Kibroth-hattaavah is the twelfth camp site.

Meaning *Kibroth-hattaavah* is a compound word consisting of קָבַר (*qābar*), meaning "to bury," and אָוָה ('*āwâ*), meaning "desire," "crave," or "covet." As a whole, it means "grave of the greedy" or "the end of greedy" (Num 11:34). Greediness is a state of being unsatisfied with present circumstances and seeking to fulfill one's own desires.

Location Kibroth-hattaavah is located 18 miles (30 km) northeast of Mount Sinai and is also called Wadi Murra today. It was the first place in which the Israelites had camped since their departure from Mount Sinai.

Event After departing from Mount Sinai, the Israelites experienced an incident at Taberah before they reached Kibroth-hattaavah. The meaning of the name Taberah (תַּבְעֵרָה, *tab'ērâ*) is "burning." God was angry at the Israelites who complained of adversity. The fire of the Lord burned among them and consumed some of the outskirts of the camp (Num 11:1–3). The word *outskirts* in Numbers 11:1 is קָצֶה (*qāṣeh*) in Hebrew, meaning "end" or "extremity," referring to those who had gone astray from the martial array and fallen behind the camp. These were the people who did not wish to march onward, but were filled with grumblings and complaints; they followed behind and complained against God (Num 11:1).

Through the incident of Taberah, the Israelites experienced God's anger and the fire of His judgment. Even then, they turned around and grumbled again about the manna they had been eating for about a year, since the fifteenth day of the second month in the first year. They requested meat as they grumbled against God, testing Him, speaking against Him, and mocking Him (Num 11:4–9).

> **Psalm 78:18–19** And in their heart they put God to the test by asking food according to their desire. [19]Then they spoke against God; they said, "Can God prepare a table in the wilderness?"

In response, God caused the east wind to blow in the heavens, and by His power He directed the south wind, so that quails would fall into the Israelite camp like dust. Thus, they ate according to their desire and were filled (Ps 78:26–29). Even then, their greed was not satisfied (Ps 78:30), and God struck the greedy people with a very severe plague while the meat was still between their teeth, before it was even chewed (Num 11:31–34; Ps 78:31). That is why the place was named *Kibroth-hattaavah* ("grave of the greedy").

Lesson The rabbles were the people instigating the Israelites' demand for meat. They were "a mixed multitude" who left Egypt with them during the exodus (Exod 12:38). They were the people who prompted the Israelites to commit sin. There are rabbles in churches today. They are the ones who do not commit to or participate in the work of the gospel, but always grumble and complain in the back.

The rebellious acts at Kibroth-hattaavah remind us that the end of greed is only the grave. Those who hate unjust gain will prolong their lives (Prov 28:16). We need to be on our guard against every form of greed, for it is an act of worshiping idols (Luke 12:15; Col 3:5). Moreover, we must not let greed even be named among us (Eph 5:3).

13	Hazeroth	חֲצֵרֹת / Numbers 33:17

Hazeroth is the thirteenth camp site.

Meaning *Hazeroth* means "enclosure," "village," or "settlement," and is derived from the Hebrew verb חָצַר (*hāṣar*), meaning "to draw a border" or "to surround with fences."

Location Located   35 miles (56 km) northeast of Mount Sinai, this is the second place where the Israelites camped since the departure from Mount Sinai. It is known as Ain Khadra today.

Event Moses took a Cushite woman as his wife at Hazeroth. Miriam and Aaron spoke against Moses because of this, and Miriam became leprous (Num 11:35; 12:1–16). Because Miriam was isolated outside the camp for seven days, the Israelites' march was delayed for as long (Num 12:15).

Lesson Moses was a man with a special mission, unlike Aaron or Miriam. Despite this fact, Aaron and Miriam claimed equality with Moses, saying that God spoke to them also (Num 12:2). When God heard this, He suddenly summoned Miriam, Aaron, and Moses to the tent of meeting (Num 12:4). Then, He called Aaron and Miriam aside from Moses (Num 12:5) and explained to them clearly how Moses was different from them. He disclosed the fact that He speaks to Moses directly, face to face, while Aaron and Miriam receive revelations in dreams and visions (Num 12:6–8). In other words, the revelations that Aaron and Miriam receive are indirect, whereas the revelations that Moses received are direct.

No one could compare with Moses in terms of his closeness to God and the authority of the Word (Exod 33:11; Num 12:8; Deut 34:10). Aaron and Miriam were leaders of the Israelites, but it was clear that they were appointed as close subordinates so that they could help Moses (Exod 7:1). In other words, there was a feeling of an enclosure around Aaron and Miriam as "Moses' helpers." Nevertheless, although they held this subordinate position, they overstepped their authority by joining forces and attempting to act as "the leader" of the Israelites. As a result, they received God's wrath. Miriam became leprous and was shut up outside the camp for seven days, causing a delay in the journey of all the Israelites (Num 12:14–16).

Sinful mankind can never become a mediator between God and man. Jesus, who shed His blood, died on the cross, and rose again on the third day, is our only mediator (1 Tim 2:5). However, there are times when sinful mankind crosses over the boundary (or fence) by acting in arrogance and claiming that they can do the work of mediation. Such people will not be able to avoid God's judgment of wrath.

(3) The Journey from Rithmah (Kadesh-barnea) and back to Kadesh (1445–1407 BC, first month; approximately 38 years)—18 camps
(Route indicated in red on the map of the wilderness journey)

The Israelites finally arrived in Kadesh-barnea, the southern borderland of Canaan. Rithmah is presumed to be the same place as Kadesh or an adjacent area. According to Numbers 12:16, the Israelites camped in the Wilderness of Paran (Kadesh) after Hazeroth, but Numbers 33:18 states that they journeyed from Hazeroth and camped at Rithmah. Therefore, it can be presumed that Rithmah may be referring to Kadesh in the Wilderness of Paran.[43]

Kadesh is about 50 miles (80 km) from Beersheba, very close to Canaan. Located on the path toward Canaan, Kadesh was the place where the Israelites could have prepared to enter into Canaan. Right in front of Canaan, however, the Israelites received the sentence that they would wander for 40 years and perish in the wilderness (Num 14:26–35). They could not enter Canaan from Kadesh (Rithmah) in the early stage of the wilderness journey. Rather, it took the Israelites 38 years to wander around the wilderness, camping 18 times, and then returning to Kadesh.

The meaning of each camp site reflects the discipline and training through which the Israelites became God's holy people, just like the meaning of the first gateway into Canaan, Kadesh (קָדֵשׁ, qādēš). God earnestly entreated His people to remember the way in which He had led them in the wilderness, where He humbled them, tested them, and even let them be hungry (Deut 8:2–3).

The wilderness is like the contemporary churches that train and nurture God's people (Rev 12:6). Thus, Stephen referred to the 40-year journey in the wilderness as "the congregation [church] in the wilderness" (Acts 7:38).

According to Numbers 20:1, the Israelites finally returned to Kadesh in the first month of the fortieth year after wandering around in the wilderness. This was 38 years after they first arrived at Kadesh, from 1445 BC (second year of the exodus) to 1407 BC (fortieth year of the exodus).

The following are the Israelites' camp sites on the journey from Rithmah to Kadesh-barnea.

[14] **Rithmah** →	[15] **Rimmon-perez** →	[16] **Libnah**	→ [17] **Rissah**
[18] **Kehelathah** →	[19] **Mount Sepher** →	[20] **Haradah**	→ [21] **Makheloth**
[22] **Tahath** →	[23] **Terah**	→ [24] **Mithkah**	→ [25] **Hashmonah**
[26] **Moseroth** →	[27] **Bene-jaakan**	→ [28] **Hor-haggidgad** →	[29] **Jotbathah**
[30] **Abronah** →	[31] **Ezion-geber**		

14 Rithmah רִתְמָה / Numbers 33:18

Rithmah is the fourteenth camp site.

Meaning The name *Rithmah* refers to "rothem tree" (a broom tree [Job 30:4]) and is derived from רָתַם (*rātam*), meaning "to bind," "to tie up" or "to attach."[44]

Location It is speculated that Rithmah may be either the same place as Kadesh or a place nearby. The Israelites who left Hazeroth camped at Rithmah, but according to Numbers 33:49, the camp was so large (5 miles [8 km]) that it probably stretched all the way to Kadesh. It was located on the southernmost part of Canaan, so it was also called "Kadesh-barnea" or "En-mishpat" (Gen 14:7). There are three fountains at Kadesh-barnea: Ain Qadeis, Ain Quseima, and Ain el Gudeirat.

Event It was from here that the 12 spies were sent into Canaan. God counted each day of the exploration as one year and sentenced the Israelites to 40 years of wandering in the wilderness for the sin of unbelief (Num 14:34).

Lesson When the Israelites arrived at Rithmah (Kadesh-barnea), the borderland of Canaan (Deut 1:19), God commanded them to immediately take possession of Canaan.

> **Deuteronomy 1:21** "See, the LORD your God has placed the land before you; go up, take possession, as the LORD, the God of your fathers, has spoken to you. Do not fear or be dismayed."

Deuteronomy 1:8 also states, "See, I have placed the land before you; go in and possess the land which the LORD swore to give to your fathers, to Abraham, to Isaac, and to Jacob, to them and their descendants after them." However, the corrupt people did not fully believe in God's Word   and instead requested that spies explore the land first.

> **Deuteronomy 1:22** "Then all of you approached me and said, 'Let us send men before us, that they may search out the land for us, and bring back to us word of the way by which we should go up, and the cities which we shall enter.'"

The expression "let us send" is שָׁלַח (šālaḥ) in Qal imperfect, first-person common plural, cohortative in both form and meaning. This means that the Israelites already made up their minds to send spies and were asking for Moses' consent. It was not God who commanded this to be done. However, knowing that their hearts were hardened with unbelief, God remained silent and consented through Moses (Deut 1:23; Num 13:1–3).

When the Israelites heard the bad report from ten of the 12 spies, they rebelled against God's command and were unwilling to go in (Deut 1:26). The whole congregation wept all night in despair and complained about Moses and Aaron. They cried out for a leader to take them back to Egypt (Num 13:31–33; 14:1–4; Deut 1:27–28).

Thus, unbelief "tied up" and "tied down" the Israelites in the wilderness when they needed to enter Canaan. If the Israelites had gone straight into Canaan, God would have gone before them to destroy all their enemies (Deut 1:30). Unfortunately, they did not believe in God (Num 14:11; Deut 1:32), and as a result of their unbelief, they could not set foot in the land promised to their ancestors, and they were forced to wander in the wilderness (Deut 1:34–40; Heb 3:19).

15	Rimmon-perez	רִמֹּן פֶּרֶץ / Numbers 33:19

Rimmon-perez is the fifteenth camp site.

Meaning *Rimmon-perez* is a combination of the word רִמּוֹן or רִמֹּן (*rim mōn*, "pomegranate")[45] and פֶּרֶץ (*pereṣ*, "breach, bursting forth, break through, tear down").[46] The word means "burst pomegranate," "broken pomegranate," or "torn pomegranate."

Location This was the first camp site after the Israelites were sentenced to 40 years of wandering in the wilderness at Rithmah (Kadesh).

Event The Israelites "mourned greatly" after they received their sentence (Num 14:39). "Mourned" in Hebrew is אָבַל (*'ābal*), meaning "to lament."

Why did they mourn and lament? The Israelites probably were quite displeased with the punishment of having to return to the wilderness for another 38 years when Canaan was just a short distance away (Num 14:26–35). Furthermore, they saw that the ten spies who gave the bad report were killed the very next day (Num 14:36–40). Even after witnessing God's just punishment, they regarded it as unfair, and they lamented greatly.

Lesson Pomegranates were used as ornaments on the hems of the priestly robes (Exod 28:33–34) and on top of the temple pillars (1 Kgs 7:18). A well-ripened pomegranate is red and full of small seeds inside, it has been the symbol of abundant harvest since the ancient times. God wanted the Israelites to obey and enter Canaan and enjoy abundant lives like the ones symbolized by the pomegranate. However, they sent spies to Canaan out of unbelief, and they received the sentence of wandering the wilderness for 40 years.

After this the Israelites foolishly sinned against God by going up to Canaan against God's command (Num 14:40–44; Deut 1:41–43). This act of colliding against God's will was considered sinful (2 Sam 6:8; 1 Chr 13:11; Ps 106:23). Ultimately, the Israelites were shamefully struck down by the Amalekites and the Canaanites (Num 14:45; Deut 1:44). They lamented after tasting bitter defeat without being able to enter Canaan, but God did not lend His ears to their weeping (Deut 1:45).

The Israelites were like broken and crushed pomegranates when they left Kadesh for Rimmon-perez. This place, Rimmon-perez, taught the fearful lesson that anyone who becomes discontented with God's Word and disobeys it will clash with God. No matter how beautiful and successful one may be, disobedience to God's Word and self-centered obstinacy will bring destruction and despair.

| 16 | Libnah | לִבְנָה / Numbers 33:20 |

Libnah is the sixteenth camp site.

Meaning *Libnah* means "whiteness" or "transparency"[47] and is derived from לָבָן (*lābān*), meaning "white" or "to purify."[48]

Location This was the second camp site after the Israelites were sentenced to 40 years of wandering in the wilderness at Rithmah (Kadesh). It is speculated that Libnah is the same place as Laban that appears in Deuteronomy 1:1.

Event There are no biblical or historical records of Libnah, but examining the root of the word, some speculate that it was the place where the Israelites repented and vowed to obediently accept God's will and were purified by God.

Lesson The Israelites experienced disgraceful defeat at the hands of the Amalekites and the Canaanites, because they disobeyed God's command (Num 14:40–45; Deut 1:41–44). It appears that the Israelites repented of their sins as they camped at Libnah. Earnest repentance before God completely purifies both the body and soul (Ps 51:7; Isa 1:18).

Libnah illustrates how life in the wilderness was God's way of sanctifying His people. God says to those who confess their sins before Him, "Though your sins are as scarlet, they will be as white as snow; though they are red like crimson, they will be like wool" (Isa 1:18). Only those who have been cleansed by the blood of Jesus Christ and made righteous can be clothed in white robes (Rev 7:9, 14). These white robes are fine linen—bright, white and clean (Rev 19:8, 14).

Even though we momentarily take the path of disobedience, if we repent and walk the path of obedience, God will not remember our sins (Isa 43:25; Jer 31:34; Heb 8:12; 10:17), and He will sanctify us as His holy people.

| 17 | Rissah | רִסָּה / Numbers 33:21 |

Rissah is the seventeenth camp site.

Meaning *Rissah* means "fragment," "break," "crush," or "heap of ruins"[49] and is derived from רָסַס (*rāsas*), meaning "to crush to fragments" or "knead."[50]

This was the third camp site after the Israelites were sentenced to 40 years of wandering in the wilderness at Rithmah (Kadesh).

Event There are no biblical or historical records of Rissah, but it illustrates how the Israelites humbled themselves and became brokenhearted through repentance and spiritual awakening as they began their lives in the wilderness.

Lesson True repentance is softening our hardened hearts, like fine powder. We need to go through the process of being "broken" many times in order to achieve the state of being like fine powder without any lumps.

Psalm 34:18 states, "The LORD is near to the brokenhearted, and saves those who are crushed in spirit," and Psalm 51:17 states, "The sacrifices of God are a broken spirit; a broken and a contrite heart, O God, Thou wilt not despise." The expression "broken" used here means "to crush into pieces or to pulverize."

The one who has truly repented has his own fleshly thoughts, stubbornness, and pride broken and crushed as stone is crushed into powder, and it is easy for God to mold such heart according to His sovereign will. Thus, God will use us for His providence of redemption when our fleshly hearts are broken and softened.

| 18 | Kehelathah | קְהֵלָתָה / Numbers 33:22 |

Kehelathah is the eighteenth camp site.

Meaning *Kehelathah* means "assembly" or "gathering"[52] and is derived from קָהַל (*qāhal*) or קְהָל (*qāhāl*), meaning "assembly," "people," and "community" as a noun and "to assemble" and "to come together" as a verb.[53]

Location This was the fourth camp site after the Israelites were sentenced to 40 years of wandering in the wilderness at Rithmah (Kadesh). Kehelathah was located between Rissah and Mount Shepher.

Event There are no biblical or historical records of Kehelathah. The name of this place is a reminder of how the grumblings of people and divided hearts were gathered together by God's sovereign work so that they may worship as one body in the tabernacle.

Lesson God wanted the Israelites to repent and become united in their hearts in living a worship-centered life together. Worshiping together as a congregation is the emblem of a godly life and the basis of a Christian life. Furthermore, it is through worship that we meet God and experience His amazing solutions to our issues. Today, God is looking for people who worship in spirit and truth (John 4:23–24).

Jesus said, "Again I say to you, that if two of you agree on earth about anything that they may ask, it shall be done for them by My Father who is in heaven. For where two or three have gathered together in My name, there I am in their midst" (Matt 18:19–20). Even though you have a small gathering, if you believe in this message and worship with thanksgiving, God will meet with you and save you and your family from trouble (Ps 50:23).

19	Mount Shepher	הַר־שֶׁפֶר / Numbers 33:23

Mount Shepher is the nineteenth camp site.

Meaning *Shepher* means "beauty" or "goodliness" and is derived from שָׁפַר (*šapar*), meaning "to be pleasing," "to be beautiful," and "fair."[53]

Location Mount Shepher was the fifth camp site after the Israelites were sentenced to 40 years of wandering in the wilderness at Rithmah (Kadesh). It is speculated that Mount Shepher is the same place as Jebel 'Arayif en-Naqah, located 6 miles (10 km) south of Kadesh-barnea.

Event There are no biblical or historical records of Mount Shepher, but given the name of the mountain, it must have been more beautiful than the other mountains. God led His people to a beautiful place, although the wilderness is not a place where anything attractive would be expected.

Lesson The word שָׁפַר (*šapar*), from which the name of Mount Shepher originates, is found in only one place in the Bible. Psalm 16:6 states, "The lines have fallen to me in pleasant places; indeed, my heritage is beautiful [שָׁפַר, *šapar*] to me." Only God can lead us toward the beautiful and attractive places.

Jesus Christ was full of grace when He became flesh and came to this earth (John 1:14). For us, He was grace upon grace (John 1:16). In Greek, grace is χάρις (*charis*), meaning "attractiveness."[54] The most beautiful and attractive place in the world is where Jesus is. Furthermore, those who have the grace of Jesus Christ in their hearts are the most beautiful and attractive people on this earth (1 Thess 5:28; 2 Thess 3:18; Phlm 1:25).

| 20 | Haradah | חֲרָדָה / Numbers 33:24 |

Haradah is the twentieth camp site.

Meaning *Haradah* means "to tremble," "to fear," or "fright" and is derived from חָרַד (*hārad*), meaning "to quake," "to tremble," and "to move about."

Location This was the sixth camp site after the Israelites were sentenced to 40 years of wandering in the wilderness at Rithmah (Kadesh). Some people speculate that it is the same place as the Wadi Lussan, which is located 5 miles (8 km) southwest of Kadesh-barnea.

Event There are no biblical or historical records of Haradah. The wilderness is a place where the lions, lionesses, vipers, flying serpents, and scorpions live (Deut 8:15; Isa 30:6). It is a land where people cannot dwell or cross (Jer 2:6). Furthermore, there were occasional pits throughout the endless desert that could swallow up people or beasts in one fell swoop (Jer 2:6). Thus, the Israelites probably were captured by fright because of these unexpected circumstances.

Lesson Here we see that God, who had led His people to an unexpectedly beautiful place, has now led them again to a rugged place fraught with dread. The word חָרַד (*hārad*), the root of *Haradah*, refers to extreme anxiety or uncontrollable fear and fright (see 1 Sam 13:5–7). Through this place where the shadow of death lurked (Ps 23:4) and brought fear like Haradah, God tried His people (Job 23:10) so that they may have faith like gold and possess absolute trust only in God. Even in the most adverse situations in the wilderness, God poured out the grace of Immanuel and chased away the darkness and led the people until they reached safety in Canaan (Deut 1:31; 32:10–12).

Jesus Christ is the only one we need to seek when we feel extreme fear. He gives true peace to those who believe and casts aways all fear (Mark 4:35–41; Luke 8:50; John 6:19–20; 14:27).

| 21 | Makheloth | מַקְהֵלֹת / Numbers 33:25 |

Makheloth is the twenty-first camp site.

Meaning *Makheloth* means "place of gathering" or "place of assembly" and is derived from קָהָל (*qāhāl*), meaning "a gathering with a specific purpose."[55]

Location ▸ This was the seventh camp site after the Israelites were sentenced to 40 years of wandering in the wilderness at Rithmah (Kadesh).

Event ▸ There are no biblical or historical records of Makheloth, but it is speculated that this was the place where all of Israel gathered for a memorial worship.

Lesson ▸ The word appears one time in Psalm 26:12 and is used to refer to a gathering or a choir.

The words קְהֵלָתָה (qĕhēlātâ [the eighteenth camp site]) and מַקְהֵלֹת (maqhēlōt) are derived from the same word, קָהָל (qāhāl). The difference is that קְהֵלָתָה (Kehelathah) is the singular noun in feminine form, while מַקְהֵלֹת (Makheloth) is the plural noun in feminine form. This signals a change of worship style since the Israelites began their 40-year wilderness journey, from that of a nuclear family unit style of worship to that of a whole congregation coming together.

It appears that the Israelites began to focus more on congregational worship after they passed through fearsome Haradah. The source of power for the early church was the gatherings of people with one heart (Acts 1:14; 2:1, 46; 5:12). As the Second Coming of the Lord draws nearer, we must take care of one another, encourage one another, and assemble together with our focus on the church (Heb 10:24–25).

When God's believers assemble, His Word is proclaimed and the Holy Spirit works vigorously (Acts 5:12–13; 10:33; 13:44). Ezra the scribe's reading aloud of the Word of God and his subsequent explanation of it resulted in a movement of great repentance when the Israelites gathered in front of the Water Gate (Neh 8:1–12).

In the Old Testament, the gathering of all of the Israelites was called "the congregation" (Exod 12:3; Num 27:17; 31:16; Josh 22:16–17, 20). The root of this word is עֵד (ʿēd), meaning "witness." Those who worship at the sanctuary must scatter to the different parts of the world and become His witnesses.

22	Tahath	תַּחַת / Numbers 33:26

Tahath is the twenty-second camp site.

Meaning ▸ Tahath means "to go down," "low place," "at the bottom of," or "in place of" and is derived from תַּחַת (taḥat), meaning "beneath."

Location This was the eighth camp site after the Israelites were sentenced to 40 years of wandering in the wilderness at Rithmah (Kadesh). Tahath is thought to have been a low desert area.

Event There are no biblical or historical records of Tahath. It is located at the end of a wadi, so one can presume that God led the Israelites to a very low desert area.

Lesson The Israelites moved down to this low desert area and camped there. They must have moved lower in order to avoid the fierce desert winds or to find more readily accessible water.

Tahath, which means "to go down" or "low place," is reminiscent of how Jesus Christ left the glory of His throne in heaven and came in the flesh to the low, humble earth in order to save fallen mankind (John 1:14). Jesus is "He who descended from heaven, even the Son of Man" (John 3:13) and the "living bread that came down out of heaven" (John 6:51). Jesus lowered Himself and was obedient to the point of death, even death on the cross (Phil 2:8).

In addition, the meaning of Tahath—"in the place of" or "for X" (X as a variable denoting an unspecified person)—is reminiscent of how Jesus died on the cross for us, in our place. The death of Jesus Christ was a redemptive (ransom) death in our place (Matt 20:28; Mark 10:45). Thus, we must follow the example of apostle Paul, who wrote, "the life which I now live in the flesh I live by faith in the Son of God, who loved me, and delivered Himself up for me" (Gal 2:20).

23	Terah	תֶּרַח / Numbers 33:27

Terah is the twenty-third camp site.

Meaning *Terah* means "to stay" or "to delay."

Location This was the ninth camp site after the Israelites were sentenced to 40 years of wandering in the wilderness at Rithmah (Kadesh). Considering that the Israelites traveled toward Mount Hor, Terah must have been located north of Tahath.

Event The word *Terah* (תֶּרַח, *terah*) appears 13 times in the Old Testament, twice as the name of a place (Num 33:27–28) and 11 times as the name of Abraham's father, Terah (Gen 11:24–26).

There are no biblical or historical records of Terah. The Israelites camped at Tahath immediately before they arrived at Terah. God led the Israelites north to Terah in order to bring them to a place nearby Moseroth, where Mount Hor was located.

Since Rithmah had many springs, and Terah was located near a wadi, both were abundant with water. It is believed that the Israelites spent a relatively long time here, delaying the march in accordance with the meaning of *Terah*.

Terah is also the name of Abraham's father, who, like the meaning of his name, delayed and hesitated. God commanded them to leave "Ur of the Chaldeans in order to enter the land of Canaan," but he delayed in the land of Haran, where he enjoyed a life of abundant wealth. In the end, he never set foot in Canaan, where God's will rested, and he died in Haran (Gen 11:31–32; Acts 7:1–4). Today, if our hearts lean toward the abundance of this world, we also will delay God's will.

24	Mithkah	מִתְקָה / Numbers 33:28

Mithkah is the twenty-fourth camp site.

Meaning *Mithkah* means "sweet-sounding," "sweet fountain," or "a sweet spring" and is derived from מָתַק (*mātaq*), meaning "sweet," "joyful," "delightful," or "good mood."[56]

Location This was the tenth camp site after the Israelites were sentenced to 40 years of wandering in the wilderness at Rithmah (Kadesh). It was close to Mount Hor, and, judging from the meaning of its name, it must have had fountains.

Event There are no biblical or historical records of Mithkah. In contrast to the bitter waters of Marah at the beginning of their journey (Exod 15:22–23), Mithkah must have had "sweet fountains."

Lesson It was by the work of God that they encountered sweet fountains in the barren wilderness. It was His grace and the work of His hands of grace that led them to sweet springs in their difficult 40-year journey. Although we may delay God's will by becoming complacent with the riches of this world for far too long, if we repent and obey His Word, the days of refreshing will come. This is the blessing of Mithkah, the sweet springs.

Acts 3:19 "Repent therefore and return, that your sins may be wiped away, in order that times of refreshing may come from the presence of the Lord."

Only God leads our lives to the sweet springs (Isa 49:10; Rev 7:17; 21:6). God's Word is profound and as sweet as the honeycomb (Ps 19:10; 119:103; Prov 24:13–14). Only God's Word is the sweet spring in the midst of the wilderness journey of life (John 4:13–14).

25	Hashmonah	חַשְׁמֹנָה / Numbers 33:29

Hashmonah is the twenty-fifth camp site.

Meaning *Hashmonah* means "abundance of fruit," "wealthy," "plump," or "fertile" and is derived from חָשֻׁם (*ḥāšum*), meaning "abundant," "plump" and "wealthy."

Location This was the eleventh camp site after the Israelites were sentenced to 40 years of wandering in the wilderness at Rithmah (Kadesh). It was close to Mount Hor and had fountains.

Event There are no biblical or historical records of Hashmonah. The land there must have been fertile, even though fertile land was difficult to find in the wilderness. Even in the barren land God led His people to fertile soil with an abundance of fruit (Num 10:33; Ps 78:52).

Lesson God leads those who obey His Word and completely separate themselves from this world to the sweet springs and to the fertile soil land by the sweet springs so that they may bear an abundance of fruit. An abundance of fruit is obtained only from fertile land. What is "fertile land" according to the Bible?

First, fertile land is land by the stream or spring. Those whose roots are deeply planted by the eternal spring, the Word of God, will bear an abundance of fruit (Ps 1:3; Jer 17:8; 31:12; John 15:7–8).

Second, fertile land is good land. Good land bears fruit thirtyfold, sixtyfold, and a hundredfold. When likening land to people, the good land represents people "who hear the Word and accept it" (Matt 13:23; Mark 4:20). The good land represents people "who have heard the word in an honest and good heart, and hold it fast, and bear fruit with perseverance" (Luke 8:15). Those who persevere to the end are like the fertile land that bears abundant fruit.

26	Moseroth	מֹסֵרוֹת / Numbers 33:30

Moseroth is the twenty-sixth camp site.

Meaning *Moseroth* means "punishment," "yoke," "chastisement" and is derived from אָסַר (*'āsar*), meaning "to bind," "to tie," and "to tighten the waist."

Location This was the twelfth camp site after the Israelites were sentenced to 40 years of wandering in the wilderness at Rithmah (Kadesh). It is speculated that it must have been near Mount Hor.

Event *Moseroth* is the plural form of מוֹסֵרָה (*môsērâ*), and this indicates the same region as the Moserah where Aaron died (Deut 10:6). Given that Numbers 33:38–39 records the place of Aaron's death as Mount Hor, Moseroth (Moserah) must have been near Mount Hor.

Lesson After the Israelites pitched camp for the twenty-sixth time at Moseroth, God made them wander in the wilderness and camp at seven other sites before leading them back to Mount Hor, near Moseroth, for the thirty-third camp site. This leads to the speculation that the Israelites must have done something at Moseroth to upset God. Later, Aaron, who sinned against God, including the incident where he led the people to worship a golden calf, died as a punishment for his sin at the thirty-third camp site on Mount Hor, located near Moseroth (Num 20:22–29; 33:38–39). This was on the first day of the fifth month of the fortieth year, eight months prior to entry into Canaan. Aaron was not counted among the 603,550 people counted in the first census, so had he not sinned, he surely would have entered Canaan without dying.

God's compassion and mercy are truly endless, but He is just and requires punishment for sin (Exod 34:7).

27	Bene-jaakan	בְּנֵי יַעֲקָן / Numbers 33:31

Bene-jaakan is the twenty-seventh camp site.

Meaning *Bene-jaakan* means "the sons of Jaakan."

Location This was the thirteenth camp site after the Israelites were sentenced to 40 years of wandering in the wilderness at Rithmah (Kadesh).

It was considered the same place as the place 11 miles (18 km) north-east of Kadesh-barnea.

Event Deuteronomy 10:6 calls the place "Beeroth Bene-jaakan," which means "the well of the sons of Jaakan." Thus, the Israelites must have encountered springs (wells) here. Furthermore, Deuteronomy 10:6 testifies that the Israelites would pass through Beeroth Bene-jaakan to Moserah, where Aaron would die (Mount Hor is also located there).

Lesson *Jaakan* comes from יַעֲקָן (*ya'ăqān*), which means "winding" or "crooked." During the 38-year journey, the Israelites left the shortcut and took a winding and crooked route. An examination of the route that the Israelites took indicates that they made seven stops on a winding course after they left Moseroth, the twenty-sixth camp, until they arrived at Mount Hor, the thirty-third camp.

They took the winding path despite the presence of a shortcut because of their disobedience and their sin of unbelief. Their winding path was like the winding shape of a snake, like the characteristics of Satan (Isa 27:1). Satan perverts God's Word, trying to make it crooked (Hab 1:4). Thus, those who become seduced by Satan end up disobeying God's Word and suffer the consequences by wandering along a winding path. Believers are people who take the straight highway (Ps 84:5). This highway is the path of the upright and the clean (Prov 15:19; 16:17; Isa 35:8).

28	Hor-haggidgad	חֹר הַגִּדְגָּד / Numbers 33:32

Hor-haggidgad is the twenty-eighth camp site.

Meaning *Hor-haggidgad* means "Gidgad's cave" or "Gidgad's hole."

Location This was the fourteenth camp site after the Israelites were sentenced to 40 years of wandering in the wilderness at Rithmah (Kadesh). It is thought to have been the spring located at the Wadi Khadakhid, which is located 14 miles (23 km) southeast from the end of Kadesh-barnea.

Event There must have been many caves at Hor-haggidgad. It is the same place as Gudgodah, which appears in Deuteronomy 10:7. *Gudgodah* comes from the word גֻּדְגֹּדָה (*gūdgōdâ*), which means "to penetrate" or "to absorb" and refers to a "place with abundant water" or "a crack." Thus, Hor-haggidgad must have been a cave with abundant water.

Lesson The Israelites probably were greatly humbled as they passed through Moseroth and Bene-jaakan and into a winding path. They previously had wandered through a short path, but now they traveled a long path from Bene-jaakan to Hor-haggidgad. Thus, God led a people exhausted from the long journey to a safe place with much water.

Caves are safe hiding places for people. King David hid in the cave of Adullam from King Saul's oppression (1 Sam 22:1). Elijah hid in a cave on Mount Horeb from Jezebel (1 Kgs 19:9). God is a safe cave for all those who are facing hardships; He is the hiding place (Ps 32:7; 46:1; 119:114).

> **Psalm 14:6** You would put to shame the counsel of the afflicted, but the LORD is his refuge.

> **Isaiah 32:2** And each will be like a refuge from the wind, and a shelter from the storm, like streams of water in a dry country, like the shade of a huge rock in a parched land.

| 29 | Jotbathah | יָטְבָתָה / Numbers 33:33 |

Jotbathah is the twenty-ninth camp site.

Meaning *Jotbathah* is derived from the Hebrew word יָטַב (*yāṭab*) and means "to be well," "to be glad," and "to be pleasing."

Location Jotbathah is located below southwest of Ezion-geber to the west of the Gulf of Aqaba. It is the fifteenth camp site after the pronouncement of the 40-year wilderness journey at Rithmah (Kadesh).

Event There were many brooks there. Thus, Deuteronomy 10:7 states that it was "a land of brooks of water."

Lesson God led the Israelites to Hor-haggidgad, where there was a lot of water, and then to Jotbathah, where there were many brooks.

The expression "a land of brooks of water" in Deuteronomy 10:7 is the plural form of the word נַחַל (*naḥal*) in Hebrew, which refers to a riverbed that is dry except during periods of rainfall. During the rainy season there is an abundance of water, like a raging river. During the dry season water usually can be obtained by digging in the riverbed (נַחַל, *naḥal*), making it a favorable place for travelers to rest and recover their energy. Jotbathah, with its many brooks, probably brought great joy to the Israelites and reenergized them after the exhausting 38-year journey since they left Rithmah (Isa 58:11).

Those who believe in Jesus Christ have the blessing of the rivers of living water flowing from their innermost being (John 4:13–14; 7:37–38). Those who have faith can enjoy happiness and satisfaction on their wilderness journey.

30	Abronah	עַבְרֹנָה / Numbers 33:34

Abronah is the thirtieth camp site.

Meaning *Abronah* means "passage" or "migration" and is derived from the Hebrew word עָבַר (*'ăbar*), which means "to pass by" or "to cross over."

Location Abronah is an oasis located by the coast of the Red Sea and the Gulf of Aqaba, 6 miles (10 km) north of Ezion-geber in what is known today as Ain ed-Defiyeh. It is the sixteenth camp site after the pronouncement of the 40-year wilderness journey at Rithmah (Kadesh).

Event There are no historical narratives on Abronah. The Israelites continued to travel down south from Bene-jaakan to Hor-haggidgad and then to Jotbathah. Now, they were headed back up north through Abronah to Kadesh.

Lesson Abronah is a passageway that must be taken in order to enter Canaan from the Gulf of Aqaba. The Israelites who wandered through the wilderness after the pronouncement of the 40-year journey at Kadesh had to travel through Abronah in order to return to Kadesh from Jotbathah.

There is a place that we must pass through in order to reach our final destination. Without passing through it, we cannot properly reach our destination. The passageway that we must travel through in order to reach Canaan (heaven) is Jesus Christ (John 14:6; Acts 4:12). He is the only way! In John 10:9, Jesus states, "I am the door; if anyone enters through Me, he shall be saved." In Greek, "through me" is δι' ἐμοῦ (*di' emou*), and this means that Jesus is the only door to salvation.

Ezion-geber is the thirty-first camp site.

Meaning *Ezion-geber* means "hero's back" or "giant's backbone" because of the geographic shape of the area that protrudes out into the sea.

Location Ezion-geber was a harbor area located about 2 miles (3 km) northeast and at the top of the Gulf of Aqaba. It is the seventeenth camp site after the pronouncement of the 40-year wilderness journey at Rithmah (Kadesh).

Event This was where King Solomon and King Jehoshaphat built ships for trading with Ophir (1 Kgs 9:26; 22:48; 2 Chr 8:17; 20:36).

Lesson Ezion-geber was the last camp site before the Israelites arrived at Kadesh at the end of the wilderness journey.

The Israelites had suffered punishment and trials since they were sentenced to the wilderness journey 38 years ago at Kadesh. They camped at Ezion-geber just before they headed back to Kadesh. They probably reflected on their sins, their disobedience to God's Word that caused them to suffer all these years, and they renewed their pledge to live by His Word.

The name *Ezion-geber* is derived from the Hebrew word עָצֶה (ʿāṣeh), which means "spine." The spine is located at the center of the body and is the pillar that supports the whole body. The body cannot function properly when the spine deviates even just a bit. Likewise, the moment we stray from God's Word, we become unable to do God's work. The source of strength that supports our lives and the history of all mankind is God's Word. God created this world with His Word (John 1:3, 10; Heb 11:3). He upholds all things by His Word (Heb 1:3) and will judge the world with His Word (John 12:48). People who have God's Word in the center of their hearts are people who stand at the center of God's work of salvation. They are God's warriors (Exod 12:41, 51; Judg 6:12) who will be as pillars in the kingdom of God (Gal 2:9; Rev 3:12).

(4) The Journey from Kadesh to the brook Zered
(first half of 1407 BC)—six camps
(Route indicated in green on the map of the wilderness journey)

The Israelites were judged frequently for their unbelief and disobedience during their journey on this route.

Aaron transferred his duties as the high priest to his son Eleazar (Num 20:25–28) and died on Mount Hor on the first day of the fifth month of the fortieth year of the exodus (Num 33:38–39) at the age of 123.

Following Aaron's death, the Israelites went around the land of Edom, which was in close proximity, and took the distant southern route toward Canaan. This was because the Edomites did not allow the Israelites to pass through their land. Here, the people became impatient because of the long journey and grumbled against God and Moses. As a result, many people were bitten by fiery serpents and died (Num 21:4–9).

At the brook Zered, the remnant of the first generation of Israelites of the wilderness journey died when the Lord's hand struck them (Deut 2:13–16).

The six camp sites from Mount Hor until Iye-abarim were as follows:

32 Kadesh →	33 Mount Hor →	34 Zalmonah
35 Punon →	36 Oboth →	37 Iye-abarim

32	Kadesh	קָדֵשׁ / Numbers 33:36

Kadesh is the thirty-second camp site.

Meaning *Kadesh* means "sanctified place" and is derived from the Hebrew verb קָדַשׁ (*qādaš*), meaning "to make holy" or "to separate." Its original name was *En-mishpat*, meaning "the fountain of judgment."

Location Kadesh is an oasis located in the Wilderness of Sin stretching 50 miles (80 km, a three-day journey) to Beersheba on the southern border of Canaan.

Event On the twentieth day of the second month of the second year of the exodus, after the Israelites camped at Mount Sinai for about one year, they marched toward the Wilderness of Paran and camped at Kibroth-hattaavah. Then, they passed through Hazeroth and arrived at Rithmah (Kadesh [1445 BC]). At Rithmah (Kadesh), they were sentenced to the 40-year wilderness journey. After they left Rithmah, they camped eight times until Ezion-geber, and then they returned to Kadesh on the first month of the fortieth year.

Lesson The Israelites who returned to Kadesh probably were flooded with emotion as they thought back to the painful event that had taken place there 38 years prior. However, at the same time, it became a place of new hope for their departure toward Canaan. God made them repent deeply of their past unbelief and its painful consequences, and prepared them for the conquest of Canaan.

They should have obeyed God in this "holy" land of Kadesh 38 years ago as they were about to begin the "holy mission" of conquering the land of Canaan. However, they disobeyed God's Word and therefore could not become God's holy people. Eventually, they were cast out of the "holy" land of Kadesh to wander around in the wilderness for about 38 years, so that they may be trained as "holy people."

Amazingly, the names of all the places that the Israelites passed through before returning to Kadesh are full of important lessons on the process of becoming God's holy people.

The event at Kadesh teaches us, who are walking the path of faith toward heaven, about holiness. It was at Kadesh, the "holy" land, that Moses and Aaron received the pronouncement that they would not enter Canaan because they did not treat God as holy (Num 20:12).

Holiness is a mandatory virtue for the people of God's kingdom (Lev 11:44–45). Hebrews 12:14 states, "Pursue peace with all men, and the sanctification without which no one will see the Lord." 1 Peter 1:15 states, "But like the Holy One who called you, be holy yourselves also in all your behavior."

| 33 | Mount Hor | הֹר הָהָר / Numbers 33:37 |

Mount Hor is the thirty-third camp site.

Meaning *Hor* means "mountain," so *Mount Hor* means a "mountain among mountains," "a mountainous area," and "a grand mountain range."

Location Mount Hor is located near Kadesh by the border of Edom (Num 20:22; 33:37). It has been Identified with Jebel Nebi Harun, 50 miles (80 km) from the Dead Sea.

Event It is the site where Aaron died (Num 33:38–39) and where his son Eleazar became high priest in his stead. Aaron died here on the first day of the fifth month of the fortieth year of the exodus at the age of 123.

Lesson Aaron led the making of a golden calf (Exod 32:1–20) for idol-worship, and he committed the grave sin of speaking against Moses for marrying a Cushite woman (Num 12:1–16). He also aligned himself with Moses when he disobeyed God's command to speak to the rock so that it would give water and instead struck the rock twice (Num 20:2–13). Aaron died on top of Mount Hor as a consequence of these sins (Num 20:28).

Aaron was not just a priest; he was the high priest for the Israelites (Ezra 7:5). Like the meaning of *Hor*, he was a mountain among mountains. However, even a person of the highest position will lose his place if he disobeys God's Word.

> **Numbers 20:25** Take Aaron and his son Eleazar, and bring them up to Mount Hor.

Numbers 33:38 expresses this as "Aaron the priest went up to Mount Hor at the command of the LORD, and died there." God judges sin regardless of the sinner's status.

34	Zalmonah	צַלְמֹנָה / Numbers 33:41

Zalmonah is the thirty-fourth camp site.

Meaning *Zalmonah* means "shady" or "darkness."

Location Zalmonah is the first camp site on the way to Punon from Mount Hor. It is speculated that the Israelites traveled through the difficult mountainous regions south by the way of the Red Sea, because the king of Edom would not allow them to pass through the King's Highway (Num 20:17–21; Deut 2:8).

Event It is the first camp site after the Israelites mourned the death of Aaron for 30 days (Num 20:29).

Lesson Like the meaning of the name *Zalmonah*, darkness probably seeped into the hearts of the Israelites after the death of a leader worthy to be called, "a mountain among mountains." To make matters worse, the king of Edom did not allow the Israelites to take the quicker route through the King's Highway, making the hearts of the Israelites dark from having to take the longer route south by the way of the Red Sea. The longer route took them through the mountainous regions that were difficult to travel, when the faster and easier route was right before them. This situation would have made anyone's heart dark.

There is one thing we need to know as we walk our journey of faith. No matter how long and difficult the road may be, if it is the way in which the Lord is guiding us, then it is the "straight way." Only the "straight way" will lead us to our dwelling place (Ps 107:7). Life and peace are guaranteed on this "straight way" (Prov 3:17; 10:9) and there will be a clear and bright light securing the path that lies in front even in the midst of deep darkness (Ps 112:4; Isa 42:16).

| 35 | Punon | פּוּנֹן / Numbers 33:42 |

Punon is the thirty-fifth camp site.

Meaning *Punon* means "sunset" or "mine pit."

Location Punon was located in the outskirts between Zalmonah and Oboth by the border of Edom. It was located between what is today Petra and Zoar.

Event It is speculated that it was at Punon that many Israelites were bitten and killed by the fiery serpents (Num 21:4–9) after complaining about the long route. This was before they arrived at Oboth (Num 21:10) after the Israelites march out of Mount Hor.[57]

Lesson Just before Aaron died on Mount Hor, Moses asked the king of Edom if the Israelites could pass through on the King's Highway. His request was rejected (Num 20:17–21). After this, Aaron died on Mount Hor (Num 20:22–29), and the Israelites fought against and defeated Arad (Num 21:1–3). The Israelites could not pass through Edom on their journey from Mount Hor to Canaan. Thus, they headed south, following the way of the Red Sea, passing by Arad and Ezion-geber, and then headed back up north to Punon (Deut 2:8).

The people must have been deeply grieved because they had to take the difficult route through Mount Seir and the desert of Araba when all they needed to do was use the King's Highway. Numbers 21:4 recorded this situation: "Then they set out from Mount Hor by the way of the Red Sea, to go around the land of Edom; and the people became impatient because of the journey." Here, "impatient" is קָצַר (qāṣar) in Hebrew and indicates that the people were in such a great state of sorrow or despair that they could not be comforted.

However, the grumblings did not stop there. They began to complain about the manna that had been their food for almost 40 years. They said, "We loathe [קוּץ, qûṣ] this miserable [קְלֹקֵל, qĕlōqēl] food" (Num 21:5). All their thanksgiving during the 40 years turned instantly into grumblings. By being quick to grumble without understanding God's will, they spilled the precious grace that they had received for nearly 40 years.

Because of this incident, God, who had protected the people from the fiery serpents, now allowed them to be bitten, so that many people died (Num 21:6).

How many times have we grown impatient when things did not go according to our past experiences and desires or when there was a delay? How many times have we stood in God's way by trying to do things through human methods without waiting for God? Impatience and grumbling are offensive to God's will. This is a grave sin that often leads the individual and the community toward death.

Like the meaning of Punon, disobedience causes the sun to set in our lives. Obedience is the fastest way and the safest way. Proverbs 4:18-19 states, "But the path of the righteous is like the light of dawn, that shines brighter and brighter until the full day. The way of the wicked is like darkness; they do not know over what they stumble."

While the Israelites were dying from the bites of the fiery serpents, they repented, and Moses prayed to God for intercession. The God of love and compassion commanded that they make a bronze serpent and set it on the standard so that He may give life to all who look upon the serpent (Num 21:7–9). The bronze serpent on the standard represents Jesus Christ, our Savior, who died on the cross (John 3:14). Just as the people lived when they looked upon the serpent, if we believe in Jesus Christ, we can receive salvation from all sin and death (John 3:16).

36	Oboth	אֹבֹת / Numbers 33:43

Oboth is the thirty-sixth camp site.

Meaning *Oboth* means "waterskins."

Location Oboth is located between Punon and Iye-abarim (Num 21:10–11), close to the southern boundary of Moab.

Event After the Israelites had an amazing experience with death and recovery through the incident of the fiery serpent, they started their march again. They left Punon and arrived at Oboth.

Lesson The Israelites took the way of the Red Sea according to God's command, but their hearts were filled with discontent. The kind of obedience that pleases God is obedience that comes from a joyful heart, not from a grudging heart (1 Chr 28:9).

God gives us the strength to obey joyfully when we believe in the Word without doubt and value His Word as more precious than life. Through the incident of the fiery serpent, the Israelites probably realized how important it was to cherish God's Word in their hearts and obey.

The waterskins are also known as wineskins (Ps 119:83). They are made by drying the skins of the head and legs of a lamb or goat and sewing them together so that there is only one opening. These skins usually hold water, milk, or wine. Old wineskins become dry and rigid and do not stretch, but new wineskins are pliable and stretch well.

In Matthew 9:17, Jesus said, "Nor do men put new wine into old wineskins; otherwise the wineskins burst, and the wine pours out, and the wineskins are ruined; but they put new wine into fresh wineskins, and both are preserved." The new wine represents the Word of Jesus Christ, and the wineskins represent the heart of the Israelites. Just as the new wine must be poured into the new skins, Jesus' new Word (Mark 1:22, 27) must be poured into a heart that is renewed each day.

37	Iye-abarim	עִיֵּי הָעֲבָרִים / Numbers 33:44

Iye-abarim is the thirty-seventh camp site.

Meaning In the name *Iye-abarim*, Iye comes from עִי (ʿî), meaning "ruin," and abarim comes from עָבַר (ʿăbar), meaning "to pass over" or "to pass by." Thus, *Iye-abarim* means "way of ruins." In Numbers 33:45, it is recorded as Iyim (עִיִּים, *'iyyîm*).

Location Iye-abarim was the barren land located in the border areas southeast of Moab. Because this land was covered mostly with rocks and crags, Moab, Edom, and other nations showed little interest in it.

Event This place was extremely close to the Wadi Zered. Numbers 21:11–12 states that the Israelites camped at Iye-abarim and then at Wadi Zered, but in actuality, there was not enough space at Wadi Zered for them to camp.[58] The camp of the Israelites probably stretched from Iye-abarim all the way to Wadi Zered. For this reason, Numbers 33:44–45 states that the next camp after Iye-abarim was Dibon-gad, not Wadi Zered.

Lesson It was at Wadi Zered that the men of war numbered in the first census who were still alive were killed by God's hand (Deut 2:14–16). Thus, Iye-abarim became the "way of ruins," as its name implies.

Interestingly, Numbers 21:11 identifies Iye-abarim as land that faces toward the sunrise. This is because although Iye-abarim became the way of ruins because of the deaths of the men of war from the first generation, a new march toward Canaan had begun for the second generation.

Just as the dawn breaks after the darkest hour, a vigorous march toward Canaan began again after the death of the first generation. The old has passed and the new has come.

(5) The Journey until the crossing of the Wadi Zered (second half of 1407 BC)—five camps
(Route indicated in purple on the map of the wilderness journey)

---

[38] **Dibon-gad** → [39] **Almon-diblathaim** → [40] **Mountains of Abarim**
[41] **Plains of Moab** → [42] **Gilgal**

Both Numbers 21:11–20 and Numbers 33:43-44 record the same account of the journey from Oboth to Iye-abarim, but Numbers 21:12–19 records six camp sites after Iye-abarim that are not listed in Numbers 33.

The Red Sea

Mount Zin in the Negev desert

Wadi Zin (Ein Advat National Park)

Wadi Zin (moonrise)

Avdat Spring in Wadi Zin; (oasis in the Wilderness of Zin)

Above: Greek Orthodox Chapel of the Holy Trinity on top of Mt. Sinai
Opposite top: Wadi Zin (sunrise) **Left:** A view of Zin valley in the Negev

The Wilderness of Sinai viewed from Mt. Sinai

A trail to the top of Mt. Sinai

A replica of the tabernacle in the wilderness

Acacia tree in the area of Abronah (Evrona)

Doum palm trees in the area of Abronah (Evrona)

Above: Shizaf nature reserve (near Oboth)
Opposite top: The salt pool in the area of Abronah **Left:** Jordan, landscape near Petra

Above: Jordan River estuary at the Dead Sea **Opposite top:** Shizaf nature reserve (near Oboth)
Left: A view west of Mt. Nebo towards the Jordan Valley

The Dead Sea

Jericho's balsam trees in the Jordan Valley

Six Camp sites Not Listed in Numbers 33

Name of Place	Bible Verse	Meaning
Wadi Zered (זֶרֶד)	Num 21:12	Osier[59]
Arnon (אַרְנוֹן)	Num 21:13	Roaring stream[60]
Beer (בְּאֵר)	Num 21:16	Well[61]
Mattanah (מַתָּנָה)	Num 21:18	Gift[62]
Nahaliel (נַחֲלִיאֵל)	Num 21:19	Torrent of God[63]
Bamoth (בָּמוֹת)	Num 21:19	High places[64]

Among these sites, Zered is thought to have been a site close to Iye-Abarim, and Arnon is thought to have been a site close to Dibon-gad. The other sites are thought to have been short stopovers, not official camp sites. The meanings of the names of these sites illustrate the life with which the second generation of Israelites marched toward Canaan after the death of the first generation.

38	Dibon-gad	דִּיבוֹן גָּד / Numbers 33:45

Dibon-gad is the thirty-eighth camp site.

Meaning In the name *Dibon-gad*, דִּיבוֹן (*dîbôn*) means "to long for" or "desolation." It comes from דוב (*dûb*), meaning "to anxiously long for" and "to wear away."[65] Dibon is also called Dimon (Isa 15:9).

Location Dibon-gad is located 11 miles (18 km) east of the Dead Sea. It is also 3 miles (5 km) north of the Arnon River. It is speculated that it might be the same place as the "other side of the Arnon" described in Numbers 21:13 or close to it.

Event The Arnon River is 20 miles (32 km) long and flows east toward the Dead Sea. The word אַרְנוֹן (*arnôn*) means "roaring (like the cry or howling of a vicious beast) stream."[66] This river is the boundary marker between the Moabites and the Amorites (Num 21:13). Not only were the rapids swift, but also the river valley was about 1,650 feet (500 m) deep. Thus, the Israelites probably climbed upward where the water was less deep before they crossed over.

The Israelites witnessed God's judgment against the first generation of Israelites as they passed through Zered. Thus, they earnestly hoped to enter Canaan without dying, and as the meaning of *Dibon* indicates, they anxiously longed for Canaan.

2 Peter 3:12 speaks of "looking for and hastening the coming of the day of God." Those whose hearts are filled with earnest longing for the new heaven and the new earth (Isa 65:17; 66:22; Rev 21:1) and put their hope in the Second Coming will utterly overcome any suffering and hardship.

39	Almon-diblathaim	עַלְמֹן דִּבְלָתָיְמָה / Numbers 33:46

Almon-diblathaim is the thirty-ninth camp site.

Meaning *Almon-diblathaim* means "hidden lump of pressed figs" or "road sign of the two figs." It is a combination of עָלַם (ʿālam), meaning "to hide," "to be hidden," or "to be concealed," and דְּבֵלָה (dĕbēlâ), meaning "lump of pressed figs."

Location Almon-diblathaim was the camp site between Dibon-gad and the Mountains of Abarim and is thought to be the same place as the Teleilat el-Gharbiyeh, about 15 miles (25 km) east of the Dead Sea.

Event Almon-diblathaim is the same place as Beth-diblathaim, to which the prophet Jeremiah issued a warning of an impending judgment (Jer 48:22).

Lesson Almon-diblathaim was the last camp site before the Israelites went up to the mountains of Abarim. The Israelites probably were burning with anticipation because the land of Canaan was just before them. At the same time, the Israelites were also physically and mentally exhausted from the long, roundabout journey they had taken through the wilderness and the mountainous regions to avoid conflict with the surrounding nations and the war against the Amorites.

In the Old Testament, there is an old Israelite custom of serving fig clusters to people exhausted from long marches or journeys. The figs were pressed into cakes and were called, "cakes of pressed figs" or "fig cakes" (1 Sam 25:18; 1 Chr 12:40). Among the foods that Abigail brought to King David to comfort and strengthen him were cakes of figs (1 Sam 25:18). A sick Egyptian soldier found abandoned was given a piece of fig cake and two clusters of raisins, and his spirit revived (1 Sam 30:12).

The land of Canaan, which the Israelites were about to enter, was a land overflowing with milk and honey and had an abundance of figs (Num 13:23; 1 Kgs 4:25). The hidden land of Canaan, the long awaited land with an abundance of figs, was finally to be revealed just over the lofty mountains of Abarim.

| 40 | The Mountains of Abarim | הָרֵי הָעֲבָרִים / Numbers 33:47 |

The Mountains of Abarim are the fortieth camp site.

Meaning *Abarim* means "regions beyond the river or sea."[67]

Location These regions were located on the lower right side of the plains of Moab to the east of the Dead Sea.

Event The mountain from which Moses looked upon the land of Canaan before he died is referred to by many names, including to this mountain of Abarim (Num 27:12), Mount Nebo ("high mountain" or "mountain of wisdom" [Deut 32:49]), and Mount Pisgah ("pointed place" [Deut 34:1]). An examination of their relationship with one another shows that Abarim was the greater mountain range, and Mount Nebo was located on the northern segment of this range (Deut 32:49). Among the many mountain peaks constituting Mount Nebo, Mount Pisgah (Deut 34:1) was the highest.

Lesson Like the meaning "land on the other side," Canaan, the land of the Israelites' dreams, was located on the other side of the mountains of Abarim. It was here that God showed Moses all the land of Canaan.

> **Deuteronomy 34:1–3** Now Moses went up from the plains of Moab to Mount Nebo, to the top of Pisgah, which is opposite Jericho. And the LORD showed him all the land, Gilead as far as Dan, ²and all Naphtali and the land of Ephraim and Manasseh, and all the land of Judah as far as the western sea, ³and the Negev and the plain in the valley of Jericho, the city of palm trees, as far as Zoar.

Here, "Dan" refers to the borders of Mount Hermon, which is the northernmost part of Canaan; "all Naphtali and the land of Ephraim and Manasseh" refers to the land west of the Jordan River; "all the land of Judah" refers to land on the western part of Canaan all the way to the Mediterranean Sea; and "Zoar" refers to the southernmost part of the Dead Sea. Thus, Moses saw all of the land of Canaan—north, south, east and west.

However, the distance between Mount Pisgah and Dan was 100 miles (160 km), indicating that no matter how good Moses' vision was (Deut 34:7), it was a distance impossible for the human eye to span. Thus, Moses did not view the land with his vision; God opened his eyes so that he could see across the long distance.

The Hebrew word for "and [the Lord] showed" in Deuteronomy 34:1 is וַיַּרְאֵהוּ (wayyar'ēhû), from רָאָה (rā'â), meaning "to look at" or "inspect." This verb is rendered in the Hiphil form, third-person masculine singular. This means that God made Moses inspect closely. Thus, Moses closely examined all four sides of the land of Canaan as if he were looking through a telescope. This is similar to how God opened the eyes of Gehazi so that he saw a mountain full of horses and chariots of fire (2 Kgs 6:17).

Today, we can see the kingdom of God on the other side of this world only when God opens our spiritual eyes. The God of our Lord Jesus Christ, the Father of glory, has to give us the spirit of wisdom and of revelation (Eph 1:17). He has to enlighten the eyes of our hearts so that we may know the hope of His calling and the riches of the glory of His inheritance (Eph 1:18). Furthermore, when He opens our spiritual eyes, the thoughts of the world and the thoughts of the flesh disappear, and we can see the world of God's Word and experience it (Ps 119:18).

| 41 | The Plains of Moab | עֲרָבָה מוֹאָב / Numbers 33:48–49 |

The Plains of Moab are the forty-first camp site.

Meaning *Moab* means "father's offspring" or "from my father."[68]

Location Moab is the plains located in front of Jericho by the Jordan River (Num 22:1). Numbers 33:49 states, "And they camped by the Jordan, from Beth-jeshimoth as far as Abel-shittim in the plains of Moab." Since the distance between Beth-jeshimoth and Abel-shittim is about 5 miles (8 km), this is an indication of how massive the Israelites' camp was.

Event ▶ The Israelites had defeated Sihon, the king of the Amorites, and Og, the king of Bashan, and conquered their land before they arrived at the plains of Moab (Num 21:21–35). In the battle against the king of Bashan they fought all the way up to Edrei (Num 21:33).

At the plains of Moab the Israelites fell prey to the counsel of the prophet Balaam and committed immoral acts with the women of Moab (Num 25). Additionally, a second census was taken (Num 26), the Israelites fought and defeated Midian (Num 31), and they distributed the land to the east of the Jordan River (Num 32). It was also here that Moses reiterated the law to the second generation of Israelites in the wilderness (Deut 1:5).

Lesson ▶ The people of Moab originated from the son who was born to Lot through his first daughter (Gen 19:33–37). Thus, the name *Moab* means "father's offspring" or "from my father."

The Israelites camped at Mount Sinai for about one year and received the law from God in preparation for entry into Canaan. However, even after receiving the law, they disobeyed God and sent spies to the land of Canaan, resulting in about 38 years of wandering in the wilderness.

Now, God proclaimed the law to the Israelites again with the entry into Canaan before them. Deuteronomy 1:5 states, "Across the Jordan in the land of Moab, Moses undertook to expound this law." Here, the word *expound* is בָּאַר (*bā'ar*) in Hebrew, meaning "to make distinct" or "to record carefully."[69] Here, the verb is used in the Piel form, perfect tense, meaning "to explain in detail," or "to make plain." Thus, God did not give them a new law; rather, He explained clearly the law that He had already given them in the past and made it comprehensible to their hearts.

The teaching of God's Word was a significant event that occurred at the plains of Moab just before the Israelites entered Canaan. The Word of grace and the Word of blessings come only from God in heaven above (Jas 1:17). If the Israelites cherish God's Word and live accordingly, then they can be blessed in the land of Canaan, multiply, and enjoy longevity (Deut 30:16).

As the day of the Lord draws near, we must continue to learn the Word of God and have conviction (2 Tim 3:14). We must be diligent in teaching God's Word to our children (Gen 18:18–19; Deut 6:7; 11:19; Prov 22:6). We must hold fast to God (Deut 30:20) and cling to Him (Deut 10:20; Josh 22:5; 23:8). In Hebrew, "to hold fast" and "to cling" is דָּבַק (*dābaq*), which means "to cleave," or "to stick to"[70]. We can boldly enter the kingdom of God when we become completely armored by drawing near to God and becoming one with the Word just as a man and a woman become one (Gen 2:24).

42	Gilgal	גִּלְגָּל / Joshua 4:19

Gilgal is the forty-second camp site.

Meaning *Gilgal* means "Today I have rolled away the reproach of Egypt from you" (Josh 5:9) and is derived from גָּלַל (*gāgāl*), which means "to roll" or "to turn."[71]

Location Gilgal is located east of Jericho and west of the Jordan, about 5 miles (8 km) away. It is the first place where the Israelites camped after entering Canaan.

Event After the Israelites crossed the Jordan River, they arrived here and set up 12 stones as a memorial (Josh 4:19–24), circumcised the sons of Israel (Josh 5:2–9), and celebrated the Passover (Josh 5:10–11). Manna ceased after the celebration of the Passover (Josh 5:12). Gilgal also acted as a bridgehead during the conquest of Canaan (Josh 9:6; 14:6).

Lesson God commanded the Israelites to perform circumcision upon those who were born during the wilderness journey (Josh 5:5) before the impending entry into Canaan. They had not performed a circumcision during the 38 years of wandering after Kadesh. Through the act of circumcision the Israelites were again acknowledged as God's people of the covenant who could possess the land of Canaan.

They demonstrated absolute obedience and faith in God by performing circumcision when a Canaanite attack was possible at any moment. They obeyed God's command with the conviction that He would protect them even though they would be unable to move as a result of the circumcision.

In commanding the circumcision at Gilgal, God said, "Today I have rolled away the reproach of Egypt from you" (Josh 5:9). What does the "reproach of Egypt" mean? It refers to the reproach of being enslaved in Egypt and to the reproach of the sin of grumbling against God for 40 years in the wilderness because the attributes of Egypt were still in them. The God of endless mercy did away with this reproach through the act of circumcision.

We too have many reproachful sins of the past. Jesus placed the reproach that we were supposed to bear upon Himself and was nailed to the cross with nothing covering His bare body (Isa 53:3–6; Heb 12:2). Jesus rolled away the shame of our sins on the cross so that we became a new creature (2 Cor 5:17).

The reproach of all the believers will disappear forever when the Lord descends from heaven with a shout and the voice of the archangel, and with the trumpet of God (1 Thess 4:16–17). At the sound of the last trumpet, we will all be changed into a spiritual body and enter heaven (Joel 2:26–27; 1 Cor 15:51–53; Phil 3:21; 1 John 3:2).

3. The Wilderness Journey without Lack

Deuteronomy 2:7 For the LORD your God has blessed you in all that you have done; He has known your wanderings through this great wilderness. These 40 years the LORD your God has been with you; you have not lacked a thing.

The definition of *wilderness* is "a wild and uncultivated region," referring to an endless barren desert (Lev 16:22; Jer 2:6). The wilderness is an uninhabited land where life-threatening danger is always present. It is a land deserted by all people. There are no roads and no resting places (Jer 2:6).

The wilderness is also a "land of pits" that appear from time to time throughout the desert to swallow up people and animals (Jer 2:6). In the phrase, "land of pits," the word *pit* is שׁוּחָה (*šûḥâ*) in Hebrew, referring to a place like sinking sand from which people cannot escape. Thus, the wilderness is a land of despair in which people cannot live and a dangerous land where the shadow of death is always lurking. This is why the wilderness is described as a "land of deep darkness" (Jer 2:6) and a "great and terrible wilderness, with its fiery serpents and scorpions" (Deut 8:15) where it is impossible to see what lies a few steps ahead.

Nonetheless, God led the Israelites safely through all the dangers of the wilderness into Canaan. God made the Israelites wander in the wilderness for 40 years to humble them and test them. Deuteronomy 8:2 states, "And you shall remember all the way which the Lord your God has led you in the wilderness these 40 years, that He might humble you, testing you, to know what was in your heart, whether you would keep His commandments or not." Here, the word *humble* is עָנָה (ʿānâ) in Hebrew, meaning "to bow down," "to abase," "to afflict," "to torment," and "to train."[72] It may appear that God afflicted the Israelites in the wilderness for 40 years, but in reality He was training them. God had planned to bless them after they endured this humbling experience.

> **Deuteronomy 8:16** In the wilderness He fed you manna which your fathers did not know, that He might humble you and that He might test you, to do good for you in the end.

In this verse, the Hebrew word for "to do good" is יָטַב (yāṭab), meaning "to be good" or "to be glad." The humbling process was part of God's ultimate plan to lead them into Canaan, the land flowing with milk and honey and to bless them.

Even in the wilderness, the land of death, God took care of their food, clothing, and shelter; intervened closely in their lives; and protected them from their enemies. The grace of Immanuel God was with them throughout the 40 years. They marched endlessly, but they did not die of thirst or hunger. Not one died because of the conditions in the wilderness. All this was the result of God's careful intervention into the lives of His covenant people.

(1) God opened the gates of heaven and poured down manna so that they did not hunger. He satisfied them with quails and quenched their thirst with living water from the rock (Exod 16; 17:1–7; Num 11:4–9; 20:11; 21:16; Deut 8:3; Ps 78:23–29; 105:40–41; Neh 9:15, 20; Isa 48:21).

Manna began to fall on the fifteenth day of the second month after their departure from Egypt (Exod 16:1–4). After they entered Canaan, they ate the produce of the land on the day after the Passover (fourteenth day of the first month on the forty-first year after the exodus), and manna stopped falling the next day (sixteenth day of the first month on the forty-first year after the exodus [Josh 5:10–12]). Thus, manna had fallen for about 39 years and 11 months.

(2) For 40 years, their clothing did not wear out nor did their feet swell. They were not in want (Deut 8:4; 29:5; Neh 9:21).

Deuteronomy 8:4 states, "Your clothing did not wear out on you, nor did your foot swell these forty years."

(3) God led them on the way with a pillar of fire by night and a pillar of cloud by day to protect them from the heat and the cold. The pillar of fire lit their way so that they did not fall into the pit of death (Exod 13:20–22; Num 9:15–23; Ps 105:39; Neh 9:19; Jer 2:6).

The pillar of fire and the pillar of cloud that continuously led them through the 40 years in the wilderness were sure indications of the grace of God, Immanuel (Exod 40:36-38).

(4) God sent hornets and drove out the Israelites' enemies (Exod 23:28; Deut 7:20; Josh 24:12).

In Hebrew, *hornet* is צִרְעָה (*ṣir'â*). Hornets have large bodies and tend to travel in large groups. They do, on occasion, sting people or animals and fatally wound them. God used these hornets to drive out the enemy.

(5) In the wilderness He carried them as a man carries his son (Deut 1:31) and guarded them as the pupil of His eye (Deut 32:10).

God's guidance and protection was like that of an eagle, which spreads its two wings and carries its young on its pinions (Exod 19:4; Deut 32:11–12).

(6) He journeyed in front of the Israelites.

The ark of the covenant of the Lord journeyed in front of the Israelites to seek out a place to camp (Num 10:33). God went before them, leading them with a pillar of fire by night and a pillar of cloud by day (Exod 13:21; Deut 1:33). The angel of God also went before the camp of Israel (Exod 14:19).

All this is the history in which God was with Israel (Deut 2:7). Since God is the source of all blessings, we will be abundant and without a lack in all aspects as long as we trust His guidance and follow in obedience (Ps 23:1; Prov 28:25).

4. Grumblings and Complaints in the Wilderness

Despite the many amazing signs of the grace of God, Immanuel, the Israelites did not cease to grumble and complain throughout the 40-year wilderness journey (Exod 14:10–12; 15:22–24; 16:1–3, 7–12; 17:1–3; 32:1; Num 11:1, 4–6; 13:31–14:4; 14:26–28; 16:1–14, 41; 20:2–5; 21:4–5; Neh 9:15–21; Ps 106:13–29). The Israelites were constant complainers. However, their grumblings against Moses were not simply grumblings against a leader; they were committing the fearful sin of grumbling against God, who had established Moses as their leader.

When the whole congregation of Israel grumbled against Moses and Aaron in the Wilderness of Sin (Exod 16:2–3), Moses said to them, "He hears your grumblings against the LORD."

> **Exodus 16:7** "And in the morning you will see the glory of the LORD, for He hears your grumblings against the LORD; and what are we, that you grumble against us?"

When they passed the Wilderness of Sin to Rephidim, the Israelites grumbled against Moses and quarreled with him because there was no water to drink. Moses said to the people, "Why do you quarrel with me? Why do you test the LORD?" (Exod 17:1–3).

There was a similar situation from the Wilderness of Paran to Kadesh. The whole congregation cried and wept all night after they heard the bad report given by ten of the 12 spies who went into the land of Canaan (Num 14:1–3). God said, "How long shall I bear with this evil congregation who are grumbling against Me? I have heard the complaints of the sons of Israel, which they are making against Me" (Num 14:26–27).

Throughout the 40 years, the Israelites rebelled against God and provoked Him to wrath with their unbelief and grumblings (Deut 9:7, 24).

> **Psalm 95:9** "When your fathers tested Me, they tried Me, though they had seen My work."

In their hearts, they continuously put God to the test (Ps 78:17–18) and fought against Him (Ps 78:19). They despised the Promised Land and did not believe in God's Word (Ps 106:24). The psalmist laments that the Israelites repeatedly grieved and pained God in the wilderness.

> **Psalm 78:40–41** How often they rebelled against Him in the wilderness, and grieved Him in the desert! [41]And again and again they tempted God, and pained the Holy One of Israel.

However, God put up with their deeds for 40 years.

Acts 13:18 "And for a period of about forty years He put up with them in the wilderness."

Today, if we become numb to the amazing grace that we have received and grumble rather than give thanks, we will cause God to grieve (Isa 63:10; Eph 4:30) and ultimately will be destroyed (1 Cor 10:9–10).

The first generation of Israelites, all 603,548 of them who had complained out of greed and lust, perished in the wilderness with the land of Canaan just before them, with the exception of Joshua and Caleb (Num 14:32–35; Deut 2:13–16).

(1) God heard the secret grumblings in their tents

Deuteronomy 1:27 "And you grumbled in your tents and said, 'Because the LORD hates us, He has brought us out of the land of Egypt to deliver us into the hand of the Amorites to destroy us.'"

Psalm 106:25–26 But grumbled in their tents; they did not listen to the voice of the LORD. ²⁶Therefore He swore to them, that He would cast them down in the wilderness.

Here, the "tents" were individual tent homes, not God's holy tent. The Israelites hid in their tents and whispered their complaints against Moses. The minor grumblings in the tents grew greater and greater, so that they stood against God's will and led them to ask for another leader besides Moses who would lead them back to Egypt (Num 14:4).

God hears even the secret grumblings under the bed covers. Thus, if we want to see good days, we must keep our tongues from uttering evil and our lips from speaking guile, and our mouths from complaining or speaking careless words (Matt 12:36–37; 1 Pet 3:10).

(2) The result of grumblings

Grumbling is the act of expressing discontent about what other people are doing or complaining so that they do not succeed. It includes the act of placing all the blame on others. Thus, grumbling against God delays His timing.

The reason the Israelites did not cease to grumble even with so many signs of Immanuel that God showed them throughout the 40 years in the wilderness is the lack of faith in God's promise about the land of

Canaan (Deut 1:32; Heb 3:19). Psalm 106:24 states, "Then they despised the pleasant land; they did not believe in His word." They could not overcome the suffering in the wilderness because of their unbelief; they could not see the blessing of the land of Canaan, the land flowing with milk and honey, beyond the wilderness. God caused all those who did not believe in the promise to fall in the wilderness so that they could not set foot in the Promised Land.

> **Numbers 14:28–30** "Say to them, 'As I live,' says the LORD, 'just as you have spoken in My hearing, so I will surely do to you; ²⁹your corpses shall fall in this wilderness, even all your numbered men, according to your complete number from twenty years old and upward, who have grumbled against Me. ³⁰Surely you shall not come into the land in which I swore to settle you, except Caleb the son of Jephunneh and Joshua the son of Nun.'"

This was a solemn display of the fact that only those who have faith can enter the Promised Land. For example, the earth opened and swallowed up Korah, Dathan, Abiram, and all their families because they rebelled against Moses and Aaron (Num 16:1–35). Even after witnessing this fearful judgment, the very next day, instead of repenting, the people blamed Moses and Aaron for causing their deaths, saying, "You are the ones who have caused the death of the LORD's people." This angered God and a plague struck them killing another 14,700 people (Num 16:41–50).

Such foolishness is best described in Proverbs 19:3: "The foolishness of man subverts his way, and his heart rages against the LORD."

(3) The leaders of the grumblings—the rabble among them

> **Numbers 11:4–6** And the rabble who were among them had greedy desires; and also the sons of Israel wept again and said, "Who will give us meat to eat? ⁵We remember the fish which we used to eat free in Egypt, the cucumbers and the melons and the leeks and the onions and the garlic, ⁶but now our appetite is gone. There is nothing at all to look at except this manna."

Behind the grumblings and complaints of the Israelites was "the rabble who were among them" (Num 11:4; cf. Exod 12:38). These people did not leave their secure lives in Egypt to head out with the Israelites because of faith. They were blinded by the material wealth and blessings they dreamt of obtaining in the Promised Land and did not consider the hardships they would face until they reached the land. They were like dangerous time bombs ready to go off and spread discontent at any time, rousing the people to grumble and complain against Moses. In Numbers 11:4–6, the rabble roused the Israelites into complaining that they could not live on just manna. In Numbers 11:6, they say, "Now our appetite is gone," meaning that all life had become exhausting.

Psalm 78:19–31 explains very well the conditions of the Israelites in Kibroth-hattaavah, where they were provoked by the greedy desires of the rabble among them (Num 11:4–6, 34).

> **Psalm 78:19–31** (NLT) They even spoke against God himself, saying, "God can't give us food in the wilderness. ²⁰Yes, he can strike a rock so water gushes out, but he can't give his people bread and meat." ²¹When the LORD heard them, he was furious. The fire of his wrath burned against Jacob. Yes, his anger rose against Israel, ²²for they did not believe God or trust him to care for them. ²³But he commanded the skies to open; he opened the doors of heaven. ²⁴He rained down manna for them to eat; he gave them bread from heaven. ²⁵They ate the food of angels! God gave them all they could hold. ²⁶He released the east wind in the heavens and guided the south wind by his mighty power. ²⁷He rained down meat as thick as dust—birds as plentiful as the sand on the seashore! ²⁸He caused the birds to fall within their camp and all around their tents. ²⁹The people ate their fill. He gave them what they craved. ³⁰But before they satisfied their craving, while the meat was yet in their mouths, ³¹the anger of God rose against them, and he killed their strongest men. He struck down the finest of Israel's young men.

The rabble that lived among them trivialised the vision regarding the Promised Land; they debased the grace of God, Immanuel. Consequently, they polluted the faith of the chosen people and made them sick. This rabble, accustomed to the idol-worshiping Egyptian culture, tempted the chosen people tirelessly throughout the wilderness journey and provoked them into corruption. The grumblings of the rabble only grew more severe, though they should have been overflowing with hope and thanksgiving as the Promised Land drew near. Their hearts were hardened like stones, and thanksgiving was nowhere to be found, only complaints everywhere.

Grumblings belong to the rabble. There is also rabble in the church today. They are people who attend church, but always stand a step behind out of fear that they would lose something if they get too involved in the church. They are people who do not serve with all their hearts.

We must always have the heart of Christ (Phil 2:5), always share fellowship with others, and devote our hearts to the church, the body of Christ, so that we do not join with the rabble. They are wicked, and there is no peace for the wicked (Isa 48:22; 57:21).

5. The Death of Three Leaders in the Wilderness

✳ The death of these three leaders in the wilderness is systematically exposited for the first time in history.

The Bible dedicates a considerable amount of space to recording the deaths of those who died at the end of the 40-year wilderness journey, just before entry into Canaan—for example, Korah and 250 of his followers who rebelled against Moses and Aaron; Miriam and Aaron; the remainder from the 603,550 people numbered in the first census, excluding Joshua and Caleb; the 24,000 people who died as a result of the adultery in Shittim; and Moses.

Among these deaths, the saddest are those of Miriam, Aaron, and Moses. They were great leaders in the wilderness, who led the Israelites to believe in the Promised Land. Yet, they had to die in the wilderness, unable to enter the land they had greatly desired. Their death, with Canaan just a short distance away, provide a solemn teaching to the believers of the end time.

(1) The Death of Miriam, the first prophetess (first month of 1407 BC, one year before entry into Canaan)

Miriam was the first prophetess in the Bible, the older sister of Aaron and Moses. Her name means "high." She played a large role in saving the baby Moses (Exod 2:4–8), and she sang the song of victory and danced as the Israelites crossed the Red Sea (Exod 15:20–21). She and Aaron were faithful leaders under Moses during the difficult wilderness journey (Mic 6:4). Numbers 20:1 states that she died on the first month of the fortieth year of the exodus, which was one year prior to their entry into Canaan. Numbers 20:1 emphasizes that she died in the Wilderness of Zin, which is Kadesh.

Miriam sang beautiful praises as the Israelites crossed the Red Sea and was full of hopes about the Promised Land, but unfortunately, she died in Kadesh in the Wilderness of Zin (Num 20:1). God allowed Miriam to live for 38 years of the journey, but made her pay the severe consequence of her sin just one year prior to entry into Canaan.

(i) Why Miriam had to die before entering Canaan

During the early part of the wilderness journey, when the Israelites departed from Mount Sinai and were camping at Hazeroth, Moses married a Cushite woman (Num 12:1, 16). Theologians propose different interpretations for Moses' marriage to the Cushite woman. However, Numbers 12 makes it clear that Moses' act was not motivated by fleshly emotions, but that he had done it in obedience to God's command.

> **Numbers 12:8** "With him I speak mouth to mouth, even openly, and not in dark sayings, and he beholds the form of the LORD. Why then were you not afraid to speak against My servant, against Moses?"

Aaron and Miriam took the initiative in speaking against Moses. They were not only trampling upon Moses' character, but also ridiculing and mocking him. It appears that Moses did not consult with Miriam or Aaron prior to his marriage. Moses probably tried to explain to them that he had done this according to God's command, but they did not want to listen because it was not something they received. In Numbers 12:2, they strongly protest, saying, "Has the Lord indeed spoken only through Moses? Has He not spoken through us as well?" As the first high priest and the first prophetess, Aaron and Miriam were confident that they were receiving the same revelations from God that Moses received.

However, God heard what Aaron and Miriam had said against Moses and suddenly called the three people together (Num 12:4). He came down in a pillar of cloud and stood at the doorway of the tent. He called Aaron and Miriam forward (Num 12:5). Here, God revealed that He appeared and spoke to Moses directly. He praised Moses as a faithful servant and reconfirmed for them that He had chosen only Moses as a spiritual leader.

> **Numbers 12:7** "Not so, with My servant Moses, He is faithful in all My household."

God did not see Moses, Aaron, and Miriam as being on the same level. Moses was the sole mediator between God and His people and was "as God" to Aaron and Miriam.

Exodus 4:16 "Moreover, he shall speak for you to the people; and it shall come about that he shall be as a mouth for you, and you shall be as God to him."

In Exodus 4:16, the words *he* and *him* refer to Aaron. Thus, Moses was "as God" to Aaron. God drew a clear line. In Exodus 7:1, God also states, "See, I make you as God to Pharaoh, and your brother Aaron shall be your prophet." Moses was as God to Pharaoh, but Aaron was just a spokesperson for Moses.

Aaron and Miriam's act of speaking out against Moses was ultimately an act of challenging the divine leadership that had been given to Moses. It is considered a grave sin because it was an act of disdaining the God-given authority. Instead of asking about the role of the marriage to the Cushite woman in God's plan of salvation, they used the opportunity as an excuse to attack his authority. Their ambition prevented them from thinking about God's Work. They thought only about the work of man. They thought only about how they could elevate themselves in the eyes of the people.

(ii) The result of Miriam's unbelief

God was angry with Aaron and Miriam and departed from them, and at this time Miriam became leprous, as white as snow (Num 12:10). Leprosy is symbolic of God's fearful judgment. Both the proud King Uzziah (2 Chr 26:19) and the greedy servant Gehazi (2 Kgs 5:27) were struck with leprosy. All lepers were relegated to the outside of the camp (Lev 13–14).

Being struck with leprosy and being removed to the outside of the camp must have been a time of personal crisis for Miriam. Aaron witnessed this and repented quickly. He acknowledged and respected Moses' spiritual authority and said, "Oh, my lord, I beg you, do not account this sin to us," (Num 12:11).

The word *lord* spoken by Aaron is אֲדוֹן (*'ādôn*), the same word used by a servant to address a master. Aaron also used the word *beg* (בִּ, *bî*), imploring Moses. At last, Aaron repented of his pride and fully acknowledged Moses as the sole spiritual leader.

Moses did not rebuke Aaron and Miriam for speaking against him. He only prayed to God on behalf of Miriam so that she might be healed (Num 12:13).

Moses was a very humble person. Numbers 12:3 states, "Now the man Moses was very meek, above all the men which were upon the face of the earth" (KJV). The word meek refers to a warm and soft disposition.

In Hebrew, the word is עָנָו (*'ānāv*) or עָנָיו (*'ānaîv*), meaning "to bend" or "to surrender." In Greek, the word is πραΰτης (*praytēs*), referring to a wild horse being controlled by reins so that it obeys its master.

As a result of Moses' prayer, Miriam spent just seven days outside the camp (Num 12:14), but during this time, more than two million Israelites could not move forward (Num 12:15).

(2) The Death of Aaron—the first high priest (first day of fifth month of 1407 BC, about eight months prior to entry into Canaan)

> **Numbers 33:38** Then Aaron the priest went up to Mount Hor at the command of the LORD, and died there, in the fortieth year after the sons of Israel had come from the land of Egypt on the first day in the fifth month.

Aaron was one of the three leaders of the wilderness and was the first holy high priest. In accordance with his position, his name means "enlightened."[73] Aaron was Miriam's younger brother and Moses' older brother. His wife was Elisheba, and his sons were Nadab, Abihu, Eleazar, and Ithamar (Exod 6:23). A fire came out from the presence of the Lord and consumed Nadab and Abihu after they offered a strange fire before the Lord (Lev 10:1–2). Both of them were childless. Eleazar and Ithamar served as priests (Num 3:4; 26:60–61), and Eleazar became high priest after Aaron (Num 20:25–28).

Aaron was called at the age of 84, and at the command of the Lord he became the spokesperson for Moses (Exod 7:7). However, he died at the age of 123 on the first day of the fifth month of the fortieth year of the exodus, about eight months prior to entry into Canaan.

(i) Why Aaron had to die before entering Canaan

The Bible points to four sins that became the reason for Aaron's death: the sin of stirring up the Israelites to make the golden calf (Exod 32:1–20); the sin of misleading the people and invoking evil (Exod 32:21–25); the sin of speaking against Moses (Num 12:1–16); and the sin of unbelief and disobedience to God's Word with regard to the waters of Meribah at Kadesh (Num 20:7–13, 24).

Aaron's first sin was in stirring up the people to make the golden calf (Exod 32:1–20). Moses was up on Mount Sinai for 40 days and nights without eating or drinking, receiving the Ten Commandments from God. While he delayed, the people assembled around Aaron and asked him to make for them a god who would lead them (Exod 32:1). They did not wait for Moses to come down. They were quick to turn their backs on the way that God had commanded (Exod 32:8; Deut 9:16).

God is above all creation (John 3:31; Rom 9:5; Eph 1:22; 4:10). He created all things (Ps 33:6; John 1:3; Heb 11:3), and He fills the heavens and the earth (Jer 23:24). Thus, no one should make and worship any gods besides God (Exod 20:23). Aaron clearly disobeyed this command. When the people cried out for a god, he should have turned the people away from their wrongful ways, but instead he told them to bring their gold rings (Exod 32:2) and fashioned a golden calf with a graving tool (Exod 32:4). Then they said, "This is your god, O Israel, who brought you up from the land of Egypt" (Exod 32:4).

Aaron contributed greatly as a leader from the exodus and throughout the wilderness journey. He was an eloquent speaker acknowledged by God (Exod 4:10–16). He was Moses' spokesperson (Exod 7:1–2) and the man who urged Pharaoh regarding the Israelites' exodus.

However, Aaron did not stand firmly upon the Word of God. That is why he was so sensitive to the people's reactions, anxious to please them and swayed by their words. When Moses questioned Aaron regarding the golden calf, not only did Aaron place the blame upon the people (Exod 32:21–22), but also he tried to hide his sins with deception and lighten the wages of his sin. Exodus 32:4 specifically states, "And he took this from their hand, and fashioned it with a graving tool, and made it into a molten calf," but he lied and said that the calf just came out when he threw gold into the fire (Exod 32:24), and he avoided the responsibility for his own actions.

Aaron's second sin was that he did not help the people walk in the way of the Lord, but allowed them to get out of control so that they became "a derision among their enemies."

> **Exodus 32:25** Now when Moses saw that the people were out of control— for Aaron had let them get out of control to be a derision among their enemies....

Here, the expression "out of control" is פָּרַע (pārâ) in Hebrew, meaning "to let go" or "to let alone." People who are out of control are not conscious of other people's eyes and do not fear anyone. The people ate, drank, and danced joyfully before the god they asked Aaron to make.

Exodus 32:6 So the next day they rose early and offered burnt offerings, and brought peace offerings; and the people sat down to eat and to drink, and rose up to play.

In this verse, the expression, "rose up to play," is translated "indulged in pagan revelry" in the NLT and the NIV with a connotation of indecent acts of dancing for idols and engaging in obscene, immoral behavior.

It is difficult to find God as angry in any other incident in the Bible. This time, God proclaimed that He would destroy everyone and start all over again with one man, Moses (Exod 32:10). Moses threw down the two tablets of the law, which then broke (Exod 32:15–16, 19), because the people were not worthy to receive the laws.

Then Moses took the calf, burned it in fire, ground it into powder, and scattered it over the water and made the people drink it (Exod 32:20). The law commands that any woman who is suspected of having sexual relations with a man other than her husband shall drink the "water of bitterness" (Num 5:12–24). Likewise, the Israelites were made to drink the "water of bitterness," which brings a curse, because they defiled themselves by committing spiritual adultery against God, their spiritual husband (Isa 54:5).

After this, God made the descendants of Levi slaughter their brothers, friends, and neighbors so that 3,000 people died (Exod 32:27–28). Even after killing their brothers, the descendants of Levi were praised for their dedication and later became the priestly tribe (Exod 32:29). On this day, because of Aaron's unbelief and sin, 3,000 lives were ruthlessly taken at the hands of their own brothers. The next day, Moses desperately cried out to God, saying that he would have his own name blotted out from the book of life (Exod 32:30–33) if the people's sins would be forgiven.

Aaron's sin, which cost the lives of so many people, was so grave that Deuteronomy 9:20 states that God was angry enough to kill Aaron (something not mentioned in Exodus). Again, Aaron's life is spared due to Moses' prayer on his behalf (Deut 9:20).

Aaron's third sin was in speaking against Moses along with Miriam (Num 12:1–16). As discussed earlier, their tainted intent to undermine Moses' spiritual authority was exposed when God suddenly intervened and spoke to them. It was at this time that Aaron acknowledged his younger brother's authority and said, "Oh, my lord, I beg you...."

Aaron's fourth sin was not believing in God's Word and disobeying Him along with Moses with regard to the waters of Meribah at Kadesh

(Num 20:7–13), and ultimately failing to treat God as holy in the sight of the people. It was after this incident that God pronounced to Aaron that he would not enter Canaan (Num 20:24).

> **Numbers 20:12** But the LORD said to Moses and Aaron, "Because you have not believed Me, to treat Me as holy in the sight of the sons of Israel, therefore you shall not bring this assembly into the land which I have given them."

(ii) The result of Aaron's unbelief

Aaron died at the age of 123 on top of Mount Hor and was gathered to his people (Num 20:22–29; Deut 10:6; 32:50) in accordance with God's Word after the episode of the Meribah waters in Kadesh (Num 20:12).

> **Numbers 33:38–39** Then Aaron the priest went up to Mount Hor at the command of the LORD, and died there, in the fortieth year after the sons of Israel had come from the land of Egypt on the first day in the fifth month. ³⁹And Aaron was one hundred twenty-three years old when he died on Mount Hor.

Aaron concluded his life in the wilderness eight months prior to entry into Canaan with the land just a short distance away. Aaron did not die of old age or of natural causes. His death was the wage that God pronounced upon him as a result of his disobedience to the will of God.

According to God's command, Moses took Aaron and his son Eleazar up to Mount Hor, where he stripped Aaron of his priestly garments (the ephod) and put them on his son (Num 20:26–28). Aaron did not remove the garments himself. Moses stripped him. Aaron was appointed the high priest according to the will of God, but he was stripped of his position as a result of his unbelief.

The congregation wept for 30 days when they saw that Aaron had died (Num 20:29). The death of the high priest whom the people had revered throughout their 40-year journey probably triggered a great fear of God among the people.

(3) The Death of Moses (eleventh month in 1407 BC, about two months prior to entry into Canaan)

Moses, who received the command to lead the Israelites out of Egypt and into the land of Canaan (Exod 3:9–10; Acts 7:30–34), had become a 120-year old man after the 40-year wilderness journey. He concluded his life on the eleventh month of the fortieth year of the exodus after a long farewell sermon that he gave on the first day of the same month

(Deut 1:3). About two months prior to entry into Canaan, Moses died before his eyes became dim and his vigor abated.

> **Deuteronomy 34:7** Although Moses was one hundred and twenty years old when he died, his eye was not dim, nor his vigor abated.

Moses prepared for Canaan for 80 years and marched toward Canaan for 40 years in all meekness. He should have been the first to set foot in the Promised Land. Tragically, Moses also concluded his life in the wilderness without setting foot on the land he so longed to enter.

(i) Why Moses had to die before entering Canaan

Numbers 20:1 states, "Then the sons of Israel, the whole congregation, came to the Wilderness of Zin in the first month." The first month refers to the first month (the month of Abib) of the fortieth year of the exodus (1407 BC [Num 33:38]).

Here in Kadesh, in the episode involving the Meribah waters, Moses disobeyed God's order to take the staff in his hand and command the rock to give forth water. Instead, he struck the rock twice and consequently was forbidden from entering Canaan. God told Moses that he could not enter Canaan because he did not treat God "as holy in the sight of the people" (Num 20:12; 27:14; Deut 32:51). What does it mean not to treat God as holy in the sight of the people? The Bible provides four explanations.

First, Moses did not believe in God (Num 20:12). Water came forth abundantly as soon as Moses struck the rock twice, but God was greatly angry with Moses and said, "You have not believed Me" (Num 20:12). No matter how great his faith was until then, God now said, "You have not believed Me." It is certain that Moses had not believed in God during this incident.

In Numbers 20:8, God said that the rock would give forth water if Moses commanded it. The word for "water" in this verse is in the plural form in Hebrew (i.e., "waters") and refers to waters great enough for two million people and their animals. It was "like a river" (Ps 105:41) and like "streams … overflowing" (Ps 78:20). However, at this moment, Moses did not wholly believe in the power of God, which caused such a great amount of water to gush out. Despite Moses' unbelief, God caused the water to gush out and quench the thirst of the people and their animals. This is God's great love and mercy in the midst of His anger.

Second, Moses rebelled against God (Num 27:14). In Numbers 27:14, God said, "You rebelled against My command to treat Me as holy before their eyes at the water." God says that Moses and Aaron rebelled against God. In Hebrew, "to rebel" is מָרָה (*mārâ*), meaning "to be stubborn about something" (Num 20:10; 1 Kgs 13:21, 26) and "to act in an obstinate manner" (Deut 9:7; 1 Sam 12:14; Job 17:2). Thus, God was saying that they were stubborn and acted in an obstinate manner.

When people become stubborn and obstinate in their ways, they refuse to listen to anyone else. God commanded them to speak to the rock so that it would bring forth water, but Moses was stubborn and struck the rock two times, disobeying God's Word. A person who is obstinate cannot obey God's Word. 1 Samuel 15:23 states that "insubordination is as iniquity and idolatry."

God wants total obedience to His Word. He wants His people to believe and to obey without adding or subtracting from His Word. Casting out our own thoughts and taking God's thoughts is the humility and the kind of obedience that pleases God.

At first, Naaman, because of his own thoughts, did not obey the prophet Elisha's command to wash himself in the Jordan River seven times (2 Kgs 5:11). However, when he cast his own thoughts aside and went into the Jordan, his leprosy was washed away. The thoughts of man are death and add nothing to the work of God; they only tear down His will (Matt 16:23; Rom 8:6).

Third, Moses broke faith with God (Num 20:8–13; 27:14; Deut 32:51). In Deuteronomy 32:51, God says to Moses that he is to die outside the Promised Land because "you broke faith with Me in the midst of the sons of Israel at the waters of Meribah-kadesh, in the Wilderness of Zin, because you did not treat Me as holy in the midst of the sons of Israel." In Hebrew, the word *broke* is מָעַל (*māʿal*), meaning "to act counter to one's duty" or "to be unfaithful." This describes how Moses had tried to covertly show himself as the one giving forth water when he was supposed to display God's glory. In Numbers 20:10, Moses failed to show God's glory by saying, "Shall we bring forth water for you out of this rock?" He undermined God's sovereign authority through this wicked act of pride. Perhaps Moses was able to veil his mistake before the people, but God who searches the hearts immediately dug through to the origin of the sin and made him pay the wages of his sin (Prov 21:2–4).

Do we have sins that we have secretly committed? God is everywhere, so there is no sin that we can hide (Ps 90:8; Jer 23:24).

Fourth, Moses spoke rashly with his lips. As Psalm 106:32–33 states, "They also provoked Him to wrath at the waters of Meribah, so that it went hard with Moses on their account; because they were rebellious against His Spirit, he spoke rashly with his lips." In Hebrew, "spoke rashly with his lips" is בָּטָא (*bāṭā*), also meaning "to speak thoughtlessly." Why did Moses, a man more humble than anyone on the face of the earth, speak in such a way?

When there was no water in Kadesh for the people, they assembled themselves against Moses and Aaron (Num 20:2). Numbers 20:3 tells us that the people "contended with Moses." In Hebrew, the word *contended* is רִיב (*rîb*) or רוּב (*rûb*), meaning "to quarrel" or "to dispute (violently)."[74] The word illustrates the level of harshness of the manner in which the people confronted Moses and Aaron and fought against them. They grumbled, asking why they did not perish along with their brothers when they were cursed by God (Num 20:3), and complained that they have been led to a "wretched place" where people cannot live (Num 20:5).

The fierce protests of the corrupt people provoked Moses so that it went hard with him after 40 years of obedience to God (Ps 106:32–33). This is what caused him to take the staff and strike the rock two times, saying, "Listen now, you rebels; shall we bring forth water for you out of this rock?" (Num 20:10). Moses did not wait after he struck the rock once. He struck the rock two times consecutively, showing how angered he was. However, James 1:20 states that "the anger of man does not achieve the righteousness of God."

The foolish are rash in speech and quick to become angry (Prov 14:29; 16:32; 29:20). "Death and life are in the power of the tongue" (Prov 18:21; 12:13; 13:3; 21:23). Tongues gone wrong are like poison and swords that kill (Ps 59:7; 64:3; Jas 3:8), and words from the tongue are like scorching fire (Prov 16:27; Jas 3:6).

In Matthew 12:36–37, Jesus states, "And I say to you, that every careless word that men shall speak, they shall render account for it in the day of judgment. For by your words you shall be justified, and by your words you shall be condemned." Thus, if we love life and want to see good days, we must keep our tongues from evil and our lips from speaking deceit (Ps 34:12-13; 1 Pet 3:10–11). Whatever we speak, we must speak in the name of Jesus Christ (Col 3:17). A perfect person is one who does not stumble with words (Jas 3:2).

Moses' prohibition from entering Canaan just one year short of the Israelites' entry is a fearful lesson for all Christians today. This shows that even those who have lived a life of obedience, those who have lived a life of faith for a long time, and those who have served faithfully and quietly can be affected by a spirit of disbelief in an instant to speak rashly, lose temper, claim deeds as their own, become self righteous, and eventually be used as Satan's tool to interfere with God's righteous will.

(ii) God's administration in the history of redemption revealed through the water from the rock

The Bible is full of testimonies about Jesus Christ and the divine administration of salvation (John 5:39; Luke 24:27). The episodes of water from the rock in the wilderness also contain God's administration in the history of redemption. In 1 Corinthians 10:4, the apostle Paul said that the rock that gave forth water in the wilderness was Christ.

Upon examination of the original text, we learn that the rock in Rephidim (Exod 17:6) and the rock in Kadesh (Num 20:8) are different in shape. The rock in Mount Horeb is צוּר (ṣûr) in Hebrew, referring to a "rock," "block of stone," or "mountain,"[75] symbolic of God's steadfastness (Ps 19:14) and eternal nature (Isa 26:4). However, the rock in Kadesh is סֶלַע (selaʿ) in Hebrew. The word סֶלַע (selaʿ) derives from an Arabic word that refers to a cleft or fissure, a rock that is steep and high with split cracks, and is translated as "rock" (Prov 30:26) or "cliff" (1 Sam 13:6).[76]

Exodus 17:6 reports, "'Behold, I [the LORD] will stand before you there on the rock at Horeb; and you shall strike the rock, and water will come out of it, that the people may drink.' And Moses did so in the sight of the elders of Israel." Here, God said, "Behold, I will stand before you there on the rock at Horeb." Thus, Moses struck the rock as God stood before him on the rock in order to make water gush out.

This episode is "a typical picture of Christ who in due time would be smitten on Calvary to provide spiritual water for the lost sinners."[77] The apostle Paul later confirmed that "the rock was Christ" (1 Cor 10:4).

However, God commanded Moses to "speak to the rock...that it may yield water" in Numbers 20:8. Here, God commanded Moses to speak to the rock unlike in Exodus 17:6, where He commanded him to strike the rock. Why? The rock in Numbers 20:8 is סֶלַע (*selaʿ*) in Hebrew, meaning that since it already has clefts, there is no need to strike it. This cleft rock is reminiscent of all the beatings and sufferings that Jesus endured on the way to the cross.

The brutal Roman soldiers placed a crown of thorns on Jesus' head with all their might (Matt 27:29; Mark 15:17; John 19:2, 5), and blood splattered everywhere as thorns thicker than human fingers pierced through Jesus' head. The blood from His head dripped into His eyes so that He could not open His eyes.

Jesus' whole face was covered with blood, and there was no place on His body unharmed from the scourging ordered by Pilate and carried out by the Roman soldiers (Matt 27:26; Mark 15:15; John 19:1). Each time they struck Him with the whip, the sharp tips dug deeply into His flesh and tore it so that His bones were revealed. There were furrows on His back from these whippings (Ps 129:3). Jesus' body shook violently each time the whip struck. His whole body was covered in blood so that He could not be looked upon.

The Roman soldiers nailed Jesus' hands and feet to the cross (Matt 27:35; Mark 15:24; Luke 23:33; John 19:18; 20:25). Jesus almost lost consciousness the moment they took His hands and nailed them to the cross. The large rough nails penetrated through Jesus' blessed hands and feet and then through the wood.

The weight of Jesus' body pulled down on the nailed hands and caused excruciating pain. As He lost too much blood, His whole body shook from the cold like aspen leaves. After He died, He shed His remaining blood and water when the soldiers pierced His side (John 19:34).

It was a brutal and gruesome death on the cross. We cannot help but feel heartbreaking sorrow as we think of how Jesus, who was without sin, faced such a horrible death because of our sins. Although the pains of life may drive us to the point of suicide, our suffering cannot compare to His pain.

There was no place on His body unharmed. If we are true believers, then we must remember that He was broken, torn, and scarred for our sins. They are the holy brand-marks of the redemption of sin; they are the brand-marks of love that can never be erased.

After His resurrection, Jesus showed His scars to Thomas, who doubted the resurrection. Jesus said to him, "Reach here your finger, and see My hands; and reach here your hand, and put it into My side; and be not unbelieving, but believing" (John 20:27). The minute Jesus spoke these words, the mountains of doubt came crumbling down.

Jesus will never be crucified again as part of God's plan of salvation. Jesus achieved eternal redemption once and for all on the cross (John 19:30; Rom 6:6–10; Heb 7:27; 9:12, 26; 10:2, 10).

The cross that Jesus bore was part of absolute predestination (Matt 26:20–24, 54–56; Mark 9:12; Luke 18:31; 22:22; 24:25–27; Acts 26:22–23; 1 Cor 15:3; 1 Pet 1:10–11). He was totally victorious (Col 2:13–15). Jesus resurrected and ascended into heaven (Acts 1:9-11), but when He comes again, He will come as the Lord of glory (1 Thess 4:16–17). This is the same Jesus who suffered on the cross (Rev 5:6).

(iii) Moses' death

Moses and Aaron were from the tribe of Levi (Exod 2:1–2), so they were not counted during the first census of Israel's army (Num 1:47, 49). Moses and Aaron surely would have entered Canaan had it not been for the event at Kadesh involving the waters. Moses and Aaron were commanded to speak to the rock so that it may yield water, but they neither believed in God nor treated God as holy in the sight of His people (Num 20:8–13; 27:14; Deut 32:50–51). As a result, both he and Aaron were forbidden from entering Canaan about one year prior to the Israelites' entry into Canaan (Num 20:12).

Imagine how much Moses longed to set foot upon the land of Canaan. Even after witnessing Aaron's death on Mount Hor according to God's Word on the first day of the fifth month of the fortieth year of the exodus, Moses could not let go of his desire to enter Canaan, and he pleaded with God with all his might. However, God firmly rejected his plea, saying, "Enough! Speak to Me no more of this matter" (Deut 3:23–27). "And when you have seen it, you too shall be gathered to your people, as Aaron your brother was" (Num 27:13; cf. Deut 32:50). Even his earnest petition to enter Canaan could not change God's Word.

When Moses died, his eyes were not dim, and his vigor was unabated (Deut 34:7). Thus, it is certain that Moses did not die of natural causes. He died exactly according to God's Word. Deuteronomy 34:5 confirms, "So Moses the servant of the LORD died there in the land of Moab, according to the word of the Lord."

Moses died at the age of 120 and was buried in the valley in the land of Moab, opposite Beth-peor, but the Bible tells us that to this day, there is no one who knows his burial place (Deut 34:6; Jude 1:9).

6. The Death of 603,548 Soldiers from Those Numbered in the First Census

When the Israelites left Egypt, there were 603,550 men over 20 years of age (Num 1:46; 2:32), although the tribe of Levi was excluded from this number (Num 26:62). All of the first generation of Israelites died within the camp before they crossed over the brook Zered (Deut 2:13–16), which was after Aaron's death in Numbers 20:28 (Num 21:12). Thus, the first generation of Israelites died after the first day of the fifth month of the fortieth year of the exodus, which was when Aaron died. With about eight months left until entry into Canaan, the remainder of the 603,548 men, with the exception of Joshua and Caleb, died according to God's Word (Deut 1:34–38; 2:13–16; Num 14:22–24, 29–30, 38; 26:63–65; 32:11–13).

(1) Why the soldiers who were numbered in the first census had to die

These soldiers died because they listened to the faithless words of the ten spies and grumbled against Moses and Aaron (Num 14:1–3, 26–30).

What was the result of the spies' 40-day reconnaissance of the land of Canaan? They brought produce from the land of Canaan, saying, "We went in to the land where you sent us; and it certainly does flow with milk and honey, and this is its fruit" (Num 13:27). They brought a branch with "a single cluster of grapes" that was so large that two men carried it on a pole between them (Num 13:23). They confirmed that Canaan was a land flowing with milk and honey.

The ten spies were struck with fear of the sons of Anak and said, "We became like grasshoppers in our own sight, and so we were in their sight" (Num 13:32–33), immediately causing the hearts of the people to waver. The congregation that heard the bad report on Canaan lifted up their voices and wept all night (Num 14:1). They grumbled, saying, "Would that we had died in the land of Egypt! Or would that we had died in this wilderness! And why is the LORD bringing us into this land, to fall by the sword? Our wives and our little ones will become plunder; would it not be better for us to return to Egypt?" (Num 14:2–3). And they became rebellious, planning to return to Egypt (Num 14:4).

Joshua and Caleb saw this faithless scene and tore their clothes, saying, "The land which we passed through to spy out is an exceedingly good land. If the LORD is pleased with us, then He will bring us into this land, and give it to us—a land which flows with milk and honey" (Num 14:6–8). Joshua and Caleb were in the same place at the same time with the other ten spies and saw the same fortified city and men of great size—the sons of Anak. Nonetheless, they considered and firmly believed that God's Word is greater. They shouted boldly to the congregation that was grumbling and crying out.

> **Numbers 14:9** "Only do not rebel against the LORD; and do not fear the people of the land, for they shall be our prey. Their protection has been removed from them, and the LORD is with us; do not fear them."

The negative and faithless words of the ten spies, however, had already seized the hearts of the congregation so that there was no room for the words of Joshua and Caleb. The congregation was ready to stone them, but at this critical moment the glory of the Lord appeared to them, and they stopped (Num 14:10).

(2) The 40-year wilderness journey mandated as the consequence of unbelief

(i) The reason why God made them wander in the wilderness for 40 years

God heard all the people's grumblings and pronounced that they would wander through the wilderness for 40 years, and that no one, except for Joshua and Caleb, would enter Canaan (Num 14:26–35). God counted each day of the 40-day exploration as one year and made them bear their guilt for 40 years (Num 14:34). In Hebrew, the phrase "for every day you shall bear your guilt a year" is written twice for emphasis:

$$\text{יוֹם לַשָּׁנָה יוֹם לַשָּׁנָה}$$

lašša̅na̅   yôm   lašša̅na̅   yôm

God also said to the prophet Ezekiel that He assigned "a day for each year" (Ezek 4:6).

(ii) The death of the ten spies who gave the negative report

The 12 spies were men chosen from each tribe out of the total 603,550 men. They were "leaders" (נָשִׂיא, *nāśîʾ*, "representative, spokesperson, herald") according to Numbers 13:2, and "heads" (רֹאשׁ, *rōʾš*, "head, beginning, peak, chief") according to Numbers 13:3.[78] In other words, they were influential men among the people, which explains why their bad report immediately caused the congregation to grumble against Moses (Num 13:30–33; 14:1–3) and to despair and weep (Deut 1:28). As a result, the ten spies died the very next day (Num 14:25, 39–40) "by a plague before the Lord" (Num 14:36–38).

In the Bible, those who died "before the LORD" include Uzzah, whom God struck down because he put out his hand to the ark (1 Chr 13:10; 2 Sam 6:8), and Nadab and Abihu, Aaron's sons, who offered strange fire before the Lord (Num 3:4; 26:61). All these people died from God's immediate judgment.

(iii) The unwavering faith of Joshua and Caleb

Joshua and Caleb became living witnesses to God's Word by becoming the only two persons to enter Canaan alive. The Bible tells us that they were able to enter Canaan as a reward for "fully" following the Lord (Num 14:24; Josh 14:8–9).

> **Numbers 32:12** "… except Caleb the son of Jephunneh the Kenizzite and Joshua the son of Nun, for they have followed the Lord fully."
>
> **Deuteronomy 1:36** "… except Caleb the son of Jephunneh; he shall see it, and to him and to his sons I will give the land on which he has set foot, because he has followed the LORD fully."

In Hebrew, the word *fully* in this verse, מִלֵּא (*millēʾ*), is derived from מָלֵא (*mālēʾ*), meaning "to fill completely," "to satisfy," and "to overflow." Their obedience was complete. Their obedience was full. Their obedience was thorough. Their obedience satisfied God. Their obedience was as thorough as Jesus' confession, "I know that His commandment is eternal life" (John 12:50).

Joshua and Caleb were captured by God's Word. Their firm belief that they would be victorious in any evil and impossible circumstance if they obeyed God's Word was deeply rooted in their lives. They did not waver or sympathize even though their families and relatives grumbled and complained.

Because they followed the Lord fully, they tasted the glory of the emotional entrance into Canaan according to God's Word. Those who did not fully follow the Lord were not able to set foot on the Promised Land.

> **Numbers 32:11** "None of the men who came up from Egypt, from twenty years old and upward, shall see the land which I swore to Abraham, to Isaac and to Jacob; for they did not follow Me fully."

When they did not fully obey, they not only prevented others from believing in God's Word, but also caused them to stumble and eventually die in distress.

(iv) The 603,548 men who ultimately fell in the wilderness

God heard the voices of those who had heard the bad report of the ten spies and wept all night. He heard them murmuring about how Moses was trying to kill them, and how they should choose someone else to lead them back to Egypt. Then, God judged them according to what they had spoken in His hearing (Num 14:27–28).

God pronounced that, except for Joshua and Caleb, they would not be able to enter the land of Canaan (Num 14:29–30). Thus, the Israelites had to continue wandering until all of the grumblers fell as corpses in the wilderness (Num 14:32–35). Because God's Word does not fall on the ground unfulfilled, all of the people, except for Joshua and Caleb, fell as corpses in the wilderness (Num 26:63–65; 32:12–13; Deut 2:14–16; Heb 3:17).

7. The Battles Fought Just Before the Entry into Canaan

The Israelites had been able to avoid war until they were about to cross the Arnon River when they began to clash with Sihon, the king of the Amorites. War with Sihon continued until they crossed the Jordan River.

(1) The Battle at Jahaz (Num 21:21–32)

After the Israelites crossed the Arnon River and camped at Dibon (Dibon-gad), they sent messengers to Sihon, king of the Amorites, and asked for permission to pass through his land, but he would not permit it. Instead, he mobilized his forces and attacked the Israelites from Jahaz, a city located in the upper northern region of the Arnon River (Num 21:23). However, the Israelites were greatly victorious against the Amorites; they took possession of the land from the Arnon to the Jabbok and lived in Heshbon and in all the cities of the Amorites (Num 21:24–26). The secret to their success, however, was not the sword or the arrow. God sent hornets before them to drive out the Amorites (Josh 24:12).

(2) The Battle at Edrei (Num 21:33–35)

After their victory against Sihon, king of the Amorites, the Israelites were able to go up from the Amorite capital city, Heshbon, straight to the mountains of Abarim. However, Israel's army did not go up into the mountains of Abarim, but turned and went up by the way of Bashan, where they battled against Og, the king of Bashan, until they reached Edrei (Num 21:33). Edrei was a chief city of King Og, located northeast of Gilead by the King's Highway. Again, the Israelites were greatly victorious. They killed all the armies of Bashan so that there was not one person left, and they possessed the land (Num 21:35).

(3) The Battle against Midian (Num 31:1–24)

The Israelites battled against the Amorites and journeyed from Dibon-gad and camped at Almon-diblathaim. They journeyed from Almon-diblathaim and camped in the mountains of Abarim. From there, they journeyed and camped in the plains of Moab (Num 33:46–49). The camp of the Israelites in the plains of Moab stretched from Beth-jeshim-oth as far as Abel-shittim.

However, the Israelites enraged God by indulging in sexual immorality with the women of Moab and worshipping their gods while they were camped at Shittim just before entering Canaan. As a result 24,000 people died of a plague and Phinehas the son of Eleazar and the grandson of Aaron the priest takes a spear and pierces the bodies of the adulterers – Zimri the son of Salu, a leader among the Simeonites and a Midianite woman Cozbi, the daughter of Zur, who was a leader in Midian. As a result, God's wrath is turned away and the plague ended (Num 25:1-18).

The Israelites and the Midianites fought as a result of this affair, and 1,000 men from each of the tribes, 12,000 in total, were sent to war and were victorious (Num 31:1–8).

(4) The Battle of Gilead (Num 32:39–42)

According to Numbers 32, after the battle against the Midianites, the land east of the Jordan River was allotted to the tribes of Reuben, Gad, and the half-tribe of Manasseh. Afterwards, the sons of Machir, a son of Manasseh, attacked Gilead and dispossessed the Amorites who were there. Moses gave Gilead to Machir (Num 32:40). Gilead is located east of the Jordan River by the King's Highway.

The Israelites were victorious in all the battles because God placed the enemy into their hands. In Numbers 21:34, God said, "Do not fear him, for I have given him into your hand, and all his people and his land; and you shall do to him as you did to Sihon, king of the Amorites, who lived at Heshbon." Here, the word *given* is נָתַן (*nātan*) in Hebrew, meaning "to give," "to put," or "to set." God gave all the enemies into the hands of the Israelites. Their victories, small and great, prior to their entry into Canaan, shaped an anticipation that their victories in the conquest of Canaan were also in God's hands. The small victories connected to great victories that ultimately led to the conquest of Canaan.

8. The Death of 24,000 People in Moab/Shittim
(Num 25:1–9)

Shittim is a region located northeast of the Dead Sea, and the name means "acacia tree." It was the last camp site before the Israelites marched into Canaan (Num 33:48–49), and many significant events occurred while they were camped there. It was there that 24,000 men were killed after indulging in sexual immorality with the women of Moab.

In Hebrew, the word *joined* in "So Israel joined themselves to Baal of Peor" (Num 25:3) is צָמַד (*ṣāmad*), meaning "to firmly fasten and bind." It means that their souls and thoughts were fixed toward Baal of Peor, and they had no intention of changing their hearts. They had become extremely corrupt.

The original cause of this event traces back to the wages of unrighteousness that the prophet Balaam received from Balak (2 Pet 2:15; Jude 11). Balaam counseled Balak to place stumbling blocks before the sons of Israel so that they would eat things sacrificed to idols and commit acts of immorality (Num 31:16; Rev 2:14). Idol worship is often accompanied by immoral acts, and the Bible treats idolatry and immorality in the same light, as the same nature of sin (Exod 34:15–17; Lev 17:7; 20:5; Deut 31:16; Judg 2:17; 8:33; Jer 3:9; 23:10; Ezek 6:9). The apostle Paul illustrates very well how the worship of creatures leads to immoral acts (Rom 1:23–27).

Both Moses and Joshua repeatedly warned the Israelites that if they worshiped the gods of Canaan, those gods would become a snare for them (Exod 23:33; 34:12; Deut 7:16, 25; 12:30; Josh 23:13). The Baal of Peor affair in Numbers 25 was the result of being ensnared by the worship of various gods. The chosen people of Israel committed immoral acts that are found in the rituals of Gentile idol worship. The people who were supposed to worship only God had defiled themselves both spiritually and physically by worshipping other gods (Exod 34:12-16; Deut 7:1-4; Josh 23:12-13).

We can learn a few things more than just a mere fact that those who worshipped idols and indulged in immoral acts died from this "Baal of Peor" affair, in which a large number of 24,000 people were killed.

The second census was taken after the plague. Most commentators consider the 24,000 who were killed by the plague to have been among the 603,548 who were counted in the first census and died in the wilderness. However, the incident in Numbers 25 occurred after the Israelites crossed the brook Zered (Num 21:12) and after all the men who were numbered in the first census had died (Deut 2:13-16). Therefore, the 24,000 who died of the plague were clearly the second generation Israelites in the wilderness and they died right before the second census of soldiers (Ps. 106:28-30; 1 Cor 10:8).

Through earlier episodes, the second generation of Israelites witnessed continually how the first generation paid the price of unbelief and fell in the wilderness. Yet, they repeated the acts of idol worship and immorality of their ancestors (Exod 34:14–16) and died before setting foot in Canaan. Although they were the generation of heirs to Canaan, they could not enter in because they sinned and did not obey the Word.

The death of the 24,000 people in Moab/Shittim teaches us the importance of keeping the body pure, keeping the bed undefiled, and holding marriage in honor, always keeping in mind that our bodies are the temple of the Holy Spirit (1 Cor 6:18–19; Heb 13:4).

9. The Second Census of Soldiers (Num 26:1–51)

Numbers 26:1–2 Then it came about after the plague, that the Lord spoke to Moses and to Eleazar the son of Aaron the priest, saying, ²"Take a census of all the congregation of the sons of Israel from twenty years old and upward, by their fathers' households, whoever is able to go out to war in Israel."

Numbers 26:51 These are those who were numbered of the sons of Israel, 601,730.

Numbers 26 is a record of the second census taken of the second generation of Israelites in the wilderness "after the plague" that was their punishment for their immoral acts at Moab/Shittim (Num 26:1). We must take heed of the fact that the second census was taken after the moral and spiritual cleansing of the Israelites. Only the pure can enter the Promised Land, the kingdom of God (Ps 24:3–4; 2 Cor 7:1). What was the purpose of the second census?

(1) The numbering of the covenantal people who would fulfill the covenant

Unlike the first census, the second census recorded the basic genealogy of each household as well as their detailed family list. This was because the purpose of the second census was closely related to the fulfillment of the covenant.

(i) To show the fulfillment of God's covenant to make the Israelites into a great nation

God promised numerous times that He would make the Israelites a great nation. Now, as the great nation of Israel made their way into Canaan, He showed that He was fulfilling His promise (Gen 12:2; 15:5; 17:2–6, 16; 18:18; 26:4; 35:11; 46:3; Acts 3:25; Gal 3:8).

(ii) To show the fulfillment of God's promise of Canaan as the Israelites' inheritance (Gen 15:8, 18-21)

God took the second census and divided the land of Canaan as an inheritance based on those figures (Num 26:52–56).

(iii) **To show the fulfillment of God's Word that those who grumbled would not enter Canaan (Num 14:26–38; 26:63–65; Ps 106:24–26; 1 Cor 10:5; Heb 3:15–19; Jude 15)**

Among those numbered in the second census, with the exception of Joshua and Caleb, there was not one person who had been part of the first census (Num 26:63–65). God's Word that He had spoken 38 years ago was fulfilled.

The second generation of Israelites in the wilderness witnessed the first generation suddenly dying and probably realized the gravity of the wages of sin. They probably were greatly amazed to see that as God had spoken, there was no one from the first generation left, except for Joshua and Caleb, to be numbered in the second census.

It was not a coincidence or a work of nature for the people of the same generation to die together on the same day at the same time. The hand of God had struck them (Deut 2:15). With His great and mighty arm and the hands of judgment, He purposely struck them and carried out His judgment of wrath (Ruth 1:13; 1 Chr 21:17; Job 19:21; Ps 39:10; 1 Sam 5:9, 11).

> **Deuteronomy 2:14–15** "Now the time that it took for us to come from Kadesh-barnea, until we crossed over the brook Zered, was thirty-eight years; until all the generation of the men of war perished from within the camp, as the LORD had sworn to them. ¹⁵Moreover the hand of the LORD was against them, to destroy them from within the camp, until they all perished."

His plan to judge them was so determined, so precise, and so stern that His hand was against them "until they all perished" (Deut 2:15) and "until the entire generation ... was destroyed" (Num 32:13).

All the 603,548 men over the age of 20 numbered in the first census died during the first 38 years of the wilderness journey. Thus, with the exception of Joshua and Caleb, all soldiers over the age of 58 were dead; that generation was gone.

Thus, the significance of the second census taken before their entry into Canaan proves that God had faithfully kept His covenant. Moreover, this census is a sign of guarantee that His covenant will continue to be fulfilled.

(2) To number the soldiers who could fight once the Israelites entered the Promised Land

The Israelites were camped in the plains of Moab with the land of Canaan before them, and they were getting ready to enter. The census taken here was in preparation for the war that they would fight in Canaan; they were counting the number of men over the age of 20 who could fight in battle.

There were 601,730 men over the age of 20 who could fight in battle (Num 26:51). This was 1,820 less than the figure for the first census taken at the start of the wilderness journey (Num 1:46). The decrease in number, despite the passage of 40 years in the wilderness, was a strong indication of the devastating consequences of unbelief and sin.

(3) To equally divide the inheritance of the land among the tribes

Another purpose of the census was to make equal allocations of land among the tribes (Num 26:53–55). Thus, the census was taken with the faith that God would fulfill His promise regarding the land, and that they would possess the land according to His Word.

In the tribe of Manasseh, the great-great-grandson Zelophehad died without an heir. He had just five daughters: Mahlah, Noah, Hoglah, Milcah, and Tirzah (Num 27:1; 36:11; Josh 17:3). Their names were mentioned in the second census (Num 26:33).

These five daughters thought that it was unjust for their father's family not to receive a portion of the inheritance, since their father had not done anything against the Lord although there were no sons in the family. They did not want their father's family to disappear from the covenantal community (ie. same concept as covenantal people). They stood at the doorway of the tent of meeting before Moses and Eleazar the priest and before the leaders and the entire congregation, and asked for a possession among their father's brothers (Num 27:2–4). Moses did not handle their case according to the patriarchal custom, but brought this case before the Lord. Then the Lord acknowledged the legitimacy of their claim and commanded Moses to give them a hereditary possession (Num 27:5–7). This case set the legal precedent for a new inheritance law among the sons of Israel (Num 27:8–11).

According to God's command, Moses also added a new law that permitted daughters who receive an inheritance to marry only within their father's tribe (Num 36:6–9). Thus, the daughters of Zelophehad, by marrying only within their father's tribe, preserved their inheritance until the end.

> **Numbers 36:10–12** Just as the LORD had commanded Moses, so the daughters of Zelophehad did: [11]Mahlah, Tirzah, Hoglah, Milcah and Noah, the daughters of Zelophehad married their uncles' sons. [12]They married those from the families of the sons of Manasseh the son of Joseph, and their inheritance remained with the tribe of the family of their father.

The daughters of Zelophehad valued the inheritance of their ancestors and complied with the instructions that Moses gave to them according to the Lord's command. Thus, after the battles in Canaan were over, when the land was being distributed to the tribes, they stood before Joshua and the leaders and boldly asked for their inheritance (Josh 17:3–4). Joshua originally had allotted six portions for the western half-tribe of Manasseh (Abiezer, Helek, Asriel, Shechem, Hepher, Shemida [Josh 17:2]), but it was increased to ten portions because each of the daughters of Zelophehad was given one portion (Josh 17:5–6).

The five daughters of Zelophehad knew the value of the inheritance of their ancestors and longed for it, reminding the Israelites of the value of such inheritance. They most likely set a good example for others when their descendants down the line became increasingly corrupt through their intermarriages with the Gentiles (Ezra 9:1–2, 11–15).

The five daughters of Zelophehad were mentioned in the second census, which numbered only men over the age of 20, demonstrating that one of the purposes of the second census was for the equal distribution of the land according to each tribe. After the second census was complete, God commanded them to divide the land according to those numbered in each tribe (Num 26:52–56).

CHAPTER 14

The Conquest of Canaan

1406–1390 BC, 676th through 692nd Year of the Covenant

The Israelites who left Egypt carrying Joseph's bones arrived in Canaan 400 years after Joseph's death on the tenth day of the first month of the forty-first year of the exodus (Josh 4:19). This was 676 years after the covenant had been ratified.

The conquest and distribution of the land of Canaan was initiated mostly by Joshua and Caleb over a period of about 16 years, which included the time of the conquest of the land and the process of allocating the land that followed.

The conquest of Canaan was the final process in the fulfillment of the covenant of the torch. "The covenant of the torch" that God had established with Abraham in Genesis 15:18 was finally fulfilled through His faithfulness as the Israelites set foot in Canaan, the Promised Land. His promise, "To your descendants I have given this land, from the river of Egypt as far as the great river, the river Euphrates" was fulfilled.

This is the land that God promised to Abraham when He first called Abraham at the age of 75 (Gen 12:7; 13:15), when He ratified the covenant of the torch when Abraham was 84 years old (Gen 15:18), and when He ratified the covenant of circumcision when Abraham was 99 years old (Gen 17:7–8). God also promised this land to Isaac (Gen 26:2–4) and to Jacob (Gen 28:13–15).

1. Joshua, a New Leader for the Conquest of Canaan

The Israelites wept for Moses for 30 days (Deut 34:8). After Moses' death, God did not delay in choosing a new leader for the fulfillment of the covenant. He chose Joshua, son of Nun, as the successor. The book of Joshua begins with "Moses My servant is dead; now therefore arise…." (Josh 1:2). Before Moses died, he had taken Joshua before Eleazar the priest and before the entire congregation and commissioned him in their sight (Num 27:18–23; Josh 1:1–2). When Moses laid his hands on Joshua, he was full of the spirit of wisdom.

> **Deuteronomy 34:9** Now Joshua the son of Nun was filled with the spirit of wisdom, for Moses had laid his hands on him; and the sons of Israel listened to him and did as the LORD had commanded Moses.

(1) God's preparation for the fulfillment of the covenant

Because Moses had been such a great leader, his absence could have caused a gap in leadership and possibly chaos. However, God prepared Joshua in advance so that there was no setback in His plan to give His people the land of Canaan and fulfill His covenant.

Joshua, who inherited Moses' leadership, carried Joseph's bones and entered Canaan. Moses was from the tribe of Levi (Exod 2:1–2), while Joshua was from the tribe of Ephraim (1 Chr 7:20–27), so there were no blood ties between Moses and his successor. Thus, Joshua's succession was based not on fleshly genealogy, but on the genealogy of faith as part of God's mission for the conquest of Canaan.

After the Israelites crossed the Red Sea, they recognized Moses as a leader for whom God was present (Exod 14:31). Likewise, they saw that God was also with Joshua when he led them over the surging waters of the Jordan River.

From the day of the miraculous crossing of the Jordan, God exalted Joshua in the sight of Israel. From that day on, the people feared Joshua the same way they had feared Moses.

> **Joshua 3:7** Now the LORD said to Joshua, "This day I will begin to exalt you in the sight of all Israel, that they may know that just as I have been with Moses, I will be with you."

> **Joshua 4:14** On that day the LORD exalted Joshua in the sight of all Israel; so that they revered him, just as they had revered Moses all the days of his life.

(2) Moses' successor, Joshua

(i) Joshua's age at his calling

Moses, just before he died, laid his hands upon Joshua in the fortieth year of the exodus (1407 BC), and at this time, Joshua was full of the spirit of wisdom (Deut 34:9). Joshua died at the age of 110 (Josh 24:29), which is known to be 1390 BC.[79]

Joshua was 93 years old when he was called as the leader of Israel, but despite his age, he successfully inherited Moses' leadership and fulfilled his duty to conquer Canaan. If Joshua was 93 years old when he was called, then he must have been 55 years old when he was sent out to spy out the land of Canaan along with the 11 others two years after the exodus (1445 BC). Since Caleb was 40 years old when he was also sent out as a spy (Josh 14:7), Joshua was 15 years older than Caleb.

(ii) Moses' servant Joshua

Considering the fact that there were over 600,000 men over the age of 20 numbered in both the first and second censuses, there must have been scholars, wise men, and heroes greater than Joshua. Nonetheless, God chose a mere servant of Moses as the leader of a nation (Exod 24:13; 33:11). God filled him with strength, courage, and the spirit of wisdom (Josh 1:1–9).

The Bible testifies that Joshua was with Moses, the leader of the nation, when he fasted and prayed in the mountain of God (Mount Sinai) 40 days and nights.

> **Exodus 24:13** So Moses arose with Joshua his servant, and Moses went up to the mountain of God.

Joshua kept watch in the tent when Moses spoke with God and did not depart from the tent even after Moses had returned to the camp.

> **Exodus 33:11** Thus the LORD used to speak to Moses face to face, just as a man speaks to his friend. When Moses returned to the camp, his servant Joshua, the son of Nun, a young man, would not depart from the tent.

Joshua was not troubled by the men of great size who are the sons of Anak, a part of the Nephilim, nor was he concerned about the surrounding environment. He focused only on God, who is faithful to His promise. Thus, even as the Israelites picked up stones to stone him in their unbelief and grumblings, he boldly shouted, "Do not fear the people of the land, for they shall be our prey" (Num 14:8–10). His faith in the covenant did not waver.

Even as death was before him, he held on to this resolute faith and confessed, "But as for me and my house, we will serve the LORD" (Josh 24:15).

(3) Joshua carried out the conquest of Canaan by fully obeying God's command

God had already commanded the battle for the conquest of Canaan to Moses (Deut 7:2; 20:16–17). Thus, throughout the whole conquest mission, Joshua did everything just as he was commanded through Moses; he did nothing on his own (Josh 8:31, 33, 35; 11:12).

> **Joshua 11:15** Just as the LORD had commanded Moses his servant, so Moses commanded Joshua, and so Joshua did; he left nothing undone of all that the LORD had commanded Moses.

A significant characteristic of the battle for the conquest of Canaan was that God intervened and gave victory. Just before the start of the battle, God appeared to Joshua as the captain of the Lord's host and said, "Remove your sandals from your feet, for the place where you are standing is holy" (Josh 5:15), just as He had done when He called Moses (Exod 3:5). This was the promise that God Himself would lead the army in the battle as an invisible captain.

In actuality, God appeared to Joshua at the start of every battle and promised victory (Josh 6:2; 8:1; 10:8; 11:6). In turn, as soon as Joshua received God's Word, he did not delay taking action according to His command; and therefore, he was able to gain victory in those times (Josh 6:2–6; 8:1–3; 10:8–9; 11:6–7).

The secret to Israel's miraculous victories from start to finish was not Joshua's courage or Israel's strategy. God Himself fought in the battle to conquer the land that He had promised to give to Abraham's descendants about 680 years ago (Josh 10:14; 23:10).

> **Joshua 10:42** And Joshua captured all these kings and their lands at one time, because the LORD, the God of Israel, fought for Israel.

> **Joshua 23:3** "And you have seen all that the LORD your God has done to all these nations because of you, for the LORD your God is He who has been fighting for you."

2. Caleb, the Godly Man Who Helped Moses and Joshua

Caleb was a leader of the post-Moses era along with Joshua. In Hebrew, his name is כָּלֵב (kāleb), derived from כֶּלֶב (keleb), meaning "dog." Thus, Caleb means "to cry out as a dog" or "aggressor." Like his name (i.e., "dog"), Caleb was a faithful helper, who followed the Lord God with a sincere zeal and hope for the Promised Land (Num 14:24; Josh 14:8–9).

Caleb is not mentioned in the Bible after the Kadesh-barnea narrative until 45 years later, when the conquest of Canaan's main regions was finished and the distribution of the land had begun. Caleb was of the old age of 85, but he was the same in his faithfulness and still displayed the power of faith (Josh 14).

(1) Caleb's affiliation

(i) He was a Kenizzite

Both Numbers 32:12 and Joshua 14:6 describe Caleb as the "son of Jephunneh the Kenizzite." Kenaz was the fifth son of Eliphaz, Esau's son, who dwelled in the regions around Palestine as one of the tribes of Edom (Gen 36:11, 15, 40–42; 1 Chr 1:36).[80] Thus, Caleb the Kenizzite was originally from the Gentile nation of Edom.

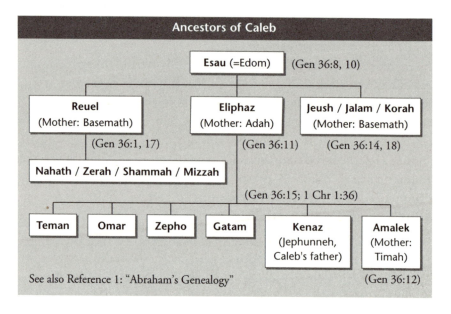

Ancestors of Caleb

Esau (=Edom) (Gen 36:8, 10)

Reuel (Mother: Basemath) (Gen 36:1, 17)

Eliphaz (Mother: Adah) (Gen 36:11)

Jeush / Jalam / Korah (Mother: Basemath) (Gen 36:14, 18)

Nahath / Zerah / Shammah / Mizzah

(Gen 36:15; 1 Chr 1:36)

Teman | Omar | Zepho | Gatam | Kenaz (Jephunneh, Caleb's father) | Amalek (Mother: Timah)

See also Reference 1: "Abraham's Genealogy" (Gen 36:12)

(ii) He belonged to the tribe of Judah

In Numbers 13:6, where Caleb is first mentioned, he is introduced as Caleb the son of Jephunneh from the tribe of Judah. Judah's genealogy is mentioned in 1 Chronicles 4:1, 13–15. However, for Caleb and his nephew Othniel (Josh 15:17; Judg 1:13; 3:9), it is only recorded that they belong to the tribe of Judah. There are no mentions of their ancestors or their roots, but only their descendants. This demonstrates that

Caleb was not originally a Hebrew, but that he was later admitted to the tribe of Judah. Regarding Caleb's roots, it is speculated that Caleb must have been one of the Gentile captives of war in Egypt who marched out along with the Israelites during the exodus.

These Gentiles were the "mixed multitude" (Exod 12:38) and the "rabble" (Num 11:4) who took part in the exodus, accepted faith in Jehovah, and were admitted to the different tribes. Given that Caleb was chosen as a spy during the early years of the exodus, his family must have accepted faith in Jehovah and was already admitted into the tribe and was living among the people of Israel. Joshua 14:7 states that Moses had handpicked Caleb as the representative of Judah to spy on the land of Canaan at Kadesh-barnea when he was 40 years old.

Although Caleb was a Kenizzite, originally of the "mixed multitude" (aka, "rabble"), he was later admitted into the tribe of Judah, which was the largest tribe with 74,600 men. Furthermore, he was chosen by Moses to represent the tribe of Judah. This probably was possible because he had succumbed to faith fully in the Lord after experiencing the ten plagues in Egypt, the miracle of parting the Red Sea, the guidance of the pillar of cloud and the pillar of fire, the manna and the quails, the living waters from the rocks, victory in war against Amalek, and all the experiences in the wilderness that demonstrated the Immanuel presence of God.

Upon his return from spying out the land of Canaan, he stood with Joshua to proclaim before the congregation that God would surely give the land to them (Num 14:6–10). In Numbers 14:24, God blessed him, "But My servant Caleb, because he has had a different spirit and has followed Me fully, I will bring into the land which he entered, and his descendants shall take possession of it." Caleb was among the first generation of the Israelites in the wilderness journey, but he received God's special promise that he would not die during the 40-year journey and go into Canaan.

(2) Caleb's resolute covenantal faith

Joshua 14 narrates the process through which Caleb receives his plot of land in Canaan with much importance. By having an unwavering faith that God would certainly fulfill His promise to give the land of Canaan to Israel, he became a paragon for all Israelites who had received the same covenant. He was able to express his volition to fight for the land by saying, "I am still as strong today as I was in the day Moses sent me;

as my strength was then, so my strength is now, for war and for going out and coming in" (Josh 14:11), because he knew the importance of the Promised Land better than anyone else. Also because he had firm faith and conviction in God's promise, "I will give the land on which he has set foot" (Deut 1:36), he took on the challenge to conquer Hebron.

Ever since he was called in Kadesh-barnea, Caleb firmly held onto God's promise steadfast even after a long time of 45 years had passed. He requested to take the rugged hill country of Hebron as his inheritance and conquered it because he confidently believed that God would surely fulfill the covenant that He had made with Abraham despite the fact that it still was not fulfilled after 682 years had already passed. He went forth with God's covenant at the forefront (Deut 1:34–36) and eventually conquered the covenantal land of Hebron (Deut 14:14) through faith and life that believed in the fulfillment of the covenant (Num 14:7–9; Josh 14:10–12).

We who live in a world of unbelief must heed to the cry of faith ringing throughout the wilderness of Kadesh; "We should by all means go up and take possession of it, for we shall surely overcome it!" (Num 13:30), "Now then, give me this hill country ... and I shall drive them out as the Lord has spoken!" (Josh 14:12).

3. The Duration of the Conquest of Canaan

Caleb made mention of his age after most of Canaan had been conquered (Josh 14:7, 10). Through Caleb's age, the duration of the conquest and settlement is estimated to have been about 16 years.

(1) Caleb was 40 years old when the twelve spies were sent into Canaan (1445 BC)

After the exodus, the Israelites remained at Mount Sinai for about one year before they marched again. This was 1445 BC, the twentieth day of the second month of the second year as Numbers 10:11 states, "Now it came about in the second year, in the second month, on the twentieth of the month, that the cloud was lifted from over the tabernacle of the testimony."

Not too long after this, Caleb was chosen to represent the tribe of Judah when the 12 spies were chosen to enter Canaan. He was 40 years old at this time.

Joshua 14:7 "I was forty years old when Moses the servant of the LORD sent me from Kadesh-barnea to spy out the land, and I brought word back to him as was in my heart."

Numbers 13:6 ... from the tribe of Judah, Caleb the son of Jephunneh.

(2) Caleb was 79 years old when the Israelites entered Canaan (1406 BC)

Caleb was called at the age of 40 in 1445 BC as one of the 12 spies. Thus, Caleb was 79 years old when the Israelites entered Canaan in 1406 BC after about 38 years of the wilderness wanderings.

Deuteronomy 2:14 "Now the time that it took for us to come from Kadesh-barnea, until we crossed over the brook Zered, was thirty-eight years; until all the generation of the men of war perished from within the camp, as the LORD had sworn to them."

(3) Caleb was 85 years old when the main regions in Canaan were conquered and the land distributed (1400 BC)

Joshua 14:10 "And now behold, the LORD has let me live, just as He spoke, these forty-five years, from the time that the LORD spoke this word to Moses, when Israel walked in the wilderness; and now behold, I am eighty-five years old today."

Caleb was 85 years old when he received the land of Hebron as his inheritance in 1400 BC. Although 45 years had passed since he was called at the age of 40 (1445 BC), he demonstrated his strength by asking for the hill country of Hebron (Josh 14:10–13).

Thus, the conquest of the main regions lasted from the time the Israelites entered Canaan in 1406 BC until the beginning of the land distribution process in 1400 BC (Caleb was age 85)—about six years. Joshua 11:18 states, "Joshua waged war a long time with all these kings." The phrase "a long time" is estimated to have been about six years.

(4) The structure of the Book of Joshua

The book of Joshua is divided largely into three parts according to the conquest period.

(i) Part 1 (Josh 1:1–12:24)

Part 1 is a narrative about the completion of the six-year period of preparation and conquest of the main regions from 1406 BC to 1400 BC.

(ii) Part 2 (Josh 13:1–21:45)

Part 2 is a narrative of the ten years it took for the land to be distributed and and for the 12 tribes to settle (from 1400 BC to 1390 BC).

(iii) Part 3 (Josh 22:1–24:33)

Part 3 is a narrative of the return of the tribes of Reuben, Gad, and the half-tribe of Manasseh; Joshua's dying instructions regarding Israel's permanent settlement in Canaan; Joshua's death (at the age of 110 [1390 BC]); and the burial of Joseph's bones in Shechem.

(5) The battles for the main regions of Canaan—(about six years)

After the long 40-year wandering in the wilderness, the Israelites finally arrived in the land where they would be permanently settled. However, this land was not an uninhibited land. Not only were there indigenous peoples already well settled in the land, but also the land was a battleground for the surrounding nations struggling for power. Thus, the conquest and settlement took time.

Joshua 11:18 states, "Joshua waged war a long time with all these kings," and Joshua 11:23 and Joshua 14:15 state that "the land had rest from war." These verses indicate that large battles for the conquest of the main regions had been continuous during the periods covered in Joshua 6–11.

They destroyed Jericho at the center (Josh 6), captured the city of Ai (Josh 8), defeated the united forces of the Amorites in the southern region (Josh 10:1–27), and annihilated the regions of Makkedah, Libnah, Eglon, Hebron, and Debir (Josh 10:28–39). Afterwards, Joshua led the victory against the allied forces of the northern regions at the waters of Merom (Josh 11:1–15).

Joshua and the Israelites conquered the main regions of Canaan over a period of six years and distributed the land among the 12 tribes, which were responsible for individually conquering and taking possession of their land. God could have commanded the Israelites to join forces to conquer the remaining unconquered land, but He commanded the distribution of the land even before all the regions were conquered. He did so in order to demonstrate that if they had faith that God's covenant would be fulfilled and trust in His sovereign power, each tribe could independently conquer and possess the land.

(6) The Distribution of land and settlement—(about ten years)

The Israelites, exhausted after the conquest of the main regions, were filled with fear regarding the rest of the land. Furthermore, tension was on the rise among the tribes because the relatively stronger tribes had taken possession of the central regions. The distribution process was delayed for these two regions. Thus, Joshua rushed to initiate the construction of the tent of meeting in order to reconfirm God's covenant regarding the land of Canaan and to restore the people's faith (Josh 18:1).

After this, minor conquest battles for settlement continued for ten years until Joshua died at the age of 110 in 1390 BC (Josh 24:29). The distribution of the land of Canaan was part of the fulfillment process of God's covenant with Abraham.

Although the nation of Israel faced the possibility of eradication before the exodus and faced hardships and endless battles during the 40-year wilderness journey and the conquest mission, at last God gave the land of Canaan to the Israelites as their inheritance.

In the land distribution process, God established borders on all four sides, and the land within those borders were allocated by drawing lots. There was no room for human interference. Everything progressed according to God's providence.

The victory of the Israelites in the battles of conquest was completely the result of God's sovereign work. In his last word of encouragement to the people, Joshua proclaimed that it was God who led them to victory in their battles: "And the Lord drove out from before us all the peoples, even the Amorites who lived in the land" (Josh 24:18; cf. 24:8, 11, 12).

Victory and defeat in the battles we face in our lives are also completely in God's hands (1 Sam 17:47; Prov 21:31). Moreover, possession of the heavenly inheritance is also possible only through God's sovereign providence, not by human methods. The God who chose the smallest nation in the world (Deut 7:6–7) and allowed them to enter Canaan will also give us possession of heaven by His sovereign providence. However, just as the Israelites faced countless battles before they took possession of Canaan, we will also have to struggle "against the rulers, against the powers, against the world forces of this darkness, against the spiritual forces of wickedness in the heavenly places" until we possess heaven (Eph 6:10–12).

בכל דבר דעת דרך המסעות ארבעים שנה במדבר 'והרוחב והאורך של אאצן הקדושה מינה. מר

מדבר צין הוא קדש

עמלק

ים המלח

מדבר סיני

עיר כרמל

שבט

מדבר פארן

מדבר שור

באר שבע

שבט שמעון

שבט

ארץ פלשתם

ארץ גשן

פתם

שרה

צען

אלכסנדרי

לוח המסעות במדבר
אשר על פי היסעו ועל פי היחנו

טו׳ רתמה	א׳ רעמסס
טז׳ רמן פרץ	ב׳ סכת
יז׳ לבנה	ג׳ אתם
יח׳ רסה	ד׳ פיהחירת
יט׳ קהלתה	ה׳ מרה
כ׳ הרספר	ו׳ אילם
כא׳ חרדה	ז׳ ים סוף
כב׳ מקהלת	ח׳ מדבר סין
כג׳ תחת	ט׳ דפקה
כד׳ תרח	יו׳ אלוש
כה׳ מתקה	יא׳ רפידם
כו׳ חשמנה	יב׳ מרבר סיני
כז׳ מסרוה	יג׳ קברתהתאוה
	יד׳ חצרות

רט׳ הרהגדגד
ל׳ ילבתה
לא׳ עברנה
לב׳ עציןגבר
לג׳ מדברצין
לד׳ ההרהר
לה׳ צלמנה
לו׳ פונן
לז׳ אבת
לח׳ דיבןגד
לט׳ עלמן דבל
מ׳ הרי עברים
מא׳ ערבת מואב
רה׳ בני יעקן

PART FIVE

The Fulfillment of the Covenant

Thus far, we have examined, in chronological order, God's covenant made with Abraham, the migration of Jacob's 70-member family into Egypt and their 430-year stay, the exodus through Moses and the 40-year wilderness journey through Moses, and finally the triumphant entry into Canaan and possession of the land through Joshua. In actuality, all these processes were part of God's sovereign plan to establish His covenant with Abraham, and His administration to fulfill what has yet to be fulfilled.

Now, we will examine in detail all the parts of the covenant of the torch fulfilled within history. Here, we will confirm that God's Word is fulfilled to the smallest letter and stroke (Matt 5:18). Furthermore, we will learn how God used the people of faith to fulfill what He Himself promised and the faith and devotion of the people of faith that served His Will. As Hebrews 11:6 tells us, "And without faith it is impossible to please Him"; the fulfillment of the covenant was possible only by faith.

CHAPTER 15

The Fulfillment of the Prophecy Regarding Abraham and His Descendants

1. The Fulfillment of the Prophecy Regarding Abraham

(1) An heir for Abraham (Gen 15:1–5)

Abraham had his servant Eliezer of Damascus in mind as his heir, but God said, "This man will not be your heir; but one who shall come forth from your own body, he shall be your heir" (Gen 15:4). Then, God took him outside and, showing him the stars in the heavens, said, "So shall your descendants be" (Gen 15:5).

This promise was initially fulfilled when Sarah, his wife, gave birth to Isaac (Gen 21:1–7) when Abraham was 100 years old. Afterward, when the 70 members of Jacob's family entered Egypt, they received blessings so that they multiplied and became exceedingly mighty (Exod 1:7, 20). By the time they came out of Egypt, they were a great nation of more than two million people. This was the precise fulfillment of God's promise that Abraham's descendants would become as numerous as the stars.

(2) Abraham's longevity (Gen 15:15)

In Genesis 15:15, God prophesied of Abraham, "And as for you, you shall go to your fathers in peace; you shall be buried at a good old age." In accordance with God's Word, Abraham lived until he was 175 years old and was buried peacefully in the cave of Machpelah (Gen 25:7–10). Isaac was 75 years old and Jacob was 15 years old at this time (Gen 21:5; 25:26).

Genesis 25:8 states, "And Abraham breathed his last and died in a ripe old age, an old man and satisfied with life; and he was gathered to his people." In Hebrew, the words corresponding to the phrase "died in a ripe old age, an old man" is בְּשֵׂיבָה טוֹבָה זָקֵן וְשָׂבֵעַ (běśêbâ ṭôbâ zāqēn wěśābēaʿ) and refer not only to a long lifespan, but also to a very satisfying life without regrets. Furthermore, the phrase "breathed his last" in Hebrew is וַיִּגְוַע וַיָּמָת (wayyigwa' wayyāmot), meaning that he had filled all the years that God had allotted to him and ended his life satisfied.

Abraham lived exactly according to God's Word: "With a long life I will satisfy him, and let him behold My salvation" (Ps 91:16). Thus, the New Living Translation of Genesis 25:8 states, "And he died at a ripe old age, having lived a long and satisfying life. He breathed his last and joined his ancestors in death." God's blessing of longevity was fulfilled.

2. The Fulfillment of the Prophecy Regarding Abraham's Descendants

(1) Strangers in a foreign land and enslaved for 400 years (Gen 15:13)

Genesis 15:13 states, "And God said to Abram, 'Know for certain that your descendants will be strangers in a land that is not theirs, where they will be enslaved and oppressed four hundred years.'" This prophecy was fulfilled as the Israelites were enslaved for 400 years in Egypt (Exod 12:40–41; Gal 3:17).

(2) God will judge the nation whom they will serve (Gen 15:14)

Genesis 15:14 states, "But I will also judge the nation whom they will serve." The word *judge* means "to execute and govern." When God heard the groan of the Israelites, He remembered His covenant with Abraham. He fulfilled this prophecy when He Himself came down to judge Egypt (Exod 2:23–25; 4:31; 6:5–6; Acts 7:34).

God poured down ten plagues in Egypt, and through the parting of the Red Sea, Pharaoh and his entire army were drowned (Exod 14:26–31; 15:4–5, 10, 19; Ps 78:53; 106:11; 136:15). Thus, God judged Egypt and fulfilled His promise to "judge the nation whom they will serve."

(3) They will come out with many possessions (Gen 15:14)

Genesis 15:14 states, "And afterward they will come out with many possessions." God allowed the Israelites to come out of Egypt with great possessions, thereby fulfilling His promise in 636 years since the covenant was given. Ahead of the exodus, God commanded Moses, "Speak now in the hearing of the people that each man ask from his neighbor and each woman from her neighbor for articles of silver and articles of gold" (Exod 11:2). The phrase "speak now in the hearing of the people" is as follows in Hebrew:

$$\text{הָעָם} \quad \text{בְּאָזְנֵי} \quad \text{דַּבֶּר־נָא}$$

hā'ām   bĕ'oznê   dabbernā'

Here, the Hebrew word נָא (*nā'*) is a particle of entreaty or exhortation that indicates the importance of a situation.[81] Next, the word בְּאָזְנֵי (*be'oznê*), meaning "in the ears," is used when total obedience is required. Thus, God emphasized that the Israelites must totally obey His command to go and ask the Egyptians for their articles of gold and silver.

It must have been a difficult task for the Israelites who had lived practically as slaves for 400 years to go and ask for articles of gold and silver. However, when they obeyed God's command, God moved the hearts of the Egyptians so that the Israelites looked great and fearful in their sight. Consequently, the Egyptians wanted the Israelites to leave their land as soon as possible and gave to them as they requested, so in effect the Israelites plundered them (Exod 3:21–22; 11:2–3; 12:35–36).

> **Exodus 12:35–36** (NLT) And the people of Israel did as Moses had instructed; they asked the Egyptians for clothing and articles of silver and gold. [36]The LORD caused the Egyptians to look favorably on the Israelites, and they gave the Israelites whatever they asked for. So they stripped the Egyptians of their wealth!

Psalm 105:37 states, "Then He brought them out with silver and gold; and among His tribes there was not one who stumbled." The following is the Hebrew text:

$$\text{כּוֹשֵׁל} \quad \text{בִּשְׁבָטָיו} \quad \text{וְאֵין} \quad \text{וְזָהָב} \quad \text{בְּכֶסֶף} \quad \text{וַיּוֹצִיאֵם}$$

kôšēl   bišbāṭāyw   wĕ'ēn   wĕzāhāb   bĕkesep   wayyôṣî'ēm

The Hebrew text illustrates the people of Israelites coming out boldly with great possessions. Here, the word כּוֹשֵׁל (*kôšēl*) corresponds to the word *stumbled*, which means "to totter" or "to stagger." In the NKJV, this word is translated as "feeble."

While Egypt stood at the brink of ruin as a result of the ten plagues, there was not one Israelite who saw harm or stumbled as a result. Envision the scene of the Israelites, men and women, young and old, coming away with gold and silver and other precious articles and reveling in their newfound liberty. They walked out in a triumphant procession, marching in a stately manner like a general in his triumphant return from a great battle.

(i) The meaning behind the "many possessions"

The "many possessions" in Genesis 5:14 that the Israelites obtained from the Egyptians were the wages that God had accumulated for them. The Lord gave the Israelites "favor in the sight of the Egyptians, so that they let them have their request. Thus, they plundered the Egyptians" (Exod 12:36).

Although the Egyptians did not remember, God kept an account of the Israelites' labor in Egypt for 400 years and allowed them to draw their rightful wages at the time of the exodus. This is what God had promised through the covenant of the torch 636 years before the exodus (Gen 15:14).

Though unnoticed by other people, God continues with such work of justice for the righteous.

> **Proverbs 13:22** A good man leaves an inheritance to his children's children, and the wealth of the sinner is stored up for the righteous.
>
> **Proverbs 28:8** He who increases his wealth by interest and usury, gathers it for him who is gracious to the poor.
>
> **Job 27:16–17** Though he piles up silver like dust, and prepares garments as as the clay; [17]he may prepare it, but the just will wear it, and the innocent will divide the silver.

(ii) The Quantity of "many possessions"

The Hebrew word for "many" in the sentence "they will come out with many possessions" is גָּדוֹל (*gādôl*) and refers to the greatest and highest degree in magnitude, extent, number, and substance. The true quantity of these "many possessions" can be roughly estimated from all the gold that was used in the construction work for the sanctuary that Moses built in the Wilderness of Sinai.

> **Exodus 38:24–26** All the gold that was used for the work, in all the work of the sanctuary, even the gold of the wave offering, was 29 talents and 730 shekels, according to the shekel of the sanctuary. [25]And the silver of those of the congregation who were numbered was 100 talents and 1,775 shekels, according to the shekel of the sanctuary; [26]a beka a head (that is, half a shekel according to the shekel of the sanctuary), for each one who passed over to those who were numbered, from twenty years old and upward, for 603,550 men.

All the many possessions that the Israelites brought with them from Egypt were used to build the sanctuary in the wilderness. The construction cost for the sanctuary in today's terms amounts to approximately $321,501,000. Thus, the prophecy that they would come out with many possessions was fulfilled (Gen 15:14).

Amount offered	Shekels	Equivalent to today's wage[82]
Gold: 29 talents and 730 shekels	1,305,730 shekels	~$261,146,000
Silver: 100 talents and 1,775 shekels	301,775 shekels	~$60,355,000
Total: ~$321,501,000		

(4) The Israelites will possess the land of Canaan and live in it (Gen 15:18–21)

In Genesis 15:18–21, God assigned the boundaries of the land of Canaan, which the Israelites would possess. The Bible records that the Israelites conquered the land within those boundaries later when they arrived in Canaan.

> **Joshua 21:43–45** So the LORD gave Israel all the land which He had sworn to give to their fathers, and they possessed it and lived in it. ⁴⁴And the LORD gave them rest on every side, according to all that He had sworn to their fathers, and no one of all their enemies stood before them; the LORD gave all their enemies into their hand. ⁴⁵Not one of the good promises which the LORD had made to the house of Israel failed; all came to pass.

There was a portion of land that remained unconquered, but even this land was totally conquered during the reigns of King David and King Solomon (1 Kgs 4:21; 2 Chr 9:26). The complete fulfillment of the Promised Land according to the covenant of the torch was confirmed again through Joshua's last words.

> **Joshua 23:14** "Now behold, today I am going the way of all the earth, and you know in all your hearts and in all your souls that not one word of all the good words which the LORD your God spoke concerning you has failed; all have been fulfilled for you, not one of them has failed."

This was Joshua's proclamation that God's covenant of the torch with his ancestor Abraham was fulfilled. God guided history through His sovereign providence since He first ratified the covenant of the torch 692 years prior to the conquest of Canaan, and when the time came, He fulfilled every part of the covenant without exception (Ps 105:42–44).

CHAPTER 16

The Fulfillment of the Prophecy "In the Fourth Generation They Will Return Here" (Gen 15:16)

In Genesis 15:16, God said, "Then in the fourth generation they shall return here." The fourth generation mentioned in this verse begins with Abraham. Let us examine how this promise is fulfilled.

1. According to the Genealogies, How Many Generations Passed before They Returned to Canaan?

(1) According to Moses' genealogy

At a sweeping glance, it appears that there were eight generations from Abraham until his descendants returned to Canaan. This is because Moses was the seventh generation from Abraham. Abraham gave birth to Isaac, Isaac to Jacob, Jacob to Levi (one of his 12 sons), Levi to Kohath, Kohath to Amram, and Amram to Moses (Exod 6:16–20). With two months left before the grand entrance into Canaan, in the fortieth year, on the first day of the eleventh month (Deut 1:3), Moses went up from the plains of Moab to Mount Nebo, to the top of Pisgah, which is opposite Jericho (Deut 34:1–6). From there, he looked upon all the land of Canaan and died. After his death, when the Israelites entered Canaan under Joshua's leadership, Moses' son Gershom entered Canaan (Exod 2:22; 18:3). Thus, based on Moses' genealogy, it appears that the Israelites entered Canaan eight generations after the covenant was ratified.

¹Abraham ———— ²Isaac ————— ³Jacob ———— ⁴Levi ——— ⁵Kohath ———

⁶Amram ———— ⁷Moses ——— ⁸Gershom   (Exod 6:16–20)

However, as discussed in chapter 2 of this book, it is erroneous to conclude that there were only four generations from Levi to Moses during the 430 years. It is more reasonable to assume that, similar to the Ancient Near East practice of recording genealogies, there must have been generations omitted between the four generations. Thus, there must have been more than eight generations between Abraham until the entry into Canaan.

(2) According to Joshua's genealogy
According to Joshua's genealogy, which has no omissions, the Israelites entered Canaan after 14 generations. The following illustrates Joshua's genealogy from Abraham to Ephraim to Joshua:

[1]Abraham ——	[2]Isaac ———	[3]Jacob ——	[4]Joseph ——	[5]Ephraim
[6]Beriah ———	[7]Resheph ——	[8]Telah ——	[9]Tahan ——	[10]Ladan
[11]Ammihud —	[12]Elishama —	[13]Non ——	[14]Joshua	(1 Chr 7:20–27)

According to the genealogy above, starting from Abraham, the Israelites entered Canaan after 14 generations. This is an exact calculation since Joshua, who carried Joseph's bones into Canaan, was from the tribe of Ephraim, who was a descendant of Joseph (Num 13:8).

Thus, the prophecy "In the fourth generation they shall return here" is not in agreement with Joshua's genealogy. How, then, is the prophecy "In the fourth generation they shall return here" fulfilled?

2. Who Was the Fourth Generation?

We have previously validated the claim that the beginning of "in the fourth generation" is Abraham. Who, then, are the three generations after Abraham, and who is the fourth generation?

(1) Isaac—the inheritance of faith after Abraham
We have seen that Isaac inherited the faith and the will of the covenant from Abraham. This was proven from Isaac's total obedience on a mount in Moriah and his faith in his father, Abraham, and in the God whom he served. Had he not inherited Abraham's faith, he would not have been able to obey in a situation where he would be killed as a sacrifice offering. At an age when he was strong enough to carry the wood for the offering, without faith he would have resisted his father's attempt to bind him to the altar (Gen 22:9).

In addition, Isaac was Abraham's heir whom God acknowledged. In Genesis 15:4, God said, "But one who shall come forth from your own body, he shall be your heir." In Genesis 17:21, God also said, "But My covenant I will establish with Isaac, whom Sarah will bear to you at this season next year." Furthermore, Romans 9:7–9 states, "Neither are they all children because they are Abraham's descendants, but: 'through Isaac your descendants will be named.' That is, it is not the children of the flesh who are children of God, but the children of the promise are regarded as descendants. For this is a word of promise: 'At this time I will come, and Sarah shall have a son.'" When God said "through Isaac your descendants will be named," He confirmed that Isaac was the true heir to Abraham's inheritance of faith.

(2) Jacob—the inheritance of faith after Isaac

Isaac's second son, Jacob, inherited the faith after him. Between Isaac's two sons, Esau and Jacob, Jacob obtained the birthright and the blessing of the firstborn (Gen 25:22–34; 27:5–40; Mal 1:2–3).

> **Romans 9:10–13** And not only this, but there was Rebekah also, when she had conceived by one man, our father Isaac; [11]for though twins were not yet born, and had not done anything good or bad, in order that God's purpose according to choice might stand, not because of works, but because of Him who calls, [12]it was said to her, "The older will serve the younger." [13]Just as it is written, "Jacob I loved, but Esau I hated."

Although Esau was the firstborn, he despised his birthright (Gen 25:34) and did not receive the blessing of the firstborn (Gen 27:23, 35–36), which ultimately went to Jacob. Jacob became the heir to inherit the faith after Abraham and Isaac.

This was the fulfillment of the revelation that his mother, Rebekah, received while her sons were in her womb (Gen 25:23). This was also the result of the covenantal faith that Jacob, who enjoyed dwelling in tents, inherited after spending 15 years in the same tent with Abraham and Isaac (Gen 25:27; Heb 11:9).

As the third generation to inherit the covenant after Isaac, Jacob was a man of faith who held strong conviction in the covenant and expended his whole life for its fulfillment. For this reason, God said of Himself, "I am the God of Abraham, the God of Isaac, and the God of Jacob" (Gen 28:13; Exod 3:6; 4:5; 1 Kgs 18:36; Matt 22:32; Mark 12:26; Luke

20:37; Acts 3:13). This is evidence that God had acknowledged these three generations: Abraham, Isaac, and Jacob.

(3) The inheritance of faith after Jacob

Jacob, who was renamed Israel, had 12 sons who became the 12 tribes of Israel (Gen 49:1, 28). His 12 sons in the order of birth are: Reuben, Simeon, Levi, Judah, Dan, Naphtali, Gad, Asher, Issachar, Zebulun, Joseph, and Benjamin (Gen 29:31–30:24; 35:18, 23–26). Who, then, among his 12 sons, was the heir to the inheritance of faith? In other words, who was the fourth generation?

3. Reuben and the Inheritance of Faith

The Bible always refers to Reuben as "Reuben, Israel's first-born" (Exod 6:14; Num 1:20; 26:5; 1 Chr 5:1, 3). In addition, when Jacob was prophesying about Reuben's future, in just Genesis 49:3 alone, he emphasized five times that Reuben was his firstborn. He called Reuben "my first-born," "my might," "the beginning of my strength," "preeminent in dignity," and "preeminent in power." Here, "dignity" refers to an authority so great that it cannot be violated, and "preeminent" in Hebrew is יֶתֶר (yeter), meaning "excellence."

During the patriarchal age, the firstborn would inherit the position of the family priest (Exod 29:9), and the phrase "preeminent in dignity" has a connection to the firstborn taking on the role of the priest. "Preeminent in power" describes the ability to rule over the family or the firstborn's right to represent the family during wartime. No matter what anyone says, Reuben, preeminent in dignity and preeminent in power, was Jacob's firstborn.

(1) The nature of Reuben, the firstborn

Various verses in the Bible describe Reuben's nature as the firstborn.

When his violent brothers sought to kill Joseph, Reuben, as the firstborn, thought first of his father. He suggested that they not shed blood, but instead throw Joseph into a pit, thereby saving his life (Gen 37:21–22, 29–30).

> **Genesis 37:21–22** But Reuben heard and rescued him out of their hands and said, "Let us not take his life." [22]Reuben further said to them, "Shed

no blood. Throw him into this pit that is in the wilderness, but do not lay hands on him"—that he might rescue him out of their hands, to restore him to his father.

Many years later, when Jacob's sons went to Egypt to buy food because of the famine and were accused of being spies, Reuben recalls how they had attempted to kill Joseph in the past, saying, "Now comes the reckoning for his blood" (Gen 42:22).

During this first trip to Egypt, Simeon was taken captive until they brought Benjamin back with them in their second trip. When the sons recounted this story to their father, Jacob, he became very sad, fearing that he may also lose Benjamin. Here, Reuben, as the firstborn, makes a self-sacrificing gesture. He reassures Jacob saying that he would bring Jacob's beloved Benjamin back or else his two sons would be put to death.

> **Genesis 42:36–37** And their father Jacob said to them, "You have bereaved me of my children: Joseph is no more, and Simeon is no more, and you would take Benjamin; all these things are against me." [37]Then Reuben spoke to his father, saying, "You may put my two sons to death if I do not bring him to you; put him in my care, and I will return him to you."

Thus, there are many examples of Reuben's nature. As the firstborn, he had a sense of responsibility, a self-sacrificing attitude as a representative of all the sons, and a special devotion to his father, Jacob.

(2) Reuben loses the right of the firstborn

If Reuben had the character of the firstborn, why did he lose the right of the firstborn and the ability to become the heir of faith? The answer may be found in Jacob's prophecy regarding Reuben's future.

> **Genesis 49:4** (NASB) "Uncontrolled as water, you shall not have preeminence, because you went up to your father's bed; then you defiled it—he went up to my couch.

> **Genesis 49:4** (NIV) "Turbulent as the waters, you will no longer excel, for you went up onto your father's bed, onto my couch and defiled it."

Here, "you shall not have preeminence" means that Reuben was unable to fulfill his duty as the firstborn. He had all the physical characteristics. His appearance was like the choicest vine expected to produce good grapes, but he produced only worthless fruit (Isa 5:2).

Genesis 49:4 explains in clear detail why Reuben lost his right of the firstborn. He went up to his father's bed. The expression "you defiled" is in the Piel perfect form, referring to an unlawful and immoral act of harlotry. It means that Reuben lay with Bilhah, his father's concubine (Gen 35:22).

Why did Reuben commit such a sin? Genesis 49:4 states that he was "uncontrolled as water." In this verse, "uncontrolled" in Hebrew is פַּחַז (pāḥaz), meaning "to be wanton," "to be reckless," "to be insolent," or "to be undisciplined."[83] In other words, Reuben could not control the lusts of his flesh and committed the crime of incest.[84]

1 Chronicles 5:1 states, "Now the sons of Reuben the first-born of Israel (for he was the first-born, but because he defiled his father's bed, his birthright was given to the sons of Joseph the son of Israel; so that he is not enrolled in the genealogy according to the birthright," connecting the loss of the birthright to the defiling of his father's bed. Although he was Jacob's firstborn according to the flesh, he lost that birthright because of his hideous sin.[85]

Reuben was Jacob's firstborn. Hence, he indisputably would have received a double portion of the inheritance had he not sinned (Deut 21:15-17). In fact, the record states that Reuben appears after Judah precisely because Reuben, by his incestuous relationship with his father's concubine (Gen 35:22), had lost the rights of the firstborn.[86]

According to the law, a man who lies with his father's wife has uncovered his father's nakedness and must be put to death (Lev 18:6–8; Deut 22:30; 27:20).

Leviticus 20:11 "If is a man who lies with his father's wife, he has uncovered his father's nakedness; both of them shall surely be put to death, their bloodguiltiness is upon them."

Moses commanded the Israelites to hold a ritual to proclaim blessings and curses on Mount Gerizim and Mount Ebal respectively. To proclaim the blessings, they were to put Simeon, Levi, Judah, Issachar, Joseph, and Benjamin on Mount Gerizim; to proclaim the curses, they were to stand Reuben, Gad, Asher, Zebulun, Dan, and Naphtali on Mount Ebal (Deut 27:11–26). The tribes that were set on the mount of blessings were children of Jacob's wives, Leah and Rachel. Although Reuben was the first son of Jacob's wife, he was set on Mount Ebal, and among the curses proclaimed on Mount Ebal was one pertaining to an act similar to the one Reuben committed.

Deuteronomy 27:20 "'Cursed is he who lies with his father's wife, because he has uncovered his father's skirt.' And all the people shall say, 'Amen.'"

A father's bed is his authority. Thus, Reuben did not simply commit adultery; he defiled his father's bed and committed the grave sin of challenging his father's authority.

Absalom, King David's son, also committed the sin of lying with his father's concubines (2 Sam 12:11–12; 16:21–22), and he encountered a wretched end to his life. While he was riding on his mule, it went under some thick branches of a great oak, and his long hair got caught in the oak. Then, Joab pierced him with the spear, and the ten young men who carried Joab's armor gathered around and struck Absalom and killed him (2 Sam 18:9–15).

Through the account of how Reuben lost the birthright of the firstborn, we learn that although a person may be preeminent in power, with one act of adultery that person loses all the blessings and rights received from God.

(3) Reuben's end

Reuben was the first son born to Leah. He was born in the midst of happiness and love (Gen 29:31–32), and in him were Jacob's greatest expectations. When Jacob summoned his sons together to prophesy about what would befall them in the future (Gen 49:1) and bless them according to the blessing appropriate for each one (Gen 49:28), he stripped Reuben of his firstborn rights saying, "You shall not have preeminence" (Gen 49:3–4).

Just as Jacob blessed his 12 sons before he died, Moses also assembled the Israelites (more than two million) and blessed each tribe (Deut 33). Amazingly, Jacob's blessing of the 12 sons bears a connection to Moses' blessing of the 12 tribes.

Where is Reuben's blessing among the blessings of Moses? In Deuteronomy 33, before Moses blessed the tribe of Judah, Moses prayed for the tribe of Reuben. It was not so much a blessing for the tribe of Reuben, but a prayer on behalf of the tribe out of a concern that they will continue to decrease in number and disappear. It was a plea for mercy and an appeal to preserve the tribe.

Deuteronomy 33:6 (NASB) "May Reuben live and not die, nor his men be few."

Deuteronomy 33:6 (NLT) Moses said this about the tribe of Reuben: "Let the tribe of Reuben live and not die out, though they are few in number."

Toward the end of the wilderness journey, when Korah and his men rebelled against Moses and Aaron's authority out of envy, two leaders in the movement, Dathan and Abiram, were Reuben's sons (Num 16:1, 26–33; Deut 11:6). As a consequence of the rebellion, the earth opened its mouth and swallowed up the two men and their families, and all the men who belonged to Korah, as well as their possessions (Num 16:32). Furthermore, fire came forth and consumed the 250 men who were offering the incense (Num 16:35).

The immature people of Israel, even after witnessing the curse caused by the Korah rebellion, did not repent; they blamed Moses and Aaron for the incident and grumbled against them. This brought the wrath of God upon them so that a plague struck them, killing 14,700 people (Num 16:41–50). This incident probably had a large impact on the decrease in the number of the tribe of Reuben. During the second census, there were 2,770 fewer men than during the first census (Num 1:21; 26:7). This is why Moses pleaded that the tribe of Reuben should not decrease any further.

During the land allocation process after entry into Canaan, the fleshly tendencies and selfishness of the tribe of Reuben became evident yet again. With the crossing of the Jordan River ahead of them, the tribe of Reuben and the tribe of Gad discovered abundant pastureland for their exceedingly large number of livestock (Num 32:1). With little thought to the task of conquering the land of Canaan, they requested this portion of land from Moses so that they could possess the land before any of the other tribes.

Clearly, the inheritance of the land was to be decided by drawing lots (Num 33:54; 34:13; Josh 14:1–2). Furthermore, with the battle for the conquest of Canaan still ongoing, this was not the time to be requesting land. Thus, their untimely and evil request angered Moses. By using the example of the ten spies' bad report uttered 38 years earlier at Kadesh, Moses warned that God might once more abandon the Israelites in the wilderness on account of the disobedience of the two tribes (Num 32:6–15).

Numbers 32:13–15 "So the LORD's anger burned against Israel, and He made them wander in the wilderness forty years, until the entire generation of those who had done evil in the sight of the LORD was destroyed. [14]Now behold, you have risen up in your fathers' place, a brood of sinful men, to add still more to the burning anger of the LORD against Israel. [15]For if you turn away from following Him, He will once more abandon them in the wilderness; and you will destroy all these people."

The descendants of Reuben, like their ancestor, were disinterested in the spiritual blessings and had their eyes set on being first in terms of worldly blessings.

Likewise, those who claim to be Christians today, but are apathetic and lazy in doing God's work because they are so engrossed in their selfish lives and fleshly pleasures, will be excluded from the blessing of becoming God's firstborn (Matt 7:21-23; Rom 8:5-8).

4. Joseph and the Inheritance of Faith

1 Chronicles 5:1–2 Now the sons of Reuben the first-born of Israel (for he was the first-born, but because he defiled his father's bed, his birthright was given to the sons of Joseph the son of Israel; so that he is not enrolled in the genealogy according to the birthright. [2]Though Judah prevailed over his brothers, and from him the leader, yet the birthright belonged to Joseph)....

In Hebrew, "birthright" is בְּכוֹרָה (bĕkôrâ), referring to the birthright of the firstborn, the right of the primogeniture (Gen 25:31–34; 27:36). This is clear evidence that following Abraham, Isaac, and Jacob, the birthright is with Joseph.

The Bible provides much evidence supporting the belief that Joseph is the "fourth generation" with regard to the fulfillment of the covenant of the torch.

(1) Evidence that Joseph has the birthright

(i) Joseph was the son born to Rachel as a result of God's remembrance When Rachel and Jacob were childless after seven years of marriage, God remembered Rachel and opened her womb so that she gave birth to Joseph (Gen 30:22–24). God heard Rachel's prayers and gave her a child when she could not conceive. Also, Rachel was Jacob's most beloved wife. He loved her so much that the seven years he served for her seemed to him but a few days (Gen 29:20). Rachel was the only woman whom Jacob called his wife, and he showed special affection for the children that she bore (Gen 29:21; 44:27).

> **Genesis 44:27–28** "And your servant my father said to us, 'You know that my wife bore me two sons; ²⁸and the one went out from me, and I said, "Surely he is torn in pieces," and I have not seen him since.'"

This is evident in Genesis 37:3, which states, "Now Israel loved Joseph more than all his sons," noting that Israel made Joseph a multicolored tunic. In Hebrew, "loved" is אָהֵב (*'āhēb*), which refers to an unconditional exclusive love. In addition, in this verse the word is used in the Qal perfect form, indicating that Israel did not love Joseph just once, but that the love continued for a long time. According to the custom of those times, only the father and his firstborn wore multicolored tunics.

(ii) The name Zaphenath-paneah[87]

> **Genesis 41:45** Then Pharaoh named Joseph Zaphenath-paneah; and he gave him Asenath, the daughter of Potiphera priest of On, as his wife. And Joseph went forth over the land of Egypt.

Zaphenath-paneah (צָפְנַת פַּעְנֵחַ) was Joseph's Egyptian name, meaning "God has spoken" or "he who holds this name lives." There are other interpretations for this name, such as "savior of the world" and "governor of the district of the place of life." This name given by Pharaoh is a clear expression of how he had fully trusted Joseph.

On the other hand, Pharaoh's description of Joseph, "in whom is a divine spirit" (Gen 41:38) and "since God has informed you of all this" (Gen 41:49), clearly indicates that Pharaoh's trust was not in the man Joseph, but in the God who was with him. Pharaoh probably believed that Joseph was a person sent by God to save the world, or that the mystery of what God has planned to do would be revealed through him.

For this reason, without hesitation, Pharaoh yielded to Joseph a position of superior authority, second only to himself. He took off his signet ring and put it on Joseph's hand, clothed him in linen garments, and put a gold necklace around his neck. Pharaoh also made Joseph ride in his second chariot, and he required all the Egyptians to bow before Joseph. In addition, he gave to Joseph as a wife, Asenath (whose name means "gift of the sun-god"), the daughter of Potiphera, priest of

On, a man of power during those times (Gen 41:45), thus further so-lidifying Joseph's position.

> **Genesis 41:44** Moreover, Pharaoh said to Joseph, "I am Pharaoh, yet without your permission no one shall raise his hand or foot in all the land of Egypt."

The Egyptian name *Zaphenath-paneah*, with its implied meaning "sus-tainer of life" (from its literal meaning, "he who holds this names lives"), is the name that Pharaoh gave to Joseph with the intent of naturalizing him into Egypt. The meaning of the name, however, demonstrates God's great providence of redemption entrusted to Joseph in Egypt.

Although the main duty of the firstborn is to sustain his family, Joseph's responsibility surpassed that of sustaining Jacob's family (Gen 45:11). His responsibility broke through national boundaries; he was the sustainer of life (Gen 41:54–57) and thus the firstborn among all the people.

> **Genesis 50:20** "And as for you, you meant evil against me, God meant it for good in order to bring about this present result, to preserve many people alive."

As the famine grew increasingly severe, the people of the world had to go to Joseph to live. Likewise, only Jesus can save the people of this world from famine (Acts 4:12). He is the only "way" for all mankind (John 14:6), and He is the only food for the life of the world (John 6:51). Just as the people had to come before Joseph during the famine in order to live (Gen 41:56–57), in the end time, we too must draw closer to Jesus to live. This is the only way to sustain life and live spiritually and physically during the wretched famine of the end time (Amos 8:11).

(iii) The account in Hebrews 11

Hebrews 11 is the chapter on faith. Hebrews 11:1–3 is an introduc-tion describing the essence of faith. Hebrews 11:4 begins the account of the acts of faith within God's plan for salvation by the ancestors. Al-though they lived in different times and in different environments, they triumphed through a complete faith in God. Hebrews 11:8–21 records the three generations of faith: Abraham, Isaac, and Jacob. The record of Joseph as a man of faith follows Jacob's.

> **Hebrews 11:22** By faith Joseph, when he was dying, made mention of the exodus of the sons of Israel, and gave orders concerning his bones.

Among Jacob's 12 sons, none other besides Joseph appears in Hebrews 11, the chapter on faith. This is further biblical evidence that Joseph is the heir to the faith, the fourth generation, after Abraham, Isaac, and Jacob.

This is also evident in the structure of the Book of Genesis. Genesis is divided largely into two parts. Genesis 1–11 deals with the origin of the universe and mankind. Genesis 12–50 deals with the lives of the patriarchs Abraham, Isaac, Jacob, and Joseph. This structure is evidence that Joseph is the "fourth generation" of faith.

(iv) Because God is the God of the living

God always introduces Himself as "the God of Abraham, the God of Isaac, and the God of Jacob" (Gen 28:13; 48:15; 50:24; Exod 3:6, 15–16; 1 Kgs 18:36; 1 Chr 29:18). The New Testament states that God is not the God of the dead, but of the living. He is the God of Abraham, and the God of Isaac, and the God of Jacob (Matt 22:32; Mark 12:26–27). For God, "all live to Him" (Luke 20:37–38).

Obviously, Abraham, Isaac, and Jacob had lived, but their strength had left them, and they all died (Abraham [Gen 25:8]; Isaac [Gen 35:29]; Jacob [Gen 49:33]), yet God calls them "the living."

Why did Jesus call them "the living"? He did so because they possessed a faith that was alive (Heb 11:4, 8, 20, 21). God acknowledges those who possess living faith as being "alive." Romans 1:17 states, "But the righteous man shall live by faith." Jesus also said, "He who believes in Me shall live even if he dies, and everyone who lives and believes in Me shall never die" (John 11:25–26).

Among Jacob's 12 sons, who faithfully believed in God's Word of the covenant? Only Joseph, believed. Even at the moment of death, he believed that God would surely fulfill the covenant of the torch. He believed in its fulfillment as if it were at hand, right before his eyes. This is why just before he died, he spoke of the Israelites leaving Egypt to enter Canaan and commanded the Israelites to carry his bones with them (Gen 50:24–25). This was an act of faith based on a conviction in God's Word (Heb 11:22). Joseph's faith and hope in the fulfillment of the Word surpassed his own limited life. The genealogy of faith consisting of Abraham, Isaac, and Jacob continued to include Joseph.

(v) The content of Jacob's and Moses' blessings

Before Jacob died, he called Joseph and made him swear that he would bury his body in the land of Canaan, saying, "If I have found favor in your sight …" (Gen 47:29). The KJV translates it as, "If now I have found grace in thy sight.…" Jacob discovered that the grace of God was upon Joseph, and Jacob made him swear that he would bury his body in Canaan. This means, Jacob thought of Joseph as the one who would inherit the faith after him.

When Jacob was blessing his sons, each according to what was fitting for him (Gen 49:28), regarding Joseph he said, "The blessings of your father have surpassed the blessings of my ancestors up to the utmost bound of the everlasting hills; may they be on the head of Joseph, and on the crown of the head of the one distinguished among his brothers" (Gen 49:26).

Moses had a similar blessing for Joseph: "Let it come to the head of Joseph, and to the crown of the head of the one distinguished among his brothers" (Deut 33:16). Jacob and Moses described Joseph as "one distinguished among his brothers" (Gen 49:26; Deut 33:16). Here, "distinguished" in Hebrew is נָזִיר (nāzîr), meaning "one consecrated" or "devoted."[88] The same word was used in the Old Testament when referring to a Nazarite (Num 6:1–21).

In the NLT, the word *prince* is used in the place of "distinguished." In the Septuagint, the word *leader/ruler* is used. Thus, Joseph was consecrated as exceptional among his brothers, meaning that he was to rule over them as the firstborn. History shows that Jacob's and Moses' blessings were fulfilled so that when Joshua allocated the inheritance of the land of Canaan, Joseph's descendants, the tribe of Ephraim and the tribe of Manasseh, received blessings "distinguished" from the other tribes so that they became a "numerous people" (Josh 17:14, 17) and had "great power" (Josh 17:17).

(vi) Joseph was a man of service (a man of humility)
When Jesus' disciples asked Him, "Who then is greatest in the kingdom of heaven?" (Matt 18:1), He answered, "If anyone wants to be first, he shall be last of all and servant of all" (Mark 9:35). In Matthew 20:26, Jesus also states, "It is not so among you, but whoever wishes to become great among you shall be your servant." Jesus also taught His disciples to go and sit in the lowest place when they are invited to the wedding feast (Luke 14:10). These teachings probably awakened the disciples, who were enslaved by ambition and wanted to be served by others.

Jesus continued in Matthew 20:28, "The Son of Man did not come to be served, but to serve, and to give His life a ransom for many." On the night Jesus was captured, while He was eating His last supper with the disciples, He got on His knees to earnestly wash the feet of Judas Iscariot, who would betray Him later that night. By doing so, Jesus became the model of one who serves (John 13:4–11).

The firstborn is the great one. The one who serves others is the greatest of all (Matt 20:26). Thus, a true firstborn is one who serves and is humble. Among Jacob's sons, Joseph was the one who lived a life of service. From a young age, Joseph showed filial devotion to his father. He willingly obeyed when his father sent him to his brothers while they were pasturing the flock in Shechem, even though it was about 60 miles (100 km) from Hebron (Gen 37:13).

Later, when Joseph became a prime minister in Egypt, he still devotedly served his family by supporting his father (Gen 45:11) and by forgiving his brothers who had sold him into slavery and providing abundantly for them and their children until the end (Gen 45:5–8; 50:19–23). Through such service, Joseph displayed the true character of the firstborn.

(2) Joseph is not in the genealogy according to birthright (1 Chr 5:1)
The author of 1 Chronicles recorded the process of God's work of redemption in the history of the Israelites in a condensed genealogy. Chapter 1 covers the genealogy from Adam to Noah, and from Abraham to Jacob; chapter 2 covers the genealogy from Jacob to King David; and chapter 3 covers the genealogy from David until the deportation to Babylon. Chapter 4 covers the genealogy of the 12 tribes from the 12 sons of Jacob. Chapter 4 first introduces the genealogies of the tribes of Judah and Simeon, and then chapters 5–8 cover the genealogies of the remaining tribes, beginning with Reuben's.

However, the following startling verses are first recorded before the genealogy of Reuben is laid out.

> **1 Chronicles 5:1–2** Now the sons of Reuben the first-born of Israel (for he was the first-born, but because he defiled his father's bed, his birthright was given to the sons of Joseph the son of Israel; so that he is not enrolled in the genealogy according to the birthright. ²Though Judah prevailed over his brothers, and from him the leader, yet the birthright belonged to Joseph)....

This is clear evidence that the birthright was transferred to Joseph. However, one significant point is that the genealogies of the sons of Jacob were not recorded according to the birthright. In 1 Chronicles 5:1 its says, "so that he is not enrolled in the genealogy according to the birthright." If the birthright was transferred over to Joseph, why was Joseph not recorded as the firstborn in the genealogy?

(i) The meaning of "not enrolled in the genealogy according to the birthright"

Since Joseph obtained the birthright that Reuben had lost, it appears natural for Joseph to be recorded as the firstborn in the genealogy, and for Jesus to come through the tribe of Joseph. However, Judah appears as the firstborn, and Jesus' genealogy shows that He came through the lineage of King David of the tribe of Judah (Isa 11:1; Mic 5:2; Matt 1:1–3; Luke 3:33; Heb 7:14; Rev 5:5–6). The birthright of the firstborn was transferred from Reuben to Joseph, but the genealogy records Judah as the firstborn, not Joseph.[89]

(ii) The reason for not being enrolled in the genealogy according to the birthright

When Joseph heard that his father, Jacob, was sick in his deathbed, he brought his two sons to Jacob (Gen 48:1). Joseph did this because he desired to have his sons receive blessings from Jacob, the patriarch of the covenant. At this time, Jacob "collected his strength" and sat upon his bed (Gen 48:2) in order to accomplish his final duty of bequeathing the covenant of God.

Here, Jacob's action astonishes us. He takes Joseph's two sons (his grandsons Ephraim and Manasseh) as his own sons, and he gives each of them an inheritance in the land of Canaan.

> **Genesis 48:5–6** "And now your two sons, who were born to you in the land of Egypt before I came to you in Egypt, are mine; Ephraim and Manasseh shall be mine, as Reuben and Simeon are. ⁶But your offspring that have been born after them shall be yours; they shall be called by the names of their brothers in their inheritance."

Jacob refers to Ephraim and Manasseh as "mine." This implies that he will no longer regard Ephraim and Manasseh as his grandchildren, but as his own sons just like the rest of Jacob's children. Such action is closely linked to Joseph not being enrolled in the genealogy according to the birthright (1 Chr 5:1). Why, then, did Jacob take Joseph's two sons as his own?

First, it was to teach his grandsons of their covenantal roots, that they are the descendants of Abraham. Ephraim and Manasseh were born in Egypt, not in Canaan, through an Egyptian woman, Asenath, the daughter of Potiphera priest of On (Gen 41:45–50). Therefore, it was very possible for them to lose their covenantal roots as the descendants of Abraham. The reason lies in the fact that Egypt was the most powerful nation at that time, and they were sons of an especially powerful figure; they were the sons of the prime minister, the second-in-command in Egypt.

However, Jacob wanted them to live not as the heirs to Egypt's prime minister, but as the descendants of Abraham. For this reason, in Genesis 48:16, Jacob says, " And may my name live on in them, and the names of my fathers Abraham and Isaac; and may they grow into a multitude in the midst of the earth." Likewise, after Jacob raised his grandsons Ephraim and Manasseh to the position of his own sons, they became two independent tribes that constituted the twelve tribes of Israel.

Second, it was to acknowledge Joseph's birthright and to give him the blessing of a double portion. According to Deuteronomy 21:15–17, the blessing of a double portion is given to the firstborn. Before his death, Jacob took Joseph's two sons, Ephraim and Manasseh, as his own sons and allowed them to constitute independent tribes. Therefore, Joseph was able to receive two allotments of tribes in place of the one allotment that he was to receive if his sons had not replaced him. After this, the tribes were called "Ephraim" and "Manasseh" instead of "Joseph."

In all of this, God's profound providence to acknowledge Joseph as the true firstborn and to give him the blessing of double portion is evident. The fact that Joseph received the double portion signifies the succession of Jacob's birthright onto him (Deut 21:17; 1 Chr 5:2). As a general rule, the birthright is passed down to the firstborn; however, the actual firstborn, Reuben, lost it due to his lying with his father's concubine, Bilhah (Gen 35:22; 1 Chr 5:1). The second son Simeon and third son Levi also lost it due to the incident of the massacre at Shechem (Gen 34:25–31). Thus, the succession of the birthright according to birth order became meaningless.[90] Likewise, Jacob took in Joseph's two sons as his own sons, like Reuben and Simeon, and gave a double portion to

Joseph, thereby acknowledging his birthright.[91]

Third, it prophesied about the path through which Jesus Christ would come in God's administration in the history of redemption. Before he died, Jacob gathered his 12 sons and spoke to them about what would befall them in the future and blessed each one according to what was fitting (Gen 49:1, 28). He also prophesied about the coming of the Messiah when he blessed the fourth son, Judah, and the eleventh son, Joseph. It was a prophecy of the two paths through which the Messiah would come.

Genesis 49:10 states, "The scepter shall not depart from Judah, nor the ruler's staff from between his feet, until Shiloh comes, and to him shall be the obedience of the peoples." Here, "Shiloh" comes from the Hebrew verb שָׁלָה (*šālâ*), which means "to give rest" and "to make peace," typifying Jesus Christ. "Shiloh" refers to the Messiah, who is to come through the tribe of Judah.[92]

However, another path for the coming of the Messiah is presented, a path through the tribe of Joseph. As Jacob blesses his beloved son Joseph, he prophesies in Genesis 49:24, "But his bow remained firm, and his arms were agile, from the hands of the Mighty One of Jacob (from there is the Shepherd, the Stone of Israel)." Here, a great controversy surrounds the interpretation of the expression, "From there is the Shepherd, the Stone of Israel."

The expression "from there" in Hebrew is מִשָּׁם (*miššām*), a compound word formed from מִן (*min*), meaning "from" and שָׁם (*šām*), meaning "there" or "thence." When these parts are taken together, the word means "from there." The controversy lies in precisely how "there" is understood.

The KJV and the NASB understand "there" as Joseph himself, interpreting that from Joseph will come the Shepherd, the Stone of Israel (1 Cor 10:4; John 10:11).

> **Genesis 49:24** (KJV) But his bow abode in strength, and the arms of his hands were made strong by the hands of the mighty of Jacob; (from thence the shepherd, the stone of Israel).
>
> **Genesis 49:24** (NASB) "But his bow remained firm, and his arms were agile, from the hands of the Mighty One of Jacob (from there is the Shepherd, the Stone of Israel)."

However, the NIV renders "there" as the Shepherd, the Stone of Israel.

Genesis 49:24 (NIV) "But his bow remained steady, his strong arms stayed limber, because of the hand of the Mighty One of Jacob, because of the Shepherd, the Rock of Israel."

Regarding these two interpretations, Kwang Ho Lee states that "the latter interpretation avoids the discrepancy that arises between the Shepherd, the Stone of Israel who would come through the tribe of Joseph, and the ruler with the scepter who would come through the tribe of Judah. Yet, we must not overlook the fact that both interpretations are based on the Hebrew text. In order to resolve the complex issues in the text accurately, we must avoid interpreting the biblical text to fit its intention to our own logic."[93]

In fact, interpreting "there" as referring to Joseph (Gen 49:24) arouses a complex and contradicting problem that the Messiah would have to come both through the tribe of Judah, as prophesied in Genesis 49:10, and the tribe of Joseph. Hence, many people seem to avoid interpreting "there" as referring to Joseph in order to avoid this complex problem. However, when the Bible is perceived from the perspective of God's administration in the history of redemption, it becomes a clear prophecy without any complication at all.

The prophecy that the Messiah would come as a descendant of Judah means that He would come according to the lineage of the tribe of Judah (Heb 7:14). In actuality, Jesus came in the lineage of King David from the tribe of Judah, and thus Jacob's prophecy was precisely fulfilled (Matt 1:2–3). Romans 1:3 states that Jesus "was born of a descendant of David according to the flesh." Moreover, the interpretation of the prophecy that the Messiah would come from Joseph ("there") can be explained that although the Messiah would come physically from the line (of the tribe) of Judah, He was to come according to an order that surpasses the boundaries of a fleshly lineage.

In regard to this, Sung-Doo Kang notes that Jacob prophesied to Judah regarding the Messiah, "The scepter shall not depart from Judah, nor the ruler's staff from between his feet, until Shiloh comes, and to him shall be the obedience of the peoples" (Gen 49:10). For what reason, then, does he repeat his prophecy of the Messiah to Joseph, saying, "from there is the Shepherd, the Stone of Israel" (Gen 49:24)? His prophecy about Judah was a prophecy concerning the fleshly lineage, implying that Judah would be granted rule over Israel. Regarding the prophecy about Joseph, since his life was like the life of the Messiah, it meant that the Messiah would emerge from his lineage of faith.[94]

Jesus was conceived by the Holy Spirit and born of a virgin (Isa 7:14; Matt 1:18, 20). This is God's providence, which surpasses all human imagination. Outwardly, Jesus came as a descendant of Judah, but He was actually conceived by the Holy Spirit without regard to physical lineage, according to the order of Melchizedek (Ps 110:4; Luke 3:23; John 1:14, 18; 17:5; Col 1:15–19; 2:9; 1 Tim 6:14, 16; Heb 5:10; 6:20; 7:11, 17). Melchizedek was an actual historical figure (Gen 14; Heb 7:1–2) and someone who is quite a mysterious figure because he was without genealogy (Heb 7:3). Surely, Jesus came according to the order of Melchizedek, without regard to genealogy.

Hence, the apostle Paul, in Romans 1:3, says of Jesus that he "was born of a descendant of David according to the flesh" and thereby illustrates that Jesus Christ was perfectly human (His humanity). Furthermore, Paul continues, in Romans 1:4, to confirm and declare that Jesus Christ Himself, who overcame the power of death by His resurrection, is perfectly God (His divinity).

> **Romans 1:3–4** … concerning His Son, who was born of a descendant of David according to the flesh, [4]who was declared the Son of God with power by the resurrection from the dead, according to the Spirit of holiness, Jesus Christ our Lord.

Jesus, in whom humanity and divinity are one, is perfectly man and perfectly God (John 1:14, 18). This does not mean that He was not the Son of God prior to His resurrection, but that He has proven to be the Son of God even more clearly through His work of atonement on the cross and His resurrection.

Jacob prophesied, through Judah and Joseph, about the two paths by which the Messiah was to come according to the divine administration for redemption. Indeed, when Jesus came to this earth, all those prophecies were fulfilled.

5. The Fulfillment of the "Fourth Generation" through Joseph

Up to this point, we have studied that Joseph was the firstborn who fits in the place of the "fourth generation" of faith promised in the covenant of the torch. The promise God made through the covenant of the torch—that the Israelites will return to Canaan in the "fourth generation" (Gen 15:16)—was fulfilled through Joseph, the fourth generation from Abraham (Abraham, Isaac, Jacob, Joseph). Joseph died in Egypt at the age of 110 (Gen 50:26).

How, then, was this prophecy that they would return to Canaan in the fourth generation fulfilled?

(1) The fulfillment through Joseph's final request made by faith

In the year that Joseph died (1806 BC), it had already been 276 years since the covenant of the torch. Joseph firmly held onto the covenant that God swore to Abraham, Isaac, and Jacob. In his final words, he said that there would come a day when God will surely visit them and bring them to the land that He swore on oath to Abraham, Isaac, and Jacob (Gen 50:24).

The content of his final words was also what Joseph had heard from his father's last will and testament. As Jacob approached the end of his life, he called Joseph from among his 12 sons and made him put his hands under his thigh and swear that he would bury him in the family burial ground in Canaan (Gen 47:28–31). Then Jacob proclaimed with conviction, "Behold, I am about to die, but God will be with you, and bring you back to the land of your fathers" (Gen 48:21). Joseph never once forgot this promise with Jacob; even upon his own death, he held firmly on to the hope of fulfilling God's promise by entering Canaan. Thus, he made his descendants swear that they would carry his bones with them to Canaan when God visits them (Gen 50:25). Among Joseph's numerous achievements of faith, the author of Hebrews recorded only his final words about the Israelites' exodus from Egypt and his bones (Heb 11:22).

Although Abraham, Isaac, and Jacob were physically dead, God acknowledged their living faith and called them "the living" (Matt 22:32; Mark 12:26–27; Luke 20:37–38). Likewise, Joseph is physically dead, but his faith is alive. Thus, God's promise that they would return in the fourth generation was fulfilled through the four generations of living faith: Abraham, Isaac, Jacob, and Joseph. Just as Abel's faith still speaks even though he is dead (Heb 11:4; cf. Gen 4:10–11), the faith of these four generations is still alive today, crying out to this unbelieving and perverted generation.

Luke 20:38 "Now He is not the God of the dead, but of the living; for all live to Him."

(2) The fulfillment through Joseph's bones

Unlike Jacob, whose body was returned and buried in Canaan immediately after his death, Joseph requested that his bones not be buried but placed in a coffin and kept together with the Israelites in Egypt (Gen 50:24–25). Remembering the prophecy, "Know for certain that your descendants will be strangers in a land that is not theirs, where they will be enslaved and oppressed four hundred years" (Gen 15:13), and believing without a doubt that it would unmistakably be fulfilled, Joseph had demonstrated his wisdom by preserving his bones in Egypt until that time arrived. The bones of Joseph represented his unwavering faith in the covenant and thereby became a great sign of faith for the Israelites. To the Israelites who were deeply groaning under the oppression of Egypt, the very presence of Joseph's bones among them probably gave them the hope and expectation for the promised day even as they suffered through endless days of labor.

Joseph's bones were a symbol of the flaming torch shining brightly into the distant Promised Land of Canaan and even into the darkness of this present time. For this reason, John Sailhamer states, on the basis of Ezekiel 37:11, that "the bones of the faithful serve as a sign that the promise of the land still awaits its fulfillment."[95]

(i) Moses takes Joseph's bones

After 360 long years had passed since Joseph's last words, the Israelites finally came out of Egypt. Even in the midst of the difficulties of the exodus, Moses remembered what Joseph had implored of his descendants (Gen 50:24–25), and he did not forget to take up the coffin of Joseph's mummified remains (Exod 13:19). Moses' action was a sign of proclamation that showed that the exodus was not just merely a sudden liberation of a nation but rather an administration of God's providence to fulfill the covenant of the torch made from long ago.

(ii) Joseph's bones buried in Shechem

Joseph's bones, which Moses took up at the time of the exodus, passed through the 40 years of wilderness and the approximately 16-year period of the Canaan conquest and finally were buried in the land of Shechem in 1390 BC, after Joshua's death at the age of 110 (Josh 24:29–32). Indeed, Joseph's bones were buried according to his faith, based on God's words. Just as his body was embalmed as a mummy to be preserved without decay, so, too, was his living faith kept alive without decay over hundreds of years. In this way, Joseph entered the land of Canaan as the fourth generation of faith in fulfillment of God's covenant.

Despite the fact that the people who carried Joseph's bones changed and the years passed, the covenant that they would return in the fourth generation was finally fulfilled, precisely, at the destined time and through profound providence.

Early on, as God brought Jacob up to Egypt, He promised that He would surely lead Jacob back to Canaan (Gen 46:4). However, Jacob died in Egypt, and he could not return to Canaan. Did that prevent the fulfillment of God's promise? No. Although Jacob died, Joseph took his body and buried it in the cave of Machpelah, thus fulfilling God's promise (Gen 50:12–13). Likewise, although Joseph died in Egypt, through the burial of his bones in the land of Canaan, God's covenant of the torch was fulfilled by Joseph, the fourth generation succeeding Abraham, Isaac, and Jacob.

So profound is the redemptive administration of God found in the promise that they would return in the fourth generation! The bones of Joseph—the emblem of Israel's birthright—have now been buried in the land of Canaan just as Joseph had made the Israelites swear before his death. Thus, the promise of their return in the "fourth generation" (Gen 15:16) in God's covenant of the torch was fulfilled.

The covenant of the torch was fulfilled 692 years after it was made in 2082 BC. It was a proclamation to the whole world that the Word of the living God is always fulfilled no matter how much time passes by. Over the long haul of 692 years, God led the history by His sovereign providence and absolutely fulfilled every promise at the fullness of time. Hallelujah!

Joseph's bones! They were more than just dead and dried-up pieces of bones; they were the crucial reminder of God's everlasting trustworthiness and faithfulness in keeping His covenants. Thus, Joseph's tomb confirms the promise that the Israelites will return in the "fourth generation" (Gen 15:16) and God's promise will be fulfilled (Ps 105:9–11, 42–44).

✳ Here, the fact that the covenant of the torch is fulfilled in 692 years is revealed for the first time in history.

6. The Covenant of the Torch Fulfilled in Shechem

✳ The two contradictory accounts regarding Shechem are exposited for the first time in history.

Shechem, a city between Mount Ebal (3,000 feet [915 m] above sea level) and Mount Gerizim (2,800 feet [850 m] above sea level), was the hub of transportation centrally located between the Jordan River and the Mediterranean Sea. Unlike other Palestinian regions, this was a land abundant in water. It was located about 40 miles (65 km) north of Jerusalem and had Bethel on the west and Ai on the east (Gen 12:8).

After entering Canaan, Joshua renewed the covenant with the people of Israel and proclaimed the statute and ordinance as Moses had commanded at Shechem (Deut 27:1–26; Josh 8:30–35). It was also at Shechem that the Israelites rededicated themselves as the chosen people of God (Josh 24:1–28). Joseph's bones were promptly buried at Shechem.

> **Joshua 24:32** The bones of Joseph, which the children of Israel had brought up out of Egypt, they buried at Shechem, in the plot of ground which Jacob had bought from the sons of Hamor the father of Shechem for one hundred pieces of silver, and which had become and inheritance of the children of Joseph.

Joseph's bones were buried in Shechem approximately 416 years after he made the request for his bones to be buried in Canaan. The covenant of the torch was finally fulfilled when Joseph's bones were buried in Shechem.

Why was Shechem chosen as the burial place for Joseph's bones? What significance does the place hold that the Israelites journeyed so long to bury Joseph's bones there? Shechem was a profoundly important place in the history of redemption.

(1) Jacob and the land of Shechem
(i) Jacob purchases land

After Abraham was called, he passed through the land of Canaan and arrived in the land of Shechem, at the oak of Moreh. It was here that Abraham received God's covenant: "I will give this land to your descendants." Then, Abraham built an altar there for God, who established the covenant (Gen 12:5–7). As the place where the first covenant was received following the entry of the Israelites into Canaan, Shechem must have been an unforgettable, special place for both Abraham and his descendants.

Years later, Abraham's grandson Jacob left Paddan-aram and arrived at Shechem, where he camped. He bought a piece of land from the sons of Hamor, Shechem's father, for 100 pieces of silver and pitched his tent. There, he erected an altar to sanctify the place (Gen 33:18–20). Jacob called the altar where he worshiped before God "El-Elohe-Israel," meaning "God, the God of Israel."

> **Genesis 33:18–20** Now Jacob came safely to the city of Shechem, which is in the land of Canaan, when he came from Paddan-aram, and camped before the city. [19]And he bought the piece of land where he had pitched his tent from the hand of the sons of Hamor, Shechem's father, for one hundred pieces of money. [20]Then he erected there an altar, and called it El-Elohe-Israel.

Also, Shechem was the memorial place where Jacob, after receiving God's revelation, "Arise, go up to Bethel, and live there; and make an altar there to God" (Gen 35:1), along with his household and all who were with him, buried their foreign gods under the oak near Shechem (Gen 35:2–4).

(ii) Jacob's last will about the land of Shechem

When Jacob called Joseph and spoke of his last will, he stated that although he was about to die, God surely would bring Joseph along with the Israelites back to the land of Canaan, and Joseph would possess Shechem. In Genesis 48:21–22, Jacob states, "Behold, I am about to die, but God will be with you, and bring you back to the land of your fathers. And I give you one portion more than your brothers, which I took from the hand of the Amorite with my sword and my bow."

Here, it seems as if Jacob had undergone a battle to possess Canaan and won the land of Shechem. It was as if he himself had achieved what was later to be achieved by his descendants. By identifying himself with his descendants, Jacob assured them that the covenant of the torch surely will be fulfilled.

Genesis 48:22 in the Hebrew text is as follows:

אֲשֶׁר עַל־אַחֶיךָ אַחַד שְׁכֶם לְךָ נָתַתִּי וַאֲנִי

ʾăšer ʿal ʾaḥêkā ʾaḥad šĕkem lĕkā nātattî waʾănî

וּבְקַשְׁתִּי בְּחַרְבִּי הָאֱמֹרִי מִיַּד לָקַחְתִּי

ûbĕqaštî bĕḥarbı̄ hāʾĕmōrî miyyad lāqaḥtı̄

Here, Jacob included Joseph among those who will enter Canaan and used the word *you*, and especially in Genesis 48:22, by saying give "you" (singular) the land of Shechem, he validated that Joseph undoubtedly will enter the land of Shechem to possess it. In accordance with Jacob's last will, Joseph's bones later were buried in Shechem, and his descendants took possession of that land.

These last words that Jacob spoke in faith probably echoed in Joseph's heart throughout the remainder of his life. Joseph must have believed and Jacob's final words of faith probably echoed in Joseph's heart throughout his life, reminding him of the faith and hope that the covenant of the torch will be fulfilled through him.

(2) Two different burial accounts

A comparison of Genesis 33:18–20 and Acts 7:14–16 shows two conflicting accounts about where Joseph's bones were buried. Such a conflict can be explained only in light of God's administration in redemptive history.

(i) The issue concerning Jacob's burial place

According to Genesis 50:13, Jacob was buried in the cave of Machpelah, which "Abraham had bought along with the field for a burial site from Ephron the Hittite." Before Jacob died, he asked that his body be buried "in the cave that is in the field of Ephron the Hittite" (Gen 49:29), and in accordance with his will, Jacob's sons did for him just as he had commanded them; they buried him in the cave of Machpelah in the field of Ephron (Gen 50:12–13). This cave was the territory that Abraham bought from the Hittites for 400 shekels of silver (Gen 23:15–20).

However, Stephen called this burial place of Jacob "Shechem."

> **Acts 7:15–16** "And Jacob went down to Egypt and passed away, he and our fathers. [16]And there they were removed to Shechem, and laid in the tomb which Abraham had purchased for a sum of money from the sons of Hamor in Shechem."

Where, then, was Jacob actually buried?

Stephen was one of the seven deacons who were full of the Holy Spirit and wisdom (Acts 6:3). He was full of faith and power (Acts 6:8) and was a great preacher with such spiritual insight that the people were "unable to cope with the wisdom and the Spirit with which he was speaking" (Acts 6:8). The sermon in Acts 7, the longest chapter in

Acts, superbly justifies Jesus Christ by interpreting the history of the Old Testament from the perspective of God's administration in the history of redemption. Thus, Stephen, being such a man, could not have mistakenly identified Shechem as Jacob's burial place.

According to the vow that Joseph had made before Jacob, his father, he carried Jacob's bones to Canaan and indeed buried them in the cave of Machpelah (Gen 50:12–13). Why, then, did Stephen preach that Jacob was buried in Shechem and not in the cave of Machpelah (Acts 7:15–16)?

Actually, the only patriarch buried in the land of Shechem was Joseph. However, behind Joseph's burial in Shechem stood Jacob's faith, which God so highly acknowledged that He spoke as if Jacob was buried in Shechem also. In what way did Jacob's faith influence Joseph?

First, through his last will, Jacob passed down God's covenant that the Israelites would return to Canaan. In Genesis 48:21, Jacob delegates his final wish to Joseph: "Behold, I am about to die, but God will be with you, and bring you back to the land of your fathers" (Gen 48:21). Similarly, Joseph also speaks to his descendants just as Jacob had spoken: "I am about to die, but God will surely take care of you, and bring you up from this land to the land which He promised on oath to Abraham, to Isaac and to Jacob" (Gen 50:24).

Second, Jacob bought the land of Shechem where his firstborn, Joseph, would later be buried and passed that land down to him. Jacob was going to die in Egypt, but in the assurance of inheriting the land of Canaan as God had promised, Jacob gave the land of Shechem to Joseph (Gen 48:22).

Thus, the land of Shechem where Joseph was buried was the land that Jacob had personally purchased (Gen 33:18–20). By purchasing in advance the land of Shechem where Joseph's bones would eventually be buried, Jacob practically paved the way for the fulfillment of the covenant. Joshua 24:32 confirms that the land where Joseph's bones were buried was obviously the land that Jacob had bought in the past from the sons of Hamor, the father of Shechem.

As noted above, Joseph was buried in Shechem on the basis of Jacob's faith. Hence, Stephen was able to preach that Jacob was buried in Shechem even though Joseph was the only one buried there because Jacob was the one who had the insight of faith to purchase the land of Shechem and prepare it for Joseph.

In the New Testament, the "principle of representation" similarly appears during the healing of the centurion's servant. According to Matthew 8:5, the centurion personally came to Jesus, but the paralleling account in Luke 7:3 states that the centurion sent some Jewish elders to Jesus. The centurion himself did not actually come, but instead sent some elders on his behalf. Yet in Matthew, the faith of the centurion who had sent the elders was so greatly esteemed that it was narrated as if the centurion himself had come.

(ii) The issue concerning who purchased Shechem

Jacob was the one who purchased the land in Shechem. Genesis 33:18–20 makes it evident that Jacob had bought the land where he pitched his tent before the city of Shechem from the sons of Hamor, Shechem's father, for 100 pieces of silver. After purchasing the city of Shechem from the sons of Hamor and erecting an altar there, Jacob called it "El-Elohe-Israel," which means "God, the God of Israel" (Gen 33:18–20).

However, in the New Testament, Stephen, while preaching just before his martyrdom, explains that Abraham had purchased the land from the sons of Hamor (Acts 7:14–16). Who, then, really bought the land, Abraham or Jacob?

> **Acts 7:14–16** (NASB) "And Joseph sent and invited Jacob his father and all his relatives to come to him, seventy-five persons all. ¹⁵And Jacob went down to Egypt and passed away, he and our fathers. ¹⁶And there they were removed to Shechem, and laid in the tomb which Abraham had purchased for a sum of money from the sons of Hamor in Shechem."

> **Acts 7:14–16** (NLT) "Then Joseph sent for his father, Jacob, and all his relatives to come to Egypt, seventy-five persons in all. So Jacob went to Egypt. He died there, as did our ancestors. Their bodies were taken to Shechem and buried in the tomb Abraham had bought for a certain price from Hamor's sons in Shechem."

Why, then, would Stephen preach that Abraham had purchased the land, when actually it was Jacob who purchased it? In Stephen's sermon, the land of Canaan was, by all means, the land that God had promised to Abraham (Acts 7:3–5). Even though Jacob bought the Shechem burial ground, which was a mere parcel in the land of Canaan, it is possible to see it from a covenantal perspective as being the equivalent of Abraham purchasing it. Jacob, having lived in the same tent with Abraham for 15 years (Heb 11:9), was the one who inherited Abraham's covenantal faith in its entirety. Jacob bought the land in Canaan with the faith inherited from Abraham, believing in God's sure promise that He would give them the land of Canaan as an inheritance.

In particular, when Abraham, following God's command, left Haran and arrived in Canaan, it was here, at the land of Shechem, that he received the first covenant: "I will give this land to your descendants." Here, Abraham built an altar for God, who made the covenant (Gen 12:5–7). Yoon Sun Park states, "Although there is no written account of Abraham purchasing Shechem, Abraham couldn't have worshipped in someone else's territory, without having purchased the land then.... It seems that Abraham purchased the land, but later, the sons of Hamor seized the area. By the time Jacob reached that land, it was already one hundred years since the time of Abraham, and thus he repurchased the land."[96]

Although there is no verse in the Bible that explicitly maintains that Abraham actually purchased the land in Shechem, the fact that "he built an altar" is a validation of his faith; because he believed, he had already possessed the land promised by God.

The later generations of the Israelites, including Jacob, must have reaffirmed their faith in the covenant, which was given to Abraham and his descendants, when they saw the altar in Shechem and remembered Abraham.

Stephen must have understood this when he preached and said that Abraham purchased a land in Shechem. Although Jacob actually purchased the land, it can be seen from the covenantal perspective that Abraham fundamentally began the purchase. Jacob purchased the land, but Stephen must have said that Abraham purchased the land because he was a decisive influence in the purchase. Hence, this issue about the purchase of the land in Shechem is a mystery that can be understood only through faith in God's administration in the history of redemption.

(3) The redemptive significance of Shechem

The redemptive significance of Shechem, which holds the bones of Joseph, becomes clear through the studying of the origin of the name *Shechem*.

First, *Shechem* in Hebrews means "shoulder, bearing burdens."[97] *Shechem* originates from the verb שָׁכַם (*šākam*), which originally referred to loading something up early on one's shoulders or on the back of an animal. Just as in the meaning of the word *Shechem*, Jesus came to this earth and bore the heavy cross on behalf of all mankind. In Matthew 11:28, Jesus says, "Come to Me, all who are weary and heavy-laden, and I will give you rest." On His way to Golgotha, Jesus, with a heavy cross weighing down on Him, collapsed repeatedly. Eventually, He was crucified with the utmost cruelty; yet, he underwent all of this to unleash every burden from the entire human race.

> **Psalm 55:22** Cast your burden upon the LORD, and He will sustain you; He will never allow the righteous to be shaken.

> **Psalm 68:19** Blessed be the LORD, who daily bears our burden, the God is our salvation. Selah.

Second, the root word of *Shechem*, םכֶֽשְׁ (*šākam*), means "to rise early in the morning" or "to start early." Not only did Jesus bear our burdens and die on the cross, but also He rose again in the dawn of the third day, thereby breaking forth a new morning of hope for all humanity (Matt 28:1–6). By the cross, He resolved all of our burdens (Isa 14:25), and by the bright morning star, the resurrected Jesus shall return (Rev 22:16).

Hence, the root-meaning of the word *Shechem* brings to light Jesus' crucifixion and resurrection in view of the redemptive history. Today, those who have an assured faith in Jesus Christ's cross and resurrection will be able to completely fulfill the divine covenant of the torch.

CHAPTER 17

The blessing of Covenant of the Torch

The main character of the covenant of the torch is Joseph. Through his final wish on his deathbed, Joseph prophesied that although he would die, God surely would visit the Israelites and bring them up to the land of Canaan (Gen 50:24). Besides this prophecy, Joseph made his descendants swear that they would carry his bones out on the day that God visits them (Gen 50:25; Heb 11:22). This was because he was certain, even after 276 years since the covenant of the torch was made, that the covenant, unbroken and perpetual, would be passed down to his descendants and would surely be fulfilled. Hence, Joseph asked that when he died, a grand funeral like Jacob's be omitted and instead his body be embalmed and preserved (Gen 50:26).

Finally, in 1446 BC, 360 years after Joseph's death, God visited the Israelites, and they were delivered out of Egypt. At this time, Moses took Joseph's bones with him out of Egypt (Exod 13:19). Joseph's bones were buried at last in Shechem, after having endured 40 years in the wilderness and 16 years of war in Canaan (1390 BC, 692 years since the covenant of the torch) (Josh 24:32). The bones of Joseph were an unmistakable sign of the fulfillment of the covenant, and Joseph became the final hero to fulfill the covenant of the torch.

In this way, the life of Joseph, who believed in God's promise without any doubt, was a life bestowed with amazing blessings under God's exceptional protection and His absolute love. Joseph's unwavering faith, which looked forward to the land of Canaan, renders a great paradigm for today's Christians who are seeking after the kingdom of God. The blessings that Joseph received are also the blessings granted to the Christians who believe and follow God's Word today.

1. The Blessing That Joseph Received

In Genesis 49:22 Jacob describes Joseph's blessing: "Joseph is a fruitful bough, a fruitful bough by a spring; its branches run over a wall."

(1) The blessing described by "the fruitful bough"

In Genesis 49:22, the word for "fruitful" is פָּרָה (*pārâ*) in Hebrew, meaning "to bear fruit." Joseph's blessings of overflowing abundance did not only apply to the leaves, but also to the fruits on the boughs.

According to this analogy, Abraham would be the root since he is the father of faith, Isaac the sprout, and Jacob the stem. Twelve boughs came out of this stem and the most fruitful was the bough of Joseph.

Joseph's life was like that described in Psalm 1:3: "And he will be like a tree firmly planted by streams of water, which yields its fruit in its season, and its leaf does not wither." He prospered in whatever he did (Gen 39:2–3; 23). Also, Joseph lived a blessed life like that described in Jeremiah 17:8: "For he will be like a tree planted by the water, that extends its roots by a stream and will not fear when the heat comes; but its leaves will be green, and it will not be anxious in a year of drought nor cease to yield fruit."

Sure enough, Joseph's sons—Ephraim and Manasseh—became exceedingly great in their numbers: 72,700 in the first census and 85,200 in the second census. They had become so abundant that other tribes could not even come close in comparison (Num 2:18-21; 26:34-37). This is none other than the testimony of the "blessings of the breasts and of the womb" mentioned in Genesis 49:25. Moreover, Joseph's descendants inherited the most fertile land in the center of Canaan, and thus had abundant produce from the land (Josh 16:1–4). This was the result of the "blessings of heaven above" and the "blessings of the deep that lies beneath" as declared in Genesis 49:25. Therefore, the timely rain and dew along with an abundant water supply allowed them to enjoy the blessing of fecundity.

(2) The blessing described by "run over a wall"

Joseph lived a life that always overflow (i.e., "ran over") to plentifully profit others. Because of Joseph, God's blessings came upon Potiphar and all that grew in his field. Potiphar witnessed how God was with Joseph and how He made him to prosper in all he did (Gen 39:3). From the time that Joseph was made overseer of the house, "the LORD blessed the Egyptian's house on account of Joseph; thus the LORD's blessing was upon all that he owned, in the house and in the field" (Gen 39:5). Joseph's blessing of prosperity had come upon Potiphar and his house as well.

While Joseph was in prison, the entire prison and all the inmates were blessed. Because Joseph prospered in all that he did, the chief jailer did not supervise anything under Joseph's charge (Gen 39:20–23). Thus, the entire prison and its inmates enjoyed blessings with Joseph.

Furthermore, when Joseph was a governor in Egypt, Pharaoh and all of the Egyptians and the nearby nations were blessed. The people said, "You have saved our lives! Let us find favor in the sight of my lord, and we will be Pharaoh's slaves" (Gen 47:25). Since Joseph had provided them food through the severe famine, they felt grateful enough to become slaves.

In addition, on account of Joseph's wise ruling, Egypt grew, and Pharaoh's authority became increasingly strengthened. By making everyone in the nation cultivate the land, Joseph caused the lives of the people to become more abundant, and order was established in the society. Because of one person, Joseph, the entire nation was greatly blessed.

On account of Joseph, Joseph's father, his brothers, and their families were blessed. Pharaoh commanded that Jacob and his family be given the land of Goshen, "the best of the land" for their "possession" (Gen 47:6, 11). He did not spare "the best of the land of Egypt" and allowed them to "eat the fat of the land" (Gen 45:18). Genesis 47:12 states, "And Joseph provided his father and his brothers and all his father's household with food, according to their little ones."

Genesis 50:21 states that even after Jacob's death, Joseph provided for his 11 brothers and even their children. Since this one man, Joseph, saved the lives of his entire family, he was indeed, as Jacob had prophesied, the firstborn distinguished from his brothers, the one who is standing at the apex, the "crown of the head" (Gen 49:26).

(3) The blessing of continuous growth

Genesis 49:22 states that the "branches run over a wall." Here, "run" is צָעַד (ṣāʿad) in Hebrew, meaning "climb out," "step," "extend out," and "march."[98] This expression illustrates the fact that Joseph's abundant blessings did not stay within the house, but ran over and continued to extend out and above boundaries to enrich and benefit others also.

Even strangers passing by could reach out to pick the fruits for food. A fruitful bough is a delight to the eyes, brings joy to the mouth, and satisfies the heart.

Such blessing is described by Jacob in Genesis 49:26 as "an infinitely continuing everlasting blessing."

> **Genesis 49:26** "The blessings of your father have surpassed the blessings of my ancestors up to the utmost bound of the everlasting hills; may they be on the head of Joseph, and on the crown of the head of the one distinguished among his brothers."

Here, in the phrase "utmost bound of the everlasting hills," the word *bound* is תַּאֲוָה (ta'ăwâ) in Hebrew, meaning "boundary,"[99] and *up to* is עַד ('ad) in Hebrew, meaning "up to" or "until."[100] Thus, "up to the utmost bound of the everlasting hills" means "up to the boundaries of the everlasting hills," implying that the blessings bestowed upon Joseph are eternal and boundless. This is because there are no boundaries in the everlasting hills. The fountain of all such blessings is indeed God Himself (Ps 16:2; 133:3). In Genesis 49:25, Jacob says that Joseph's blessings come "from the God of your father who helps you, and by the Almighty who blesses you." To those who totally trust in God, from whom the blessings flow, God will abundantly bestow the blessings like those of Joseph (Ps 84:12).

2. Joseph's Faith

As the main figure in the covenant of the torch, Joseph indeed has received tremendous blessings. At the foundation of these blessings is Joseph's great faith toward God.

(1) Faith that overcomes sufferings

Genesis 49:22 states that Joseph's bough will have "its branches run over a wall." The expression "run over" does not mean an effortless flow over a wall, but it connotes a laborious process of climbing up against a high wall. In other words, it is prophesying that blessings will not easily and automatically come to Joseph without toil. Regarding the life of Joseph, Jacob prophesied in Genesis 49:23–24, "The archers bitterly attacked him, and shot at him and harassed him; but his bow remained firm, and his arms were agile, from the hands of the Mighty

One of Jacob." Here, "harassed" in Hebrew is שָׂטַם (śāṭam) and means "to push into a trap." This indicates the many afflictions and sufferings that Joseph had to undergo. Nevertheless, Joseph has overcome all afflictions and triumphed by the hands of the Mighty One of Jacob (Gen 49:25).

When Joseph was despised by his brothers and sold into slavery, he probably felt completely hopeless and fell into deep despair. To make matters worse, under false accusations, he was shut in a prison as cold as ice; his feet were afflicted with fetters, and his body was laid in irons (Ps 105:17–18). He had fallen to the bottom of life's pit. Who was there to understand this wretched man and deliver him from such crisis? Even in midst of such misery, Joseph did not complain against God. Rather, he trusted in the hand of the Lord Almighty and waited for the day when God's promise would be fulfilled.

What we also need as believers who are seeking after the kingdom of God until the perfection of our salvation is patience. We must trust in the Almighty God, wait for His time, overcome our suffering, and endure to the end (Matt 10:22; 24:13). In Luke 21:19, Jesus says, "By your endurance you will gain your lives," and James 5:7–8 advises, "Be patient, therefore, brethren, until the coming of the Lord. Behold, the farmer waits for the precious produce of the soil, being patient about it, until it gets the early and late rains. You too be patient; strengthen your hearts, for the coming of the Lord is at hand."

(2) Faith by a spring (God-first faith)

As the main character in the covenant of the torch, what was Joseph's secret in receiving the blessing of fulfilling the covenant of the torch? Regarding this, the Bible informs us that it was because of his faith "by a spring."

Genesis 49:22 states, "Joseph is a fruitful bough, a fruitful bough by a spring; its branches run over a wall." Here, the phrase "by a spring" is עֲלֵי־עָיִן ('ălê-'āyin) in Hebrew, meaning "just above the spring" or "next to the spring." If a tree is not planted by a spring, it may momentarily look fruitful and alive, but soon it will whither, and the fruits will not ripen. However, Joseph's life never panted from the lack of water, but was abundantly renewed with living waters. How was that possible? His roots were deeply planted in God (Jer 17:7-8), who is the fountain of living waters (Isa 49:10; Jer 2:13; 17:13; John 4:14).

The special attributes of Joseph's faith "by a spring" were proven at various times throughout his life. When the wife of Potiphar seduced him, Joseph refused Potiphar's wife by saying, "How then could I do this great evil, and sin against God?" demonstrating that he always lived a God-centered life (Gen 39:9). Also, when he interpreted the dreams of Pharaoh's wine steward and baker while he was imprisoned, he said, "Do not interpretations belong to God?" (Gen 40:8), revealing only God and none of himself. Even when he was interpreting Pharaoh's dream, he replied, "God will give Pharaoh a favorable answer" (Gen 41:16) and "God has told to Pharaoh what He is about to do" (Gen 41:25), thus exhibiting well his belief that all matters are in God's sovereign hands and His hands only.

By naming his second son *Ephraim*, meaning "God has made me fruitful in the land of my affliction," Joseph confessed that all the blessings bestowed upon him came not through his own effort, but were given entirely by God (Gen 41:52).

Even when he was second-in-command of Egypt and had access to great wealth, he employed no deception; he brought all the money into Pharaoh's house (Gen 47:14, 20, 23). The principle of Joseph's faith that was deeply rooted by the spring was pure and clear, and he was upright and faithful before God.

Furthermore, he believed that his brothers' hatred against him was also a part of God's sovereign providence (Gen 45:5, 7). Thus, he said to them, "And as for you, you meant evil against me, but God meant it for good" (Gen 50:20). This was his confession of faith in God's absolute sovereignty, that God works through man's plans and strategies to fulfill His providence in salvation (Prov 16:9, 33; 19:21; 20:24).

Even in his last hour, Joseph said to his brothers, "I am about to die, but God will surely take care of you, and bring you up from this land to the land which He promised on oath to Abraham, to Isaac and to Jacob" (Gen 50:24), and thus he kept his God-first faith, yearning for the fulfillment of God's covenant to the very end.

In short, Joseph never left God's side, but lived by completely attaching himself to God. He served God from the bottom of his heart and communed with God; he lived just as God led him and with the wisdom God gave him. Psalm 73:28 states, "But as for me, the nearness of God is my good," and in James 4:8, God promises that He will draw near to us when we draw near to Him.

The greatest secret in drawing near to God is prayer. God comes near to us when we pray (Deut 4:7; Ps 145:18). Also, He draws near to us when we listen to His Word (Luke 10:39). This is because the Word from the beginning was with God, and the Word is God (John 1:1; Rev 19:13).

I am certain that when we keep watching and praying and deeply root our faith in the spring of God's Word, which never runs dry, the blessings that Joseph received—the "fruitful bough by a spring"—will be upon all of us (Jer 31:12).

לכל בר דעת דרך המסעות ארבעים שנה במדבר 'והרוחב והאורך של אוג הקדושה מנהר בן

עמלק

מדבר צין הוא קדש

ים המלח

עיר כרמל

שבט יהודה

מדבר סיני

מדבר פארן

באר שבע

מדבר שור

שבט שמעון

שבט יהודה

ארץ פלשתים

ארץ גשן

פתם

שורה

צען

אלכסנדרי

לוח המסעות במדבר
אשר על פי ה' יסעו ועל פי ה' יחנו

א' רעמסס'	טז' רתמה
ב' סכת	טז' רמן פרץ
ג' אתם	יז' לבנה
ד' פי החירת	יח' רסה
ה' מרה	יט' קהלתה
ו' אילם	כ' הר ספר
ז' ים סוף	כא' חרדה
ח' מדבר סין	כב' מקהלת
ט' דפקה	כג' תחת
יו' אלוש	כד' תרח
יא' רפידם	כה' מתקה
יב' מדבר סיני	כו' חשמנה
יג' קברות התאוה	כז' מסרות
יד' חצרות	כח' בני יעקן

כט' הר הגדגד
ל' יטבתה
לא' עברנה
לב' עציון גבר
לג' מדבר צין
לד' הר ההר
לה' צלמנה
לו' פונן
לז' אבת
לח' דיבן גד
לט' עלמן דבל'
מ' הרי עברים
מא' שבת מואב

Conclusion

The Covenant of the Torch
to Be Fulfilled in the Future

1. The Covenant of the Torch Yet to Be Fulfilled

Thus far, we have studied the process in which the covenant of the torch was fulfilled from the perspective of God's administration in the history of redemption. Although the covenant was fulfilled when the Israelites entered the land of Canaan and the bones of Joseph were buried in Shechem of Canaan in the fourth generation from Abraham, it is a covenant that needs to be fulfilled today in all believers of God who are striving toward the spiritual Canaan, the kingdom of heaven. Thus, the covenant is still valid to us and yet to be fulfilled to its completion in each of us.

How can we say that the covenant of the torch is yet to be fulfilled?

(1) It is because of the eternal attributes of the covenant of the torch.

Psalm 105:8–45 is a historical poetry that reflects upon the history of the birth and growth of the chosen people of Israel as a nation. The passage addresses the events from the time the covenant was established with Abraham until it is fulfilled in the Book of Joshua. Here, it closely describes the covenant of the torch in particular. Psalm 105:9 mentions, "the covenant which He made with Abraham." Here, the Hebrew word for "make a covenant" is כָּרַת (kārat), meaning "to cut, to ratify a covenant, to establish" (Gen 15:18). It reflects the custom involved in the ratification of covenants in the ancient times, during which the person making the covenant must pass between two pieces of an offering (Jer 34:19), and more specifically, it refers to the covenant of the torch in Genesis 15 (Gen 15:17).

Psalm 105 contains many expressions that exhibit the eternal attributes of the covenants that God made with Abraham (especially the covenant of the torch).

Psalm 105:8 He has remembered His covenant forever, the word which He commanded to a thousand generations.

זָכַר לְעוֹלָם בְּרִיתוֹ דָּבָר צִוָּה לְאֶלֶף דּוֹר

dôr lĕʾelep ṣiwwâ dābār bĕrîtô lĕʿôlām zākar

"His covenant" in Hebrew is בְּרִיתוֹ (*bĕrîtô*), which refers to "the covenant of the Lord." It implies that God will keep His covenant eternally, for this covenant with Abraham was given unilaterally according to His sovereign will.

A "thousand generations" in Hebrew is לְאֶלֶף דּוֹר (*lĕʾelep dôr*), and it does not refer to a literal 1,000 generations; rather, it is an emblematic illustration of a boundless, infinite period—that is, an eternity (Exod 20:6; Deut 7:9; 1 Chr 16:15). Also, "forever" in Hebrew is עוֹלָם (*ʿôlām*), an expression of infinity (an eternity).

Likewise, the words *His covenant, thousand generations,* and *forever* all emphasize the truth that God will not forget His covenant forever. This is why Psalm 105:10 identifies the covenant of the torch as an "everlasting covenant" (cf. 1 Chr 16:17). Therefore, the covenant is not a covenant of the past made exclusively for Abraham and his descendants; its efficacy holds for the believers today, who are the descendants of Abraham by faith (Rom 4:16; Gal 3:7–9, 26–29). Thus, the covenant still awaits fulfillment in the spiritual sense. This covenant undoubtedly will be fulfilled through the spiritual descendants of Abraham. This is because God does not lie and He fulfills what He has spoken (Num 23:19), and He has commanded it and He has remembered His covenant (Ps 105:8).

(2) It is because the Israelites did not obtain all the land of Canaan promised through the covenant of the torch

God promised the land of Canaan to the Israelites, the descendants of Abraham. Psalm 105:11 records God saying, "To you I will give the land of Canaan as the portion of your inheritance." And Genesis 15:18 states, "On that day the LORD made a covenant with Abram, saying, 'To your descendants I have given this land, from the river of Egypt as far as the great river, the river Euphrates.'" God thus confirmed the borders of Canaan that the Israelites were to possess. However, at the time of the Israelites' conquest of Canaan under the leadership of Joshua, they were unable to possess all of these regions (Num 34:3–5).

It was not until the reigns of King David and King Solomon that the borders, which God had promised through the covenant of the torch, were conquered (1 Kgs 4:21; 2 Chr 9:26). However, after the reign of King Solomon, because of their transgression against God, the Israelites could not move on to entirely possess Canaan, the land promised by God. What God required after granting Canaan was that they wholly keep His statutes and observe His laws (Ps 105:44–45). Nevertheless, upon entering Canaan, the people of Israel neglected His laws, and as a result, they were once again expelled from Canaan, shackled and taken away as captives to Babylon.

The land of Canaan is a shadow of the kingdom of heaven, which the descendants of Abraham through faith in Jesus Christ must take possession of in the future (Rom 4:16; Gal 3:7–9, 26–29). Just as God gave the land of Canaan as an inheritance to Abraham's descendants (Ps 105:11), the kingdom of heaven is an inheritance given to His believers. This inheritance is the "kingdom which He promised to those who love Him" (Jas 2:5), "your nation" (Ps 106:5), "kingdom of God" (1 Cor 6:9–10; 15:50; Gal 5:21), and "an inheritance which is imperishable and undefiled and will not fade away" (1 Pet 1:4).

Hence, the covenant of the torch is a covenant that is to be fulfilled by the people of God today and continues to be valid until the fulfillment of God's Kingdom.

2. Faith Needed for the Future Fulfillment of the Covenant

Until that day of the complete fulfillment of the covenant of the torch, what kind of faith should the believers in Jesus Christ, the descendants of Abraham by faith, possess?

(1) The faith of the "living"

The four generations of faith that begin with Abraham possessed faith of the "living."

In Matthew 22:31–32, Jesus said, "Have you not read that which was spoken to you by God, saying, 'I am the God of Abraham, and the God of Isaac, and the God of Jacob?' He is not the God of the dead but of the living." Joseph, the fourth generation of faith who had inherited the faith of Abraham, Isaac, and Jacob, likewise possessed this faith of the "living." As he died at the age of 110, he commanded his bones be carried to Canaan. His body was dead, but his faith lived on. Joseph's faith to enter Canaan by all means, even as mere bones, never died; it lived, and at last he was buried and laid to rest in the Promised Land, in Shechem, thus bringing closure to the four generations and fulfilling the covenant of the torch.

The faith of the "living" that Abraham, Isaac, Jacob, and Joseph possessed never halted or ended at their generations, but became the beacon of hope toward Canaan for their descendants who were afflicted in Egypt for 400 years.

The faith of the "living" was not to be possessed exclusively by the Israelites only; it is indispensable even for believers today. God is searching for the "living," those who possess the four generations of faith—that is, the faith of Abraham, the faith of Isaac, the faith of Jacob, and the faith of Joseph. He is searching for those who will obey without doubt, believing in the truth that God will fulfill all that He has spoken so that not a single word of His falls to the ground unaccomplished. God will fulfill His eternally imperishable providence through those who possess such a faith..

Today, those who cherish Jesus Christ in their hearts and believe without doubt in the gospel of His cross are the spiritual descendants of Abraham and the godly descendants who will continue the inheritance as promised (Gal 3:29). They are "living" beings. Ecclesiastes 9:4 states, "For whoever is joined with all the living, there is hope; surely a live dog is better than a dead lion." With dead faith, even a hero, patriot, or a person as mighty as a lion is lower than the lowliest person who has living faith. Only those who possess "living" faith have hope no matter how inadequate they may be (Eccl 9:4).

To walk the path of life, the path of the "living" until the end, we must die to this world (Gal 6:14) and be "dead" to sin (Rom 6:11). Only such people can be "alive" to God in Jesus Christ (Rom 6:11). The only way for us to escape the power of death and obtain life is by living through faith in the Son of God, who gave up His divine body on the cross for us sinners (Gal 2:20).

I pray that we may only speak in faith, think in faith, and do good deeds in faith now until God's administration in the history of redemption is fulfilled (Eph 2:10; Titus 2:14). I firmly believe that the blessings of the final grace, which was promised in the Old and New Testaments, will be bestowed upon those who have long-persevered in hope of heaven on the day when His promise, "heaven and earth will pass away, but My words shall not pass away" (Matt 24:34-35), is fulfilled (1 Pet 1:13).

(2) The devoted labor of carrying Joseph's holy bones

The Israelites pitched tents 41 times during the wilderness journey and then crossed the Jordan River, pitching tent one more time in Gilgal, for a total of 42 times. This journey was the course of discipline and trials that the Israelites had to endure in order to be made holy as godly people who were to soon possess the land of Canaan.

The Israelites carried Joseph's bones through the 40-year wilderness journey and the 16-year conquest of Canaan for a total of 56 years. Despite Joseph's heavy coffin and the walk through the vast and frightening wilderness with unending desolate tracts and rocks, they cautiously cared for and protected Joseph's coffin. They had devoted themselves to the labor of personally carrying Joseph's coffin to the very end.

His body not only was embalmed and placed in a wooden coffin, but most likely was plastered with stone or basalt on the outside.[101] The wooden coffin alone was fairly heavy, so it must have been difficult to care for it each time they moved camp from place to place.

Furthermore, after they entered Canaan, carrying Joseph's coffin and caring for it through the continuous battles in Canaan day after day must have been a life-threatening task. Yet, the people did not bury or cremate his bones on the way for they did not regard their duty cumbersome. Rather, they fulfilled their duty with devotion and faith in the covenant of God.

Carrying the bones of Joseph was indeed, in its essence, a great symbol of Immanuel to the Israelites, reminding them that the "God who was with Joseph" is with them. Through his bones, they probably felt the presence of Joseph who had once delivered Israel from their crisis. They still vividly remembered their ancestor's request from long ago— even after 360 years had passed—and dedicated themselves to carrying the bones of Joseph. This truly was a march of faith in obedience to the word of God, who is the faithful One.

We, who are daily pressing on toward the kingdom of heaven this day, must also carry the spiritual bones and march on in faith to fulfill the covenant of God (Matt 10:38; 16:24; Mark 8:34; Luke 9:23; 14:27).

3. God's Zeal for the Fulfillment of the Covenant

Abraham, Isaac, Jacob, and Joseph (who became the "fourth genera-tion"); Moses, Joshua, Caleb, and the other great leaders of the wilder-ness; and the people who carried Joseph's heavy coffin all the way to Shechem, are all people who participated primarily in fulfilling the cov-enant of the torch.

Despite the extreme suffering and affliction they endured, like that of a smoking iron furnace under the oppression of Egypt for 400 years (Deut 4:20; 1 Kgs 8:51; Jer 11:4), their hearts were flaming as ever be-fore this undying torch of the covenant.

Such an inextinguishable torch! The flaming torch was indeed the zeal of God (2 Cor 11:2) and His fervent love that desires to save His people. Hence, the true hero of the covenant of the torch is indeed none other than God Himself, for He fulfills His covenant in the his-tory of redemption.

(1) The zeal of God, who fulfills through dreams

Joseph had two dreams (Gen 37:5–11). In the first dream, the 11 sheaves bowed before Joseph. In the second dream, the sun, the moon, and the 11 stars bowed down before Joseph.

The sheaves of grain, the sun, the moon, and the stars are not objects that can arise on their own or bow down the way people can. Thus, the fact that they either arose or bowed down means that someone made them do so, revealing that the one who gave this dream surely was God. Sure enough, Joseph's dreams were great revelations from God, which encompassed everything that lies in the covenant of the torch to be ful-filled in course of time.

(i) Joseph's dream and the preparation to enter Egypt

Through God's fervent zeal to fulfill the covenant of the torch, He gave the dreams to Joseph and prepared the way for the Israelites to enter Egypt. These dreams caused Joseph to become the object of his brothers' envy and hatred (Gen 37:8, 11). When Joseph went to see his brothers as they were tending the flocks in Dothan, "they saw him from a dis-tance and before he came close to them, they plotted against him to put him to death. They said to one another, 'Here comes this dreamer!'" (Gen 37:18–19). This clearly shows that Joseph's dream was the fac-tor that caused his brothers to sell him to Egypt. Although Joseph's brothers sold him over to Egypt out of their hatred and jealousy, God employed such evil in his brothers to send Joseph to Egypt in advance, thereby preparing the conduit for Jacob's household to later enter Egypt (Gen 45:5; 50:20). This portrays God's providence and zeal, brought forth in His administration of the redemptive history, in order to fulfill the prophecy of the covenant of the torch: "Know for certain that your descendants will be strangers in a land that is not theirs, where they will be enslaved and oppressed four hundred years" (Gen 15:13).

(ii) Joseph's dream and the Israelites' slavery in a foreign land

The common thing about the two dreams of Joseph is that he is bowed to by others. The act of bowing is an expression of respect. When people see something worthy of respect or reverence, they naturally bow before it. Hence, the 11 sheaves, the sun, moon and 11 stars that bowed to Joseph in his dreams will come to respect Joseph. The 11 sheaves and 11 stars represent Joseph's 11 brothers, and the sun and moon represent his parents (Gen 37:8, 10). Therefore, Joseph's dreams were a revelation that the entire household of Israel would voluntarily pay respect to Joseph, and that he would save them.

However, after being sold into slavery to Egypt, Joseph had to experience the suffering that took him to the bottom of life's pit. He worked as a slave in Potiphar's house, and he was unjustly accused of trying to violate Potiphar's wife and was imprisoned.

In the prison Joseph met Pharaoh's wine steward and baker and interpreted their dreams, providing the circumstance by which later he would interpret Pharaoh's dream. Although he faced the suffering of his feet being bound with fetters and his body lying in irons in a dark prison (Ps 105:18), it was all part of the process to fulfill Joseph's dreams in accordance with God's Word—that is, God's providence to eventually make Joseph the governor of Egypt.

When at last it was time for God's Word to come to pass (Ps 105:19), God called Joseph out of prison and opened the path for him to interpret the dream of Pharaoh, who thereby granted Joseph governorship in Egypt (Ps 105:20–22). Then, by sending a famine upon all the earth so that there was no food, God planned for Joseph's 11 brothers and Jacob, their father, to bring their entire households into Egypt (Ps 105:23). It is written in Genesis 15:13, "And God said to Abram, 'Know for certain that your descendants will be strangers in a land that is not theirs, where they will be enslaved and oppressed four hundred years,'" and thus began the fulfillment of the covenant of the torch through Joseph, in accordance with the dreams that God had given to Joseph.

(iii) Joseph's dreams and the blessing of the crown of the head granted to Joseph

Joseph's dreams did not stop here. The sun, the moon, and the stars do not simply represent his parents and brothers; they encompass far more, representing the whole universe. Indeed, Joseph received the blessing of the whole universe. What lies in his blessing is also illustrated in Genesis 49:26 and Deuteronomy 33:16.

Jacob's Prophecy

Genesis 49:26 "The blessings of your father have surpassed the blessings of my ancestors up to the utmost bound of the everlasting hills; may they be on the head of Joseph, and on the crown of the head of the one distinguished among his brothers."

Moses' Blessing

Deuteronomy 33:16 "And with the choice things of the earth and its fullness, and the favor of Him who dwelt in the bush. Let it come to the head of Joseph, and to the crown of the head of the one distinguished among his brothers."

In both Genesis 49:26 and Deuteronomy 33:16, the "head of Joseph" and "the crown of the head of the one distinguished among his brothers" are couplets. That is, "head" forms a symmetry with "crown of the head." It implies that Joseph's place among his brothers is at the highest place on the head, the crown. The top of the head is, metaphorically speaking, a place even higher than the peak, such as "the highest tip of the peak." This is why, when we commonly refer to the entirety of our body, from the bottom to the top, we use the expression "from the sole of your foot to the crown of your head" (Deut 28:35; 2 Sam 14:25; Job 2:7).

The blessing of the entire universe that Joseph received was the blessing of the crown, signifying the highest of the blessings. Genesis 49:25 speaks of this blessing as "the blessings of heaven above" and as the "blessings of the deep that lies beneath."

Also, Genesis 49:26 describes this blessing as "the blessing surpassing the blessings of the ancestors." Here, the word *ancestors* is הַרְ *hārâ*) in Hebrew, and it shows that the blessing Joseph received from Jacob surpasses the blessings of his "ancestors." These "ancestors" include Abraham, Isaac, and Jacob and therefore Joseph's blessing is far superior to the blessings they received. Surely, the blessings that Joseph received were like the highest mountain among all the mountains standing tall on a plain.

Why were Joseph's blessings greater than the blessings his ancestors received? It was because the covenant of the torch, which began with Abraham, would eventually be completed through Joseph. The covenant grew its roots during Abraham's time, formed the stem during Isaac's time and the leaves during Jacob's time, and then it flowered and bore abundant fruit during Joseph's time. Surely, Joseph received a combination of all of Abraham, Isaac and Jacob's blessings.

This amazing truth is also vividly displayed in Psalm 105. Psalm 105 reconfirms the grand promise that the land of Canaan would be given to Abraham and his descendants as an inheritance (see 1 Chr 16:7–36). This is also a foreshadowing of how the spiritual descendants of Abraham, the believers of Jesus Christ, would come to inherit the kingdom of God.

Here, God's covenant with Abraham is further reinforced through Isaac and Jacob.

> **Psalm 105:8–10** He has remembered His covenant forever, the word which He commanded to a thousand generations, ⁹the covenant which He made with Abraham, and His oath to Isaac. ¹⁰Then He confirmed it to Jacob for a statute, to Israel as an everlasting covenant.

Here, God's "covenant" with Abraham is described for Isaac as the "oath" that absolutely guarantees the covenant's certainty, and for Jacob as the "statute" ("everlasting covenant") that holds the unchanging efficacy of objective law, both through which the declaration increasingly became more powerful and definite.

But, following closely after the reference to Abraham, Isaac, and Jacob, Psalm 105:17 speaks of Joseph: "He sent a man before them, Joseph, who was sold as a slave." This is a clear proclamation to the whole world that Joseph is the "fourth generation" of faith succeeding to Abraham, Isaac, and Jacob, and that the covenant of the torch is at last fulfilled through Joseph.

(iv) Joseph's dream and Jesus Christ

The "crown" in the expression "the crown of the head" in Genesis 49:26 refers to the "summit, peak, top," describing the highest part of the head. Customarily, a crown is worn on the head of a king, and thus Joseph's blessing of the crown of the head was the "blessing of a king."

Jesus is our King of kings (Rev 17:14; 19:16). Therefore, Joseph is a type of our Lord, Jesus Christ. When we dwell in Jesus Christ, we can receive the "blessing of the crown of the head."

If the sun, the moon, and the stars represent the entire universe, then there is only one to whom the entire universe should bow and that is Jesus Christ. Herein lies the amazing providence of redemption. Joseph is indeed a type of Jesus Christ. From the life and character of Joseph, which surely compels all to bow before him, we discover an image of Jesus Christ. We are reminded of Jesus Christ through Joseph's suffering and patience, wisdom and love, sinless and flawless perfection, abundant works of life, and the final glory in which all people bow down before him.

If the final person who fulfilled the covenant of the torch given by God was Joseph, then the one who will fulfill the everlasting covenant of the torch to give us the kingdom of heaven is indeed our Lord, Jesus Christ. Through His Second Coming, He will defeat all powers of darkness and will completely and eternally fulfill the covenant of the torch by granting the new heaven and the new earth to the saints, the descendants of Abraham's faith.

(2) God's zeal fulfills the divine administration in the history of redemption

We have examined in detail how the covenant of the torch was fulfilled through God's administration in the history of redemption. Behind all the historical achievement was the flaming fire of God's zeal, flowing from His love and mercy, to save His people whom he chose. Neither the power of darkness nor any obstacle could extinguish the flames of His zeal.

There was nothing in this world that could put out His burning desire to save His people from bondage in Egypt and lead them to the land of Canaan. Egypt's mighty army and Pharaoh's hardened heart were no match for God's devotion. Even the raging waves of the Red Sea roaring up to engulf God's people were parted before His zeal. The fierce desert winds and the dusty wilderness, the scorching heat of day and the skin-piercing cold of night, and the miles of rocky wilderness and the mountains with harsh rocks, through which God's people could pass only by walking, could not deter God's diligence. Even the recurring doubts of the Israelites, who crucified the heart of God with their persistent grumblings and betrayals, could not extinguish the flames of His zeal for His people. Even the horrifying swords and attacks by Sihon, the king of the Amorites, the king of Bashan, and other countless enemies were all like falling autumn leaves before the zeal of God.

The One who ratified the covenant is our living God, and He is the One who has fulfilled and at last completed it (Isa 55:11; Jer 33:2). This fervency of God was burning brightly in the hearts of those who were part of His work of fulfilling the covenant of the torch.

Those who believe and follow Jesus Christ today also have a duty to complete the covenant of the torch in their lives. This is the time of heightened darkness, for the night is almost gone and the daybreak is near (Rom 13:12). Everywhere we go, lawlessness is at its peak and love has grown cold (Matt 24:12). The end of all things is near (1 Pet 4:7), and all creation is groaning (Rom 8:22). As we live in the time when even the spiritual world becomes dark, we must brighten our hearts with God's Word and continuous prayers. We must become fervent with God's zeal and become diligent stewards for His good work (Eph 2:10; Titus 2:14).

Why did God establish us as stewards of His church? It is so that we may bear God's zeal in our hearts in accordance with the administration of redemptive history and carry out the Word of God.

> **Colossians 1:25-27** Of this church I was made a minister according to the stewardship from God bestowed on me for your benefit, that I might fully carry out the preaching of the word of God, 26that is, the mystery which has been hidden from the past ages and generations; but has now been manifested to His saints, 27to whom God willed to make known what is the riches of the glory of this mystery among the Gentiles, which is Christ in you, the hope of glory.

Jesus Christ is the mystery of God (Eph 3:4; Col 1:27; 2:2). If there is one thing that we must do, it is to spread the abundance of the glory of Jesus Christ to the entire world. We must persevere in our ministry to preach God's Word in season and out of season (Eph 6:19; 2 Tim 4:2).

Churches, which are the body of our Lord, will have to face much persecution and tribulation in witnessing the Word of God. However, no tribulation is greater than the suffering of the cross. I sincerely hope that we may live our lives, "do[ing] our share on behalf of His body (which is the church) in filling up that which is lacking in Christ's afflictions" as the apostle Paul confessed (Col 1:24). When we rejoice in sharing the sufferings of Christ in enduring all sorts of suffering for Jesus Christ and His gospel until the end, God's Spirit of the glory will rest upon us (1 Pet 4:13–14). As no power of unrighteousness could hold back God's zeal to save His people from Egypt, there is no one who will be able to hold back God's fervent zeal to save His people from the sinful world in the end (Rom 8:35–39).

We have hope as long as this zeal burns unquenchably in our hearts. This hope is the blessed hope (Titus 2:18), the hope in which we will not be ashamed (Ps 119:116; Phil 1:20), and the hope that will not be cut off (Prov 23:18; 24:14). This is the hope that becomes grounded even more in the midst of life-threatening tribulations (2 Cor 1:7-8) and the hope of the eternally steadfast Gospel (Col 1:23). This is the hope of inheriting the incorruptible and imperishable kingdom of heaven through Jesus Christ, who is the only Lord of salvation (1 Pet 1:3-4).

I wholeheartedly pray that the fervent zeal of God and the covenantal torch burn brightly through our lives, and that this wonderful encounter with God may continue eternally through the redemptive grace of Jesus Christ. Hallelujah!

Commentaries and References

COMMENTARY FROM DR. JAE-YONG JOO

Emeritus Professor of Hanshin University, Chair of the Theological
　Research Center
Former President and Professor of Hanshin University
President of Korean Professor Mutual Society

Initially, upon receiving a request to provide a commentary for Rev.
Park's *The Covenant of the Torch*, I hesitated, thinking that I was not the
right person, and so I politely declined.

First, I neither knew the author nor had much recollection of his writ-
ings. Not only do Rev. Park and I belong to different denominations,
but also we have significant differences in our views on Scripture, theology, and distinctives of the faith. Rev. Park is a pastor who has spent all
of his life serving a church of conservative faith and theology, whereas
I am a professor who has spent his life teaching progressive theological
views in lecture halls. Hence, he probably understood the Scriptures as
God's Word and a historic documentation of God's administration from
the perspective of his pastoral work and experience, whereas I came to
understand the Scriptures as a historic documentation of God's administration from the perspective of mere theological reasoning.

Second, Rev. Park's book is about Old Testament Scriptures. Therefore, for me, whose expertise is in church history, writing a review of
this book seemed to exceed my scholarly limits. I thought that a proper
commentator on this book must be an expert in the Old Testament.

Why, then, did I decide to write this commentary? Primarily, it was
because of my curiosity and intellectual craving for a book that stood
in stark contrast with my theological camp, my faith expression, and
my academic expertise. I also want to grow theologically and spiritually
through this book.

Consequently, I now feel greatly honored and ever more thankful to
have met Rev. Park and built a friendship with him, albeit through the
printed word. Most of all, as stated in his book *The Genesis Genealogies*,
he confesses that the patriarchs' footsteps of faith had come alive and
moved before him. He stayed awake for many nights, overwhelmed
and inspired by God's grace. He also confesses in the foreword of *The
Covenant of the Torch* that he vowed before God 47 years ago that he
would pray for two hours and read the Scriptures for three hours daily.

To this day, he has not missed a single day of fulfilling that promise. He has uncompromisingly walked on a solitary road, focusing only on the Scriptures. In the face of these confessions of faith, I cannot help but feel a sense of shame as a theologian, and I have acquired an admiration for the author's life of faith.

Moreover, a pastor's life in Korea is overwhelmingly busy and physically demanding, sparing little if any time to write books. Yet, despite his advanced age of over 80 years, Rev. Park has published a second book soon after his first one. His scholarly passion truly inspires me. Having experienced God's grace, he has lived such an inspirational walk of faith that he would give up his own life for God. In *The Genesis Genealogies*, he states that these books are not a work of theological research, but a compilation of his sermons of grace that he had received, illuminated by the Holy Spirit, as he prayed and read the Scriptures hundreds of times. However, after seeing the books' contents, I now realize that they are a work of revealed theology, attained through a deep meditation of the Scriptures and prayer.

From *The Genesis Genealogies* and *The Covenant of the Torch*, it becomes evident that the author views the Old Testament Scriptures through God's administration in redemption history. In truth, not just the Old Testament, but all 66 books of the Scriptures—from Genesis to Revelation—encompass dissimilar generational histories and mankind's disparate societal, political, and economic living environments. These books were written by unrelated scribes or authors. Even so, the Scriptures are confessions of faith by those who received God's revelation and experienced His administration in redemption history. Hence, God's administration in redemption history is the theme above all themes in the Scriptures. God desired to reveal His administration in redemption history through the patriarchs, the prophets, His chosen servants, and Jesus Christ. Calling upon God as the Creator is the expression and the basis for God's administration in redemption history. At the center of this divine administration stands Jesus Christ. From this perspective, it is especially remarkable that *The Covenant of the Torch* begins with a section titled "Jesus Christ, the Center of the Divine Administration of Redemption History."

In his series covering God's administration in redemption history, the author places a special emphasis on covenants, particularly the "covenant of the torch," which God established with Abraham. God established various covenants with the Israelites. Among them, their core belief is "I will be your God, and you will be my people." The relationship between God and the Israelites is a contractual relationship. The history of Israelites begins with this contract, of which the most tangible incident is the exodus. The principle of a contract is keeping it; a contract is not meant to be breached. Therefore, both God and man must keep this contract. The reason why the author places a special emphasis on the covenant of the torch established with Abraham is that God's administration of redemptive history is most evident in this covenant.

Through his exploration of the covenant of the torch, the author strives to assure the readers that God never breaches a covenant once it is entered. Even when the Israelites breached it, God kept it to the end. After settling in Canaan, the Israelites sinned by forgetting God and worshiping Baal. Israelite rulers sinned with their unrighteousness and corruption by politically and economically oppressing and exploiting their people. The prophets cried out that they must remember their God, and they prophesied about His judgment. However, because of the contract that God had entered with them, He had to forgive and receive them again. This is the way of God's "covenantal love."

Man, preciously created in God's image, had fallen and was expelled from the Garden of Eden, thereby losing the image of God, the blessings contained in God's covenant, and the memory of his beautiful life of grace. Therefore, the author stresses that finding what had been lost and meeting God again is the ultimate purpose in human life. An encounter with God is the most crucial beginning and the living force that will determine human lives. At the center of this lies the covenant of the torch.

The Covenant of the Torch is composed of five parts and a conclusion. The author covers God's administration, His covenant in redemptive history, its final fulfillment, and in conclusion, the future fulfillment of the covenant. The author reviews the history of the covenant revealed through the lives of the patriarchs Abraham, Isaac, Jacob, and Joseph, covers events within this history from the exodus to the conquest of Canaan, and then describes the covenant's final fulfillment through Abraham and his descendants. However, the author emphasizes that the covenant of the torch does not end here. The covenant continues perpetually through Psalm 105. This is the blessing contained in God's administration in the history of redemption. Hence, we who live in the present are not excluded from this blessing. However, one must faithfully keep the contract with God, which is to observe God's commandments until the day of the coming of His kingdom.

Rev. Park notes that he is a pastor, not a theologian, and is also over 80 years old. Nevertheless, it is astonishing that he is interpreting the important words in the Old Testament from the original scriptural language and is using the Scriptures to interpret the Scriptures. Furthermore, the various charts and tools provided by the author, including a map that he composed after having personally explored the actual sites in Israel, add to the merit of this book, remaining as precious resources that will greatly assist its readers. These resources abundantly assist in carrying out his intentions in the chronological composition of this book.

If I were to point out the difference between my own historical views and those of the author, I would say that he seems to describe God's history of redemption as a chronology, viewing "problems in the chronology" as the most fundamental and significant issue in God's history of redemption. Thus, most of his work shows his research on the chronology of the patriarchs; the history of Abraham, Isaac, Jacob and Joseph; the period of life in Egypt; and the chronology of the exodus. Through such a chronological approach, God's work of redemption seen in the Old Testament may be understood as historical facts. However, I would point out, from the perspective of historical science, that chronological research is a measure, a tool for understanding history, and is not the actual history in itself. Hence, in my opinion, the importance lies in the interpretation of the contents of the chronology. From that interpretation, God's administration can become the history of redemption. God's redemptive history is based not on *chronos* (man's time), but on *kairos* (God's time). God's redemptive history is really a study of eschatology. Eschatological events bear implications beyond being merely chronological events.

However, because *The Covenant of the Torch* is thoroughly based on the revelation that the Scriptures are the Word of God, my differing viewpoint removes no merit from this book. It is my wish that other pastors of the churches around the world would, like the author, search for unfathomable valleys of grace through deep meditations on the Scriptures along with their ministry, sincerely preach what they have discovered before God, and then publish their works. This is because I am quite certain that the more such books are published for believers to read, the more the churches can grow into God-fearing churches firmly grounded in the Scriptures. The faith of a believer must be rational, but at the same time, a believer must be able to experience the dimension of a world that transcends rationality. In other words, one must experience heaven on this earth. From the beginning to the end of this book, the author stresses and places his concern upon the sincerity toward the Scriptures. The scriptural content clearly imparts its redemptive implications through the history of humanity.

Through this book, I, along with Rev. Park, have great anticipation for all its readers: "Through their remaining years, may the passionate encounter perpetually continue by the grace of Jesus Christ's redemption in the interminable, flaming torch of God's never-ending love."

COMMENTARY FROM DR. ANDREW J. TESIA

President, Research Institute of Reformed Theology

Everyone who has received salvation, including laypeople, pastors with a special calling, and theologians, must continue to study the inspired revelation, the Word of God, throughout their lives and apply what they have learned. Just as food is essential for the sustenance of life, this effort is essential for our spiritual survival. Among the various approaches available for correct understanding and application of the Word, total trust and faith in the Word as well as persistent effort and research are imperative. This is an absolute calling that all Christians must respond to in gratitude for the Lord's grace and love. Therefore, all Christians (including pastors and theologians), as debtors to God's grace, must always walk with the Word as the deer pants for the water brooks (Ps 42:1). It is not an easy task to discover a coherent theme and gain penetrating insight on the revealed Word. This is because of the role that the long duration of time, historical circumstances, and the varied experiences and educational backgrounds of the authors played during the recording of the inspired Word. It is impossible to comprehend God's profound will with our limited capacity, even through persistent readings and studies of the Word. At the Second Coming of the Lord, in the last days, when the perfect comes, the partial will be done away (1 Cor 13:10). I sincerely long for the day of the Lord's coming. Maranatha!

Recently, Rev. Abraham Park attempted something that no one has attempted before through two books: *The Genesis Genealogies* and *The Covenant of the Torch*. They are sure to astonish the world.

I first met Rev. Park about ten years ago at a world missions conference that I attended through the invitation of my friend Rev. Andrew Phipps. I was greatly blessed as I listened to Rev. Park, through the powerful work of the Holy Spirit, preach vividly about Jesus Christ's suffering and crucifixion. I later heard some negative criticism against Rev. Park, and so I became reserved and watched him from a distance to discern what kind of person he is. Over the past ten years, I have heard his sermons about four times. I was greatly inspired and truly received grace each time I heard his messages. My soul, which had dried up from conventional faith, felt revived, like a fish thrown back into the water. The more I observed Rev. Park, the more I lamented that such a godly and faithful man and true pastor has to go through the frustration of being misunderstood. Then one day, Rev. Phipps gave me the two books that Rev. Park authored. I read them right away. I could not put them down until I finished reading them. They are simply marvelous. After reading the books, I was deeply ashamed that I had not completely accepted Rev. Park as a true servant of God. Hence, with an apologetic heart, I write this commentary.

Rev. Park uses the covenantal links to dynamically unfold the enormous biblical discourse, which no one can come close to endeavoring, from the perspective of God's redemptive plan. He logically and perfectly depicts this theme as the central theme of Christian theology as well as the theme of his own faith and theological belief. This surely is the result of his life-long devotion to prayer and his study of the Word with gratitude for the Lord's grace. He has read the Bible hundreds of times since his calling, and his books are compilations of the Word of God and the spiritual mysteries of the Bible that he was awakened to through the process. Through the two books, we pastors and theologians will have to examine ourselves to see if we have lived our lives fulfilling the tasks we were given. At times, we must lend our ears to his discussions and confront the challenges.

First, by clearly organizing the Bible from the salvation and covenant perspective, Rev. Park has attempted something that has not been attempted during the two thousand years of the church's history. There are countless biblical commentaries and interpretations available. Furthermore, many pastors are studying and preaching the Bible based on various existing theological frameworks, typically those based on Calvinism and orthodox theology founded upon conservative faith. Nevertheless, one cannot help but be amazed at Rev. Park's work, which approaches the Bible, the original text of Christianity, as a great discourse and unfolds it coherently from the covenantal perspective. His two books truly reveal the essence of his immense theological beliefs and the perfect and logical development of his competence. More than anything, it is shocking to see a man of little scholarship (as he confesses to be) explain the profound Word in such a clear and easy way. It is amazing to see how both *The Genesis Genealogies* and *The Covenant of the Torch* are so perfectly arranged and harmonized. The mathematical calculations of the chronological years in history since the time of Adam cause readers to marvel at his immense effort and achievement, although further discussions may be needed as new archaeological discoveries are made. His achievement is truly a stern admonition to pastors and theologians who profess to be what they call "conservative" but have spent and are spending their time in denominational power struggles rather than working to fulfill their God-given tasks! A tearful, contrite heart is required.

Second, Rev. Park is now in his early eighties, but in both *The Genesis Genealogies* and *The Covenant of the Torch* he pours out the spiritual mysteries of the Bible that he was awakened to in a clear, detailed, and powerful literary style. Readers will be overtaken by a magical spell of continuous tension and anticipation that leaves them breathless and motionless. Above all, his literary style has powerful spiritual charisma that attracts the readers' attention. I believe that this is because Rev. Park himself has lived his whole life captured by the Word. Hence, his sermons call to mind the great "Prince of Preachers" who shook up not only England but also all the rest of the world in the mid-nineteenth century, Charles Haddon Spurgeon. Spurgeon was faced with the challenges of a time that was rapidly inclining toward the liberal left, and solitarily he poured out the Word of God into the minds of people through his sermons from the pulpit and his written works. The thousands who congregated at the London Central Baptist Church were captivated by his sermons as they listened breathlessly, with the exception of occasional bursts of acclamation and shouts of joy. The Word of grace that he had received he proclaimed with great strength and zeal, like a spiritual lion's roar. Unfortunately, he spent long, heartbreaking years facing much dissension, misunderstandings, disputes, and refutations. Nevertheless, with conviction in the Word of God, he pushed on with his pastoral ministry, standing firmly upon the orthodox belief of Calvinism.

Language represents one's beliefs. In that respect, Rev. Park may actually be the wizard of language that the Lord has sent to us during these turbid times where the Word of God has become scarce, and good and evil hard to distinguish. Despite his advanced age, his skill and ability to freely narrate the Word of God in his own words stand unrivaled. He is undeniably a faithful servant of God, completely captured by the Word and inspired by salvation.

Third, the foundation of his faith and theology was established through unspeakable suffering and affliction. Through times of trial and isolation he looked only upon God and trusted only in Him. He concentrated solely on faithfully raising his sheep—the congregation entrusted to him. He was captivated by a strong sense of calling and was unable to escape God's hands even for one moment. He spent many years in solitude as a result of unfounded accusations and jealousy. Nevertheless, he fully dedicated himself to the Lord and is a guardian of Calvinism, which holds biblical inspiration in one hand and God's sovereign authority in the other. As is well known, St. Augustine spent his youth in dissipation and pagan philosophy. He was even dedicated to Manichaeism at one time. However, after he met the Lord, he put an end to his old way of life and completely dedicated himself to the Lord. He gave thanks for the grace and love of the Lord of creation and found peace through repentance. Who among us today can criticize him, ostracize him, and condemn him as a libertine or a heretic? The grace and blessings that the church has received through him over the past fifteen hundred years of church history is immeasurable. How his *Confessions* have consoled many Christians, especially those who were struggling! He is considered one of the few preeminent figures of church history. There is no such thing as a perfect person in this world. I find Rev. Park's two books to be as moving as St. Augustine's *Confessions*, and readers will discover a yearning for God burning like an active volcano.

Fourth, the core of Christian theology is the progression from prophecy to fulfillment toward completion through the interpretation of the Bible using the Bible. At the center of this development is the variety of types that appear in the Old Testament, Christ's suffering and crucifixion, and completion through the Second Coming in the end. Through his great suffering and trials Rev. Park has developed a strong yearning for the return of the Lord and His glory. This is illustrated in his description of the patriarchs from Abraham to Isaac, Jacob, and Joseph, and to Moses and Joshua after the exodus. It will be depicted in greater detail in books to follow. Therefore, his understanding of the biblical history of redemption, which is the covenantal belief, is based completely on the Bible. This is possible because he was educated and trained in a conservative theological seminary and denomination. That is why, even in his advanced age, he has embarked on this great project that no one has dared to attempt. Truthfully, who among us, whether pastor or theologian, can coherently unravel this great discourse?

Rev. Park's well-versed knowledge of God's Word, the Bible, throws a great challenge to theologians whose knowledge is limited to one area of theology, for the Bible needs to be understood thoroughly and in its entirety. Theologians generally are very proficient in the areas of their study and research, but Rev. Park shows his spiritual power and knowledge in all areas of theology, which enables him to freely and appropriately use different parts of the Bible.

This is a lifelong project that Rev. Park has solely endeavored as part of his unyielding vow with God in response to the grace and love that he has received. His head and heart are filled with the Bible and the fervent zeal to think and live with the Word. In this sojourner's world we have discovered an old servant struggling to pour himself out as a drink offering on the Lord's altar, just like the apostle Paul.

Fifth, the well-organized logic and real challenges and applications of Rev. Park's work are distinguished yet natural. The details and motivating power come from his many years of experience and lifelong pastoral ministry.

His applications are concise and entirely based on the Bible. Although he uses very concise and plain language, his sentences contain a concentrated form of theological depth that no other pastor or theologian can mimic. He addresses highly debated issues that even theologians cannot easily address, such as the relationship between Abraham and Jacob, the relationship between Judah and Joseph, and the various themes that develop through Moses' life. His discoveries that the duration of the construction of Noah's ark was less than the well-accepted 120 years and of the 42 camp sites during the Israelites' wilderness journey are the first of their kind since the time of Noah and Moses. This is a marvelous and celebrated achievement unimaginable even for a scholar who has dedicated his entire life to the study of the Bible and theology.

Unfolding the great discourse using a concise sermon format and storytelling style stands out in the world of theology, which places importance on logic and proof based on scholarship. Rev. Park unravels this discourse smoothly and with the sincerity of a grandfather narrating a story to his grandchild. His thorough insight of the Bible gives him the agility to maneuver through it and the ability to visually illustrate the Old and New Testaments as with a computer. His analysis of heretofore unresolved theological issues can easily be considered a masterpiece.

Finally, what is most urgently needed in the church today? Proper understanding of the Bible and its application in life are necessary to overcome the long period of stagnation. This is the goal that the church needs to pursue in the rapidly changing twenty-first century in order to recover the lost glory of old. For this purpose, we must first learn to live out the Word of God, develop our theological awareness, and revitalize the redemptive movement. Frankly, an understanding of the inspired Word of revelation, the Bible, and effective application in life are the universal hope of all pastors. Learning to effectively deliver the Word from the pulpit is a lifelong assignment for pastors. To be able to do this, they must first gain thorough knowledge of the Bible. This knowledge refers not merely to literal interpretation, but also to the ability to see the entire flow and to accurately reveal the meaning of each part. Another crucial task is to shed light on how the revelations of the Bible are fulfilled in history. Paradoxically, we are living in an age where the Word of God is overflowing and scarce at the same time. Thus, we must fathom the depth of God's will through the redemptive and covenantal approach. Thus, I joyfully recommend Rev. Park's *The Genesis Genealogies* and *The Covenant of the Torch* to all the churches of the world, for not only do they satisfy the spiritual aspirations of thirsting Christians, but also they are an absolute necessity for those who desire a more mature life of faith. I pray that you may receive a double portion of blessings by reading and studying these books!

Andrew J. Tesia

COMMENTARY FROM DR. YEONG-SU YE

President of the International Christian Academy
President of the International Council of Churches and Ministries
Former President of Hanshin University Graduate School

Recently, I received a letter from a pastor asking me to theologically evaluate *The Genesis Genealogies* written by Rev. Abraham Park in order that he can correctly guide his parishioners. This became an opportunity for me to start researching about Rev. Abraham Park and read his book carefully. Through my studies, I came to know the fact that Rev. Park has experienced a great deal of heartache and suffering for a long time because of libelous accusations and misapprehensions. When I found out that some of those slanderers even fabricated a picture of Rev. Park with his congregation in order to attack him, I could not suppress my righteous indignation. I learned that he persevered endless accusations with an attitude of turning the other cheek. I was saddened to learn that many years of mental affliction caused him to lose most of his teeth, and now he has to use dentures.

As I was reading *The Genesis Genealogies*, I was strongly convicted that he is a man of sound and profound faith based on absolute Christ-centered beliefs and redemptive theological viewpoint.

I was able to discover the author's true qualities through *The Covenant of the Torch*, the second book he has published. Although he is an 82-year old man, he has authored a 297 page book as a second volume in the History of Redemption Series. I could not but admire his persistency in studying and reading the Bible over and over, the amount of data and accuracy of his knowledge, his complete devotion to the Word of the Bible, his godly faith and theology, and the keen eyes to see and understand God's administration of redemption in history by studying the genealogies of the biblical patriarchs.

There are several fortes that stand out in this book.

First, this book allows the readers to easily see and grasp Israel's history from Abraham until the conquest of Canaan. The book organizes a vast amount of information including Abraham's family tree and genealogy, all the historical events that happened in each generation, God's prophecy about Jacob's twelve sons and the fulfillment through the blessings given in the time of Moses, the death of the leaders in the wilderness, wars before and after the entry in to Canaan, and the redemptive significance for not recording the firstborns according to their birth order in the genealogy, etc. I was impressed at the author's concentrated effort in organizing so much information in a way that is simple and easy-to-understand.

Second, the map of "The Exodus and Wilderness Journey" is probably the first in the world. It is a compilation of a great amount of data that has been published up until now and the author's on-site surveys. The map includes the details of the 42 camp sites of the 40 years in the wilderness, the meaning of their names, location, events that happened, and the lessons we can learn. I can boldly say that this is a splendid achievement in the Church history.

Third, the author clearly resolves the biblical dilemma concerning the fulfillment of the covenant of the torch by examining the matter from a history of redemption perspective. God promised Abraham in the covenant of the torch. "Then in the fourth generation they (Abraham's descendants) shall return here...." However, the actual generation that returned from Egypt to Canaan was much later than the fourth generation. The author explicitly answers this dilemma in the Bible. This is truly a highlight in the studies of the Bible.

The subtitle for this book, *A Forgotten Encounter in the History of the Exodus and Wilderness Journey* is also very intriguing. This book connects the biblical events according to their historical flow in a way that the events and characters come alive. Those who read this book will be inspired and feel as though God's covenant of the flaming torch is being fulfilled today through their very lives.

I sincerely pray that the Church and all Christians may recover the forgotten encounter with God and have a heartfelt reunion.

As an 85-year old Caleb conquered and triumphed like a 40-year old warrior, I pray and bless that Rev. Abraham Park would conquer and become triumphant.

Recommending Rev. Park and *The Covenant of the Torch*.

Yeong-Su Ye

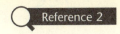

A Single Blessing of the Firstborn

✳ Isaac's faith in blessing Jacob is explained here for the first time in history.

Genesis 27 narrates the process through which Isaac, when he was advanced in age (approx. 136 years old), bequeaths God's covenant and the blessings of the firstborn to Jacob (approx. 76 years old). According to this narration of the account, Isaac gave the blessings without knowing whom he was blessing because he was deceived by his wife Rebekah and the second son Jacob.

> **Genesis 27:1** Now it came about, when Isaac was old, and his eyes were too dim to see...
>
> **Genesis 27:23** And he did not recognize him ... so he blessed him.

However, the book of Hebrews records that Isaac blessed Jacob and Esau by faith regarding things to come, and it emphasizes Isaac's faith (Heb 11:20).

Now, was Isaac aware or unaware of whom he was blessing?

1. Initially, Isaac was unaware that he was blessing Jacob.

Isaac gave all the blessings of the firstborn to Jacob when he disguised himself as Esau and brought the food that Isaac loved. According to Genesis 27:23 "He did not recognize him, because his hands were hairy like his brother Esau's hands; so he blessed him." In Hebrew, the expression "he did not recognize him" is לֹא הִכִּירוֹ (lōʾ hikkîrô). The root of הִכִּירוֹ (hikkîrô) is נָכַר (nākar), meaning, "to point out," "identify," "to contemplate," and "to investigate in detail" (Gen 31:32). With the addition of a Hebrew negative particle לֹא (lōʾ), it is evident that Isaac gave the blessings without a careful effort to identify which son he was blessing. Isaac did not give much thought to this when he gave the blessings because he assumed, without a doubt, that the son he was blessing was Esau.

Genesis 27:33 speaks of Isaac's response when Esau came in with the food that he loved and asked for his blessings after Jacob had left: "Then Isaac trembled violently, and said, 'Who was he then that hunted game and brought it to me, so that I ate of all of it before you came, and blessed him? Yes, and he shall be blessed.'"

2. Later, Isaac blessed Jacob through faith.

According to Genesis, it appears that Isaac was unaware of whom he was blessing when he blessed Jacob since he was deceived by Rebekah and Jacob. Contrarily, however, Hebrew 11:20 states, "By faith Isaac blessed Jacob and Esau, even regarding things to come," as though Isaac knew whom he was blessing. How can these contradicting verses be reconciled?

(1) Isaac immediately put away his own thoughts.

Isaac initially wanted to bless Esau. The obvious reason was that Esau was the first-born, but also Isaac loved Esau more. Genesis 25:28 states, "Now Isaac loved Esau, because he had a taste for game." If Isaac had been caught up in his personal human love, he could have given the blessings of the firstborn to Esau again. Nevertheless, Isaac refused Esau when he tearfully pleaded with him for a blessing (Gen 27:34, 37–38). In Genesis 27:33, Isaac says to him, "Who was he then that hunted game and brought it to me, so that I ate of all of it before you came, and blessed him? Yes, and he shall be blessed."

The Hebrew word for "shall" here is גַּם (*gam*), meaning "truly" or "no matter what happens." Isaac declared that the blessings that Jacob had received could not be changed by human effort. This event clearly demonstrates Isaac's faith. Isaac's resolution to subdue his own fleshly affection, when he realized that it was God's will for Jacob to receive the blessing of the firstborn, is the true faith that God acknowledged.

Without faith, it is impossible to completely subdue or cut off human affection (Matt 12:50). In his commentary on this verse, John Calvin said, "For he [Isaac], renouncing the affections of the flesh, now yields himself entirely to God, and, acknowledging God as the Author of the benediction which he had uttered, ascribes due glory to him in not daring to retract it."

Esau was certainly the first son to whom Isaac gave all his heart and hope according to human affection (Gen 25:28; 27:1–4). When God's will became clear to him, Isaac immediately put away his own thoughts and pushed forth to follow God's will with a firm conviction in his heart. Witnessing Isaac's great faith, the author of Hebrews said, "By faith Isaac blessed Jacob and Esau, even regarding things to come" (Heb 11:20).

(2) Isaac understood and obeyed God's sovereign providence.

There was a very short period of time between when "Jacob had hardly gone out" and when Esau came in (Gen 27:30). The Word of God that Isaac had forgotten all this time probably flashed in his head as soon as he realized that the son before him was Esau. It was the Word that God had spoken when Rebekah prayed about the struggle between the twins in her womb (Gen 25:22).

> **Genesis 25:23** And the older shall serve the younger.

Although Isaac had blessed Jacob without an awareness of whom he was blessing, he realized that it was by God's sovereign determination, wholly dissimilar from his own thoughts, and he "trembled violently" with great shock (Gen 27:33). The NLT for this verse says, "Isaac began to tremble uncontrollably." Outwardly, it seems like he was trembling out of anger after being deceived into giving the blessings of the firstborn to Jacob. However, Jacob's trembling contains a greater significance. In Hebrew, the phrase "then Isaac trembled violently" in Genesis 27:33 is וַיֶּחֱרַד יִצְחָק חֲרָדָה גְּדֹלָה עַד־מְאֹד (*wayyeḥĕrad yiṣḥāq ḥărādâ gĕdōlâ ʿadmĕʾōd*), meaning "Isaac trembled violently in great fear." This fear was not simply from the thought that he had made a mistake by blessing Jacob; it was a holy fear from the realization that he had almost blessed Esau against God's marvelous providence because of his own prejudice and stubbornness.

God's sovereign will regarding Jacob and Esau is explained well in Romans 9:10–13 (cf. Mal 1:2–3).

Romans 9:10 And not only this, but there was Rebekah also, when she had conceived twins by one man, our father Isaac; [11]for though the twins were not yet born, and had not done anything good or bad, in order that God's purpose according to His choice might stand, not because of works, but because of Him who calls, [12]it was said to her, "The older will serve the younger." [13]Just as it is written, "Jacob I loved, but Esau I hated."

Isaac came to an understanding that it was God's absolute will for Jacob to receive the blessing of the firstborn. Isaac's spiritual eyes were opened to see that Jacob was the true firstborn, and thus he resolutely refused Esau's request for the blessing of the firstborn. Later, just before he died, Jacob's eyes became dim from old age so that he could not see (Gen 48:10). Yet, he realized God's providence and gave the blessing of the firstborn to the younger son, Ephraim, by placing his right hand on his head. Upon seeing that his father had laid his right hand on Ephraim's head, Joseph grabbed his father's hand to move it from Ephraim's head to Manasseh's head. Nevertheless, Jacob said, "I know, my son, I know," and gave the blessing of the right hand to Ephraim (Gen 48:17–20). This was possible solely because God had opened Jacob's spiritual eyes. Before Moses, the leader of the wilderness, died, he was able to see all the land of Canaan from the top of Pisgah, which was about 100 miles (160 km) away, because God had opened Moses' spiritual eyes (Deut 34:1–3).

Rather than blessing Esau, Isaac declared that it was God's will for Jacob to receive the blessing of the firstborn.

Genesis 27:37 But Isaac answered and said to Esau, "Behold, I have made him your master, and all his relatives I have given to him as servants; and with grain and new wine I have sustained him. Now as for you then, what can I do, my son?"

Here, the word "master" is גְּבִיר (*gĕbîr*) in Hebrew, meaning "lord" or "governor." Hence, it is evident that Isaac realized that giving Jacob the blessing of the firstborn was the crucial providence of God for salvation, and so he told Esau, who was pleading for the blessing, "Behold, I have made him your master [governor]."

True faith is following the will of God completely without hesitation like Isaac, even if God's providence contradicts one's own thoughts or preference.

3. There is only one firstborn that God will acknowledge.

When Esau asked, "Have you not reserved a blessing for me?" (Gen 27:36), Isaac replied that there was nothing that he could do for him (Gen 27:37). Essentially, Isaac's reply meant that there was only one blessing. Although there was no possibility of receiving a blessing, Esau repeatedly cried and pleaded, "Do you have only one blessing, my father? Bless me, even me also, O my father" (Gen 27:38).

Isaac responded to Esau's cry with a curse: "Behold, away from the fertility of the earth shall be your dwelling, and away from the dew of heaven from above. And by your sword you shall live, and your brother you shall serve" (Gen 27:39–40).

Esau's bitter cry (Gen 27:34, 38) was merely the regret for considering the God-given birthright with negligence and contempt. Hebrews 12:17 says of Esau that "he found no place for repentance." This is a great lesson for us. We may weep out loud and repent, but it is no use if we lose our ability to repent. Even Esau, who was so loved, was refused by Isaac, and the blessing of the firstborn could not be returned.

God's prophecy that "the older shall serve the younger" (Gen 25:23) was fulfilled without fail. There is no regret or change in God's decisions and will (Num 23:19; Rom 11:29; Heb 6:18). All things are predestined in the Word of God. Psalm 139:16 states, "Thine eyes have seen my unformed substance; and in Thy book they were all written, the days that were ordained for me, when as yet there was not one of them."

Outwardly, Isaac appeared to have been momentarily deceived; however, God certainly is never deceived by man, and His Word is always fulfilled just as He had planned. This is nothing else but the absolute sovereignty, strength, and power found in the Word of God.

May we also give up our human thoughts and let go of our fleshly affections before the presence of God's definite will and providence so that we can become great people of faith like Isaac, who held on to only God's Word. Hallelujah!

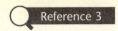
Chart: The Number of Years that Abraham, Isaac, Jacob, and Joseph Lived Together

✳ Organized and illustrated for the first time in history

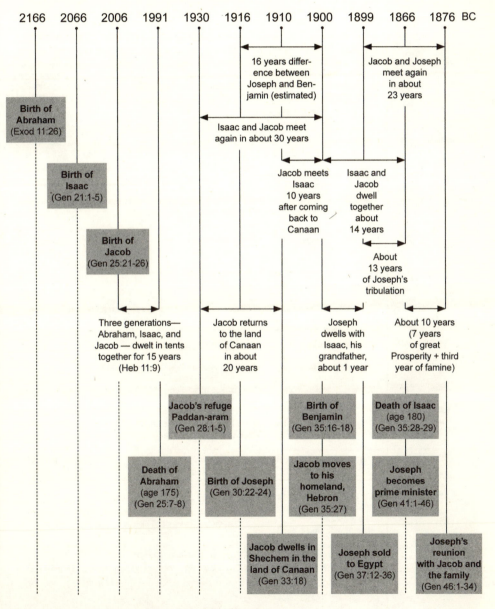

The years above are estimated and may have slight differences.

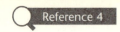
Chart: The 40-Year Journey at a Glance

✳ Organized and illustrated for the first time in history

1st year, 1st month, 15th day	**The Exodus** "And they journeyed from Rameses in the first month, on the fifteenth day of the first month" (Num 33:3).
1446 BC	רַעְמְסֵס / **Rameses** (Exod 12:37, Num 33:3)
636th year since the covenant of the torch	The first year—"This month shall be the beginning of months for you, it is to be the first month of the year to you." (Exod 12:2)

① סֻכּוֹת / **Succoth** (Exod 12:37; Num 33:5)	② אֵתָם / **Etham** (Exod 13:20; Num 33:6)	③ פְּנֵי מִגְדֹּל / **Before Migdol** (Exod 14:2, 9; Num 33:7)

Crossing of the **Red Sea** (Exod 14:15-31)

④ מָרָה / **Marah** (Exod 15:23; Num 33:8)	⑤ אֵילִם / **Elim** (Exod 15:27; Num 33:9)	⑥ עַל יַם סוּף / **By the Red Sea** (Num 33:10)

⑦ מִדְבַּר סִין / **The Wilderness of Sin** (Exod 16:1; Num 33:11)

1ˢᵗ year, 2ⁿᵈ month, 15ᵗʰ day	**Manna** starts falling (Exod 16:1-13). It falls for 39 years and 11 months until the 41st year, 1st month, 15th day (Josh 5:10-12).
1446BC	

⑧ רְפְקָה / **Dophkah** (Num 33:13)	⑨ אָלוּשׁ / **Alush** (Num 33:13)	⑩ רְפִידִים / **Rephidim** (Exod 17:1; 19:2; Num 33:14)

Water provided from the rock (Exod 17:1-7)

1st year, 3rd month ~ 2nd year, 2nd month, 20th day (approx. 1 year)	⑪ מִדְבַּר סִינַי / **The Wilderness of Sinai** (Exod 19:1-2; Num 33:15)	Law given and Sinai Covenant ratified (Exod 20:1-24:18)
1446 ~ 1445BC	2ⁿᵈ year, 1ˢᵗ month, 1ˢᵗ day	Establishment of the tabernacle (Exod 40:17)
	2ⁿᵈ year, 1ˢᵗ month, 14ᵗʰ day	First Passover in the wilderness (Num 9:1-5)
637ᵗʰ year since the covenant of the torch	2ⁿᵈ year, 2ⁿᵈ month, 1ˢᵗ day	First census of soldiers – 603,550 excluding the tribe of Levi (Num 1:1-46; 47~49)
	2ⁿᵈ year, 2ⁿᵈ month, 20ᵗʰ day	After about 1 year of stay at Mt. Sinai, Israel departs to the Wilderness of Paran (Num 10:11-12)

⑫ קִבְרוֹת הַתַּאֲוָה / **Kibroth-hattaavah** (Num11:34; 33:16)	⑬ חֲצֵרוֹת / **Hazeroth** (Num 11:35; 33:17)	⑭ רִתְמָה / **Rithmah** (Num 33:18)

	קָדֵשׁ בַּרְנֵעַ / **Kadesh-barnea** 40 days of spying out the land of Canaan (Num 13:1-33; Deut 1:19-33)	Because of the negative reports of 10 spies, people of Israel sin against God by grumbling and receive the judgment that they will wander around the wilderness for 40 years and perish (Num 14:26-35).
After the 2ⁿᵈ year, 5ᵗʰ month (estimated)	**Pronouncement of the 40 years in the wilderness** "According to the number of days which you spied out the land, forty days, for every day you shall bear your guilt a year, even forty years." (Num 14:34)	

15 רִמֹּן פֶּרֶץ / Rimmon-perez (Num 33:19)	16 לִבְנָה / Libnah (Num 33:20)	17 רִסָּה / Rissah (Num 33:21)
18 קְהֵלָתָה / Kehelathah (Num 33:22)	19 הַר שֶׁפֶר / Mt. Shepher (Num 33:23)	20 חֲרָדָה / Haradah (Num 33:24)
21 מַקְהֵלֹת / Makheloth (Num 33:25)	22 תַּחַת / Tahath (Num 33:26)	23 תֶּרַח / Terah (Num 33:27)
24 מִתְקָה / Mithkah (Num 33:28)	25 חַשְׁמֹנָה / Hashmonah (Num 33:29)	26 מֹסֵרוֹת / Moseroth (Num 33:30)
27 בְּנֵי יַעֲקָן / Bene-jaakan (Num 33:31)	28 חֹר הַגִּדְגָּד / Hor-haggidgad (Num 33:32)	29 יָטְבָתָה / Jotbathah (Num 33:33)
30 עַבְרֹנָה / Abronah (Num 33:34)	31 עֶצְיוֹן גֶּבֶר / Ezion-geber (Num 33:35)	

40th year, 1st month 1407 BC

675th year since the covenant of the torch

32 קָדֵשׁ / Kadesh (Num 13:26; 20:1-13; 33:36)	**Death of Miriam** (Num 20:1)—about 1 year before the entry into Canaan Water given from the **rock** (Num 20:2-13)—By disobeying God's command and striking the rock twice, Moses and Aaron are banned from entering Canaan (Num 20:7-13).
33 הֹר הָהָר / Mt. Hor (Num 20:22; 33:37)	**Death of Aaron** (Num 20:22-29; 33:38-39)—about 8 months before the entry into Canaan

34 צַלְמֹנָה / Zalmonah (Num 33:41)	35 פּוּנֹן / Punon (Num 33:42)	36 אֹבֹת / Oboth (Num 21:10; 33:43)
37 עִיֵּי הָעֲבָרִים / Iye-abarim (Num 21:11; 33:44)		

After the 40th year, 5th month (estimated)

נַחַל זֶרֶד / Brook Zered
All 603,550 soldiers who were counted in the first census and were still living until this time perished here except Joshua and Caleb (Deut 2:14-16; Num 26:63-65)

Perishing of the first generation in the wilderness	"Now the time that it took for us to come from Kadesh-barnea, until we crossed over the brook Zered, was thirty-eight years; until all the generations of the men of war perished from within the camp." (Deut 2:14)

38 דִּיבוֹן גָּד / Dibon-gad (Num 33:45)	39 עַלְמֹן דִּבְלָתָיְמָה / Almon-diblathaim (Num 33:46)	40 הַר עֲבָרִים / Mountains of Abarim (Num 27:12; 33:47)

41 עַרְבֹת מוֹאָב / Plains of Moab (Num 33:48-49)	As a result of "playing the harlot" with the daughters of Moab, 24,000 were killed by a plague (Num 25:1-9). Second census of soldiers—601,730 excluding the tribe of Levi (Num 26:1-51, 62)

40th year, 11th month, 1st day

Reiteration of the Law to the second generation in the wilderness (Deut 1:3-5)
Death of Moses—about 2 months before the entry into Canaan (Deut 34:1-8)
Rise of the new leader, Joshua (Num 27:18-23; Deut 34:9)

Crossing of the **Jordan River** (Josh 3:14-17)

41st year, 1st month, 10th day

42 גִּלְגָּל / Gilgal (Josh 4:19)	Total duration of the wilderness journey - 5 days less of 40 years

1406 BC

676th year since the covenant of the torch

Entry into Canaan, the Promised Land	"Now the people came up from the Jordan on the tenth of the first month and camped at Gilgal...." (Josh 4:19)

Simeon, Levi, and Judah

Simeon, Levi, and Judah are the second, third, and fourth sons of the same mother, Leah (Gen 29:33–35). Simeon and Levi were especially close, so much so that they were even called "two of a kind" (Gen 49:5 NLT). They became accomplices in a heinous crime of murder and were cursed by Jacob as a result. However, they did not continue on the same path in the end. Furthermore, Judah, the fourth son, received many more blessings compared to the other sons.

1. The Rape of Dinah at Shechem (Gen 34)

After 20 years of residing in Paddan-aram, Jacob passed Succoth and safely arrived at the city of Shechem in Canaan, where he settled (Gen 33:18). One day, Jacob heard the shocking news that his daughter Dinah had gone out to visit the daughters of the land and was raped by Shechem, the son of Hamor the Hivite, the prince of that land (Gen 34:3–5). This event is described in great length in Genesis 34.

Dinah was the daughter that Leah bore after bearing Issachar and Zebulun. It appears that she went out secretly "to visit the daughters" of Shechem by herself without the knowledge of her family (Gen 34:1). Here, "to visit" in Hebrew is רָאָה (rāʾâ), the word used to describe the act of closely observing or carefully inspecting in order to have a direct experience or relationship. It seems that Dinah did not go out just once to look around but many times, most likely to enjoy and get to know the things around.

Dinah's frequent outings captured the heart of Shechem, the chief of the Hivite tribe. After raping Dinah, Shechem longed for her (Gen 34:3, 8) and told his father, Hamor, to request intermarriage with Jacob's family (Gen 34:4–12). Jacob's sons replied, deceitfully, that they would intermarry if all the males of the Hivite tribe received circumcision. Upon hearing this, the Hivites lost no time in circumcising all the men who had entered their city gates (Gen 34:18–24). However, on the third day after the circumcision, while they were still in enormous pain and recovering, Simeon and Levi broke their promise and took their swords and killed every man who was circumcised, including Hamor and Shechem, and brought Dinah back (Gen 34:25–26).

2. Jacob's Prophecy Regarding Simeon and Levi

Simeon and Levi's act of mass murder doubled and even tripled the anxiety in their father, who was already immersed in deep sorrow because of what had happened to his daughter Dinah. Later, in Genesis 49:5–7, Jacob calls Simeon and Levi "implements of violence" (NASB), "weapons of violence" (NAB), or "instruments of cruelty" (NKJV) and proclaims his intense anger toward them.

Genesis 49:5–7 "Simeon and Levi are brothers; their swords are implements of violence. Let my soul not enter into their council; let not my glory be united with their assembly; because in their anger they slew men, and in their self-will they lamed oxen. Cursed be their anger, for it is fierce; and their wrath, for it is cruel. I will disperse them in Jacob, and scatter them in Israel."

This can be understood as God's proclamation of anger. If so, why did Simeon and Levi receive such great wrath?

(1) The brothers committed brutal murder

Genesis 34:25–26 Now it came about on the third day, when they were in pain, that two of Jacob's sons, Simeon and Levi, Dinah's brothers, each took his sword and came upon the city unawares, and killed every male. They killed Hamor and his son Shechem with the edge of the sword, and took Dinah from Shechem's house, and went forth.

"Edge of the sword" in Hebrew is לְפִי־חָרֶב (lĕpiḥāreb), and it depicts the ruthless slaughter as the blade of the sword devouring the flesh and swallowing the blood (Gen 34:26). Killing anyone they could lay their hands on, Simeon and Levi committed brutal mass murder, a massacre. Furthermore, they did not stop there; they looted the livestock inside the city and the fields, captured women and children as prisoners, and plundered household articles (Gen 34:27).

Thus, in their cruel retaliatory massacre against Shechem, besides committing such inhumane murder, Simeon and Levi added detestable deception—lies and stealing. They even went even further by defiantly rebelling and arguing with their father who rebuked them (Gen 34:31). As hatred and loathing consumed them, sin brought on more sin, causing their sin to gradually intensify.

(2) Unable to control their anger, they became implements of violence

When Jacob's sons heard that Dinah was violated, they became furious. Genesis 34:7 states that "the men were grieved, and they were very angry." Apparently, not only were their minds deeply grieved, but also they became furious beyond their control, such that their rage violently exploded outward.

Furthermore, in Genesis 49:5–7, Jacob emphasized Simeon and Levi's anger four times: "in their anger," "in their self-will," "their anger is fierce," and "their wrath is cruel." Because they took lives out of anger, they became "implements of violence." It seems that Jacob wanted to expose what was behind this horrid bloodshed: the angry nature that had always been inside Simeon and Levi. Indeed, they were "men of bloodshed" (Ps 55:23) and "men with feet swift to shed blood" (Rom 3:15).

Jacob harshly rebuked Simeon and Levi for what they did in secret. Because Jacob's family was only a small nation in a Gentile land, Simeon and Levi's act of slaughter in the city of Shechem could have put them in great danger.

Genesis 34:30 Then Jacob said to Simeon and Levi, "You have brought trouble on me by making me a stench to the Canaanites and Perizzites, the people living in this land. We are few in number, and if they join forces against me and attack me, I and my household will be destroyed."

Genesis 34:5 states that Jacob heard of Dinah's disgrace, but Jacob "kept silent." A literal translation of the corresponding Hebrew word here, וְהֶחֱרִשׁ (wĕhehĕriš), is "conducted like a deaf person." The word conveys that although Dinah's defilement brought about surges of unspeakable grief and shock to her father, he remained silent and chose not to seek revenge. Jacob had acted prudently because God's providence in redemptive history—to raise up a pure and holy nation through his family—might collapse in an instant.

Because they did not control their anger and committed brutal murder, they could not become the "generation of faith" that succeeds Jacob.

3. The Fate of the Tribe of Simeon

(1) The tribe with the lowest population

Psalm 55:23 states that bloodthirsty and deceitful men will not live out half their days. In accordance with this word, the second census, executed after 40 years in the wilderness, shows that the tribe of Simeon had decreased in number by as much as 63 percent compared to the first census. In the first census, it was the third strongest tribe among the 12 tribes, with 59,300 people, but in the second census, it had become the tribe with the lowest population with only 22,200 people (Num 1:23; 26:14). Though it would be normal for the number of people to increase in the 40-year duration of time, the tribe of Simeon came out as the weakest and least productive in their fruit of life according to the tribal census.

(2) The leader of the Simeonites worships Baal of Peor

When we closely examine the account of the Baal of Peor event, we see that at the end of the wilderness period at Shittim in Moab, the leader of the Israelites was not a common person but an actual patriarch, Zimri, who was a Simeonite (Num 25:6–15). Therefore, it can be assumed that many people from the Simeon tribe participated in worshiping Baal of Peor.

(3) The tribe of Simeon was excluded from Moses' blessing

In Deuteronomy 33, Moses blesses the Israelites by their tribes just before his death. As Jacob had prophesied about each of his 12 sons when he blessed them, Moses also gave prophecies about each tribe as though he was blessing his own children. However, the astonishing fact is that Moses did not mention anything about the tribe of Simeon. It must have been a great disgrace and tragedy for the people in that tribe to be excluded.

The tribe of Simeon was excluded from Moses' blessings! They became a dispersed tribe that is destroyed and forgotten just as Jacob had prophesied. Adding onto the despair, the tribe of Simeon was not given an allotted inheritance. They barely managed to take a little portion of the land that the tribe of Judah had received as their inheritance, which was the largest, but it was the most barren land in the Negev Desert (Josh 19:1). During the time of the King Hezekiah, they became dispersed through the entire territory of Israel (Josh 21:9; 1 Chr 4:42–43; 2 Chr 15:9).

4. The Fate of the Tribe of Levi (a Tribe Restored)

The tribe of Levi, which Jacob condemned as committing the same sin as Simeon, received the same wrath with identical consequences. However, the descendants of the Levites were, fortunately, different from the tribe of Simeon and were cleansed from that curse. Although Jacob had definitely prophesied wrath against the Levites, after 450 years had passed and before they entered the land of Canaan, Moses proclaimed his blessing upon the tribe of Levi.

According to the blessings given through Moses, the tribe of Levi received more than other tribes (Deut 33:8–11). Deuteronomy 33:9 states, "He said of his father and mother, 'I have no regard for them.' He did not recognize his brothers or acknowledge his own children, but he watched over your word and guarded your covenant" (NIV). This refers to the account of when all Israelites faced a crisis of their impending destruction due to their idolatry while Moses was up on the mountain. The tribe of Levi alone stood on God's side and took the lead in destroying anyone who disobeyed God's will, whether it was their parents, siblings, friends, or neighbors (Exod 32).

Through this incident, the tribe of Levi was not only set free from the curse that they had received from Jacob, but also received blessings from Moses (Exod 32:29). Indeed, one's resolution and determination to dedicate oneself before the Lord can become the passageway to the restoration of lost blessings and the cleansing of wrath. By receiving the greatest blessing of the Lord as their eternal inheritance, they became an example of those who recover from their sins and curse.

Even during the event of Baal Peor that broke out toward the end of the life in the wilderness, the tribe of Levi distinguished itself. At the time when Israel was sinning with their idolatry and lewdness, the person who took God's side and felt God's jealousy was Phinehas, Aaron's grandson among the descendants of the Levites (Exod 6:16–25). By piercing Zimri, the leader of the Simeonites, and Cozbi, the Midianite woman, with a spear and killing them, he turned away God's wrath and atoned for the Israelites (Num 25:7–13). Ironically, the tribe of Simeon and the tribe of Levi, which used to be tribes that were "two of a kind," appear as enemies in this event.

The ends of these two tribes are in obvious contrast. Surely, the ancestors of these two tribes were the very ones who became the implements of violence and massacred the clan of Shechem. Even though the tribe of Levi had a feeble beginning, its change was great such that it became the everlasting tribe of priests called "the shining tribe." In contrast, Simeon was the son of "the heard," born in response to Leah's prayers, and in the early days of the wilderness it was the third most powerful tribe. However, after receiving the wrath of God, it gradually lost its power and was finally destroyed, becoming "the forgotten tribe."

Just as Jacob had prophesied, "the tribe of Levi will be scattered among Israel" (Gen 49:7); the tribe of Levi was allocated to 48 cities throughout the nation and lived scattered. Moreover, just as Moses prophesied, the Levites were entrusted with a precious commission to carry out God's rule on his behalf as priests in each region. The Levites, who were dispersed throughout the nation, were then appointed the important task of ensuring that all Israelites do not sin against God and forsake Him. Through the ends of the Simeonite and Levite tribes, we can see that God's prophecy is fulfilled without fail. The Levites accomplished this positively, and the Simeonites accomplished it negatively. Our lives must become lives that positively accomplish God's prophecy.

5. The Blessing That Judah Received

Jesus' genealogy states that Abraham was the father of Isaac, Isaac the father of Jacob, and Jacob the father of Judah and his brothers (Matt 1:2). Judah had received the marvelous blessing of having Jesus come as his descendant (Matt 1:1–3; Heb 7:14). Even though Judah was the fourth son, he became the leader of the 12 tribes.

Jacob repeatedly emphasized that the Messiah will come through the "tribe of Judah," underlining the fact that Judah will become the bloodline ancestor for the Messiah amongst other things, prophesying much more about him than for the rest of his sons. If so, what is the blessing that Judah received from his father Jacob?

(1) Your brothers will praise you (Gen 49:8)

This is the very first blessing that Jacob had prophesied to Judah. Undoubtedly, Jacob gave such a blessing while keeping in mind that the Messiah will come through Judah. Looking back at Judah's life, Jacob proclaimed, "Judah, your brothers shall praise you" (Gen 49:8). In fact, at every crucial moment, he saved his family from crisis with a sacrificial and devotional attitude and carried out an important role in God's redemptive history.

Judah said to his brothers who were about to kill Joseph, "What profit is it for us to kill our brother and cover up [hide away, keep it a secret] his blood?" (Gen 37:26). He persuaded his brothers and saved Joseph from the threat of death.

Also, during the brothers' second visit to Egypt, when Jacob did not want to allow them to take Benjamin with them even though their families were starving to death due to the famine, Judah gave his life as a surety for Benjamin's life, thereby moving his father's heart and receiving his permission (Gen 43:8–10).

Later, when Benjamin faced the threat of becoming a slave in Egypt forever due to Joseph's test with a silver cup, Judah fervently pleaded that he be made slave in Egypt in place of Benjamin. This was a decisive moment that brought forth the great reconciliation between Joseph and his brothers (Gen 44:18–34; 45:1–15). Here, Judah's plea, which rose up from his passionate love for his brothers and consideration for his father, stirred up and touched Joseph's heart so powerfully that Joseph finally broke down and cried. Among the seven incidents of Joseph's cries recorded in Genesis (Gen 42:24; 43:30; 45:2, 14–15; 46:29; 50:1, 17), the cry after Judah's plea was especially described as a weeping that is so loud that even the Egyptians and the household of Pharaoh heard of it (Gen 45:1–2).

Seeing that Jacob had sent ahead his fourth son, Judah, to Joseph before Jacob led his family to Egypt, it is perceivable that Jacob had firm trust in Jacob to represent the family (Gen 46:28).

(2) Your hands shall be on the neck of your enemies (Gen 49:8)

Following the prophecy "Your brothers will praise you," Jacob added, "Your hands shall be on the neck of your enemies" (Gen 49:8). "Grasping the enemy's neck" is the image of causing a powerful enemy to surrender, or of a conqueror triumphing a battle (Job 16:12). The prophecy was fulfilled when Israel became a powerful nation by Judah's descendants David and Solomon. However, ultimately it refers to when Jesus, who would come as a descendant of the tribe of Judah, bruises the head of Satan, our enemy (Gen 3:15).

(3) Your father's sons shall bow down to you (Gen 49:8)

The statement "Your father's sons shall bow down to you" signifies that Judah will become a leader. 1 Chronicles 5:2 states that "Judah prevailed over his brothers."

The meaning of this statement goes beyond the thought that Judah will become a leader over his brothers; it implies that the descendant to succeed to the royal power will come from the descendants of Judah, hence making the tribe of Judah eminent. In reality, King David emerged from among Judah's descendants and ruled over the tribe of Judah, which approved of him as their king in Hebron for seven years and six months (2 Sam 2:4–11); and after, he was crowned as the king of a unified Israel and reigned in Jerusalem for 33 years (2 Sam 5:5). Ultimately, this statement signifies the prophecy that Jesus Christ, who comes as a descendant of the tribe of Judah, as the Son of David, will reign over the universe by all the powers of heaven and earth (Matt 28:18; Phil 2:9–11).

(4) Like a lion, like a lioness (Gen 49:9)

To emphasize the image that the tribe of Judah was the "king's tribe" which has strong authority and power, Jacob figuratively described him as a lion and a lioness (Gen 49:9). The comparison of Judah to a lion was made to imply that defeating Judah is as difficult as conquering a lion, and that to compete with him is like offending a lion. Such characteristics of Judah—the image of a conqueror who does not surrender the chastity of his faith and fights triumphantly to the end—symbolize the coming Messiah.

(5) Neither the scepter nor the ruler's staff will depart from Judah (Gen 49:10)

The "scepter" is a rod that symbolizes a king's ruling sovereignty and power (Num 24:17; Esth 4:11; Heb 1:8). It implies that Judah's descendants will continue to be in succession to royal authority. In fact, King David, King Solomon, and all the kings from the southern Judah dynasty came from the tribe of Judah. Furthermore, even Jesus Christ, the King of kings, was from the tribe of Judah, according to the genealogy (Matt 1:2–3; Heb 7:14).

(6) Shiloh arises from the tribe of Judah (Gen 49:10)

"Shiloh," meaning "the one who brings peace," is a symbol of the coming Messiah as "the king of peace" or "the prince of peace" (Isa 9:6; Luke 1:79; 19:42). Surely, through the tribe of Judah, Israel's sovereign ruler, Jesus Christ was born (Ps 78:68–70; Heb 7:14; Rev 5:5). 1 Chronicles 5:2 also states that "Judah prevailed over his brothers, and from him came the leader."

(7) Be blessed with a peaceful and abundant life (Gen 49:11–12)

Grapevines are so plentiful that a donkey is fastened to one, and when threshing the grape, the thresher is drenched because of its abundance. Also, the eyes are reddened (חַכְלִילִי, *ḥaklīlī*, "lively, glistening, shining") due to the abundant wine, and the teeth are whitened from the endless drinking of milk from the fat cattle (Gen 49:11–12). Such are the great blessings of abundance that Judah received. The donkey is a symbol of peace (Zech 9:9), and the grapevine is a symbol of abundance (Ps 4:7). It was prophesied that the descendants of the tribe of Judah and their land would enjoy peace and materialistic abundance. Furthermore, this is a prophecy that points to the peace and abundance that will come upon mankind through the Messiah (John 10:10).

In fact, the tribe of Judah was blessed with the greatest prosperity and peace during the periods of their descendants David and Solomon (2 Sam 7:11–12; 1 Kgs 4:24–25; 5:4; 15:14). Since Judah was the ancestor ten generations before David, and the Messiah came through the descendants of David, the blessings upon the kingdom that had begun from Judah reached their climax at the birth of the Messiah.

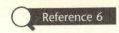

Chart: Jacob's Twelve Sons Who Became the Twelve Tribes of Israel

Genesis 49:28 All these are the twelve tribes of Israel, and this is what their father said to them when he blessed them. He blessed them, everyone with the blessing appropriate to him.

There are diverse accounts of the twelve tribes recorded in the Bible. In Genesis 49, prior to Jacob's death (1859 BC), he prophesied about his 12 sons and "what will befall them in the days to come" (Gen 49:1) and blessed "every one with the blessing appropriate to him" (Gen 49:28). Jacob was not acting on his own initiative. He bequeathed the blessings of the covenant to his sons because he foresaw that God's work of salvation in Abraham and Isaac's times would now continue through his 12 sons.

In 1407 BC, 452 years after Jacob's prophecy, Moses, "the man of God," also blessed the 12 tribes in Deuteronomy 33 (Deut 33:1). Prior to going up to Mount Nebo to face his deathbed, he gave the blessing in the presence of over two million people. The contents of the blessings that Moses gave to each tribe were identical to Jacob's prophecy and were not of Moses' own thoughts but originated from God (Deut 33:1–5). The timing of Jacob's prophecies was before the nation of Israel had been constituted; however, the timing of Moses' blessings was after the nation of Israel had been divided into the 12 tribes and the nation's identity was established. Thus, in comparison to Jacob's prophecy, the contents in Moses' blessings were more developed in terms of the progress of the revelation. Furthermore, in Revelation 7, the 144,000 made up of the 12,000 chosen from each tribe would come to receive God's seal.

The order of birth (Gen 29:31–35; 30:1–24; 35:16–18)	The order of Jacob's prophecy (Gen 49)	The order of Moses' blessing (Deut 33)	The order of the tribes sealed (Rev 7:4–8)
Reuben	Reuben	Reuben	Judah
Simeon	Simeon, Levi	Judah	Reuben
Levi	Judah	Levi	Gad
Judah	Zebulun	Benjamin	Asher
Dan	Issachar	Joseph (Ephraim, Manasseh)	Naphtali
Naphtali	Dan	Zebulun, Issachar	Manasseh
Gad	Gad	Gad	Simeon
Asher	Asher	Dan	Levi
Issachar	Naphtali	Naphtali	Issachar
Zebulun	Joseph	Asher	Zebulun
Dinah (daughter)	Benjamin	(excluding the tribe of Simeon)	Joseph
Joseph			Benjamin
Benjamin			(excluding the tribe of Dan and Ephraim)

The interesting fact is that the order of the 12 sons' births, the order of Jacob's prophecy for each son, the order of Moses, blessings for the 12 tribes, and the order of the sealed tribes are all different from one another, and there are tribes that have been excluded from the orders (see the table that follows).

Later, during the formation of the 12 tribes, Levi was excluded because they were of the priest tribe. Joseph was also excluded, but his two sons, Ephraim and Manasseh, were raised up and became two tribes, thereby completing the 12 tribes. It was done exactly according to Jacob's blessing in Genesis 48:5–6 (Josh 14:4–5; 17:17–18).

The following is a summary of Jacob's 12 sons and the 12 tribes based on the order of birth.

The First Son **Reuben**	① Meaning: "Behold! The vision of the son" (Leah's first son)
	② **Confession at time of birth** (Gen 29:32) Once Reuben was born, Leah confessed, "Because the LORD has seen my affliction; surely now my husband will love me."
	③ **Jacob's prophecy** (Gen 49:3–4) The prophecy symbolizes "boiling water" (Gen 49:4). Reuben was born with the birthright of the firstborn, but Reuben went and lay with Bilhah, depriving himself of his birthright as the first son (Gen 35:22; 1 Chr 5:1). The law strictly forbids violating a stepmother (Lev 18:8; 20:11; Deut 22:30; 27:20).
	④ **Moses' blessing** (Deut 33:6) As the tribe of Reuben gradually became weaker, Moses implored for an increase in population to prevent the possible extinction of the tribe.
	⑤ **Numbering of the soldiers** From 46,500 in the first census (Num 1:21) to 43,730 in the second census (Num 26:7), there was a decrease of 2,770 people.
The Second Son **Simeon**	① **Meaning:** "that is heard" (Leah's second son)
	② **Confession at time of birth** (Gen 29:33) Once Simeon was born, Leah confessed, "Because the Lord has heard that I am unloved, He has therefore given me this son also."
	③ **Jacob's prophecy** (Gen 49:5–7) The prophecy symbolizes "implement of violence" (Gen 49:5). As a result of the frightful and brutal sin that Simeon committed along with Levi, the sudden attack on Shechem and the killing of all its men (Gen 34:18-27), they received the curse that they would be scattered among Israel.
	④ **Moses' blessing** (excluded) This is the only tribe that was excluded from the distribution of the inheritance after the entry into Canaan. Thus, they lived a portion of the land that Judah had received, which was the largest (Josh 19:1–9).

⑤ **Numbering of the soldiers**
From 59,300 in the first census (Num 1:23) to 22,200 (Num 26:14) in the second census, there was a decrease of 37,100 people.

The Third Son
Levi

① **Meaning:** "associated with him" (Leah's third son)

② **Confession at time of birth** (Gen 29:34)
Once Levi was born, Leah confessed, "Now this time my husband will become attached to me, because I have borne him three sons."

③ **Jacob's prophecy** (Gen 49:5–7)
The prophecy symbolizes "implement of violence" (Gen 49:5).
As a result of the frightful and brutal sin that Levi committed along with Simeon, the sudden attack on Shechem and the killing of all its men (Gen 34:18–27), they received the curse that they would be scattered among Israel.

④ **Moses' blessing** (Deut 33:8–11)
When Israel made an idol of the golden calf, this tribe followed God's commandment with righteous anger and took their sword to slaughter the idolaters, which included their own siblings, friends, and neighbors (Exod 32:25–29). Following this event, the tribe of Levi, which had been cursed by Jacob, dispersed into each of Israel's 48 towns and taught the the law and commandments to the Israelites, took possession of Urim and Thummim, and became a righteous priest tribe in charge of religious services (Num 35:2–8). Therefore, they received the great honor and blessings of having the Lord as their eternal inheritance (Deut 10:9; 18:1–2; Josh 13:33; 18:7).

⑤ **Numbering of the soldiers**
As a priest tribe, the tribe of Levi was not included in the numbering of soldiers (Num 1:47–49; 2:33; 26:62); however, males "a month old and upward" were counted (Num 3:15, 39; 26:62). From 22,000 in the first census (Num 3:39) to 23,000 in the second census (Num 26:62), there was an increase of 1,000 people.

Fourth Son
Judah

① **Meaning:** "the praise of the Lord" (Leah's fourth son)

② **Confession at time of birth** (Gen 29:35)
Once Judah was born, Leah confessed, "This time I will praise the Lord."

③ **Jacob's prophecy** (Gen 49:8–12)
The prophecy symbolizes "the lion" (Gen 49:9).
The blessing of "the scepter" represents a king's governing authority and power. We have received the blessing of the coming of the Messiah (the Prince of Peace) symbolized by "Shiloh," the giver of peace and harmony (Gen 49:10). In fact, Jesus Christ came through the tribe of Judah (Matt 1:1–3; Luke 3:33).

④ **Moses' blessing** (Deut 33:7)
God heard Judah's voice and petitioned the blessing and victory of Israel's ruling authority. King David came through the tribe of Judah, and furthermore, the King of all kings, Jesus Christ, also came through this tribe (Matt 1:1–3; Luke 3:33).

⑤ **Numbering of the soldiers**
From 74,000 in the first census (Num 1:27) to 76,500 in the second census (Num 26:22), there was an increase of 1,900 people.

The Fifth Son	
Dan	

① **Meaning:** "he that judges" (first son of Bilhah, Rachel's servant)

② **Confession at time of birth** (Gen 30:6)
Once Dan was born, Rachel confessed, "God has vindicated me, and has indeed heard my voice and has given me a son."

③ **Jacob's prophecy** (Gen 49:16–18)
The prophecy symbolizes "snake and serpent" (Gen 49:17).
Jacob prophesied, "Dan shall be a serpent in the way, a horned snake in the path." The snake and the serpent are indicative of Satan's distinctive qualities (Gen 3:1; Job 20:16; Ps 140:3; Jer 8:17; Rom 3:13; Rev 12:9).
The religious leaders of Jesus' time were prejudiced by eternal ideologies and formalism, and he rebuked them by saying, "You serpents, you brood of vipers, how will you escape the sentence of hell?" (Matt 23:33). Just as Jacob prophesied, in later days during the times of the judges, the fortress town of the tribe of Dan became the center for idolatry and Satan's passageway for the whole of Israel (Judg 18:1–31).

④ **Moses' blessing** (Deut 33:22)
Moses said, "Dan is a lion's cub, springing out of Bashan." A lion is an imposing animal that sets justice in the woods, but instead, a lion cub gets rowdy and harms others.
The tribe of Dan received an allotment in the Promised Land (Josh 19:40–46), but as soon as they lost this to the Amorites (Judg 1:34), they rushed out from this place and moved to the land of Laish, a land that has no relation to God's covenant (Josh 19:47–48; Judg 18:7, 27–29). In later days, the land of the tribe of Dan became the center of idolatry (Judg 18:30; 1 Kgs 12:25–30; 2 Kgs 10:29). It is not a coincidence that the tribe of Dan was excluded from the number of those who were sealed (Rev 7:4–8).

⑤ **Numbering of the soldiers**
From 62,700 in the first census (Num 1:39) to 64,400 in the second census (Num 26:42–43), there was an increase of 1,700 people.

The Sixth Son	
Naphtali	

① **Meaning:** "that struggles or fights" (second son of Bilhah, Rachel's servant)

② **Confession at time of birth** (Gen 30:8)
Once Naphtali was born, Rachel confessed, "With mighty wrestlings I have wrestled with my sister, and I have indeed prevailed."

③ **Jacob's prophecy** (Gen 49:21)
The prophecy uses metaphor to describe Naphtali – "a doe let loose" (Gen 49:21).
A "doe let loose" symbolizes the agility to leap swiftly even to places that are too high or difficult for people to go on foot.

With their agility and swift courage, the tribe of Naphtali contributed largely in defeating Israel's enemies in wars (Judg 4:10; 5:18; 7:23).

Naphtali also had the blessing of speaking beautiful words that people admire. This may also be a foreshadowing of the wonderful and blessed words (the good news) that the Messiah will later proclaim in Galilee (Isa 40:9; 52:7; 61:1; Ps 40:9), which is in the land of Naphtali (Isa 9:1-2).

④ **Moses' blessing** (Deut 33:23)

There was an abundance of grace. They had received a blessing filled with the Lord's favor and received the blessing of acquiring the west side (the west coast of the Sea of Galilee) and the south side (the southern coast of the Sea of Galilee) (Josh 19:32–39). In later days, Jesus mainly remained here and proclaimed God's grace and blessed news of salvation (Matt 4:12–16).

⑤ **Numbering of the soldiers**

From 53,400 in the first census (Num 1:43) to 45,400 in the second census (Num 26:50), there was a decrease of 8,000 people.

The Seventh Son Gad	

① **Meaning:** "blessed" (first son of Zilpah, Leah's servant)

② **Confession at time of birth** (Gen 30:11)

Once Gad was born, Leah confessed, "How fortunate."

③ **Jacob's prophecy** (Gen 49:19)

The prophecy symbolizes "warrior" (Gen 49:19).

He prophesied about their military valor despite invasions from foreign countries. In the records of the brave soldiers who rendered service to King David, the tribe of Gad's valor and agility are especially prominent (2 Chr 12:8–15). The famous judge, Jephthah, was also a "valiant warrior" (Judg 11:1).

④ **Moses' blessing** (Deut 33:20–21)

Gad received the blessing of giving praise to God who made him vast, the blessing of victory over powerful enemies by becoming brave like a lion and tearing the enemy's arms and the crown of their heads, and the blessing of executing God's justice and ordinances.

⑤ **Numbering of the soldiers**

From 45,650 in the first census (Num 1:25) to 40,500 in the second census (Num 26:18), there was a decrease of 5,150 people.

The Eighth Son Asher	

① **Meaning:** "happiness" (second son of Zilpah, Leah's servant)

② **Confession at time of birth** (Gen 30:13)

Once Asher was born, Leah confessed, "Happy am I! For women will call me happy."

③ **Jacob's prophecy** (Gen 49:20)

The prophecy symbolizes "rich food" (Gen 49:20).

Asher had abundance of food; therefore, he received the blessing of presenting food fit for the king's table. In the later days, the food that originated from this place was procured for the royal palace.

④ **Moses' blessing** (Deut 33:24–25)
Asher's descendants prospered, and he received the blessing of many children, the blessing of becoming a joy to his brethren, and the blessing of having his feet dipped in oil. Just as Moses prophesied, second to Manasseh's tribe, Asher's tribe increased numerously in population. Moreover, Asher's tribe obtained a fortress town and received the blessing that they would become a competent tribe.

⑤ **Numbering of the soldiers**
From 41,500 in the first census (Num 1:41) to 53,400 in the second census (Num 26:47), there was an increase of 11,900 people.

The Ninth Son Issachar	

① **Meaning:** "reward, recompense" (Leah's fifth son)

② **Confession at time of birth** (Gen 30:18)
Once Issachar was born, Leah confessed, "God has given me my wages because I gave my maid to my husband."

③ **Jacob's prophecy** (Gen 49:14–15)
The prophecy symbolizes a "strong donkey" (Gen 49:14).
A donkey is used for carrying heavy goods and for plowing land for farming, and thus it symbolizes strength and labor power. Jacob prophesied, "Issachar is a strong donkey, lying down between the sheepfolds." The tribe of Issachar produces "great warriors" because it is strong like a donkey (1 Chr 7:1–5); however, they will be relegated to serving others because of their excessive optimism and obedience.

④ **Moses' blessing** (Deut 33:18–19)
The tribe of Issachar received the blessing of calling people together from other countries while residing in their tents. In later days, the tribe received great blessing upon its cattle breeding and agriculture, gaining wealth, so that many people came to them seeking provisions.

⑤ **Numbering of the soldiers**
From 54,400 in the first census (Num 1:29) to 64,300 (Num 26:25) in the second census, there was an increase of 9,900 people.

The Tenth Son Zebulun	

① **Meaning:** "dwelling" (Leah's sixth son)

② **Confession at time of birth** (Gen 30:20)
Once Zebulun was born, Leah confessed, "God has endowed me with a good gift; now my husband will dwell with me, because I have borne him six sons."

③ **Jacob's prophecy** (Gen 49:13)
The prophecy symbolizes "the seashore" (Gen 49:13).
It was prophesied that the tribe of Zebulun would dwell at the seashore. In fact, the tribe of Zebulun engaged in the trade and commerce industry while residing between the Mediterranean and Galilee (Josh 19:10–16).0

④ **Moses' blessing** (Deut 33:18–19)
In accordance with the blessing, "Rejoice in your going forth," the tribe of Zebulun, working at seaborne trade, acquired copious treasure. Moreover, the blessing, "They will call peoples to the mountain; there they will offer righteous sacrifices," is seen in later days of Jesus Christ. In the region of Galilee, where the tribes of Zebulun and Issachar resided, Jesus called together vast numbers of the people of the kingdom of heaven.

⑤ **Numbering of the soldiers**
From 57,400 in the first census (Num 1:31) to 60,500 in the second census (Num 26:27), there was an increase of 3,100 people.

The Eleventh Son
Joseph

① **Meaning:** "increase, addition" (Rachel's first son)

② **Confession at time of birth** (Gen 30:23–24)
Once Joseph was born, Rachel confessed, "God has taken away my reproach. May the Lord give me another son."

③ **Jacob's prophecy** (Gen 48:15–16; 49:22–26)
The prophecy symbolizes "a fruitful bough by a spring" (Gen 49:22). Joseph's life was rooted in God, who is the source of living water; hence, the boughs were always fruitful and he received the blessing of the branches running over the wall (Gen 49:22). Furthermore, Joseph received the most prominent blessing of the birthright: "the crown of the head of the one distinguished among his brothers" (Gen 49:26; cf. 1 Chr 5:1–2).

④ **Moses' blessing** (Deut 33:13–17)
In accordance with Jacob's prophecy about Joseph being "the one distinguished among his brothers," the outcome of having received the blessing of birthright was material abundance (the treasures of the heavens, the treasures of the sun and the moon, and the treasures of the everlasting mountain). Additionally, having "the majesty of the first-born ox" and "the horns of the wild ox," he received the blessing of leading the people and reaching the ends of the earth.
Moses, like Jacob (Gen 48:15–16), did not speak about the blessing regarding Manasseh and Ephraim, but rather pronounced it upon them under the name of Joseph (Deut 33:16–17). Because Ephraim and Manasseh each received his share, Joseph ultimately received double the blessing (Deut 21:17).

⑤ **Numbering of the soldiers**
There is no record of the numbering of the soldiers regarding Joseph. There are only records of the number of soldiers for Ephraim and Manasseh.

The Twelfth Son **Benjamin**	① **Meaning:** "son of the right hand" (Rachel's second son)

① **Meaning:** "son of the right hand" (Rachel's second son)

② **Confession at time of birth** (Gen 35:18)
Rachel named him *Ben-oni* ("the son of sorrow") as she was dying and her soul was departing, but Jacob changed the name to *Benjamin* ("the son of the right hand").

③ **Jacob's prophecy** (Gen 49:27)
The prophecy symbolizes "a ravenous wolf" (Gen 49:27). This describes the aggressive nature that must accomplish a set goal (Judg 3:15–30; 20:12–16, 19–25).
Furthermore, Jacob prophesied that in the morning Benjamin would eat what was snatched and in the evening share it. This is prophesying that those from the tribe of Benjamin would make a surprisingly great contribution to Israel's history (e.g., the left-handed judge Ehud [Judg 3:15]; the first king, Saul [1 Sam 9:1–2, 21]; Esther and Mordecai [Esth 2:5–7]; the apostle Paul [Phil 3:5]).

④ **Moses' blessing** (Deut 33:12)
Moses' blessing was that Bejamin would be clothed in God's love and be safely protected between God's shoulders. Historically, the tribe of Benjamin had been given the land of Jerusalem, which was to be the site of the temple, thus receiving God's protection (Josh 18:28).

⑤ **Numbering of the soldiers**
From 35,400 in the first census (Num 1:37) to 45,600 in the second census (Num 26:41), there was an increase of 10,200 people.

Joseph's First Son Manasseh

① **Meaning:** "forgetfulness" (first son of Asenath, Joseph's wife)

② **Confession at time of birth** (Gen 41:51)
Once Manasseh was born, Joseph confessed, "God has made me forget all my trouble and all my father's household."

③ **Jacob's prophecy** (Gen 48:8–20)
The prophecy symbolizes "a male calf and the horns of the wild ox" (Deut 33:17).
Although Manasseh was the firstborn, he received Jacob's left hand, thus he received the blessing of the second son. This was done through God's sovereign and providential work.

④ **Moses' blessing** (Deut 33:16–17)
In his blessing Moses said, "Those are the thousands of Manasseh." Despite having received the blessing of the second son, Manasseh was not disappointed but must have been content with the blessing he received. As time passed, Manasseh continuously developed. Jacob's blessing was that Manasseh "also will be great" (Gen 48:19). Just as Moses said, "Those are the thousands" (Deut 33:17), the tribe of Manasseh showed the greatest population growth among the 12 tribes (an increase of 20,500 from the first census).

⑤ **Numbering of the soldiers**
From 32,200 in the first census (Num 1:35) to 52,700 (Num 26:34) in the second census, there was an increase of 20,500 people.

① **Meaning:** "fruitful, increasing" (second son of Asenath, Joseph's wife)

② **Confession at time of birth** (Gen 41:52)
Once Ephraim was born, Joseph confessed, "God has made me fruitful in the land of my affliction."

③ **Jacob's prophecy** (Gen 48:8–20)
The prophecy symbolizes "a male calf and the horns of the wild ox" (Deut 33:17).
Ephraim was Manasseh's younger brother, but due to the crossing of Jacob's hands, he received the blessing of the firstborn. Ephraim became the eldest son not through any meritorious service of his, but because of God's sovereign and providential work.

④ **Moses' blessing** (Deut 33:16–17)
In his blessing Moses said, "Those are the ten thousands of Ephraim." Worthy of a tribe that had received the blessing of the firstborn and the blessing of the ten thousands, the tribe of Ephraim produced many leaders. For example, there was Joshua, Moses' successor and the leader during the occupation of Canaan (Num 13:8); the judge Deborah (Judg 4:4–5); and Jeroboam, the first king of the northern kingdom of Israel (1 Kgs 11:26). As a large tribe, Ephraim represented the north of Israel, and the Bible calls northern Israel "Ephraim" (Ezek 37:16; Zech 9:10).

⑤ **Numbering of the soldiers**
From 40,500 in the first census (Num 1:33) to 32,500 (Num 26:37) in the second census, there was a decrease of 8,000 people.

Reference: Israel's First and Second Census of the Soldiers

First census of the soldiers: This was taken on the first day of the second month in the second year after the exodus from Egypt (Num 1:1; 10:11-12). The total number of people was 603,550 (Exod 38:26; Num 1:46; 2:32).

Second census of the soldiers: This was taken approximately 39 years after the first census, which numbered the soldiers at the final camp prior to entering Canaan, in the plains of Moab by the Jordan River, opposite Jericho (Num 26:2-4). The total number of people was 601,730 (Num 26:51).

Notes

1. The word John uses is σπεῖρα (*speira*): "cohort, battalion, a Roman military technical term for the tenth part of a legion, normally containing 600 troops" (Timothy Friberg, Barbara Friberg, and Neva F. Miller, *Analytical Lexicon of the Greek New Testament* [Grand Rapids, MI, 2000], 353).

2. Erich Sauer, *The Dawn of World Redemption: A Survey of Historical Revelation in the Old Testament*, trans. G. H. Lang (Grand Rapids: Eerdmans, 1951), 98.

3. "The period of the judges was about 340 years, since the completion of the Canaan conquest in 1390 BC until the beginning of Saul's reign in 1050 BC" (Disciples Publishing House, *The Grand Bible Commentary: With Comprehensive and Synthetic Exegetical Study Methods* [Seoul: Bible Study Material Publisher, 1991–1993], 1:80–81).

4. Gerhard von Rad, *Genesis: A Commentary* (London: SCM Press, 1972), 187.

5. James Montgomery Boice, *Genesis: An Expositional Commentary*, vol. 2 (Grand Rapids: Baker, 1982), 565.

6. Peter S. Ruckman, *The Book of Genesis* (Pensacola, FL: Bible Believers Press, 1969), 182.

7. H. L. Willmington, *Complete Guide to Bible Knowledge* (Wheaton, IL: Tyndale House, 1990), 52.

8. S. R. Driver, *The Book of Genesis* (London: Methuen, 1904), 177.

9. C. F. Keil and F. Delitzsch, *Commentary on the Old Testament*, vol. 1, *The Pentateuch* (Peabody, MA: Hendrickson, 1989), 470.

10. Disciples Publishing House, *Grand Bible Commentary*, 3:28–29.

11. See Reference 1: "The Chronology of the Patriarchs" in Abraham Park, *The Genesis Genealogies: God's Administration in the History of Redemption* (North Clarendon, VT: Periplus Editions, 2009).

12. Daniel H. King, "Archaeology: Abram: The Man to Whom God Revealed Himself," *TruthMagazine.com*, http://truthmag.seekye1st.net/archives/volume20/GOT020218.html.

13. Park, *The Genesis Genealogies*, 167–68, 235.

14. Thompson Bible Editing Committee, *The Thompson Commentary Study Bible II* (Seoul: Christian Wisdom Publishing, 1990), 26.

15. H. C. Leupold, *Exposition of Genesis* (Grand Rapids: Baker, 1942), 2:885–86.

16. Ibid., 2:1148.

17. Keil and Delitzsch, *The Pentateuch*, 311.

18. Ibid., 315–16.

19. H. D. M. Spence and Joseph Exell, eds., *The Pulpit Commentary*, vol. 1, *Genesis* (Peabody, MA: Hendrickson, 1950), 416–17.

20. Keil and Delitzsch, *The Pentateuch*, 319.

21. Spence and Exell, *Genesis*, 417.

22. J. P. Lange, *Commentary on the Holy Scriptures: Critical, Doctrinal and Homiletical*, vol. 1, *Genesis*, trans. and ed. Philip Schaff (Grand Rapids: Zondervan, 1978), 571.

23. Henry M. Morris, *The Genesis Record: A Scientific and Devotional Commentary on the Book of Beginnings* (Grand Rapids: Baker, 1976), 508.

24. "We can conclude, then, that Jacob's bowing at the head of his bed is an acknowledgement of divine care that has allowed him to pass clan leadership successfully to his son Joseph" (John H. Walton, *Genesis*, NIV Application Commentary [Grand Rapids: Zondervan, 2001], 710).

25. According to Matthew 10:10 and Luke 9:3, the parallel verses to Mark 6:8, taking a staff as ῥάβδος (*rhabdos*) is absolutely prohibited. These verses seem to contradict Matthew 10:10, but Jesus was speaking according to the different uses of the staff. *Rhabdos* was generally the staff used as a weapon to protect from outside attacks or as a leaning staff that takes away exhaustion in traveling. In Mark and Luke, the Lord prohibited the *rhabdos* from being used as a weapon. He also prohibited the *rhabdos* from being used for protection; this was to show His strong will in that the Lord Himself would protect His people who go out to evangelize.

26. Jacob and Joseph are the only people in the Bible whose bodies were known to have been preserved as mummies (Gen 50:2-3, 26).

27. Lange, *Genesis*, 14–15.

28. Françoise Dunand and Roger Lichtenberg, *Mummies and Death in Egypt*, trans. David Lorton (Ithaca, NY: Cornell University Press, 2006), 46–48.

29. Joseph S. Exell and Thomas H. Leale, *Genesis*, vol. 1 of *The Preacher's Complete Homiletic Commentary on the Books of the Bible* (Grand Rapids: Baker, 2001), 730.

30. Disciples Publishing House, ed. *The Oxford Bible Interpreter* (Seoul: Bible Study Material Publisher, 2002), 112:598.

31. Ibid., 112:598.

32. Ibid., 3:697.

33. Robert Jamieson, A. R. Fausset, and David Brown, *A Commentary: Critical, Experimental, and Practical on the Old and New Testaments*, Vol. 1 (Grand Rapids: William B. Eerdmans, 1945) 274..

34. *Encyclopaedia Judaica* (Jerusalem: Keter, 1972), 10:212.

35. The King's Highway: an ancient trade route that extends north and south on the east side of the Jordan River and the Dead Sea. Its north end is Damascus on the northeast side of the Jordan and leads down through ancient states, including Ammon, Moab, and Edom, to Ezion-geber by the the Gulf of Aqaba. There, it is connected to another route that leads to Egypt. When Moses asked the king of Edom to let them pass through that path, he refused and the Israelites turned away from Edom (Num 20:17-21, Ref: Deut 2:5). Moses requested Sihon, king of the Amorites, also to let them pass through their border. When Sihon would not permit Israel to pass through his border, but rather went out against Israel, Israel struck them with the edge of the sword (Num 21:21-26, Ref: Deut 2:24-25). Thus, they followed the King's Highway and camped in the plains of Moab (Num 22:1). (see endpapers: "Map of The Exodus and Wilderness Journey")

36. According to Egyptian history, the works of Amenhotep II were recorded for about 20 years since 1446 BC, and his mummy was discovered near the Valley of the Kings in Egypt in AD 1898 by biblical archaeologist Victor Loret. How, then, does the body that was buried under the Red Sea remain until now? The first answer can be found in Exodus 14:30: "and Israel saw the Egyptians dead on the seashore." Based on this statement, it can be construed that Amenhotep's dead body was found on the shore by the Egyptians and preserved as a mummy. Also, archaeological records reveal that Amenhotep II had no military activities other than two large-scale wars in the early years of his reign (1450 BC and 1446 BC). The

reason as to why the records of his military campaigns were cut short cannot be explained without the record of the Exodus in the Bible (Eui Won Kim, *The History of the Old Testament* [Seoul: The Korea Society for Reformed Faith and Action, 1998], 140).

37. "It is uncertain how long the Israelites remained encamped at Pi-hahiroth. They would wait as long as the pillar of the cloud did not move (Num. ix. 18–20). It must have taken Pharaoh a day to hear of their march from Etham, at least another day to collect his troops, and three or four days to march from Tanis to Pi-hahiroth. The Jewish tradition that the Red Sea was crossed on the night of the 21st of Nisan (Abib) is therefore, conceivably, a true one" (H. D. M. Spence and Joseph Exell, eds., *The Pulpit Commentary*, vol. 1, *Exodus* [Peabody, MA: Hendrickson, 1950], 321).

38. Storage city: cities (supply bases) with large fortified storages usually located in places of strategic importance or near borders to store up food and weapons for times of emergency (cf. Gen 41:35; Exod 1:11; 1 Kgs 9:19; 2 Chr 17:12; 32:28).

39. Rameses to Succoth is about 32 miles (52 km), and it probably took the Israelites at least two days because they had over two million people. It probably also took them over one day to travel from Succoth to Etham, although it is normally a one-day journey. Thus, it is estimated that the Israelites journeyed about four days from Rameses to Etham.

40. *Wadi* is the Arabic term traditionally referring to a valley; in some cases it refers to a dry riverbed that contains water during times of heavy rain or simply an intermittent stream.

41. An omer is approximately 2.5 quarts (2.3 l).

42. For details on the meaning of the rock, see the section on "Death of Moses" in chapter 13.

43. "It is as natural as it well can be to seek for this place of encampment in the desert of Paran or Zin at Kadesh under the name of *Rithmah*, which follows Hazeroth in the present list (ver. 18)" (C. F. Keil and F. Delitzsch, *Commentary on the Old Testament*, vol. 1, *The Pentateuch* [Peabody, MA: Hendrickson, 1989], 243).

44. BDB 958; HALOT 2:1299.

45. TDOT 13:504-505.

46. BDB 829; TDOT 12:104-105.

47. TDOT 7:440.

48. BDB 526; TDOT 7:438-440.

49. *Nelson's Illustrated Bible Dictionary*. Edited by Herbert Lockyer (Nashville: Thomas Nelson 1897), 919.

50. HALOT 2:1249–50.

51. *Nelson's Illustrated Bible Dictionary* 612.

52. BDB 874; TDOT 12:546-561.

53. BDB 1051.

54. BDAG 877.

55. BDB 874.

56. Willem A. VanGemeren, *New International Dictionary of Old Testament Theology & Exegesis* (Grand Rapids: Zondervan, 1997) 2:1150.

57. *Oxford Bible Interpreter*, 12:434.

58. Keil and Delitzsch, *The Pentateuch*, 143.

59. A. R. Fausset, *Fausset's Bible Dictionary* (Grand Rapids: Zondervan, 1979), 730.

60. BDB 75.

61. TDOT 1:463-466.

62. *Nelson's Illustrated Bible Dictionary*, 684.

63. TDOT 9:335-340.

64. TDOT 2:139-145.

65. HALOT 1:215.

66. BDB 75.

67. BDB 720.

68. Fausset, *Fausset's Bible Dictionary*, 480.

69. BDB 91; HALOT 1:106.

70. TDOT 3:79-84.

71. HALOT 1:193–94; TDOT 3:20-23.

72. HALOT 1:851–54; TDOT 11:230-252.

73. BDB 14.

74. HALOT 2:1224–26; TDOT 13:473-479.

75. TDOT 12:311-321.

76. TDOT 10:270-277.

77. George Ernest Wright, *Biblical Archaeology* (Philadelphia: Westminster, 1957), 65.

78. TDOT 10:44-53.

79. *Oxford Bible Interpreter*, 16:28.

80. Besides Esau's grandson Kenaz, there is another Kenaz in the Bible. He appears in Joshua 15:17; Judges 1:13; 3:9. He is a brother of Caleb and the father of Othniel the judge. Clearly, he is not the grandson of Esau.

81. TWOT 2:541.

82. 1 talent of silver = 3,000 shekels; 1 talent of gold = 45,000 shekels (15 times the silver); 1 shekel of silver (4 denarii) = 4 days' average wage (since 1 denarius was 1 day's wage). Considering 1 day's average wage is 50.00 USD today, 1 shekel of silver would be equivalent to about 20.00 USD.

83. HALOT 2:923.

84. H. C. Leupold, *Exposition of Genesis* (Grand Rapids: Baker, 1942), 2:1170–71.

85. Roddy Braun, *1 Chronicles*, Word Biblical Commentary 14 (Waco, TX: Word, 1986), 75.

86. Eugene H. Merrill, *1, 2 Chronicles*, Bible Study Commentary (Grand Rapids: Lamplighter Books, 1988), 30.

87. The ancient documents of Egypt prove the historicity of the narration about Joseph. The name *Zaphenath-paneah* was found in a document as a name of a high official of Egypt (Sun Lin Theological Research Institute, *DTP Researching for Dogmatic Pulpit* [Seoul: Sun Lin, 1994], 196).

88. BDB 634.

89. Disciples Publishing House, *The Grand Bible Commentary: With Comprehensive and Synthetic Exegetical Study Methods* (Seoul: Bible Study Material Publisher, 1991–1993), 1:799; 7:72.

90. Ibid., 1:799.

91. Yune-Sun Park, *Yune-Sun Park's Bible Commentaries: Genesis* (Seoul: Young Eum, 1994), 397.

92. Thompson Bible Editing Committee, *The Thompson Commentary Study Bible II* (Seoul: Christian Wisdom Publishing, 1990), 79.

93. Kwang Ho Lee, *Genesis*, CNB Series (Seoul: Calvin, 2007), 505:483.

94. Sung-Doo Kang, *Study of People in the Old Testament*, vol. 1 (Seoul: Pastors' House, 2005), 217–18.

95. John H. Sailhamer, *The Pentateuch as Narrative: A Biblical-Theological Commentary* (Grand Rapids: Zondervan, 1992), 268.

96. Yune-Sun Park, *Yune-Sun Park's Bible Commentaries: Acts* (Seoul: Young Eum, 1994), 167–68.

97. BDB 1014.

98. VanGemeren, 3:823-5.

99. TWOT 2496.

100. TWOT 1565.

101. Robert Jamieson, A. R. Fausset, and David Brown, *A Commentary: Critical, Experimental, and Practical on the Old and New Testaments.* Vol. 1 (Grand Rapids: William B. Eerdmans, 1945), 274.

Bibliography

Boice, James Montgomery. *Genesis: An Expositional Commentary*. Vol. 2. Grand Rapids: Baker, 1982.

Braun, Roddy. *1 Chronicles*. Word Biblical Commentary 14. Waco, TX: Word, 1986.

Cho, Paul Yonggi. *Genesis Exegesis*. Vol. 1. Seoul: Seoul Word Press, 1998.

Chun, Samuel. *The Christian Literature Society of Korea 100th Year Anniversary Bible Commentary Series*. Vol. 1. Seoul: Christian Literature Society of Korea, 2001.

Chung, Il-Oh. *Interpretation of Genesis*. Seoul: Solomon, 2004.

Delitzsch, Franz. *New Commentary on Genesis*. Vol. 2. Minneapolis: Klock & Klock Christian Publishers, 1978.

Disciples Publishing House, ed. *The Grand Bible Commentary: With Comprehensive and Synthetic Exegetical Study Methods*. 16 vols. Seoul: Bible Academy, 1991–1993.

The Oxford Bible Interpreter. 130 vols. Seoul: Bible Study Material Publisher, 2002.

Driver, S. R. *The Book of Genesis*. London: Methuen, 1904.

DTP Researching for Dogmatic Pulpit. Seoul: Sun Lin, 1994.

Dunand, Françoise, and Roger Lichtenberg. *Mummies and Death in Egypt*. Translated by David Lorton. Ithaca, NY: Cornell University Press, 2006.

Encyclopaedia Judaica. 16 vols. Jerusalem: Keter, 1972.

Exell, Joseph S., and Thomas H. Leale. *Genesis*. Vol. 1 of *The Preacher's Complete Homiletic Commentary on the Books of the Bible*. Grand Rapids: Baker, 2001.

Fausset, A. R. *Fausset's Bible Dictionary*. Grand Rapids: Zondervan, 1979.

Friberg, Timothy, Barbara Friberg, and Neva F. Miller. *Analytical Lexicon of the Greek New Testament*. Victoria, BC: Trafford, 2005.

Jamieson, Robert, A. R. Fausset, and David Brown, *A Commentary: Critical, Experimental, and Practical on the Old and New Testaments*. Vol. 1. Grand Rapids: William B. Eerdmans, 1945.

Kang, Sung-Doo. *Study of People in the Old Testament*. Vol. 1. Seoul: Pastors' House, 2005.

Keil, C. F. and F. Delitzsch, *Commentary on the Old Testament*. Vol. 1, *The Pentateuch*. Peabody, MA: Hendrickson, 1989.

Kim, Eui-Won. *The History of the Old Testament*. Seoul: The Korea Society for Reformed Faith and Action, 1998.

King, Daniel H. "Archaeology: Abram: The Man to Whom God Revealed." *TruthMagazine.com*. http://truthmag.seekye1st.net/archives/volume20/GOT020218.html.

Lange, J. P. *Commentary on the Holy Scriptures: Critical, Doctrinal and Homiletical*. Vol. 1, *Genesis*. Translated and edited by Philip Schaff. Grand Rapids: Zondervan, 1978.

Lee, Kwang-Ho. *Genesis*. CNB Series.

Lee, Sang-Ho. *Hebrew Morphology* and *Exegesis Bible Series: Genesis*. Sung Kwang Culture, 1996.

Leupold, H. C. *Exposition of Genesis*. 2 vols. Grand Rapids: Baker, 1942.

Merrill, Eugene H. *1, 2 Chronicles*. Bible Study Commentary. Grand Rapids: Lamplighter Books, 1988.

Morris, Henry M. *The Genesis Record: A Scientific and Devotional Commentary on the Book of Beginnings*. Grand Rapids: Baker, 1976.

Nelson's Illustrated Bible Dictionary. Edited by Lockyer, Herbret, Nashville: Thomas Nelson, 1986.

Pang, Ji-Il. *The Exegesis of Genesis*. Seoul: Dong Jin Culture, 1989.

Park, Abraham. *The Genesis Genealogies: God's Administration in the History of Redemption*. North Clarendon, VT: Periplus Editions, 2009.

Park, Yune-Sun. *Yune-Sun Park's Bible Commentaries:* Acts. Seoul: Young Eum, 1994.

Yune-Sun Park's Bible Commentaries: Genesis. Seoul: Young Eum, 1994.

Ruckman, Peter S. *The Book of Genesis*. Pensacola, FL: Bible Believers Press, 1969.

Sailhamer, John H. *The Pentateuch as Narrative: A Biblical-Theological Commentary*. Grand Rapids: Zondervan, 1992.

Sauer, Erich. *The Dawn of World Redemption: A Survey of Historical Revelation in the Old Testament*. Translated by G. H. Lang. Grand Rapids: Eerdmans, 1951.

Spence, H. D. M., and Joseph S. Exell, eds. *The Pulpit Commentary*. Vol. 1, *Genesis, Exodus*. Peabody, MA: Hendrickson, 1950.

Suk, Won-Tae. *A Commentary on Genesis*. Seoul: Gyung Hyang, 2002.

A Commentary on Hebrews. Seoul: Gyung Hyang, 2005.

Sun Lin Theological Research Institute. *The Complete Biblical Library: The Old Testament Study Bible*. Vol 1., *Genesis*. Springfield, MO: World Library Press, 1994.

The New Thompson Thompson Reference Commentary Bible Editing Committee, ed. *The Thompson Reference Commentary Bible*. Seoul: Bible Text Publisher, 1989.

The Thompson Commentary Study Bible II. Seoul: Christian Wisdom Publishing, 2000.

VanGemeren, Willem A. *New International Dictionary of Old Testament Theology & Exegesis*. Grand Rapids, MI: Zondervan, 1997.

Von Rad, Gerhard. *Genesis: A Commentary*. London: SCM Press, 1972.

Walton, John H. *Genesis*. NIV Application Commentary. Grand Rapids: Zondervan, 2001.

Wenham, Gordon J. *Genesis 1–15*. Word Biblical Commentary 1. Waco, TX: Word, 1987.

Willmington, H. L. *Complete Guide to Bible Knowledge*. Wheaton, IL: Tyndale House, 1990.

Wone, Yong-Kuk. *A Commentary of Genesis*. Seoul: Se Shin Culture, 1990.

Wood, Leon J. *A Survey of Israel's History*, rev. David O'Brien. Grand Rapids: Zondervan, 1986.

Wright, George Ernest. *Biblical Archaeology*. Philadelphia: Westminster, 1957.

Index

Rimmon-perez, 171–72; Rissah, 173–74; Rithmah, 170–71; Succoth, 152–53; Tahath, 177–78; Terah, 178–79; Wadi Zered, 192, 193; The Wilderness of Sin, 159–60; The Wilderness of Sinai, 150, 151, 165–66; Zalmonah, 188–89

Canaan, battle between kings of, 47; conquest by Israelites, 48, 124, 173, 236–39, 247; geography of, 195–96; shown to Moses, 195; spies sent to, 170–71, 219–21, 236

caves, 182–83

census, first, 123, 151, 164, 165, 219–20, 255, 278, 324, 330, 331–37; second, 123, 225–29, 255, 278, 324, 330, 331–37

Chosen People. *See* Israelites

Christ. *See* Jesus Christ

1 Chronicles 5:1–2, 256, 261

chronology, of patriarchs, 65–71

circumcision, covenant of, 66, 76–77; during exodus, 198–99; forced on Hivite men, 94–95; performed at Gilgal, 198

Colossians 1:20, 28; 1:25–27, 296; 1:26–27, 20; 1:27, 20

covenant, animal slaughter in, 38; divine administration and. *See* redemption, history of; expansion of revelations of, 36–39; in Old Testament, 36–39; meaning of, 31–32; new, Jesus as, 30, 32, 34–35, 39; of circumcision, 76–77; of grace, 35–36; of redemption, 34–35; of the torch. *See* torch, covenant of; of works, 33–34; ratification of, 49–50; ratified at Mount Sinai, 166; types of, 33–36; with Abraham, 37; with God, 32–33

cross, gospel of, 29; Jesus' words on, 26–27; redemptive work of, 21–23

Dan, head of tribe, 251, 332

David (king), covenant with, 36; dates of reign, 48; hid in cave, 183

Deuteronomy 1:21, 170; 1:22, 171;

1:27, 203; 1:36, 221; 2:7, 199; 2:14, 237; 2:14–15, 227; 8:16, 200; 27:20, 254; 33:6, 255; 33:16, 293; 34:1–3, 195; 34:7, 213; 34:9, 231

devil, 18

Dibon-gad camp site, 193–94

Dinah, birth of, 89; rape of, 94–95, 322

Dophkah camp site, 160–61

dreams, of Joseph, 97–98, 99–100, 282, 291–93

Eber, father of Peleg, 56; longevity of, 54

Edom, 186, 189

Edrei, battle at, 197, 223

Egypt, building projects in, 127–28; famine in, 99–100; increase of Israelites in, 125–27; Israelites' departure from, 134, 139–40; Israelites' entry into, 49, 57–58; Jacob's resettlement in, 102–05; Joseph in, 98–105, 257–58, 279; oppression of Israelites in, 127–28, 135–36; ten plagues in, 136–39

Egyptians, armies destroyed in Red Sea, 155–57; sins against Israelites by, 135–36

18th Dynasty, 127–28

Eleazar, 186, 188; made priest by Moses, 212

Elijah, 183

Elim camp site, 158

Ephraim, blessed by Jacob, 110, 317; head of tribe, 337

Ephesians 2:13, 28

Esau, birth and youth of, 84–85; marriage of, 86; reconciliation with Jacob, 93; sells birthright to Jacob, 87, 250

Etham camp site, 153–154

Eve, disobedience of, 18, 33–34

Exodus 1:7, 125; 1:8, 127; 2:2, 129; 2:23–25, 134; 4:16, 207; 4:22–23, 139; 10:2, 138; 12:12, 138; 12:35–36, 245; 13:17, 143; 13:18, 139, 142; 13:18, 139, 142;

Naphtali, head of tribe, 251, 332–33
Nehemiah 9:10, 136
New Testament, as covenant, 30
Noah, covenant with, 36, 74; father of Shem, 56; longevity of, 54; time since Abraham, 54
Numbers 11: 4–6, 204; 12:7, 207; 12:8, 207; 13:6, 237; 14:9, 220; 14:28–30, 204; 20:12, 212; 20:25, 188; 26:1–2, 226; 26:51, 226; 32:11, 222; 32:12, 221; 32:13–15, 256; 33:1, 139; 33:2, 148; 33:4, 138; 33:8, 209; 33:38–39, 212; 36:10–12, 229

Oboth camp site, 191
Og (king), 197, 223
Old Testament, as covenant, 30

Paran wilderness, 79–80, 186
patriarchs, chronology of, 65–71; longevity of, 54–55
Peleg, father of Reu, 56; longevity of, 55
Peter (apostle), 22
Paul (apostle), 21, 224
Pilate, at Jesus' trial, 24, 25
pillars of cloud and fire, 153–154, 201
Plains of Moab camp site, 196–98
plagues, in Egypt, 136–39
predestination, absolute, 19
principle of representation, 274
Proverbs 16:7, 93; 13:22, 246; 28:8, 246
Psalm 14:6, 183; 22:6, 25; 55:22, 276; 68:19, 276; 78:8, 149; 78:18–19, 167; 78:19–31, 205; 28:40–41, 202; 95:9, 202; 105:7–10, 37; 105:8–10, 294; 105:25, 135; 106:25–26, 203; 129:3, 25; 136:15, 145
Punon camp site, 189–90

quails, 167, 200

rabble, as leaders of grumblers, 204–06
Rachel, birth of Benjamin, 95, 101; birth of Joseph, 91, 256–57; death of, 95–96; marries Jacob, 89

rainbow, covenant of, 74
Rameses, Israelites' departure from, 121, 152, 151
ratification, of covenant, 49–50
Rebekah, birth of Jacob and Esau, 84; marriage to Isaac, 83
reconciliation, 27–29
Red Sea, camp site, 159; Israelites' crossing of, 142–46, 155–57
redemption, covenant of, 34–35; definition of, 18–29; history of, divine administration in, 30–31, 42–43, 264, 286–97; Jesus Christ in, 18–21, 178
repentance, 174
Rephidim camp site, 162–65
Reu, father of Serug, 56; longevity of, 55
Reuben, as firstborn of Jacob, 251–54; head of tribe, 251, 330; Moses' prayer for, 254; recklessness of, 252–54; selfishness of, 255–56
Rimmon-perez camp site, 171–72
Rissah camp site, 173–74
Rithmah camp site, 170–71. See also Kadesh

Roman soldiers, at Jesus' crucifixion, 25–26
Romans 1:3–4, 266; 5:11, 28; 9:10, 317; 9:10–13, 250

saints, redeemed, 29
Samuel, 48
1 Samuel 1:19, 91; 2:21, 91
Sarah, death and burial of, 81–82; renamed from Sarai, 76–77
Saul (king), 48
salvation, God's plan of, 21–22, 44–46
Sanhedrin, at Jesus' trial, 24
sea of reeds, 159
serpent, in Garden of Eden, 34
Serug, father of Nahor, 56; longevity of, 55
Seti I (pharaoh), 47
scapegoat, 23
Shechem, Abraham at, 270, 275–76;

Jacob's land purchase at, 271; Joseph's bones buried in, 124, 268–70; rape of Dinah at, 94–95, 322; redemptive significance of, 275–76

Shelah, father of Eber, 56; longevity of, 54

Shem, longevity of, 54

Shittim, 224–25

Sihon (king), 197, 222–23

Simeon, fate of tribe, 324–25; head of tribe, 251, 330–31; Jacob's prophecy regarding, 322–23

Sinai. *See* Mount Sinai, The Wilderness of Sinai

smoking oven, in covenant of the torch, 43–45

soldiers, death of, 123; first census of, 123, 164, 219–20, 337; second census of, 123, 225–29, 337

Solomon (king), 48–49

speech, 215–16

spies, sent to Canaan, 170–71, 219–21, 236

Stephen, 272–73

straight way, 182, 189

Succoth camp site, 152–53

suffering, of Jesus, 23–27

Taberah, fire at, 166–67

tabernacle, building of, 165–66

Tahath camp site, 177–78

Ten Commandments, 165

tent of meeting, 149–50, 165

Terah, longevity of, 55

Terah camp site, 178–79

Thessalonians, 5:24, 46

Thutmose I, 121, 127, 128

Thutmose III, 47–48, 131, 132, 133

Timothy, 2:13, 46

torch, covenant of, 33, 38–39, 42–45, 74, 280–88; and Abraham's age, 47; fulfillment of, 230, 243–47, 277–83; future fulfillment of, 288–90, 296–97; ratification of, 49–50; smoking oven in, 43–45

Tower of Babel, 54–55, 64

tribes, 12 of Israel, 228–29, 239, 251, 329–37

unleavened bread, at Succoth, 152

Wadi Zered camp site, 192, 193

water, at Jotbathah, 183–84; at Meribah, 163, 213; from rock, differences in, 216–17; springs at Elim, 158; springs at Mithkah, 179; springs at Terah, 179; sweetened at Marah, 157–58

wilderness journey, God's care during, 199–201

The Wilderness of Sin camp site, 159–60

The Wilderness of Sinai camp site, 150, 151, 165–66

wineskins, 191

Word of God, 18, 34, 185, 191, 197–98; disobedience to, 188; faithfulness of, 45; obedience to, 214, 216, 221–22

works, covenant of, 33–36

worship, 174–75, 177

Zalmonah camp site, 188–89

Zebulun, head of tribe, 251, 334–35

Zelophehad, daughters of, 228–29

Zered brook, 151, 185–86; death of soldiers at, 123

Zoar, 195–96

Oral traditions recounted by indigenous peoples during site visits were taken into consideration for the location of a few camp sites.

Map of the Ex
AND WILDERNESS JOU

"And Moses recorded their starting places according to their journe
Lord, and these are their journeys according to their starting
Exod 13:17–19:3; 40:17; Num 10:11–12:16; Deut 1:1–3:29; 34:

1390 BC, Joseph's bo
entry into Canaan. (

Mediterranean Sea

1406 BC, ~ 1st month, 1
"Now the people came u
day of the first month and
edge of Jericho.' (Josh 4

The Battle of Hormah
The early stage of the wilder
disobedience. (Num 14:39–
The last stage of the wildern
the king of Arad in southern

1446 BC, 1st month, 15th day
"And they journeyed from Rameses in the first month, on the fifteenth day of the first month; on the next day after Passover the sons of Israel started out boldly in the sight of the Egyptians." (Num 33:3)

The Death of Aaron
1407 BC, 5th month, 1st day, ~ 8 months before ent
"Then Aaron the priest went up to Mount Hor at the
there, in the fortieth year after the sons of Israel h
on the first day in the fifth month." (Num 33:38)

"Now it came about when Pharaoh had let the pe
them by the way of the land of the Philistines, eve
said, 'Lest the people change their minds when th
Egypt.'" (Exod 13:17)

Goshen

Rameses

EGYPT

The Way of the Land of the Philistines (Exod 13:17)

The Death of Miriam
1407 BC, 1st month, ~ 1 year before entry into Canaa
"Then the sons of Israel, the whole congregation, ca
wilderness of Zin in the first month; and the people sta
Now Miriam died there and was buried there." (Num

Succoth
1

2 **Etham** The Way of Shur

Rimmon

Bitter Lake **The Wilderness of Shur (Eth**
(Exod 15:22; Num 33:8)

Lib

"Hence God led the people around by the way of the wilderness to the Red Sea; and the sons of Israel went up in martial array from the land of Egypt." (Exod 13:18)

On

The Way of Mt. Seir

Nile River

Baal-zephon (uncertain)

3 **Before Migdol**

Pi-hahiroth

"Tell the sons of Israel to turn back and camp before Pi-hahiroth, between Migdol and the sea; you shall camp in front of Baal-zephon, opposite it, by the sea." (Exod 14:2)

4 **Marah**

The Wilde

Crossing the Red Sea
(Exod 14:15–31)

Elim 5

6

7 **The**

8 **D**

By the Red Sea

The Battle against Amalek (Exod 17:8–16)
"So Joshua overwhelmed Amalek and his people with the edge of the sword... I will utterly blot out memory of Amalek from under heaven... And Moses built an altar, and named it 'The Lord is My Banner.'" (Exod 17:13–17)

Rephi

N
W E
S

Gulf of Suez

Scale 1 : 2,850,000

0   25   50   75km
0   25   50miles